REA's Test Prep Books A

(a sample of the <u>hundreds of letters</u> REA receives each year)

" This book [REA's AP Spanish Language prep] is an excellent source
of information for all material covered on the exam. The audio CDs were
essential . . . and made studying more fun. I am grateful to the authors of the
book, since their work helped me to score a 5 on the exam. I would strongly
recommend this book to test-takers. "
AP Spanish Language Student, Glendora, CA

" One of the best books [REA's AP Spanish Language prep] for studying
the Spanish language . . . the most user-friendly, well designed, and
comprehensive book for learning Spanish on the market today . . .
Please do yourselves a favor and buy this book. "
AP Spanish Language Student, Snowflake, AZ

" Your book was such a better value and was so much more complete than
anything your competition has produced — and I have them all! "
Teacher, Virginia Beach, VA

" Compared to the other books that my fellow students had, your book was
the most useful in helping me get a great score. "
Student, North Hollywood, CA

" Your book was responsible for my success on the exam, which helped me get
into the college of my choice... I will look for REA the next time I need help. "
Student, Chesterfield, MO

" Just a short note to say thanks for the great support your book gave me in
helping me pass the test... I'm on my way to a B.S. degree because of you! "
Student, Orlando, FL

(more on next page)

(continued from front page)

" I just wanted to thank you for helping me get a great score
on the AP U.S. History exam... Thank you for making great test preps! "
Student, Los Angeles, CA

" Your *Fundamentals of Engineering Exam* book was the absolute best
preparation I could have had for the exam, and it is one of the major
reasons I did so well and passed the FE on my first try. "
Student, Sweetwater, TN

" I used your book to prepare for the test and found that the advice and the
sample tests were highly relevant... Without using any other material, I earned
very high scores and will be going to the graduate school of my choice. "
Student, New Orleans, LA

" What I found in your book was a wealth of information sufficient to shore up
my basic skills in math and verbal... The section on analytical ability was
excellent. The practice tests were challenging and the answer explanations most
helpful. It certainly is the *Best Test Prep for the GRE*! "
Student, Pullman, WA

" I really appreciate the help from your excellent book. Please keep up
the great work. "
Student, Albuquerque, NM

" I am writing to thank you for your test preparation... your book helped me
immeasurably and I have nothing but praise for your *GRE* preparation."
Student, Benton Harbor, MI

(more on back page)

The Best Test Preparation for the

AP
Spanish
Language Exam

6th Edition

Practice Exams Updated by

Suzanne Varner
AP Spanish Instructor and
Foreign Language Department Chairperson
St. Christopher's School, Richmond, VA

Erica R. Hughes
Spanish Instructor
James S. Rickards High School, Tallahassee, FL

Lana Robb Craig, M.A.
AP Spanish Instructor
Ithaca High School, Ithaca, NY

Cristina Bedoya
Spanish Instructor
Conackamack Middle School, Piscataway, NJ

Candy Rodo
Spanish Journalist
New York, NY

George Wayne Braun, M.A.
Spanish Instructor
Seminole High School, Seminole, TX

Diane Senerth
Spanish Consultant
Lawrenceville, NJ

Research & Education Association
Visit our website at
www.rea.com

Research & Education Association
61 Ethel Road West
Piscataway, New Jersey 08854
E-mail: info@rea.com

The Best Test Preparation for the
AP SPANISH LANGUAGE EXAM
With Audio CDs

Library of Congress Control Number 2006935885

International Standard Book Number 0-7386-0294-9

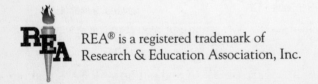

The AP Expert Behind Our Updated Practice Exams

Suzanne Varner chairs the Foreign Language Department and teaches Advanced Placement Spanish Language at St. Christopher's School, Richmond, Va. Ms. Varner has been a College Board AP Spanish Language reader since 2001. In 2002, she was named an Arthur Vining Davis Fellow of the Center for Liberal Arts at the University of Virginia.

About Research & Education Association

Founded in 1959, Research & Education Association (REA) is dedicated to publishing the finest and most effective educational materials—including software, study guides, and test preps—for students in middle school, high school, college, graduate school, and beyond.

REA's Test Preparation series includes books and software for all academic levels in almost all disciplines. Research & Education Association publishes test preps for students who have not yet entered high school, as well as high school students preparing to enter college. Students from countries around the world seeking to attend college in the United States will find the assistance they need in REA's publications. For college students seeking advanced degrees, REA publishes test preps for many major graduate school admission examinations in a wide variety of disciplines, including engineering, law, and medicine. Students at every level, in every field, with every ambition can find what they are looking for among REA's publications.

REA presents tests that accurately depict the official exams in both degree of difficulty and types of questions. REA's practice tests are always based upon the most recently administered exams, and include every type of question that you can expect on the actual exams.

REA's publications and educational materials are highly regarded and continually receive an unprecedented amount of praise from professionals, instructors, librarians, parents, and students. Our authors are as diverse as the fields represented in the books we publish. They are well-known in their respective disciplines and serve on the faculties of prestigious high schools, colleges, and universities throughout the United States and Canada.

Today REA's wide-ranging catalog is a leading resource for teachers, students, and professionals.

We invite you to visit us at *www.rea.com* to find out how "REA is making the world smarter."

REA Staff Acknowledgments

In addition to our authors, we would like to thank Larry B. Kling, Vice President, Editorial, for his editorial direction; Pam Weston, Vice President, Publishing, for setting the quality standards for production integrity and managing the publication to completion; John Paul Cording, Vice President, Technology, for his coordination of media revisions; Molly Solanki, Associate Editor, for coordinating revisions to this edition; Christine Saul, Senior Graphic Designer, for cover design; Jeff LoBalbo, Senior Graphic Designer, for coordinating pre-press electronic file mapping; Rachel DiMatteo, Graphic Designer, and Kathy Caratozzolo of Caragraphics, for typesetting revisions.

We also thank Simone Gatto and Teri Gatto for technical advice; Jannette Ball, Lesley Breuer, Edward Cologna, and the voice talents at Amazing Voice for their professional recordings on our audio CDs; and Robyn Catania, Patricia Dempsey, Blanca E. Goyo-Shields, Gene Hammitt, and Dagoberto Muniz for their editorial contributions.

CONTENTS

STUDY SCHEDULE

AP Spanish Language

STUDY SCHEDULE

AP Spanish Language

The following study schedule will help you become thoroughly prepared for the Advanced Placement Spanish Language exam. Although the schedule is designed as a six-week study program, it can be condensed into three weeks if less time is available by combining two weeks into one. Be sure to set aside enough time each day for studying purposes. If you choose the six-week program, you should plan to study for at least one hour per day. If you choose the three-week program, you should plan to study for at least two hours per day. Keep in mind that the more time you devote to studying for the Spanish exam, the more prepared and confident you will be on the day of the exam.

Week	Activity
1	Read and study the introduction on the following pages. Then, take and score Practice Test 1 in this book to determine your strengths and weaknesses. When you grade your exam, you should determine what types of questions cause you the most difficulty, as this will help you determine what review areas to study most thoroughly. For example, if you incorrectly answer a number of questions dealing with Reflexive Pronouns, you should carefully study this section in our subject review. Begin studying the Spanish Review and try to finish through the section on the Future and Conditional.
2	Continue studying the Review sections. Try to finish through Object Pronouns. Be sure to answer all of the drill questions.
3	Finish the remainder of the Review section and answer all drill questions. Be sure to look up the explanations for questions you answer incorrectly.
4	Study the dictionary of Spanish words.
5	Take and score Practice Test 2 in this book. Make sure to review all of the detailed explanations of answers. Restudy the section(s) of the review for any area(s) in which you are still weak.
6	Take and score Practice Test 3 in this book. Make sure to review all of the detailed explanations of answers. Restudy the section(s) of the review for any area(s) in which you are still weak.

CHAPTER 1

Excelling on the AP Spanish Language Exam

EXCELLING ON THE AP SPANISH LANGUAGE EXAM

WHY THIS BOOK IS FOR YOU

This book will help you master the AP Spanish Language Exam, which was revamped in 2007, with complete coverage fully embracing the exam's new format and question types. REA offers *the* total test prep package with comprehensive printed and audio materials that take you through the newly integrated listening, speaking and writing portions of the exam. As you may already know, the test covers subject matter deemed to be comparable to an advanced-level college course in Spanish Composition and Conversation.

Why use this book? Because you don't want to leave anything to chance on test day. While our prep is designed to be effective for self-study, this book also lies at the heart of hundreds of AP Spanish classrooms in schools across the United States.

Our targeted subject review—specially designed to complement your textbook—and three full-length practice tests, featuring detailed explanations for each answer, will put you in the best possible position to succeed on the exam. We also provide a 500-word English-to-Spanish and Spanish-to-English glossary.

It's all about giving you the confidence you need to score well on the AP Spanish Language Exam come May.

ABOUT THE REVIEW SECTION

This book begins with a substantive review of the Spanish language. This review includes conjugations of regular and irregular verbs, pronouns, idioms, as well as other parts of speech. After each new topic, we offer drills to enable you to practice the vocabulary and rules you have just reviewed.

At the end of the practice tests is our 500-word English-to-Spanish and Spanish-to-English glossary. With it, you will not only be able to locate Spanish words you do not know from the reading passages but you can also review words that will help you provide a more detailed answer to the essay or speaking parts of the exam. (Please note that no dictionaries will be allowed at the time of the actual exam.)

ABOUT OUR AUDIO CDs

At various points throughout the practice tests, you will need to stop the test CD and record your responses on a recording device. Make sure to have a recording device available.

Follow the directions carefully by listening to the directions on the CD as well as following the tests in this book.

ABOUT THE AP PROGRAM

The Advanced Placement Program is intended to provide high school students with the opportunity to pursue college-level studies and, if they test sufficiently well, gain actual college credit or placement for that work. In fact, most colleges and universities in the United States and in more than 30 other countries grant incoming students credit, placement, or both according to their AP Exam scores.

SSD ACCOMMODATIONS FOR STUDENTS WITH DISABILITIES

Many students qualify for extra time to take the AP Spanish Language exam. For information, contact:

College Board Services for Students with Disabilities
PO Box 6226
Princeton, NJ 08541-6226
Phone: (609) 771-7137 Monday-Friday, 8 a.m. to 6 p.m.
          (Eastern time)
TTY: (609) 882-4118
Fax: (609) 771-7944
E-mail: ssd@info.collegeboard.org

WHAT'S ON THE EXAM?

The AP Spanish Language exam is divided into two sections. The first section is a 90-minute multiple-choice section that tests listening and reading comprehension. The second section, a free-response section, is approximately100 minutes long and tests the student's speaking and writing skills.

Section I.   Multiple choice (50% of your grade):

This section is composed of two parts. **Part A** is the listening comprehension portion of the test. You will listen to a series of dialogues, narratives, and lectures on audio CD. You will then answer questions based on each.

Part B is the reading comprehension part of the exam. Students read several passages and answer questions about each.

Section II.   Free response (50% of your grade):

Part A of the free-response section consists of four distinct parts.

The first exercise requires the student to read a paragraph and fill in the correct form of the root words that have been provided. The second exercise also requires the student to fill in correct and appropriate words, but the root word is not provided.

The next part of Section II, Part A, is a writing component. The first task, an informal writing task, requires the student to read a prompt and write a response to that prompt. Prompts may require the student to address an e-mail message, a letter, or a postcard, for example. Students are allowed 10 minutes to complete this part.

The last section is the formal writing component. Students are asked to read documents, listen to a related recording, and respond to a writing prompt. Students are allowed 55 minutes to complete this part and their written response should contain at least 200 words.

Part B of the free-response section consists of two distinct parts.

In the first part, the informal component, students are asked to interact with a recorded conversation. There are five or six opportunities for a student to respond and a response can last up to 20 seconds.

The second part, the formal component, requires the student to read one document and listen to a recording. Students then have 2 minutes to prepare for an oral presentation and 2 minutes to answer a question related to the sources.

AP SPANISH EXAM FORMAT

Section	Item Type	Number of Questions	Time
Section I	Multiple Choice	70	85–90 min.
Part A: Listening	Short Dialogues and Narratives	30–35	30–35 min.
	Long Dialogues and Narratives		
Part B: Reading	Reading Comprehension	35–40	50–60 min.
Section II	Free Response		Approx. 100 min.
Part A: Writing	Paragraph Completion (with root words)	10 questions 7 minutes	Approx. 80 min.
	Paragraph Completion (without root words)	10 questions 8 minutes	
	Informal Writing	1 prompt 10 minutes	
	Formal Writing (Integrated Skills)	1 prompt Approx. 55 minutes	
Part B: Speaking	Informal Speaking— Simulated Conversation	5–6 response prompts 20 seconds to respond to each	Approx. 20 min.
	Formal Oral Presentation (Integrated Skills)	1 prompt 2 minutes to respond	

ABOUT THE EXAM'S SPOKEN PORTION

In Section II, Part B of the exam, the student will be required to record all answers on audio tape. For the actual exam you will have either a second recorder provided for you or you will be instructed to replace the test tape with a blank audio tape. You should familiarize yourself with the recording equipment before the exam. If you should make an error while speaking, make the correction. You will score better by correcting yourself than by leaving an error in place.

SCORING THE EXAM

The multiple-choice section of the exam is scored by computer. Each correct answer is credited with one point; one-third of a point is deducted for each incorrect answer. Unanswered questions receive neither credit nor deduction.

Hundreds of college and secondary school teachers are brought together every June to grade the free-response portion of the exams. These readers are chosen from around the country for their familiarity with the AP program, their knowledge of the subject matter and their ability to be impartial. Each essay booklet and tape is evaluated and scored. The fill-in answers are scored objectively. When the free-response answers have been graded by all of the evaluators, the scores are then converted.

Once raw scores have been obtained for each section, they are weighted to form a composite score. Then the composite scores for each section are added together to form a total composite score for the exam. The range for the composite score is from 0 to 180.

Finally, the composite score is translated into a range from 1 to 5, with 1 being the lowest and 5 being the highest. This correlation between the composite score and the scoring range varies from administration to administration. It is determined by comparing the examinees' performance on a core group of questions. When overall student performance is strong, the range of scores is narrowed; when it is weak, the scoring ranges are widened.

For the free-response portion of the exam, it would be extremely helpful to find someone who is willing to score your informal and formal writing tasks and oral presentations. Your teachers, friends, or anyone familiar with the Spanish language and the test material would be excellent candidates to grade your responses.

If you must grade your own speaking and writing, try to be objective. You may want to give your responses three different grades, as if you did well, average, and poorly. This will give you a safe estimate of how you will do on the actual exam. By underestimating what your score may be, you are more likely to receive a better score on the actual exam.

SCORES THAT RECEIVE COLLEGE CREDIT AND/OR ADVANCED PLACEMENT

AP grades are reported on a 5-point scale and are interpreted as follows:

    5—extremely well qualified
    4—well qualified
    3—qualified
    2—possibly qualified
    1—no recommendation

Your grade will be used by your college of choice to determine placement in its Spanish language program. This grade will vary in significance from college to college, and is used with other academic information to determine placement. Normally, colleges participating in the Advanced Placement Program will recognize grades of 3 or better. Contact your college admissions office for more information regarding its use of AP grades.

STUDYING FOR YOUR AP EXAMINATION

It is never too early to start studying. The earlier you begin, the more time you will have to sharpen your skills. Do not procrastinate! Cramming is not an effective way to study, since it does *not* allow you the time needed to review the test material.

It is very important for you to choose the time and place for studying that works best for you. Some students may set aside a certain number of hours every morning to study, while others may choose to study at night before going to sleep. Other students may study during the day, while waiting on a line, or even while eating lunch. Only you can determine when and where your study time will be most effective. But, be consistent and use your time wisely. Work out a study routine and stick to it!

When you take the practice exam(s), try to make your testing conditions as much like those of the actual test as possible. Turn your television and radio off, and sit down at a quiet table free from distraction. Make sure to time yourself.

As you complete the practice test(s), score your test(s) and thoroughly review the explanations for the questions you answered incorrectly. But don't review too much during any one sitting. Concentrate on one problem area at a time by reviewing each question and explanation, and by studying our review(s) until you are confident that you completely understand the material.

Since you will be allowed to write in your test booklet during the actual exam, you may want to write in the margins of this book when practicing. However, do not make miscellaneous notes on your answer sheet. Mark your answers clearly and make sure the answer you have chosen corresponds to the question you are answering.

Keep track of your scores! By doing so, you will be able to gauge your progress and discover general weaknesses in particular sections. You should carefully study the reviews that cover the topics causing you difficulty, as this will build your skills in those areas.

TEST-TAKING TIPS

Although you may be unfamiliar with tests such as the Advanced Placement exams, there are many ways to acquaint yourself with these exams and help alleviate your test-taking anxieties. Listed below are ways to help you become accustomed to the AP exam, some of which may also be applied to other standardized tests as well.

Become comfortable with the format of the AP Examination in Spanish Language. When you are practicing to take the exam, simulate the conditions under which you will be taking the actual test. You should practice under the same time constraints as well. Stay calm and pace yourself. After simulating the test only a couple of times, you will boost your chances of doing well, and you will be able to sit down for the actual test much more confidently.

Know the directions and format for each section of the exam. Familiarizing yourself with the directions and format of the different test sections will not only save you time, but will also ensure that you are familiar enough with the AP exam to avoid nervousness (and the mistakes caused by being nervous).

Read all of the possible answers. Just because you think you have found the correct response, do not automatically assume that it is the best answer. Read through each choice to be sure that you are not making a mistake by jumping to conclusions.

Work on the easier questions first. If you find yourself working too long on one question, make a mark next to it in your test booklet and continue. After you have answered all of the questions that you can, go back to the ones you have skipped.

Use the process of elimination when you are unsure of an answer. If you can eliminate two of the answer choices, you have given yourself a fifty-fifty chance of getting the item correct since there will only be two choices left from which to make a guess. If you cannot eliminate at least two of the answer choices, you may choose not to guess, as you will be penalized one-third of a point for every incorrect answer. Questions not answered will not be counted.

Be sure that you are marking your answer in the circle that corresponds to the number of the question in the test booklet. Since the multiple-choice section is graded by machine, marking the wrong answer will throw off your score.

CONTACTING THE AP PROGRAM

For more information on the exams, contact Educational Testing Service or the College Board.

AP Services - Educational Testing Service
P.O. Box 6671
Princeton, NJ 08541-6671
Phone: (609) 771-7300
    or 888-225-5427 (toll-free in the U.S. and Canada)
Fax: (609) 530-0482
E-mail: apexams@info.collegeboard.org
Website: *www.collegeboard.com*

CHAPTER 2

AP Spanish Review

AP SPANISH REVIEW

THE ALPHABET

Spanish uses the same Latin alphabet as English except for the addition of one letter: *ñ*. Spanish letters use the following pronunciation guidelines[*]:

ch pronounced like "ch" in "chief"

ll pronounced like the "y" in "beyond"

ñ pronounced like "ni" in "opinion"

c sounds like "s" before "e" and "i," and like "k" in all other cases.

g sounds like the "h" in "humid" before "e" and "i," and like the "g" in "go" or "get" in front of "a," "o," and "u." In order to obtain the hard sound before "e" and "i," Spanish interpolates the vowel "u": *guerra, guión*. In these cases the "u" is silent; a dieresis indicates that it must be pronounced: *vergüenza, güero*.

h is always silent: *ahora, húmedo, horrible*.

v is pronounced like "b" in all cases.

y sounds like "ll" at the beginning of a word or syllable. When it stands alone or comes at the end of a word, it is equivalent to the vowel "i."

z is pronounced like "s."

[*] This pronunciation guide follows Latin American usage. In Castilian Spanish the soft "*c*" and the "*z*" are pronounced like "th" in "thin." Either pronunciation is acceptable on the spoken portion of the exam.

Letter		Spanish Example	English Example
b	[b]	*bomba*	boy
c	[k]	*calco*	keep
	[s]	*cero*	same
ch	[tʃ]	*mucho*	chocolate
d	[d]	*andar*	dog
f	[f]	*fama*	fake
g	[x]	*general*	humid
	[g]	*rango*	get
h	always silent	*hombre*	honor
j	[x]	*justo*	humid
k	[k]	*kilogramo*	kite
l	[l]	*letra*	light
ll	[ʎ]	*ella*	beyond
m	[m]	*mano*	mad
n	[n]	*pan*	no
ñ	[ŋ]	*uña*	onion
p	[p]	*padre*	poke
q	[k]	*que*	kite
r	[r]	*rápido*	(this is a trilled or "rolling" sound with no English equivalent)
s	[s]	*casa*	some
	[z]	*mismo*	rose
t	[t]	*patata*	tame
v	[b]	*vamos*	boy
x	[ks]	*máximo*	fox
y	[j]	*yo*	yes
z	[s]	*zapato*	same

The sounds of the Spanish vowels are invariable.

a   sounds approximately like "a" in "ah."
e   sounds approximately like "e" in "men."
i   sounds approximately like "ee" in "eel."
o   sounds approximately like "o" in "or."
u   sounds approximately like "oo" in "moon."

Letter		Spanish Example	English Example
a	[a]	*pata*	father
e	[e]	*pelo*	men
i	[i]	*filo*	eel
o	[o]	*poco*	or
u	[u]	*luna*	moon

A combination of one strong (a, e, o) and one weak vowel (i, u) or of two weak ones is a diphthong and counts as one syllable:

ai, ay	*aire, hay*	pronounce like "eye"
ei, ey	*reino, ley*	pronounce like "may"
oi, oy	*oigo, hoy*	pronounce like "toy"
iu	*triunfo*	pronounce like "you"
ui, uy	*cuidar, muy*	pronounce like "Louie"
ue	*hueso, muerte*	pronounce like "west"

RULES FOR STRESS IN SPANISH

There are two rules that indicate stress in Spanish. If either of these two rules is broken, a written accent mark will appear on the word.

1. If a word ends in a vowel, *–n,* or *–s,* the **normal** stress is on the penultimate (next to last) syllable.

mano (over the *–a*)	*tribu* (over the *–i*)
esposa (over the *–o*)	*hablan* (over first *–a*)
clase (over the *–a*)	*tomaban* (over first *–a*)

2. If the word ends in any other letter (than those mentioned above), the **normal** stress will fall on the last syllable.

hablar (over the *–a*)	*papel* (over the *–e*)
comer (over the *–e*)	*ejemplar* (over the *–a*)
vivir (over the *–i*)	*nivel* (over the *–e*)

3. Spanish words will have an accent for the following specific reasons:

   a. There is another identical word and the accent distinguishes the one from the other.

de (of, from)	vs.	*dé* (give—formal command)
se (reflexive pronoun)	vs.	*sé* (I know, verb)

<table>
<tr><td>mas (but, conjunction)</td><td>vs.</td><td>más (more, adverb)</td></tr>
<tr><td>si (if)</td><td>vs.</td><td>sí (yes)</td></tr>
</table>

b. A pronoun has been added to a verb form.

diciéndolo	saying it
diciéndomelo	saying it to me
explíquelo	explain it
explíquemelo	explain it to me
decírselo	to say it to him

Note: Infinitives require two pronouns before an accent is necessary.

c. The accent is the result of a stem-change.

reunir (ú) – The *ú* will appear in the first, second, and third person singular and third person plural of the present indicative/subjunctive.

Other examples:

continuar (ú),   *enviar (í)*
graduarse (ú)

d. There may be a diphthong (two weak vowels or a weak with a strong) where the weak vowel (*u* or *i*) needs to be stressed.

Examples:

divertíos	Enjoy yourselves!
creíste	you believed

SYLLABIC DIVISION

A consonant between two vowels joins the second vowel to form a syllable: *li-te-ra-tu-ra, e-ne-mi-go, a-ho-ra.*

- Two consonants together must be separated: *cuer-no, pac-to.*

- "*ch*," "*ll*," and "*rr*" are considered one letter and are not separated.

- "*l*" or "*r*" preceded by "*b*," "*c*," "*d*," "*f*," "*g*," "*p*," and "*t*" are not separated: *ha-blar, a-brup-to, te-cla, pul-cri-tud, me-lo-dra-ma, in-flu-jo, a-gra-de-cer.*

- "*ns*" and "*bs*" are not separated in groups of three or four consonants: *ins-cri-bir, obs-tá-cu-lo.*

- In words formed with prefixes, the prefix stands alone as one syllable: *sub-ra-yar, in-ú-til, des-a-gra-dar.*

ARTICLES

The forms of the definite article are:

	Masculine	**Feminine**
Singular	*el*	*la*
Plural	*los*	*las*

El is used instead of *la* before feminine nouns beginning with stressed "a" or "ha": *el agua*, *el hacha*, *el alma*, *el hambre*.

El contracts to *al* when the article follows the preposition *a* (*a + el*) and to *del* when the article follows the preposition *de* (*de + el*).

Uses of the Definite Article

The definite article is used in Spanish (but not in English):

- when the noun represents an abstraction: **life** is short; **time** is money; **freedom** is worth fighting for; **politics** is a practical art. (*la vida*, *el tiempo*, *la libertad*, *la política*)

- when the noun includes the totality of a category: **books** are good; **man** is mortal; the Incas were acquainted with **gold**; **bread** is a staple. (*los libros*, *el hombre*, *el oro*, *el pan*)

- with the days of the week (except after a form of the verb *ser*) and the seasons of the year: *el lunes* (but *hoy es lunes*), *la primavera*, *el otoño*

- with the hours of the day: *son las tres de la tarde; a las doce del día* (or *al mediodía*)

- with personal or professional forms of address in the third person: *el señor Jiménez*, *la señorita Méndez*, *el doctor Márquez*, *el licenciado Vidriera*. (It is omitted when the individual is directly addressed and in front of titles such as *Don, Doña, San*, or *Santo[a]*: *venga, señor Jiménez; no se preocupe, señorita Méndez*.)

- with the parts of the body or articles of clothing instead of the possessive adjective: I brushed **my** teeth. *Me cepillé los dientes.* I put on **my** shirt. *Me puse la camisa.*

- with the names of languages except after the prepositions *en* and *de* and the verb *hablar*: *el francés es difícil* (but *no hablo francés; ese texto está en francés*)

- with weights and measures: *un dólar la libra*, one dollar per pound; *diez pesos la docena*, ten pesos per dozen

- with infinitives used as nouns (gerunds): Lying is a vice. *El mentir es un vicio.* (This use is optional, especially in proverbs.) Seeing is believing. *Ver es creer.*

- with names of "generic" places: jail, *la cárcel*; class, *la clase*; church, *la iglesia*; market, *el mercado*

- with family names: The Garcías, *los Garcías*

- with adjectives to make them nouns: the pretty one, *la bonita*; the poor, *los pobres*; the old man, *el viejo*

- with nouns in apposition with a pronoun: We Americans... *Nosotros los americanos...*

Omission of the Definite Article in Spanish

The definite article in Spanish is omitted in the following cases:
1. With fields of knowledge, in general, one needs an article unless one...

    a. gives a **definition**   *¿Qué es astronomía?*
                                      Astronomía es una ciencia.

    b. uses *estudiar* or *examinar*   *Estudiamos química.*

2. With the expressions *de...a*

En casa comemos *de seis a ocho.*
At home we eat from 6:00 to 8:00.

3. With expressions such as

por primera vez	for the first time
por segunda vez	for the second time
en primer lugar	in the first place

4. With *con* and *sin* before an unmodified abstract noun.

No puedo vivir sin libertad.
I cannot live without liberty.

Con amor la vida tiene sentido.
With love life has meaning.

5. With a numeral that denotes the order of a monarch.

Carlos Quinto   Charles the Fifth

The Neuter Article *Lo*

This article is used exclusively in the singular as follows:

1. *Lo* + adjective = **part/thing**

   Examples: *lo importante*   the important thing/part
              lo mejor   the best thing/part

2. *Lo* + adj/adv + *que* = **how**

   Examples: *Tú no sabes lo importante que es.*
              You don't know **how** important it is.

              Él no entiende lo despacio que va.
              He doesn't know **how** slowly it goes.

3. *Lo de* = All that or everything that (happened)

   Example: *Vamos a cubrir lo de ayer.*
              We'll cover everything we did yesterday.

4. *Lo* is used in sentences with the pronoun *todo* as the direct object.

   Example: *Lo entiendo todo.*
              I understand everything.

5. *Todo lo que* = All that

   Example: *Todo lo que oí no es verdad.*
              All that I heard isn't true.

6. *Lo* is used as a complement to replace adjectives, pronouns, or nouns with *ser, estar,* and *parecer*.

   Examples: *Pareces enojada.* [adj-*enojada*]
              You seem angry.

              —*Quizás **lo** parezca, pero no **lo** estoy.*
              Perhaps I seem it, but I'm not.

              ¿Estas llaves son tuyas? [noun-*llaves*]
              Are these keys yours?

              —*No, no **lo** son.*
              No, they're not.

Forms of the Indefinite Article

The indefinite article must agree in gender and number with the noun it modifies. Its forms are the following:

	Masculine	Feminine
Singular	*un*	*una*
Plural	*unos*	*unas*

Examples: *un perro* – a dog
unos perros – some dogs

Note: Feminine nouns beginning with a stressed "*a*" or "*ha*" take *un* instead of *una*: **un** *alma,* **un** *hacha,* **un** *hada madrina*. This rule only applies if the noun is singular.

Uses of the Indefinite Article

Spanish *omits* the indefinite article (but not English) as follows:

- after the verb *ser* with nouns denoting profession, religion, or nationality: *soy profesor, son católicos, es española*. (This rule does not apply when the noun is followed by an adjective or some other modifier: *soy* **un** *profesor exigente* (I'm a demanding teacher).)

- with words such as *otro* (other), *medio* (half), *cien* (one hundred or a hundred), *mil* (one thousand or a thousand), *tal* (such a), *cierto* (a certain), and *qué* (what a): *cierta mujer* (a certain woman), *¡qué día!* (What a day!), *cien libros* (a hundred books), *mide un metro y medio* (it measures one and one-half meters), *otra respuesta* (another answer), *tal hombre* (such a man).

- after **sin**:

  Salió sin abrigo.   He left without a coat.

- after **haber** used impersonally, **buscar,** and **tener** (otherwise it means **one**):

No hay respuesta.	There isn't **an** answer.
Estoy buscando trabajo.	I'm looking for **a** job.
No tiene coche.	He doesn't have **a** car.

GENDER

In Spanish nouns are either masculine or feminine. Most nouns ending in *-o* or *-or* are masculine and most of those ending in *-a ,-d, -ión, -umbre, -ie, -sis, -itis* are feminine.

Masculine	Feminine
el dinero – money	*la muchedumbre* – crowd
el otoño – autumn	*la serie* – series
el amor – love	*la crisis* – crisis
	la presencia – presence
	la bronquitis – bronchitis
	la acción – action

Note: Drop the accent on *–ión* words when made plural: *nación, naciones*

Many masculine nouns become feminine by changing the *-o* ending to *-a* or by adding an *-a* if the word ends in a consonant:

Masculine	Feminine
el escritor – the writer	*la escritora* – the writer
el doctor – the doctor	*la doctora* – the doctor
el hijo – the son	*la hija* – the daughter
el muchacho – the young man	*la muchacha* – the young woman

Exceptions

A few common words ending in *-o* are feminine:

la mano – the hand
la foto (la fotografía) – the photo, picture
la moto (la motocicleta) – the motorcycle

There is a large number of words ending in **-ma**, **-pa**, and **-ta** that are masculine. For the most part, if these are easily identifiable in English, they are probably masculine.

el clima – climate	*el problema* – problem
el diploma – diploma	*el sistema* – system
el drama – drama	*el mapa* – map
el poema – poem	*el profeta* – prophet
el tema – theme	*el aroma* – aroma

There are also other ways of forming the feminine than by adding an *-a* ending:

Masculine	Feminine
el rey – the king	*la reina* – the queen
el actor – the actor	*la actriz* – the actress
el poeta – the poet	*la poetisa* – the poet
el gallo – the rooster	*la gallina* – the hen

Sometimes the masculine and feminine words corresponding to a matched pair of concepts are different:

Masculine	Feminine
el yerno – the son-in-law	*la nuera* – the daughter-in-law
el varón – the male	*la hembra* – the female
el toro – the bull	*la vaca* – the cow

Masculine words that appear to be feminine:

el día – day	*el césped* – turf
el sofá – sofa	*el colega* – colleague
el ataúd – coffin	*el tranvía* – trolley

Nouns of Invariable Gender

Some nouns can be either masculine or feminine depending on their content or reference, without undergoing any formal alterations:

Masculine	Feminine
el artista – the artist	*la artista* – the artist
el estudiante – the student	*la estudiante* – the student
el joven – the young man	*la joven* – the young woman

Gender and Meaning Change

There are nouns that have different meanings depending on whether they are used as masculine or feminine:

el policía – the policeman	*la policía* – the police (force)
el papa – the Pope	*la papa* – the potato
el cometa – the comet	*la cometa* – the kite
el orden – order (as in a command)	*la orden* – the order (to do something)
el cura – the priest	*la cura* – the cure
el guía – the guide (person)	*la guía* – the guide (book, as in *guía de teléfonos*)
el frente – the front	*la frente* – the forehead

Use of *El* Before a Feminine Noun

If the feminine noun begins with a stressed *a* or *ha*, the singular forms of the article used are *el* or *un*. If anything intercedes between these two items, use the normal *la* or *una*.

el águila (eagle)	*las águilas*	*la gran águila*
un hacha (hatchet)	*unas hachas*	*una gran hacha*

Other examples: *el alma* – soul, *el aula* – classroom, *el agua* – water, *el ala* – wing, *el alba* – dawn, *el hada* – fairy, *el hambre* – hunger.

Note: On AP exams this concept is tested by asking students to write the correct form of an adjective that follows, as in these examples. Observe that the adjective is feminine because the nouns is, despite the masculine article.

el agua tibia	the warm water
el alba bonita	the pretty dawn
el águila maravillosa	the marvelous eagle

Other Feminine Words (Often Used on AP Exams)

la pirámide – pyramid	*la vez* – time
la torre – tower	*la razón* – reason
la leche – milk	*la imagen* – image
la carne – meat	*la luz* – light
la gente – people	*la catedral* – cathedral
la frase – sentence	*la suerte* – luck

NUMBER

In Spanish, as in English, nouns can be singular or plural. The most common way to form the plural is by adding the *-s* ending to the singular form of the word. (Note that the following examples are of words ending in an unstressed vowel.)

Singular	Plural
hombre – man	*hombres* – men
niño – boy	*niños* – boys
perro – dog	*perros* – dogs

Formation of the Plural by Addition of -es

In other cases (words ending in a consonant or in a stressed vowel other than -*é*), the plural is formed by adding an -*es* ending to the singular form of the word:

Singular	Plural
mujer – woman	*mujeres* – women
razón – reason	*razones* – reasons
jabalí – boar	*jabalíes* – boars

Exceptions: *mamá* (mother), pl. *mamás; ley* (law), pl. *leyes*.

Nouns of Invariable Number

Nouns ending in -*s* are the same in the singular and the plural if the final syllable is unstressed:

el (los) rascacielos – the skyscraper(s)
el (los) paraguas – the umbrella(s)
el (los) lunes – Monday(s)

Diminutives

The Spanish endings -*ito, -cito*, and their feminine forms are used to indicate affection or to emphasize smallness of size:

*Tú eres mi **amor**.*
You are my **love**.

*Tú eres mi **amorcito**.*
You are my **sweetheart**.

*Quiero chocolate. Dame un **poco**.*
I want chocolate. Give me **some**.

*Quiero chocolate. Dame un **poquito**.*
I want chocolate. Give me **a little**.

*Ese **hombre** tiene buen aspecto.*
That **man** is good looking.

*Ese **hombrecito** debe ser muy desgraciado.*
That **poor man** must be very unfortunate.

Augmentatives

The endings -*ote, -ón,* and -*ona* are added to express increased size:

hombre – man	*hombrón* – big man
mujer – woman	*mujerona* – big woman
casa – house	*casona* – big house

ADJECTIVES

Adjectives agree in gender and number with the noun they modify.

a) Adjectives ending in *-o* change their ending to *-a* when they modify a feminine noun:

   bueno, buena – good; *malo, mala* – bad; *bello, bella* – beautiful

b) Adjectives ending in *-or* (or *-on* or *-an*) add an *-a* to become feminine:

   hablador, habladora – talkative; *alemán, alemana* – German

   Exceptions:

mejor – better	*peor* – worse
superior – upper, superior	*inferior* – lower, inferior
exterior – outer, external	*interior* – inner, internal
anterior – earlier, anterior	*posterior* – later, posterior

c) Most other adjectives have the same ending for both genders:

verde – green	*grande* – big, great
azul – blue	*frágil* – fragile
cortés – courteous	*soez* – mean, vile

d) Adjectives of nationality have four forms. If they end in *-o*, they follow the normal pattern of change. All others may be changed by adding *-a* to make them feminine and *-as* to make them feminine plural:

   inglés, inglesa, ingleses, inglesas
   alemán, alemana, alemanes, alemanas
   español, española, españoles, españolas

Number

a) Adjectives ending in a vowel add an *-s* to form the plural:

   bello, bellos – beautiful; *grande, grandes* – big, great

b) Adjectives ending in a consonant add *-es* to form the plural:

   azul, azules – blue; *débil, débiles* – weak; *vulgar, vulgares* – vulgar

c) If an adjective modifies more than one noun and one of those nouns is masculine, the adjective must be **masculine** and **plural**:

*Mis tíos y tías eran **ricos**.* My uncles and aunts were **rich.**
*Los hombres y las mujeres **viejos**…* **Old** men and women…

Shortening of Adjectives

Some adjectives that directly precede the noun lose their final vowel or syllable:

ciento → cien	*grande → gran**
*bueno → buen***	*malo → mal***
*Santo → San***	*primero → primer***
*tercero → tercer***	*alguno→ algún***
*ninguno→ ningún***	*cualquiera→ cualquier**

* The shortening of this adjective only happens in front of singular nouns, either masculine or feminine. Compare:

*El acontecimiento fue **grande**.*
The event was **big.**

*el **gran** acontecimiento* – the **big** event

** These adjectives only shorten in front of masculine singular nouns. Compare:

*El hombre es **bueno**.*
The man is **good.**

*el **buen** hombre* – the **good** man

Qualifying Adjectives

Qualifying adjectives usually follow the noun:

*un día **frío*** – a **cold** day
*unas sábanas **limpias*** – some **clean** sheets

Change of Meaning with Location

Some common adjectives change their meaning with their location:

*el hombre **pobre*** – the poor man (having no money)
*el **pobre** hombre* – the poor man (pitiable)

*un cuadro **grande*** – a large painting
*un **gran** cuadro* – a great painting

*el policía **mismo*** – the policeman himself
*el **mismo** policía* – the same policeman

ciertas palabras – certain words (specific words from among many)
palabras ciertas – certain (sure)

nueva casa – new house (different)
casa nueva – new house (brand new)

un simple empleado – a mere employee
un empleado simple – a simple-minded employee

COMPARISON OF ADJECTIVES AND ADVERBS

Adverbs modify verbs, adjectives, and other adverbs and are invariable.

The following is a list of frequently used adverbs:

bien – well	*mal* – badly
más – more	*menos* – less
siempre – always	*nunca* – never
cerca – near	*lejos* – far
antes – before	*después* – afterwards
bastante – enough	*demasiado* – too much
temprano – early	*tarde* – late
así – thus, so	*casi* – almost
entonces – then	*luego* – later, afterward
todavía – still	

Aún is a common adverb whose meaning depends on whether the sentence is affirmative or negative:

Aún quiere trabajar.
He **still** wants to work.

Aún no está despierta.
She's not **yet** awake.

Aun (no accent) normally has the meaning **even** and commonly precedes the word it modifies.

¿Aun no ha llegado Juan?
Juan hasn't even arrived?

Adverbs Ending in -mente

Many adverbs are derived from the **feminine** form of the adjective (when such a form is available) by the addition of *-mente:*

claro/claramente – clearly
rápido/rápidamente – quickly

feliz/felizmente – happily
hábil/hábilmente – skillfully
dulce/dulcemente – sweetly

When two or more adverbs are used in a sequence, only the last adverb ends in *–mente*. All others are written as feminine adjectives (if they have a feminine form).

*Habla lenta y elocuente**mente**.*
He speaks slowly and eloquently.

*Juan corre rápida y hábil**mente**.*
Juan runs rapidly and skillfully.

Con, Sin + Noun

At times an adverb can be formed by using the preposition *con* (with) or *sin* (without) + a noun.

con cuidado – carefully
sin cuidado – carelessly
con rápidez – rapidly

Recientemente vs. Recién

Recientemente becomes *recién* before a past participle.

los recién llegados – the recent arrivals
los recién casados – the newlyweds

Adverbs Replaced by Adjectives

Adverbs may be replaced by adjectives with verbs of motion.

Ellos van y vienen silenciosos.
They come and go silently.

Comparison of Equality

This is constructed in the following ways:

Tanto, a, os, as + (noun) + *como*
Tan + (adverb or adjective) + *como*

*Tuve **tantas** deudas **como** el mes pasado.* I had **as many** debts **as** last month.

*Su música es **tan** clara **como** el agua.*
Her music is **as** clear **as** water.

*Llegué **tan** tarde **como** ayer.*
I arrived **as** late **as** yesterday.

Tanto como (without intervening expressions) means "as much as."

*Tu amigo estudia **tanto como** yo.*
Your friend studies **as much as** I [do].

Comparison of Inequality

The formula for describing levels of superiority is:

más + (noun, adjective, or adverb) + ***que***

*Tengo **más** dinero **que** tú.*
I have **more** money **than** you.

*Su auto es **más** caro **que** el mío.*
His car is **more** expensive **than** mine.

*Me levanto **más** temprano **que** ella.*
I get up **earlier than** she does.

The above formula changes to ***más de*** if a numerical expression is involved and the sentence is in the affirmative:

*Vimos **más de** mil estrellas en el cielo.*
We saw **more than** a thousand stars in the sky.

But:

*No tengo **más que** cinco dólares en el bolsillo.*
I don't have **more than** five dollars in my pocket.

The formula for describing levels of inferiority is:

menos + (noun, adjective, or adverb) + ***que***

*Nos dieron **menos** tiempo **que** a ustedes para completar el examen.*
They gave us **less** time **than** they gave you to finish the exam.

*Eres **menos** pobre **que** ella.*
You are **less** poor **than** she is.

*Tiene **menos** problemas **que** su madre.*
She has **fewer** problems **than** her mother.

The same change applies to the comparison of inferiority **except** that even in negative sentences *de* is used instead of ***que***:

*No eran **menos de** cinco los asaltantes.*
The assailants were no **fewer than** five.

If the second part of the comparison has a different verb from the first, **than** is expressed in one of five ways: *del que, de la que, de los que, de las que* (which all have gender and refer to nouns that are objects of both verbs), and *de lo que* (which is used when adjectives or adverbs are being compared).

*Ella gasta más dinero **del que** gana su esposo.* [*dinero*]
She spends more money **than** her husband earns.

*Tengo más coches **de los que** puedo contar.* [*coches*]
I have more cars **than** I can count.

*Es más fácil **de lo que** crees.* [*fácil*]
It is easier **than** you believe.

*Anda más despacio **de lo que** corre.* [*despacio*]
He walks more slowly **than** he runs.

Special Comparatives

Adjective (Adverb)	Comparative
bueno (bien) – good, well	*mejor* – better
malo (mal) – bad, badly	*peor* – worse
grande – big	*mayor** – older
pequeño – small	*menor** – younger

* *Mayor* and *menor* only refer to age; otherwise, *más (menos) grande (pequeño) que* is used.

*Mi padre es **mayor** que yo; mi hijo es **menor**.*
My father is **older** than I; my son is **younger.**

*Esta ciudad es **más grande que** la capital.*
This city is **bigger than** the capital.

Superlatives

In English the true or relative superlative is rendered by **the most (least) of** a category:

El, la, los, las + más (menos) + (adjective) + de
Lo + más (menos) + adverb + de

*Estos anillos son **los más** caros **de** la tienda.*
These rings are **the most** expensive **in** the store.

*Tienes **los** ojos **más** lindos **del** mundo.*
You have **the prettiest** eyes **in** the world.

*Corre **lo más** rápidamente **de** todos.*
He runs **the most** quickly **of** all.

Previously the special comparatives noted have a superlative form:

El, la, los, las + (special comparatives) + *de*
*Mi hijo es **el mayor de** la clase.* My son is **the oldest in** the class.

Absolute Superlative

Superlatives can also be formed by adding the *-ísimo* ending to adjectives and adverbs. (Some spelling adjustments may be necessary.)

The absolute superlative is usually rendered in English as "very pretty," "very ugly," etc.

lindo/lindísimo (a) – very pretty
feo/feísimo (a) – very ugly
tarde/tardísimo (a) – very late
cerca/cerquísimo (a) – very near
rico/riquísimo (a) – very rich
fácil/facilísimo (a) – very easy

The adjective *malo* has the special superlative *pésimo* in addition to the more informal *malísimo*.

☞ Drill 1

1. Ramiro es más guapo...Felipe.

   (A) que   (C) de

   (B) como   (D) tan

2. ...arma de fuego es peligrosa.

   (A) El   (C) Los

   (B) La   (D) Las

3. Mercedes lavó los platos...

   (A) rápidamente y cuidadosamente.

   (B) rápida y cuidadosa.

   (C) rápida y cuidadosamente.

   (D) rápidamente y cuidadosa.

4. Los explicaron...nosotros.

   (A) menor que   (C) mayor que

   (B) tanto   (D) mejor que

5. Elena tiene más amigas...puede contar.

   (A) de los que   (C) de las que

   (B) que   (D) de lo que

6. Pablo trabaja mejor...usted cree.

   (A) que   (C) del que

   (B) de lo que   (D) de la que

7. Anita es menos alta...Elena.

   (A) tan   (C) como

   (B) de   (D) que

8. Estas películas son...interesantes como ésas.

   (A) tan   (C) tantas

   (B) tantos   (D) como

9. Roberto y Ana son...inteligentes de la clase.

   (A) las más   (C) más

   (B) los más   (D) menos

10. Ellos corren...y hábilmente.

    (A) rápida   (C) rápidamente

    (B) rápido   (D) rápidos

11. Las chicas hablan...lentamente de todos.

    (A) el más   (C) lo más

    (B) las más   (D) más

12. Hay...torres como palacios en aquel país.

    (A) tan   (C) tan muchos

    (B) tantos   (D) tantas

13. ...persona puede estudiar este curso.

    (A) Algún   (C) Ningún

    (B) Cualquier   (D) Cualquiera

14. Wilhelm y Kerstin son...

    (A) alemanas.   (C) alemanes.

    (B) de alemanes.   (D) alemanos.

15. La Reina Isabela I ...

    (A) una gran mujer.   (C) una mujer gran.

    (B) una grande mujer.   (D) mujer grande.

16. Mis notas son...las de Juan.

    (A) mayor que

    (B) mayores de

    (C) mejores que

    (D) mejores de

17. Tú no sabes...importantes...son las tareas.

    (A) los...que

    (B) las...que

    (C) lo...que

    (D) lo...de

18. ¿Estas llaves son tuyas? –No, no...son.

    (A) las

    (B) lo

    (C) ellas

    (D) nothing needed

19. Juan lo hizo...ayer.

    (A) para primera vez

    (B) por primer vez

    (C) por primera vez

    (D) por la primera vez

20. Todo...oí ayer no es verdad.

    (A) que

    (B) lo que

    (C) la que

    (D) de

Drill 1—Detailed Explanations of Answers

1. **(A)** The most common pattern to express a **comparison** of superiority (i.e., to show that one thing or person is superior to another in some respect) is "más...que" (more than); for example, "Yo soy más delgado que tú" (I am thinn**er than** you); "Hablas español más fácilmente que yo" (You speak Spanish more easily than I); "Tengo más años que ella" (I am older than she). Notice from these three examples that we may use either adjectives, adverbs, or nouns between the words "más" and "que." The only time we use "de," as in (C) after "más" is when there is a number immediately afterwards: "Tenemos más de tres pesos" (We have more than three pesos).

2. **(A)** "Arma de fuego" means "firearm." Of the possible choices, we can immediately eliminate (C) and (D) because they are plural definite articles and cannot be placed before a singular noun such as "arma." This reduces our choices to "El" or "La." We know that most nouns that end in -a are feminine. By looking at the sentence carefully, we also see that the adjective "peligrosa" (dangerous) is feminine and most certainly modifies "arma." Therefore, you might have been tempted to choose (B), "La." This is not correct, however. Feminine singular nouns which end in -a but begin with "a" or "ha" and have their **stress** on the **first syllable**, as in "arma," require that we use the masculine singular definite article in front of them. This does not change the gender of the noun, however. It still stays feminine. We can see this in our sentence because we used the feminine adjective "peligrosa" to describe "arma." Remember that this rule applies only to feminine **singular** nouns. In the plural, we use the feminine plural definite article: "Las armas de fuego son peligrosas."

3. **(C)** When two or more adverbs are used together to refer to the same verb, the last one is the only one with the **–mente** ending.

4. **(D)** The verb "explicaron" in our sentence means "they explained." Comparisons of superiority, i.e., comparisons which show that in some respect someone or something is superior to someone or something else, are usually formed according to the following pattern: "más" + adjective or adverb or noun + "que." Example: "Enrique es **más rico que** yo." (Enrique is richer than I.) There are some adjectives and adverbs which have irregular comparatives. For example, "menor," which appears in (A), is the comparative form of "pequeño." "Mayor," in (C), is the comparative for "grande." Neither of these could be used in the blank because we are

not talking about size. On the other hand, "mejor que" would mean "better than" and makes sense in our sentence. The word "tanto," in (B), means "as much" or sometimes "so much." It is usually followed by "como" to form comparisons of equality, i.e., to show that two persons or things are equal in some respect: "Tengo **tanto dinero como** tú" (I have as much money as you). In (B), however, we have omitted the word "como," which is obligatory in comparisons of equality.

5.   **(C)**   When the verbs in each half of the comparison are both refer-ring to the same noun ("amigas"), the longer form of **than** is required. Because "amigas" is a feminine noun, "de las que" is used. For this reason (A) would be incorrect because it is masculine plural, and (D) is also in-correct because it is neuter. Answer (B) would be used in a simple com-parison where the verb is not repeated in the second half.

6.   **(B)**   Because an adjective is the point of comparison for each verb ("trabaja" and "cree"), the neuter form of **than** is used. Therefore, (C), the masculine form, and (D), the feminine form, are not correct. Answer (A) would be used in a simple comparison where the verb is not repeated in the second half.

7.   **(D)**   This is a simple comparison where the verb in the second half of the comparison is not stated but understood to be from the same infini-tive (**ser** in this case). Choice (A) is used in the first half of an equal com-parison and means **as**. Choice (C) is used in the second half of an equal comparison to mean **as**. Choice (B) is used in an unequal comparison when followed by a number.

8.   **(A)**   When there is an equal comparison that involves using an ad-jective or adverb, the word preceding this adjective or adverb is **tan** mean-ing **as**. The second half of this comparison requires using **como**, which is already in the sample. Therefore, choice (D) cannot be used to precede the adjective. Choices (B) and (C) each have gender and would precede nouns.

9.   **(B)**   Superlative statements require the use of the definite article and are followed by **de**. In this sample, because Roberto is masculine and Ana is feminine, the masculine plural "los" is required. Therefore, choice (A), the feminine plural, is incorrect. In order to use either choice (C) or (D), the sentence would need to be in the comparative form (not the superla-tive) and **que** would then need to follow the adjective.

10. **(A)** Whenever there are two or more adverbs modifying a verb, only the last adverb ends in **-mente**. The other must be written in the feminine form of the adjective (if there is one). This would eliminate choice (B), which is a masculine adjective, and (D), which is a masculine plural adjective. Choice (C) is incorrect because it ends in **-mente**.

11. **(C)** When dealing with the superlative forms of adverbs instead of using the definite article, which has gender, **lo** is used with **más** or **menos**. Therefore, (A), which is masculine, and (B), which is feminine plural, are incorrect. Choice (D) is incomplete because **lo** is needed.

12. **(D)** Because "torres" is a feminine plural noun, the feminine plural form of **tanto** is required. Choice (A) means **as** and does not translate correctly with a noun after it. Choice (C) is a completely incorrect form since forms of **tanto** mean **as much** or **as many**.

13. **(B)** Before any singular noun, "cualquiera" apocopates (drops the -a). Therefore, (D) is incorrect. Choices (A) and (C), although apocopated, are used with masculine singular nouns. To be correct, each would need to end in -a.

14. **(C)** Adjectives of nationality have four forms. The masculine plural form is required here because the adjective is modifying both a masculine and feminine subject. Because the masculine singular form is **alemán**, the plural adds -**es** to that form. (Note that the accent is dropped on the plural form.) This would eliminate (A), which is feminine plural, and (D), which is nonexistent. Choice (B) is incorrect because adjectives of this sort are not preceded by **de**.

15. **(A)** There are two grammatical points here: "grande" becomes "gran" before any singular noun and means **great**; the indefinite article ("una") is required before predicate nouns of occupation that are modified (have adjectives). Choice (B) is incorrect because "grande" is not apocopated, and (C) is incorrect because the apocopated form precedes, not follows, the noun. Choice (D) requires an indefinite article.

16. **(C)** This answer requires knowing the meaning of "mejor" (better) and "mayor" (older). Also, a comparison is followed by **que** not **de**. "Mejor" must be plural in this sample to match "notas." Although choices (B) and (D) are plural, they are followed by **de**. Choices (A) and (B) also mean "older," which doesn't make sense in this context. Although (D) is plural, it is also followed by **de** and is, therefore, incorrect.

17. **(C)** To express **how** followed by an adjective or adverb, use **lo** before that adjective/adverb and follow it with **que**. This would eliminate (A), (B), and (D) as correct choices.

18. **(B)** **Lo** is used as a complement to replace adjectives, pronouns, or nouns used with **ser**, **estar**, and **parecer**. In this sample, the noun "llaves" (keys) is being replaced in the answer with **lo**. **Lo** used in this sense is invariable and will not, therefore, have the same gender and number as the noun it replaces.

19. **(C)** The definite article is omitted with expressions such as this one (por primera vez, en primer lugar, etc.) Also, "vez" is feminine.

20. **(B)** "Todo lo que" is an expression meaning "all that."

PRESENT INDICATIVE

	amar **to love**	***comer*** **to eat**	***vivir*** **to live**
yo	*amo*	*como*	*vivo*
tú	*amas*	*comes*	*vives*
él/ella/Ud.	*ama*	*come*	*vive*
nosotros, –as	*amamos*	*comemos*	*vivimos*
*vosotros, –as**	*amáis*	*coméis*	*vivís*
ellos/ellas/Uds.	*aman*	*comen*	*viven*

* This pronoun and corresponding forms of the verb are used in Spain only.

Verbs irregular in *yo* form only:

caber	to fit	*quepo*	*saber*	to know	*sé*		
caer	to fall	*caigo*	*salir*	to leave	*salgo*		
dar	to give	*doy*	*traer*	to bring	*traigo*		
hacer	to make/do	*hago*	*valer*	to be worth	*valgo*		
poner	to put	*pongo*	*ver*	to see	*veo*		

Verbs irregular in more than one form:

decir **to tell or say**	***estar*** **to be**	***haber*** **to have (auxiliary)**	***ir*** **to go**
digo	*estoy*	*he*	*voy*
dices	*estás*	*has*	*vas*
dice	*está*	*ha*	*va*
decimos	*estamos*	*hemos*	*vamos*
decís	*estáis*	*habéis*	*vais*
dicen	*están*	*han*	*van*

oír **to hear**	***ser*** **to be**	***tener*** **to have**	***venir*** **to come**
oigo	*soy*	*tengo*	*vengo*
oyes	*eres*	*tienes*	*vienes*
oye	*es*	*tiene*	*viene*
oímos	*somos*	*tenemos*	*venimos*
oís	*sois*	*tenéis*	*venís*
oyen	*son*	*tienen*	*vienen*

Verbs Ending in -cer, -cir

The *yo* form ends in *–zco* if preceded by a vowel. If the ending is preceded by a consonant, the form ends in *–zo*.

conocer	to know	*cono**zco***
traducir	to translate	*tradu**zco***
vencer	to conquer	*ven**zo***

Others:

merecer – to deserve	*crecer* – to grow
carecer – to lack	*convencer* – to convince
aparecer – to appear	*nacer* – to be born
parecer – to seem	

Verbs that Have Stem Changes

There are five types of stem-changes that may occur in the present tense: (*ie*), (*ue*), (*i*), (*ú*), (*í*). This will occur in all forms except nosotros/vosotros and appears in the stressed syllable.

ie	ue	i	ú	í
pensar	*dormir*	*pedir*	*actuar*	*enviar*
to think	to sleep	to ask for	to act	to send
pienso	duermo	pido	actúo	envío
piensas	duermes	pides	actúas	envías
piensa	duerme	pide	actúa	envía
pensamos	dormimos	pedimos	actuamos	enviamos
pensáis	dormís	pedís	actuáis	enviáis
piensan	duermen	piden	actúan	envían

Other examples:

ie: *comenzar/empezar* – to begin, *nevar* – to snow, *cerrar* – to close, *apretar* – to tighten, *perder* – to lose, *querer* – to want, *mentir* – to lie, *sentir* – to feel, *herir* – to wound

ue: *morir* – to die, *dormir* – to sleep, *volar* – to fly, *poder* – to be able, *volver* – to return, *rogar* – to beg, *jugar* – to play

i: *elegir* – to elect, *repetir* – to repeat, *servir* – to serve, *corregir* – to correct

ú: *graduarse* – to graduate, *continuar* – to continue

í: *confiar* – to confide, *guiar* – to guide, *variar* – to vary

Verbs Ending in -ger, -gir

In the *yo* form there will be a spelling change because the **-go** combination will produce a **g** sound and the infinitive has an **h** sound.

coger	to catch	***cojo***
elegir (i)	to elect	***elijo***

Others:

escoger	to choose	***escojo***
corregir	to correct	***correjo***
recoger	to gather	***recojo***

Verbs Ending in -uir

All forms except *nosotros/vosotros* have a **y**.

huir **to flee**	***construir*** **to build**
huyo	*construyo*
huyes	*construyes*
huye	*construye*
huimos	*construimos*
huís	*construís*
huyen	*construyen*

Verbs Ending in -guir

The *yo* form drops the *u*.

seguir (i) – to follow	***sigo***
perseguir (i) – to pursue	***persigo***

Uses of the Present Indicative

There are three possible translations for the present tense as expressed below with the verb to eat (*comer*).

I eat./I do eat./I am eating. = *Como*.

Immediate Future

The present tense is commonly used to express the immediate future.

Mañana voy a casa.
Tomorrow I will go home.

The "Hace" Sentence

When an action began in the past and is still continuing in the present, the Spanish sentence is rendered with the following formula:

hace + time + *que* + Present/Present Progressive

Hace dos horas que comemos/estamos comiendo.
We have been eating for two hours.

¿Cuánto tiempo hace que ella canta/está cantando?
How long has she been singing?

PRETERITE AND IMPERFECT

Preterite Indicative—Regular: -ar, -er, -ir

	amar to love	*comer* to eat	*vivir* to live
yo	*amé*	*comí*	*viví*
tú	*amaste*	*comiste*	*viviste*
él/ella/Ud.	*amó*	*comió*	*vivió*
nosotros, –as	*amamos*	*comimos*	*vivimos*
vosotros, –as	*amasteis*	*comisteis*	*vivisteis*
ellos/ellas/Uds.	*amaron*	*comieron*	*vivieron*

Preterite Indicative—Irregular

The following group of preterites shares the same set of irregular endings: *–e, –iste, –o, –imos, –isteis, –ieron.*

andar to walk	*caber* to fit	*estar* to be	*haber* to have	*hacer* to make/do
anduve	*cupe*	*estuve*	*hube*	*hice*
anduviste	*cupiste*	*estuviste*	*hubiste*	*hiciste*
anduvo	*cupo*	*estuvo*	*hubo*	*hizo*
anduvimos	*cupimos*	*estuvimos*	*hubimos*	*hicimos*
anduvisteis	*cupisteis*	*estuvisteis*	*hubisteis*	*hicisteis*
anduvieron	*cupieron*	*estuvieron*	*hubieron*	*hicieron*

*poder** to be able	*poner* to put	*querer** to want
pude	puse	quise
pudiste	pusiste	quisiste
pudo	puso	quiso
pudimos	pusimos	quisimos
pudisteis	pusisteis	quisisteis
pudieron	pusieron	quisieron

*saber** to know	*tener** to have	*venir* to come
supe	tuve	vine
supiste	tuviste	viniste
supo	tuvo	vino
supimos	tuvimos	vinimos
supisteis	tuvisteis	vinisteis
supieron	tuvieron	vinieron

* These verbs have an altered translation in the preterite and will be discussed later in this chapter.

Irregular Preterites with a –J

decir to say/tell	*traer* to bring to drive	*–ducir* types *conducir*
dije	traje	conduje
dijiste	trajiste	condujiste
dijo	trajo	condujo
dijimos	trajimos	condujimos
dijisteis	trajisteis	condujisteis
dijeron	trajeron	condujeron

Note: The third plural does not have an *i* after the *j*.

Irregulars of *Dar, Ir, Ser*

Dar is irregular in that it takes the endings of the *-er/-ir* verbs (without accents). *Ser* and *ir* are identical in this tense.

dar to give	*ir/ser* to go/to be
di	fui
diste	fuiste
dio	fue
dimos	fuimos
disteis	fuisteis
dieron	fueron

Stem-Changing Verbs

Stem-changes commonly occur in the preterite for –*ir* verbs that have a stem-change in the present. These changes have a pattern (*ue/u*), (*ie/i*), and (*i/i*). The second vowel in parenthesis will surface in the preterite third person singular and plural.

dormir (ue, u) to sleep	*sentir* (ie, i) to regret or feel	*pedir* (i, i) to ask for
dormí	sentí	pedí
dormiste	sentiste	pediste
durmió	sintió	pidió
dormimos	sentimos	pedimos
dormisteis	sentisteis	pedisteis
durmieron	sintieron	pidieron

Others:

morir — to die	*divertirse* — to enjoy oneself	*servir* — to serve
	herir — to wound	*repetir* — to repeat
	mentir — to lie	*seguir* — to follow

Verbs ending in –car, –gar, –zar

Verbs ending in –*car*, –*gar*, and –*zar* are affected in the **yo** form of the preterite by the final –*é*. This vowel will cause the consonants before it (*c, g, z*) to change in sound. To maintain the original sound of the infinitive, these verbs will require a spelling change in that form as follows.

–*car* = *qué*	–*gar* = *gué*	–*zar* = *cé*

Examples:	*atacar = ataqué*	I attacked.
	entregar = entregué	I delivered.
	rezar = recé	I prayed.

Verbs that Change I to Y

All *–er* and *–ir* verbs with double vowels in the infinitive (with the exception of *traer/atraer*) will require this change in the third person singular and plural.

oír **to hear**	*creer* **to believe**	*leer* **to read**
oí	*creí*	*leí*
oíste	*creíste*	*leíste*
oyó	*creyó*	*leyó*
oímos	*creímos*	*leímos*
oísteis	*creísteis*	*leísteis*
oyeron	*creyeron*	*leyeron*

An added requirement for these verbs is the accent mark over the *i* in the *tú*, *nosotros*, and *vosotros* forms to split the diphthong.

Verbs Ending in –ller, –llir, –ñir, –ñer

Although these verbs are used with less frequency, they can surface on an AP exam. Because of the double *l* and the tilde over the *ñ*, these verbs in the third person singular and plural do not need the *i* of those endings.

bruñir **to polish**	*bullir* **to boil**
bruñí	*bullí*
bruñiste	*bulliste*
bruñó	*bulló*
bruñimos	*bullimos*
bruñisteis	*bullisteis*
bruñeron	*bulleron*

Verbs Ending in –uir

Just like the present tense of these verbs, the preterite also needs a *y*. It will occur in the third person singular and plural only.

huir	*construir*
to flee	**to build**
huí	*construí*
huiste	*construiste*
huyó	*construyó*
huimos	*construimos*
huisteis	*construisteis*
huyeron	*construyeron*

Verbs Ending in –guar

In this particular combination of letters, the **u** is heard as a separate letter, not treated as a diphthong with the **a** that follows. This sound will be altered in the **yo** form because of the final *–é*. To maintain the sound of the **u**, a dieresis mark is placed over it.

averiguar (to verify) = *averi**güé***

Note: This also occurs in other Spanish words:

la vergüenza (shame), *el agüero* (omen)

Imperfect Indicative–Regular: –ar, –er, –ir

This tense may be translated as "used to + verb," "was or were verb + ing," or the normal past tense ending "–ed."

	amar	*comer*	*vivir*
	to love	**to eat**	**to live**
yo	*amaba*	*comía*	*vivía*
tú	*amabas*	*comías*	*vivías*
él/ella/Ud.	*amaba*	*comía*	*vivía*
nosotros, –as	*amábamos*	*comíamos*	*vivíamos*
vosotros, –as	*amabais*	*comíais*	*vivíais*
ellos/ellas/Uds.	*amaban*	*comían*	*vivían*

Imperfect Indicative–Irregulars

There are only three irregular verbs in this tense.

ser to be	*ir* to go	*ver* to see
era	*iba*	*veía*
eras	*ibas*	*veías*
era	*iba*	*veía*
éramos	*íbamos*	*veíamos*
erais	*ibais*	*veíais*
eran	*iban*	*veían*

Continuation vs. Completion of an Action

The imperfect is used for an action **continuing** in the past; the preterite designates a **finished** action or an action whose beginning, duration, or end is emphasized by the speaker.

Estaba nublado. (Imperfect)
It was cloudy. (No indication of when it got that way.)

Estuvo nublado. (Preterite)
It was cloudy. (But now it has changed.)

Ella quería a su marido. (Imperfect)
She loved her husband. (Indefinitely in the past.)

Ella quiso a su marido. (Preterite)
She loved her husband. (While he was alive, while she was married to him, etc.)

Description vs. Narration

The imperfect is used to **describe** a quality or a state in the past; the preterite is used to **narrate** an action.

*Los soldados **marcharon** (pret.) toda una mañana y **llegaron** (pret.) al fuerte enemigo al mediodía cuando **hacía** (imp.) mucho calor. Se **sentían** (imp.) cansados y **necesitaban** (imp.) descansar. Se **sentaron** (pret.) a la sombra de un árbol.*
The soldiers marched one full morning and arrived at the enemy fort at noon when it was very hot. They were tired and needed to rest. They sat down in the shade of a tree.

"Used to" Followed by Infinitive

The English expression **used to** followed by an infinitive is rendered by the imperfect, as this is the tense that designates a habitual action in the past.

Pasábamos las vacaciones en la costa.
We **used to spend** the holidays on the shore.

Eran amigos.
They **used to be** friends.

Alternatively, the verb *soler* (to be in the habit of) may be used in the imperfect to render the sense of "used to." *Soler* must be accompanied by an infinitive: *solíamos pasar las vacaciones en la costa; solían ser amigos,* etc.

"Was" or "Were" Plus Present Participle

Expressions formed with the past tense of "to be" followed by the present participle of another verb (**was** or **were** doing, singing, studying, etc.) are rendered by the imperfect.

*Él **conducía** cuando ocurrió el accidente.*
He **was driving** when the accident occurred.

Pensaban visitarnos ese verano.
They **were thinking** of visiting us that summer.

Telling Time in the Past

The imperfect (of *ser*) is used to tell time in the past.

Eran las tres.
It was 3 o'clock.

Era tarde cuando se fueron los invitados.
It was late when the guests left.

Special Preterites

The preterite of some verbs (such as *conocer, saber, poder, poner, tener,* and *querer*) has a special meaning:

*Yo la **conocí** el año pasado.*
I **met** her last year.

*Cuando **supimos** la noticia nos pusimos tristes.*
When we **learned/found out** the news we felt sad.

*El fugitivo **pudo** abandonar el país a última hora.*
The fugitive **managed to** abandon the country at the last minute.

*Jamás **tuvo** noticias de su familia.*
She never **received** news of her family.

*El ladrón **quiso** abrir la puerta con una barra.*
The thief **tried to** open the door with a bar.

*Juan no **quiso** pagar la cuenta.*
Juan **refused** to pay the bill.

States of Mind

Normally verbs indicating state of mind (*saber, creer, pensar, comprender, convencerse*, etc.) are expressed using the imperfect unless there is an indication of change in that state. Look for words to indicate this change like *de pronto* (soon), *de repente* (suddenly), *luego que* (as soon as), *cuando* (when), *al* + infinitive (upon + ing).

Juan creía la verdad.
Juan believed the truth.

But:

__De pronto__ Juan la creyó.
Suddenly Juan believed it.

"Ago" Statements

"Ago" statements are normally expressed with this formula:

Hace + time + *que* + preterite

Hace dos años que fuimos allí.
We went there two years ago.

"Hacía" Statements

To express "had been + ing," use the formula:

hacía + time + *que* + imperfect/past progressive

Hacía dos horas que cantaba/estaba cantando.
He had been singing for two hours.

FUTURE AND CONDITIONAL

Future/Conditional Indicative–Regular: –ar, –er, –ir

Since these two tenses use the entire infinitive as their stem, only two examples are given here.

	amar **to love**	*comer* **to eat**
yo	*amaré/ía*	*comeré/ía*
tú	*amarás/ías*	*comerás/ías*
él/ella/Ud.	*amará/ía*	*comerá/ía*
nosotros, –as	*amaremos/íamos*	*comeremos/íamos*
vosotros, –as	*amaréis/íais*	*comeréis/íais*
ellos/ellas/Uds.	*amarán/ían*	*comerán/ían*

Future/Conditional Indicative–Irregulars

Verbs that drop the *–e* of the infinitive.

caber **to fit**	*haber* **to have–** **auxiliary**	*poder* **to be able**
cabré/ía	*habré/ía*	*podré/ía*
cabrás/ías	*habrás/ías*	*podrás/ías*
cabrá/ía	*habrá/ía*	*podrá/ía*
cabremos/íamos	*habremos/íamos*	*podremos/íamos*
cabréis/íais	*habréis/íais*	*podréis/íais*
cabrán/ían	*habrán/ían*	*podrán/ían*

querer **to want**	*saber* **to know**
querré/ía	*sabré/ía*
querrás/ías	*sabrás/ías*
querrá/ía	*sabrá/ía*
querremos/íamos	*sabremos/íamos*
querréis/íais	*sabréis/íais*
querrán/ían	*sabrán/ían*

Verbs that change the vowel (*e* or *i*) to a *d*.

poner **to put**	*salir* **to leave**	*tener* **to have**
pondré/ía	*saldré/ía*	*tendré/ía*
pondrás/ías	*saldrás/ías*	*tendrás/ías*
pondrá/ía	*saldrá/ía*	*tendrá/ía*
pondremos/íamos	*saldremos/íamos*	*tendremos/íamos*
pondréis/íais	*saldréis/íais*	*tendréis/íais*
pondrán/ían	*saldrán/ían*	*tendrán/ían*

valer **to be worth**	*venir* **to come**
valdré/ía	*vendré/ía*
valdrás/ías	*vendrás/ías*
valdrá/ía	*vendrá/ía*
valdremos/íamos	*vendremos/íamos*
valdréis/íais	*vendréis/íais*
valdrán/ían	*vendrán/ían*

Verbs that drop the *e* and *c* of the infinitive.

decir **to tell/say**	*hacer* **to make/do**
diré/ía	*haré/ía*
dirás/ías	*harás/ías*
dirá/ía	*hará/ía*
diremos/íamos	*haremos/íamos*
diréis/íais	*haréis/íais*
dirán/ían	*harán/ían*

Note: Compounds of the above words are conjugated in the same manner (*proponer, detener, contener*). However, **maldecir** and **bendecir** are conjugated as regular verbs in these two tenses and do not follow the pattern for **decir**.

Uses of Future/Conditional

Common translations include **will/shall** for the future and **would** for the conditional.

Saldré en seguida.	I shall leave immediately.
Me gustaría saberlo.	I would like to know it.
Juan vivirá conmigo.	Juan will live with me.

Probability Statements or Conjecture

The future tense is used to express **present** probability statements while the conditional expresses **past** probability. These statements in English may be expressed a number of ways.

Present Probability	Past Probability
He **is** probably ill.	He **was** probably ill.
Estará enfermo.	*Estaría enfermo.*
*[Debe de estar enfermo.]**	*[Debía de estar enfermo.]*
It **must** be 1:00.	It **must have been** 1:00.
Será la una.	*Sería la una.*
[Debe de ser la una.]	*[Debía de ser la una.]*
Where **can** he be?	Where **could** he be?
¿Dónde estará?	*¿Dónde estaría?*
I wonder who he **is**?	I wonder who he **was**?
¿Quién será?	*¿Quién sería?*

* ***Deber de*** + **infinitive** is another way to express probability statements.

Expressing *Would, Wouldn't* with the Past Tense

When **would** means **used to**, the imperfect tense is used.
When **wouldn't** means **refused**, the negative preterite of *querer* is used.

Cuando era joven, iba al cine a menudo.
When he was young, he would go to the movies often.

No quiso verme.
He wouldn't (refused to) see me.

☞ Drill 2

1. Ninguna de las ventanas está sucia porque la criada las...ayer.

    (A) limpio   (C) limpió

    (B) limpiaba   (D) limpian

2. Ayer, al levantarme por la mañana, vi que...un día estupendo.

    (A) hacía   (C) hizo

    (B) hará   (D) había hecho

3. Durante mi niñez siempre...a la casa de mis tíos.

    (A) iría   (C) fui

    (B) iba   (D) iré

4. Cuando tropezaron conmigo,...de salir del cine.

    (A) acabaron   (C) acabé

    (B) acababa   (D) acaban

5. Los jugadores no...jugar más.

    (A) tuvieron   (C) quisieron

    (B) trataron   (D) iban

6. Esta tarde mientras...el periódico, sonó el teléfono.

    (A) miraré   (C) leía

    (B) busqué   (D) estudio

7. Aunque ella vino temprano, no la...

    (A) vi.   (C) vea.

    (B) viera.   (D) veré.

8. Al despertarse Ramón se dio cuenta de que...

    (A) llovió.   (C) llovido.

    (B) llovía.   (D) había llover.

9. El ladrón entró por la ventana que…abierta.

    (A) estuvo   (C) estará

    (B) estaba   (D) estaría

10. La guerra de Vietnam…varios años.

    (A) duraba   (C) duró

    (B) durará   (D) hubo durado

11. …tres horas que regresó de su viaje.

    (A) Hacen   (C) Hace

    (B) Ha   (D) Desde

12. Yo…el colegio a los 10 años.

    (A) dejé   (C) dejara

    (B) dejaba   (D) dejase

13. Yo…dormido cuando me llamaste.

    (A) estaba   (C) estoy

    (B) estuve   (D) estaré

14. Lo…la semana que viene.

    (A) hicimos   (C) haremos

    (B) hacíamos   (D) habíamos hecho

15. Si yo fuera al centro, te…algo.

    (A) compraría   (C) compre

    (B) compré   (D) compraré

16. Cuando era niño, me…viendo pasar a la gente por las calles.

    (A) divertí   (C) divertiría

    (B) divertía   (D) divirtiera

17. ¿Cuánto tiempo...que hablabas cuando entraron?

    (A) hacía   (C) hacían

    (B) hizo   (D) había sido

18. Hacía dos horas que ellos...cuando sonó el teléfono.

    (A) charlaron   (C) habían charlado

    (B) charlan   (D) estaban charlando

19. Ayer al oír al testigo, el juez lo...

    (A) crea.   (C) creyó.

    (B) creía.   (D) creerá.

20. ...las tres cuando el tren partió.

    (A) Eran   (C) Fue

    (B) Era   (D) Fueron

21. ...dos años que terminó la guerra.

    (A) Hizo   (C) Hace

    (B) Hacía   (D) Hacen

22. Ayer yo...a Juan por primera vez.

    (A) conocía   (C) supe

    (B) conocí   (D) sabía

23. Hace dos semanas que no he visto a Ana. ¿...enferma?

    (A) Estará   (C) Va a estar

    (B) Esté   (D) Estás

24. Cuando Juan era joven,...al cine a menudo.

    (A) va   (C) iba

    (B) iría   (D) irá

25. Si tengo el tiempo,... el museo.

    (A) visitaría   (C) visitaré

    (B) visite   (D) visitaba

26. ¿Cuánto tiempo... que andas sin coche?

    (A) hacía   (C) hizo

    (B) haces   (D) hace

Drill 2—Detailed Explanations of Answers

1. **(C)** We know that a past tense is needed in this sentence because of the word "ayer" (yesterday). We must then choose between the two past tenses given among the choices: preterite and imperfect. The imperfect tense is often used to imply that a past action was incomplete, i.e., that it had not come to an end, that it was not concluded. In this sentence, however, we know that the maid finished her task of cleaning the windows because we are told that for that very reason the windows are now clean. The preterite tense is used to show that a past action, as viewed by the speaker, is considered completed, over and done with.

2. **(A)** The use of the preterite of the verb "ver" tells us that we are talking about the past. In our sentence, we are describing what the weather was like yesterday morning. The imperfect tense, rather than the preterite, is most frequently used in sentences which describe in the past, particularly if we do not wish to place undue emphasis on the idea that the situation described came to an end. This use of the imperfect tense is especially evident in contexts in which one is setting up the scene or describing the background against which other major events will take place, for example: "Era una tarde triste y lluviosa. No había nadie en la calle." (It was a sad and rainy afternoon. There was no one in the street.)

3. **(B)** In the sentence where you are to fill in the blank, the adverb "siempre" (always) is important. When we are talking about the past and we are referring to a customary or habitual action, as is the case in our sentence, we use the imperfect tense to place emphasis on the idea that the action was performed repeatedly (for an unspecified number of times). In (A), however, the verb "ir" is used in the conditional tense, not the imperfect. English speakers sometimes erroneously use the conditional tense in Spanish to express the idea of "would" in the sense of "used to" simply because English uses the word "would" both as a conditional and also to convey the concept of repeated and habitual past action. This cannot be done in Spanish. Compare the following two English sentences: If he were here, I would know it; Every Saturday when we were at the beach I would swim. Notice that only the second example has to do with a customary and habitual past action. It is in such a case that Spanish would use the imperfect tense instead of the conditional. Choice (C) is wrong because although the sentence refers to the past, it is in the preterite tense. Choice (D) is incorrect also because it is in the wrong tense, the future.

4. **(B)** The verb "tropezar" means "to stumble." The expression "tropezar **con**" means "to meet or encounter." Notice how the preposition
"con," when followed by the prepositional pronoun "mí," results in the
special form "conmigo." The same thing happens in the second person
singular (the familiar form) to produce the word "contigo." The expression "acabar de" + infinitive signifies "to have just" done something. This
expression is normally only used in two tenses, the simple present and the
imperfect. In the present it means "have or has just." In the imperfect it
means "had just." Since our sentence contains a verb in the preterite tense,
"tropezaron," we know that we are talking about the past. Therefore, we
must logically use the only form of the imperfect that appears among the
choices, "acababa."

5. **(C)** (A) is incorrect because "to have to" do something is "tener
que" + infinitive, but we have omitted the "que." (B), "trataron," is wrong
because we have not included the "de" from the expression "tratar de" +
infinitive (to try to do something). In (D), "iban," the preposition "a" is
lacking. Remember, "ir a" + infinitive means "to be going to" do something. (C), "quisieron," is the only answer which fits grammatically in our
sentence. Try to recall the special meanings which the verb "querer" may
have in the preterite tense. If the sentence is affirmative, it may be a syn-
onym for "tratar de" (to try to). "Quisieron venir" would mean "They tried
to come." If we simply mean "They wanted to come," we would use the
imperfect tense: "Querían venir." If the sentence is negative, then "querer"
in the preterite can mean "refused to," as is the case in our sentence. If we
simply mean "They didn't want to come," then we would use the imperfect
tense again: "No querían venir."

6. **(C)** In our sentence, "mientras" means "while," and "sonó" is the
third person singular of the verb "sonar" (to ring—what a telephone does).
Do not confuse "sonar" with "soñar" (to dream). Because "sonó" is a past
tense, we know that neither (A), "miraré," the first person singular of the
future of "mirar" (to look at), nor (D), "estudio" (I study), the first person
singular or the present, can be used. Then we are faced with a choice between the first person singular of the preterite of "buscar" (to look for), in
(B) "busqué," and "leía," the first person singular of the imperfect of "leer"
(to read), in (C), which are both past tenses. When we are talking about
the past and we wish to show that an action which was in progress was
interrupted by another action, the action in progress is given the imperfect
tense and the interrupting action appears in the preterite. In our sentence,
the action which was in progress when something else cut across it or interrupted is "I was reading" ("leía"). The action which caused the interrup-
tion is "rang" ("sonó").

7. **(A)** After **aunque,** if the present tense is used, the independent clause is generally in the future. In this case, since it is in the past, the preterite indicative is correct. This sentence does not express any uncertainty, but fact. She did arrive, and early. Another statement of fact is that "I did not see her." Therefore, the subjunctive is not needed.

8. **(B)** The correct choice is "llovía" since the imperfect translates a sense of an ongoing event in the past (sometimes, as in this phrase, "intersected" by another discrete event, namely, "se dio cuenta"). The preterite, on the other hand, marks the start, end, or completed duration of an event. In this context such an event is the realizing and not the raining which had already started outside the enunciation, so to speak. This is why choice (A) is incorrect. (As a rule of thumb, if a Spanish verb in the past can be translated into English by means of was + ing, then the Spanish verb can be rendered in the imperfect.) Choices (C) and (D) are wrong for other reasons: "llovido" is a past participle that requires an auxiliary verb ("haber") to function in the present context; and "había llover" is ungrammatical since compound tenses cannot be formed with the infinitive of the main verb.

9. **(B)** The window was already open. The real action of the phrase is the entering. By comparison, the reference to the window is in the mode of a **state** of things or in the mode of a **description**. This is why the correct answer involves an imperfect tense and not a preterite. Choices (C) and (D) do not correlate temporally with "entró."

10. **(C)** Again, the right answer is the preterite because the temporal function of the verb is to designate a duration. Choice (D) is a rarely used formation mostly reserved for literary style. It means the same as the preterite.

11. **(C)** The formula for this kind of expression is **hace** (never in the plural) + **time** + **que** + **preterite** (or **preterite** + **hace** + **time**). In English, this formula translates the particle "ago."

12. **(A)** Choices (C) and (D), both in the subjunctive, are ungrammatical, and (B) is not a good choice in view of the fact that the sentence is about temporal circumscription: the action of quitting school is "bound" by the point in time designated by "ten years." Remember that "imperfect" means incomplete and that an imperfect action is one that the sentence does not mark as ending (or beginning) in the past. The action described in this question, however, is complete; it is a point in time and not an open-ended line.

13. **(A)** Both (C) and (D) make no sense in terms of the temporal frame of the question. Now, the action of calling is in the preterite, which means it did not go on in time and that it is limited and complete in itself. But this is not true of sleeping, which becomes the temporal background for the instance of calling. And here we run into another criterion for learning the difference between preterite and imperfect: when there is a description in the past (as opposed to a main action), the verb used is in the imperfect.

14. **(C)** This item simply tests your understanding that the future tense must be used in the sentence and your recognition of the future tense form of the verb "hacer" (to make or do), "haremos." We know that we must use the future because of the expression "la semana que viene" (next week) in our sentence. (A) "hicimos," is the first person plural of the preterite of "hacer." (B) and (D) give us, respectively, the first person plural of the imperfect, "hacíamos," and of the pluperfect, "habíamos hecho," of the same verb.

15. **(A)** In an "if" clause in the past, using the subjunctive, the conditional is the appropriate form to follow.

16. **(B)** You should first recognize the different forms of "divertirse" given as options and realize, for example, that "divirtiera" is a subjunctive form with no place in the sentence (because there is no "que" followed by a dependent verb). You can also eliminate (C) in order to avoid the contradiction in tense that would result if you put together an imperfect ("era") and a conditional. So the final choice boils down to a choice between the preterite form (A) and the imperfect one (B). The latter is correct because the action of having fun is not circumscribed temporally by any semantic element of the sentence. In other words, you may translate the second part of the sentence with "used to," and being able to do this automatically signals the use of the imperfect.

17. **(A)** In time phrases that use the imperfect tense (hablabas), the third singular of the imperfect of "hacer" is needed. This would eliminate (C) because it is plural and (B) because it is preterite. Answer (D) is a form of the verb **ser**.

18. **(D)** In time phrases beginning with "hacía" either the imperfect tense or, in this case, the past progressive is correct. This would eliminate (A) the preterite and (B) the present tense of charlar. Choice (C) could be used if it were negative.

19. **(C)** Because the action occurred yesterday and "upon hearing" the witness, the preterite of the verb is necessary. If the sentence does not have any indications of past completion, the imperfect answer (B) would be preferred. This would eliminate (A) the subjunctive and (D) the future.

20. **(A)** To express time in the past, the imperfect tense is used. Because it is "three" o'clock and, therefore, plural in Spanish, the plural form of the verb is required. Therefore, choice (B), which is singular, is incorrect. Because both (C) and (D) are in the preterite tense, they are incorrect.

21. **(C)** In order to express **"ago"** in Spanish, an "hace" statement of time will be followed by the preterite tense (in this case "terminó"). "Hace" will be written in the third person singular of the present tense in these statements. Therefore, choice (A) in the preterite, (B) in the imperfect, and (D) in the plural are all incorrect.

22. **(B)** Certain verbs change meaning in the preterite. "Conocer" means "met" in this tense. Because this happened yesterday (ayer) for the first time (por primera vez), we know that the preterite is necessary. This would make choice (A) in the imperfect incorrect. Also, to "meet or know" people requires the use of the verb **conocer**. Therefore, choice (C) "I found out" and (D) "I knew" for the verb **saber** are incorrect in this context.

23. **(A)** This question intimates probability in that it has been two weeks since Ana was seen last. To express present probability, the future tense is used. This may be translated a number of ways: I wonder if she is ill?; Can she be ill?; Is she probably ill? Choice (B), the present subjunctive, and (C), the immediate future, make no sense in this context. Choice (D) is the second singular to refer to Ana, but the third singular is required here.

24. **(C)** In English we often use "would" to refer to something we "used to" do in the past. In Spanish, however, this must be expressed with the imperfect tense, not the conditional. Choice (A), the present tense, (B), the conditional tense, and (D), the future tense are incorrect in this context.

25. **(C)** In this question an understanding of **if** clauses is needed. Commonly when the **if** clause is in the present tense, the other clause will be written in the future tense. Choice (A) is conditional and would call for a past subjunctive to be used in the **if** clause. Choice (B), the present subjunctive, and (D), the imperfect, make no sense when translated in this context.

26. **(D)**   Time expressions with **hace** have a certain formula. When asking "how long something **has been** going on," **hace** is paired up with the present tense (or present progressive tense). The other possible time expression would have **hacía** coupled with the imperfect (or past progressive tense). Since "andas" follows **que** and is in the present tense, "hace" must be used in the time expression. Choice (A), the imperfect, and (C), the preterite, are incorrect here. Choice (B) is in the wrong person to be used in an **hace** sentence.

FORMATION OF COMPOUND TENSES

Compound tenses are formed by adding an invariable past participle to the different forms of the auxiliary verb *haber*.

The Past Participle

The past participle in Spanish is formed by appending **–ado** to the stem of an *–ar* verb or **–ido** to the stem of an *–er* or *–ir* verb,

jugar – jugado (played)	*comer – comido* (eaten)
recibir – recibido (received)	

The Irregular Past Participle

There are 12 irregular past participles.

abrir — abierto (opened)	*morir — muerto* (died)
cubrir — cubierto (covered)	*poner — puesto* (put)
decir — dicho (said)	*resolver— resuelto* (solved)
escribir — escrito (written)	*romper — roto* (broken)
hacer — hecho (done)	*ver — visto* (seen)
imprimir — impreso (printed)	*volver — vuelto* (returned)

Past Participles Ending in –ido

Most double voweled infinitives will require an accent mark over the participle ending to separate the diphthong created when the weak vowel *i* follows the strong vowel of the stem.

oír – oído (heard)   *caer – caído* (fallen)   *leer – leído* (read)

Note: Verbs ending in **–uir** do not require accents in this form.

huir – huido (fled)   *construir – construido* (built)

Conjugation of *Haber*: Indicative Mood*

	Present	Preterite*	Imperfect	Future	Conditional
yo	he	hube	había	habré	habría
tú	has	hubiste	habías	habrás	habrías
él/ella/Ud.	ha	hubo	había	habrá	habría
nosotros, –as	hemos	hubimos	habíamos	habremos	habríamos
vosotros, –as	habéis	hubisteis	habíais	habréis	habríais
ellos/ellas/Uds.	han	hubieron	habían	habrán	habrían

* The preterite perfect is a literary tense not commonly used in everyday speech. It is always preceded by a conjunction of time:

luego que	as soon as	*apenas*	hardly, scarcely
en cuanto	as soon as	*cuando*	when
así que	as soon as	*después que*	after
tan pronto como	as soon as	*no bien*	no sooner

Conjugation of *Haber*: Subjunctive and Imperative Moods

	Present	**Imperfect**
yo	*haya*	*hubiera/hubiese*
tú	*hayas*	*hubieras/hubieses*
él/ella/Ud.	*haya*	*hubiera/hubiese*
nosotros, –as	*hayamos*	*hubiéramos/hubiésemos*
vosotros, –as	*hayáis*	*hubierais/hubieseis*
ellos/ellas/Uds.	*hayan*	*hubieran/hubiesen*

Names of Compound Tenses

Compound tenses are formed by combining different tenses of verbs to create a new one.

Perfect

The present indicative of *haber* with a past participle forms the **present perfect** tense:

He amado.
I **have** loved.

Habéis comido.
You **have** eaten.

Han partido.
They **have** left.

Note: Only *haber* is conjugated. *Amado, comido,* and *partido* do not have to agree in gender and number with their respective subjects.

Pluperfect

The imperfect indicative of *haber* with a past participle forms the **pluperfect** or **past perfect** tense. This tense is used for a past action that precedes another past action:

Había amado.
I **had** loved.

Habíais comido.
You **had** eaten.

Habían partido.
They **had** left.

Future Perfect

The future of *haber* with a past participle forms the **future perfect:**

Habré amado.
I **will have** loved.

Habrán partido.
They **will have** left.

Note: This tense expresses an action that will take place **before** another. But very commonly the future perfect denotes probability in the past. Compare the following examples:

a) *¿Habrán partido antes de que comience a llover?*
    Will they **have left** before it starts to rain?

b) *Ya habrán partido.*
    They **probably left** already.

Conditional Perfect

The conditional of *haber* with a past participle forms the **conditional perfect:**

Habría amado.
I **would have** loved.

Habrían partido.
They **would have** left.

Perfect Subjunctive

The present subjunctive of *haber* with a past participle forms the **present perfect subjunctive:**

*Es increíble que no **haya amado** a nadie en su vida.*
It's incredible that he **has** not **loved** anyone in his life.

*Los extrañaremos cuando **hayan partido**.*
We'll miss them when they **have left.**

Pluperfect Subjunctive

The imperfect subjunctive of *haber* with a past participle forms the **pluperfect** or **past perfect subjunctive**:

*Yo no habría conocido la felicidad si no **hubiera amado**.*
I would not have known happiness if I **had** not **loved**.

*Él siempre había dudado de que sus amigos **hubieran partido** sin despedirse.*
He had always doubted that his friends **had left** without saying goodbye.

Past Participle as Adjective

When the past participle is used with ***haber*** to form the perfect tenses it is invariable. When not accompanied by some form of ***haber***, it functions as an adjective and has four possible forms.

He roto la taza.	I have broken the cup.	[perfect]
La taza está rota.	The cup is broken	[adjective]
una ventana abierta	an open window	[adjective]

THE PRESENT PARTICIPLE

The present participle is formed by appending ***-ando*** to the stem of *–ar* verbs and ***-iendo*** to the stem of *–er* and *–ir* verbs.

andar-andando (walking)   *escribir-escribiendo* (writing)
vivir-viviendo (living)

Present Participles with a *y*

Double voweled infinitives ending in *–er* and *–ir* (*creer, leer, oír, caer*, etc.) have a *y* in the present participle. It replaces the *i* of the participle ending.

caer–cayendo   *leer–leyendo*   *oír–oyendo*   *traer–trayendo*

Exception: *reír–riendo* (laughing)

Present Participles with Stem Changes

Verbs ending in *–ir* that have preterite tense stem-changes use the same Stem-Change in the present participle.

dormir–durmiendo	*pedir–pidiendo*	*servir–sirviendo*
(ue, **u**)	(i, **i**)	(i, **i**)

Irregular Present Participles

There are four irregular present participles.

ir–yendo   *poder–pudiendo*   *venir–viniendo*   *decir–diciendo*

The Present Participle with *Estar*

The present participle denotes an action in progress and commonly follows the verb *estar*. It corresponds to the "-ing" form of the verb in English. In Spanish it is always invariable. These are called progressive tenses.

Estoy comiendo.	I am eating.
Estaban leyendo.	They were reading.
Estaremos jugando al tenis.	We will be playing tennis.

The Present Participle with Motion Verbs

The present participle may also follow verbs of motion: *ir* (to go), *venir* (to come), *andar* (to walk), *entrar* (to enter), *salir* (to go out), etc.

Ella va corriendo por la calle.
She goes running down the street.

Juan entró riendo pero salió llorando.
Juan entered laughing but left crying.

The Present Participle with *Seguir/Continuar*

Present participles also follow forms of *seguir* (*i, i*) (to keep on) and *continuar* (*ú*) (to continue). In English "to continue" is often followed by an infinitive. This will **not** occur in Spanish.

Siga leyendo.	Keep on reading.
Ellos continúan hablando.	They continue talking.
	They continue to talk.

The Present Participle Used Alone

The present participle does not need a helping verb to exist. It is often used alone.

Andando por la calle, se cayó.
Walking down the street, he fell down.

No conociendo bien la ciudad, se perdieron.
Not knowing the city well, they got lost.

When Not to Use the Present Participle

Never use the present participle as an **adjective**. Use a clause instead.

un niño que llora	a crying child
un asunto que aterroriza	a frightening event

Never use the present participle as a **noun** (gerund). Use the infinitive instead.

Ver es creer.	Seeing is believing.

Never use the present participle after a **preposition**. Use the infinitive instead.

después de comer	after eating

Never use the present participle of *ir* with the verb **estar**. Use *voy a, vas a, iba a,* etc.

Voy a salir.	I am going to leave.
Iban a comer.	They were going to eat.

REFLEXIVE PRONOUNS

Verbs whose action reflects back upon the subject are called reflexive. Infinitives of reflexive verbs in Spanish end in *–se*. Verbs of this type require the use of the reflexive pronoun group (*me, te, se, nos, os, se*). English uses pronouns such as myself, herself, themselves, etc., to designate reflexive actions. There are a number of reasons why a verb is reflexive.

1. The verb actually has a "reflexive" translation. I bathe "myself." = *Me baño*.

2. The pronoun is an inherent part of the verb and has no English translation: *atreverse a* (to dare to), *quejarse de* (to complain about), etc.

3. The pronoun alters the meaning of the verb in some way, other than reflexively: *irse* = to go **away**, *caerse* = to fall **down**, etc.

4. To render the meaning "get or become": *enfermarse* (to get ill), *casarse* (to get married), *enojarse* (to get angry), etc.

5. The pronoun is used with the verb when the subject is performing an action **on** his/her own body. *Me rompí la pierna.* = I broke my leg.

Placement of the Pronouns with Verbs

After selecting the pronoun that matches the subject of the verb, it will be placed either **before** the verb or **after** and **attached** to the verb. The following samples demonstrate the placement.

Quiero bañarme.	I want to bathe.	[infinitive]
¡Levántese!	Get up!	[+ command/formal]
¡No te sientes!	Don't sit down!	[– command/familiar]
Estás lavándote.	You are washing up.	[present participle]
Me llamo Juana.	My name is Juana.	[conjugated]

Uses of *Se*

The reflexive pronoun *se* is used a number of ways.

1. To express the impersonal **one/people/they** statement with the third person singular of the verb.

    se dice = one says/people say/they say

2. To render "non-blame" statements when used with certain verbs: *perder* (to lose), *olvidar* (to forget), *romper* (to break), *quemar* (to burn). With statements such as these the speaker is indicating that something happened that was unintentional on his/her part. The *se* will precede the indirect object pronoun (which replaces the subject in English), and the verb will match the noun that follows it.

*se **me** rompió el vaso.*	**I** broke the glass.
*se **nos** perdió el dinero.*	**We** lost the money.
*se **le** olvidaron los libros.*	**He** forgot the books.

Reciprocal Actions

The plural reflexive pronouns (*nos, os, se*) are used to express "each other" in Spanish.

Se escriben.	They write to each other (to themselves).
Nos amamos.	We love each other (ourselves).

Note: Because the above statements could have a reflexive meaning (in parenthesis) as well, one may add the following phrase to clarify:

Se escriben uno a otro	or	*el uno al otro*
una a otra	or	*la una a la otra*
unos a otros	or	*los unos a los otros*
unas a otras	or	*las unas a las otras*

This additional clarifying statement is especially useful with verbs that are already reflexive. In those cases the reflexive pronoun cannot have dual meanings—it must act as a reflexive. As is often the case with these types, there is an accompanying preposition to be dealt with. This preposition is placed in the clarifying statement.

casarse con	to get married to
*Se casan uno **con** otro.*	They get married to each other.
burlarse de	to make fun of
*Se burlan uno **de** otro.*	They make fun of each other.

Reflexive Substitute for the Passive Voice

It is more idiomatic to replace the passive construction with a reflexive construction using the pronoun *se* and the verb in the third person singular or plural. This is especially true of passive sentences that have no expressed agent.

Aquí se habla español.	Spanish is spoken here.

☞ **Drill 3**

1. Después de dos horas el orador siguió...

   (A) hablar.   (C) habla.

   (B) hablaba.   (D) hablando.

2. ...olvidó lavar la ropa por la manaña.

   (A) Me   (C) Se me

   (B) Se   (D) Me lo

3. Los alumnos están...la composición.

   (A) escrito   (C) analizando

   (B) leen   (D) escriben

4. Los vampiros no...en el espejo.

   (A) lo ven   (C) le ven

   (B) se ven   (D) les ven

5. Los trabajadores han...su labor.

   (A) terminaron   (C) terminados

   (B) terminando   (D) terminado

6. Hace mucho tiempo que yo no...con mi mamá.

   (A) he hablado   (C) estaba hablando

   (B) había hablado   (D) hablado

7. ...el trabajo, pudo salir a tiempo.

   (A) Haber terminado   (C) Al terminando

   (B) Estar terminando   (D) Habiendo terminado

8. Los problemas..., cerró el libro y salió.

   (A) resueltos   (C) resolvidos

   (B) resueltas   (D) resuelven

9. Para este viernes ellos...la película.

   (A) habían visto   (C) habrán visto

   (B) habrían visto   (D) han visto

10. Ellos vinieron...por la calle.

    (A) andando   (C) andado

    (B) andar   (D) andados

11. ..., salió del cuarto.

    (A) Decírmelo   (C) Diciéndomelo

    (B) Me lo decir   (D) Deciéndomelo

12. Juan entró...después de oír el chiste.

    (A) reír   (C) reyendo

    (B) riendo   (D) riyendo

13. No continúes...en la iglesia por favor.

    (A) hablar   (C) hablado

    (B) a hablar   (D) hablando

14. Un niño...me causa pena.

    (A) que llora   (C) llorar

    (B) llorando   (D) a llorar

15. Esto es...

    (A) vivido.   (C) viviendo.

    (B) vivir.   (D) viva.

16. Los chicos...por la calle cuando vieron al policía.

    (A) eran yendo   (C) yendo

    (B) estaban yendo   (D) iban

17. Al…el ruido, todos corrieron.

    (A) oír   (C) oído

    (B) oyeron   (D) oyendo

18. ¡Ay de mí! ¡…el vaso!

    (A) se me rompió   (C) se me rompieron

    (B) me rompí   (D) me rompieron

19. ¿Quieres…antes de ir?

    (A) bañarse   (C) bañarte

    (B) báñate   (D) bañándote

20. Es importante…la mano antes de hablar.

    (A) levantarse   (C) que te levantes

    (B) que levanta   (D) levantar

21. El sacerdote…la pareja.

    (A) se casó   (C) casó a

    (B) se casó a   (D) casó con

22. Aunque vivimos en distintos lugares,…uno a otro cada semana.

    (A) nos escribimos   (C) escribimos

    (B) se escriben   (D) nos escriben

Drill 3—Detailed Explanations of Answers

1. **(D)** The gerund in Spanish may be used after a conjugated verb, as in this case. The only answer which is correct is **hablando**. The **siguió** is translated as "kept on" or "continued," i.e., verbs of motion.

2. **(C)** There are three different forms in which the verb "olvidar" (to forget) may be used. The simplest of these is "olvidar" used non-reflexively and followed by a noun of an infinitive. For example, "Olvidé lavar la ropa" (I forgot to wash the clothes). Another form is "olvidar**se de**" + noun or infinitive: "**Me** olvidé **de** lavar la ropa." The third form is also reflexive but does not use the preposition "de." It is always accompanied by an indirect object pronoun in addition to the reflexive pronoun: "**Se me** olvidó lavar la ropa." Notice that in this sentence the verb and the reflexive pronoun both are used in the third person singular. This is because the subject of the Spanish sentence is **not** "yo" (I), but rather the infinitive "lavar." In other words, the Spanish literally says "Washing forgot itself." In this sentence, "me" is an indirect object pronoun and means "to me." Therefore, "Se me olvidó lavar la ropa" literally means "Washing the clothes forgot itself to me." One would never say that in English. Instead, we would simply say "I forgot to wash the clothes." The indirect object pronoun, when used this way with the reflexive form of "olvidar," simply shows who is affected by the action of the verb. (A) "Me" will not work here. For it to be correct, we would have to change the verb to "olvidé" and then add the preposition "de."

3. **(C)** In order to form the present progressive tense, we use "estar" + –ndo verb form, meaning "to be doing (something)." Hence, we must say "están analizando" (are analyzing). The progressive tenses place very special emphasis on the fact that the action is (was, etc.) in progress or is (was, etc.) happening at a particular moment. If we do not wish to give that decided emphasis, we just use the simple tenses (present, imperfect, etc.) We can use the progressive form in all of the tenses simply by changing the tense of "estar," for example, "estaban analizando" (they were analyzing), etc. Choice (A) "escrito" is wrong because it is the past participle, not the present participle, of "escribir" (to write). (B) "leen" will not function in our sentence because we cannot have two conjugated verbs, one immediately after the other ("están" and "leen"). The same is true for (D) "escriben."

4. **(B)** "Espejo" indicates that the pronoun needed is reflexive, and the only such pronoun among the choices is (B). The rest are direct object pronouns (A) or indirect, (C) and (D).

5. **(D)** What is needed to fill in the blank is a past participle, which eliminates the first two choices. You also must know that a past participle in a compound tense (following "haber") is invariable in person, gender, and number.

6. **(A)** "Time" statements beginning with **hace** are normally written using the present indicative or the present progressive tenses. Only in the case where the main verb is negative can a perfect tense be used. Choice (B) would be correct if the verb were negative and followed "hacía." Choice (C) also would be found in an "hacía" statement. Choice (D) makes no sense since it is the past participle by itself.

7. **(D)** The translation of this sentence indicates that a participle is required ("Having finished the work,") to make sense. In order for (A) to be correct in the infinitive form, it would have to act as a gerund (i.e., be the subject or object of the verb). Choice (C) is incorrect because **al** must be followed by an infinitive. Choice (B) makes no sense when translated and used in this context.

8. **(A)** The past participle may act as an adjective and in that capacity must match the noun it modifies. Because this noun is masculine and this participle is irregular, (A) is the correct answer. Choice (B) is feminine and (C) is an incorrect form of the past participle. Choice (D) is a conjugated verb and makes no sense in this context.

9. **(C)** By translating this sentence (By this Friday they will have seen the movie.) the proper perfect tense surfaces. Choice (A) "they had seen, (B) "they would have seen," and (D) "they have seen" make no sense in this context.

10. **(A)** Verbs of motion ("vinieron") can be followed by present participles, in this case "andando." They cannot, however, be followed by an infinitive (B) or the past participle (C) and (D).

11. **(C)** This sentence begins with the participial phrase meaning "Saying it to me." Because "Saying" is not the subject of the sentence, it will not be written as a gerund (the infinitive form in Spanish). Therefore, choice (A) is incorrect. Choice (B) is incorrect not only because it is in the

infinitive form but also because pronouns must be after and attached to infinitives. Choice (D) is misspelled.

12. **(B)** Again, verbs of motion may be followed by present participles. Choices (C) and (D) appear to be written in the present participle but are misspelled. Choice (A) is an infinitive and is, therefore, incorrect.

13. **(D)** Unlike English the verb **continue** (continuar) in Spanish cannot be followed by either the infinitive or the present participle. In Spanish, only the present participle is correct with this verb. This would eliminate (A), the infinitive, (B), the infinitive preceded by an "a," and (C) the past participle.

14. **(A)** The present participle in Spanish may not act as an adjective. Phrases such as these must be converted to clauses such as the one found in this sample. Therefore, "a crying child" becomes "a child that cries" in the Spanish sentence. Therefore, (B), the present participle, (C), the infinitive, and (D), the infinitive with "a," are all incorrect.

15. **(B)** In Spanish a verb used as a gerund, either as a subject or the object of the verb, must be in the infinitive form. Therefore, (A), the past participle, (C), the present participle and (D), the present subjunctive, are all incorrect.

16. **(D)** "Ir" may not be used in the progressive tense in Spanish. In order to say that one "is or was doing something," a form of **ir a** (either in the present or in the imperfect tense) is used with the infinitive. Choice (B) is in the progressive tense and choice (A) is a form of **ser** with a present participle, which is never correct. Choice (C) is the present participle alone and makes no sense in the context of this sentence.

17. **(A)** The idiom **al + infinitive** means **upon + –ing**. Because choices (B), the preterite, (C), the past participle, and (D), the present participle, are not in the infinitive form, they are all incorrect.

18. **(A)** This sentence is considered a "non-blame" statement. Certain verbs (such as perder, dejar, caer, romper, etc.) are used in this manner so as to indicate that the subject did not commit the action on purpose. These sentences require using the reflexive pronoun **se**, the **indirect object** pronoun for the subject, and the verb in either the third person singular or plural depending on what follows it. In this case "vaso" is singular and requires a singular verb. Choice (C) is, therefore, incorrect because the verb

is plural. Choice (D) is plural and the reflexive pronoun is missing. Choice (B) would be correct if written as "rompí" alone but would then mean that this action occurred on purpose.

19. **(C)** After a conjugated verb the infinitive is necessary. In this case the subject (tú) requires adjusting the reflexive pronoun to match it. For this reason choice (A) is incorrect because the pronoun (se) does not match the subject (tú). Choice (B) is the familiar singular command and (D) is the present participle, neither of which would follow the conjugated verb in this sample.

20. **(D)** In order to answer this question, one must know the difference between "levantar" and "levantarse." The former means "to raise" while the latter means "to get up." This would then eliminate both (A) and (C). While choice (B) appears to be correct in that it is **not** reflexive, the verb form would need to be subjunctive to fit this particular sentence since it begins with an impersonal expression and there is a change in subject. "Levanta" in this sample is the present indicative.

21. **(C)** This sentence requires knowing the difference between "casarse con" (to get married) and "casar" (to marry). Because the priest is performing the ceremony, choice (C) is correct. The personal **a** precedes the direct object "pareja." Choice (A) is incorrect because it is reflexive and the meaning would not fit this sentence and (B), which is also reflexive, is followed by the wrong preposition. Choice (D) is not correct with "con."

22. **(A)** This is a statement calling for an "each other" translation. The phrase "uno a otro" also indicates this. In Spanish the plural reflexive pronouns are used in these statements. The phrase "uno a otro" is an additional piece so that the translation of the verb will not be confused for "we write to ourselves." Choice (B) is incorrect because the subject in this sentence is **we** (intimated in the first part of the sentence with "vivimos"). Choice (C) requires the matching reflexive pronoun "nos." Choice (D) means "they write to us" and doesn't fit the meaning implied by this sentence.

THE INFINITIVE

The Infinitive as the Subject of the Sentence

When the infinitive is used as the subject of the sentence (gerund) in English, it may be written in the infinitive form or end in –ing. In Spanish this is written only in the infinitive form.

Seeing is believing.	*Ver es creer.*
Eating is important.	*Comer es importante.*

The Infinitive after Prepositions

In Spanish the only correct verb form that can follow a preposition is the infinitive.

antes de salir	before leaving
después de comer	after eating
al entrar	upon entering

The Infinitive with Verbs of Perception

The infinitive is used with verbs of perception *ver* (to see) and *oír* (to hear) when the sentence has a noun object.

Oí llorar al niño.	I heard the child cry.
Ella vio salir a Juan.	She saw Juan leave.

Verbs Requiring a Preposition Before the Infinitive

Certain verbs require an *a, en, de, por,* or *con* before the infinitive. See page 131 for a detailed listing.

Verbs Requiring No Preposition Before the Infinitive

aconsejar	advise to	*pensar (ie)*	intend to
deber	ought to	*permitir*	allow to
dejar	let, allow to	*poder (ue)*	be able to
desear	desire to	*prometer*	promise to
esperar	hope to	*querer (ie)*	wish to
impedir (i, i)	prevent from	*recordar (ue)*	remember to
lograr	succeed in	*rehusar*	refuse to
necesitar	need to	*saber*	know how to
oír	hear	*soler (ue)**	be accustomed to
pedir (i, i)	ask to	*temer*	be afraid to

*   This verb is defective and commonly used in two tenses only—the present and the imperfect.

☞ Drill 4

1. Lavé la ropa después de...

    (A) cenar.

    (B) comiendo.

    (C) comida.

    (D) había almorzado.

2. Al...la alarma, todos abandonaron el hotel.

    (A) oyen

    (B) oyendo

    (C) oír

    (D) oído

3. Orlando oyó...a la puerta.

    (A) tocó

    (B) tocar

    (C) tocando

    (D) tocándola

4. El respirar no es...

    (A) vivir.

    (B) viviendo.

    (C) la vida.

    (D) vive.

5. Al..., le dije adiós.

    (A) salir

    (B) saliendo

    (C) salí

    (D) salido

6. ...es bueno para el cuerpo.

    (A) Corriendo

    (B) Corrido

    (C) Correr

    (D) Fumar

7. ...es bueno para la salud.

    (A) Dormir

    (B) Durmiendo

    (C) Dormido

    (D) Dormí

8. Sin..., no puedo recomendar la película.

    (A) ver   (C) verla

    (B) veo   (D) verlo

9. Antes de...del autobús, Juan pagó el pasaje.

    (A) bajando   (C) bajar

    (B) el bajar   (D) baje

10. El policía vio...al ladrón del banco.

    (A) salida   (C) saliendo

    (B) salir   (D) salió

Drill 4—Detailed Explanations of Answers

1. **(A)** "Después de" (after) is a preposition. The only form of the verb we use directly following a preposition is the infinitive. Therefore, we cannot use the present participle, as in (B), "comiendo." The present participle in English is the verbal form ending in –ing: for example, "eating." In English, this form may be used as a noun, in which case we call it a gerund. In a phrase such as "after eating," "eating" is a gerund and means "the act of eating." In Spanish, the form which corresponds to the –*ing*, i.e., words ending in **–ando** and **–iendo**, do not follow a preposition. This is a mistake often made in Spanish by English speakers. Choice (C) is incorrect. If we want to say "after the meal" or "after the afternoon meal," we would have to use the definite article: "después de **la** comida." Choice (D) is also wrong. In Spanish, a conjugated form of the verb does not immediately follow a preposition. We could say, however, "después de haber almorzado" (after **having eaten** lunch). Then the verb is not in a conjugated form.

2. **(C)** Syntactically, the verb forms "oyen" (they hear), the third person plural of the present of "oír," "oyendo" (hearing), the present participle, and "oído" (heard), the past participle, will not fit correctly into this sentence. There is, however, an idiomatic construction based on "al" + **infinitive** which means "upon doing something." We find this form in (C).

3. **(B)** After verbs of perception ("oír", "ver"), the infinitive is used. Therefore, (A), the preterite, and (C) and (D), the present participles, are incorrect.

4. **(A)** Verbs used as gerunds in Spanish (either as the subject or object of the verb) must be in the infinitive form. (B) The present participle and (D) the present tense are incorrect. (C) is incorrect because the infinitive is necessary to maintain parallel structure (infinitive/infinitive).

5. **(A)** The only verbal form that can follow "al" is the infinitive. It means upon + –ing in English.

6. **(C)** The key to this question is to remember that the infinitive can function as the subject of a sentence, but not the gerund (A) or the past participle (B). (D) "to smoke" is not good for "the body."

7. **(A)** This is another example of the use of the infinitive as the subject of the sentence. Therefore, (B) the present participle, (C) the past participle, and (D) the preterite are incorrect.

8. **(C)** After prepositions in Spanish the infinitive must be used. In the context of this sentence, the translation "without seeing it" makes most sense. "It" refers to "película" which is feminine. (A) needs the direct object pronoun "la", (D) has the incorrect direct object pronoun, and (B) is the present indicative, a conjugated verb form.

9. **(C)** The correct verb form after a preposition in Spanish is the infinitive. This would eliminate the present participle (A) and the subjunctive in (D). Choice (B) is a gerund and is not used after a preposition.

10. **(B)** After verbs of perception (ver/oír) the infinitive is used in Spanish. Therefore, the present participle (C), the preterite tense (D) and the noun meaning "departure" in (A) are incorrect.

FORMATION OF THE SUBJUNCTIVE

Present Subjunctive—Regular

	amar to love	*comer* to eat	*vivir* to live
yo	ame	coma	viva
tú	ames	comas	vivas
él/ella/Ud.	ame	coma	viva
nosotros, –as	amemos	comamos	vivamos
vosotros, –as	améis	comáis	viváis
ellos/ellas/Uds.	amen	coman	vivan

Present Subjunctive—Irregular

caber	quepa, quepas, quepa, quepamos, quepáis, quepan
caer	caiga, caigas, caiga, caigamos, caigáis, caigan
dar	dé, des, dé, demos, deis, den
decir	diga, digas, diga, digamos, digáis, digan
estar	esté, estés, esté, estemos, estéis, estén
haber	haya, hayas, haya, hayamos, hayáis, hayan
hacer	haga, hagas, haga, hagamos, hagáis, hagan
ir	vaya, vayas, vaya, vayamos, vayáis, vayan
oír	oiga, oigas, oiga, oigamos, oigáis, oigan
poner	ponga, pongas, ponga, pongamos, pongáis, pongan
saber	sepa, sepas, sepa, sepamos, sepáis, sepan
salir	salga, salgas, salga, salgamos, salgáis, salgan
ser	sea, seas, sea, seamos, seáis, sean
tener	tenga, tengas, tenga, tengamos, tengáis, tengan
traer	traiga, traigas, traiga, traigamos, traigáis, traigan
valer	valga, valgas, valga, valgamos, valgáis, valgan
venir	venga, vengas, venga, vengamos, vengáis, vengan
ver	vea, veas, vea, veamos, veáis, vean

Present Subjunctive—Spelling Changes

–*car*	atacar	ataque, ataques, ataque, etc.
–*gar*	entregar	entregue, entregues, entregue, etc.
–*zar*	rezar	rece, reces, rece, etc.
–*ger*	coger	coja, cojas, coja, etc.
–*gir*	dirigir	dirija, dirijas, dirija, etc.
–*guir*	distinguir	distinga, distingas, distinga, etc.

–guar	*averiguar*	*averigüe, averigües, averigüe, etc.*
–uir	*huir*	*huya, huyas, huya, etc.*
–quir	*delinquir*	*delinca, delincas, delinca, etc.*
–cer	*conocer*	*conozca, conozcas, conozca, etc.*
	vencer	*venza, venzas, venza, etc.*
–cir	*conducir*	*conduzca, conduzcas, conduza, etc.*

Present Subjunctive–Stem Changes

If a verb has only one stem change, it will appear in all persons except *nosotros* and *vosotros*. If there are two stem-changes given, the second one will appear in the *nosotros/vosotros* forms of the present subjunctive while the first one will appear in all other persons.

(ú) *actuar* to act	(í) *enviar* to send	(ue, u) *morir* to die	(i, i) *pedir* to request	(ie, i) *sentir* to feel or regret
actúe	*envíe*	*muera*	*pida*	*sienta*
actúes	*envíes*	*mueras*	*pidas*	*sientas*
actúe	*envíe*	*muera*	*pida*	*sienta*
actuemos	*enviemos*	*muramos*	*pidamos*	*sintamos*
actuéis	*enviéis*	*muráis*	*pidáis*	*sintáis*
actúen	*envíen*	*mueran*	*pidan*	*sientan*

Past (Imperfect) Subjunctive–Regular

To form this tense, remove *–ron* from the end of the third plural of the preterite and add the following endings:

–ra	*–ras*	*–ra*	*´–ramos*	*–rais*	*–ran*
–se	*–ses*	*–se*	*´–semos*	*–seis*	*–sen*

Either set of endings is correct, with the first set being the more widely used.

Past Subjunctive–Irregular

andar	*anduviera or anduviese, etc.*
caber	*cupiera or cupiese, etc.*
dar	*diera or diese, etc.*
decir	*dijera or dijese, etc.*
estar	*estuviera or estuviese, etc.*
haber	*hubiera or hubiese, etc.*
hacer	*hiciera or hiciese, etc.*

ir	*fuera or fuese, etc.*
poder	*pudiera or pudiese, etc.*
poner	*pusiera or pusiese, etc.*
querer	*quisiera or quisiese, etc.*
saber	*supiera or supiese, etc.*
ser	*fuera or fuese, etc.*
tener	*tuviera or tuviese, etc.*
traer	*trajera or trajese, etc.*
venir	*viniera or viniese, etc.*
conducir	*condujera or condujese, etc.*
huir	*huyera or huyese, etc.*

Past Subjunctive–Verbs with Stem Changes

Because the stem for the past subjunctive comes from the third plural of the preterite, it will be affected by verbs that have stem changes in the preterite.

dormir (ue, u) to sleep	*sentir* (ie, i) to feel/regret	*pedir* (i, i) to ask for
durmiera	*sintiera*	*pidiera*
durmieras	*sintieras*	*pidieras*
durmiera	*sintiera*	*pidiera*
durmiéramos	*sintiéramos*	*pidiéramos*
durmierais	*sintierais*	*pidierais*
durmieran	*sintieran*	*pidieran*

Past Subjunctive–Verbs Like *Leer*

Because *–er* and *–ir* verbs with double vowels (*leer, oír, creer, caer,* etc.) have a *y* in the third person of the preterite, this *y* will be found in all forms of the past subjunctive.

oír	*oyera, oyeras, oyera, oyéramos, oyerais, oyeran*

COMMANDS: FORMAL AND FAMILIAR

The Formal Command

Formal commands (*Ud.* and *Uds.*) are always expressed by the present subjunctive. Some samples follow.

comer: (eat)	*(no) coma Ud.*	*(no) coman Uds.*
volver: (return)	*(no) vuelva Ud.*	*(no) vuelvan Uds.*
tener: (have)	*(no) tenga Ud.*	*(no) tengan Uds.*
atacar: (attack)	*(no) ataque Ud.*	*(no) ataquen Uds.*

The Familiar Command

Unlike the formal commands which are derived from the same form (the present subjunctive), the familiar commands come from several different verb forms to cover the positive, negative, singular and plural forms.

1. The singular (*tú*) form of the affirmative command is the same as the third person singular of the present indicative.

leer = lee (tú)	*lavar = lava (tú)*	*vivir = vive (tú)*
Read!	Wash!	Live!

2. The plural (*vosotros*) form of the affirmative command is formed by changing the *–r* ending of the infinitive to a *–d*.

leer = leed	*lavar = lavad*	*vivir = vivid*
Read!	Wash!	Live!

3. The negative forms come from the *tú* and *vosotros* forms of the present subjunctive.

leer = no leas (tú)	*lavar = no laves (tú)*
no leáis (vosotros)	*no lavéis (vosotros)*
Don't read!	Don't wash!

Familiar Commands–Irregulars

The only irregular familiar commands occur in the affirmative singular. All other forms follow the rules stated above.

	tú	*vosotros*	*tú*	*vosotros*
decir	**di**	decid	no digas	no digáis
hacer	**haz**	haced	no hagas	no hagáis
ir	**ve**	id	no vayas	no vayáis
poner	**pon**	poned	no pongas	no pongáis
salir	**sal**	salid	no salgas	no salgáis
ser	**sé**	sed	no seas	no seáis
tener	**ten**	tened	no tengas	no tengáis
valer	**val**	valed	no valgas	no valgáis
venir	**ven**	venid	no vengas	no vengáis

Commands of Reflexive Verbs

Reflexive verbs require the use of reflexive pronouns. The formal command, singular and plural, uses *–se*. The familiar command uses *te* (singular) and *os* (plural). These pronouns **precede** the **negative command** and are **after** and **attached** to the **positive command**. Any time a pronoun is appended to a command form an accent mark is required. Without it, the stress automatically moves to the next syllable thus affecting the pronunciation.

Bañarse:	*báñese Ud.*	*no se bañe Ud.*
	báñense Uds.	*no se bañen Uds.*
	báñate tú	*no te bañes tú*
	*bañaos vosotros**	*no os bañéis vosotros*

* When *os* is appended to the affirmative plural command, the final *–d* is dropped (**exception**: *idos*). If using an *–ir* verb, an accent is required over the *i* (*divertid* + *os* = *divertíos*) to split the diphthong and allow for the *i* to be pronounced separately.

"Let's" Statements

There are two ways to express this statement:

1. *Vamos a* + infinitive:

Vamos a comer.	Let's eat.
Vamos a sentarnos.	Let's sit down.
Vamos a leérselo.	Let's read it to him.

2. First plural present subjunctive:

comamos	Let's eat.	(*no comamos*)
*leámoselo**	Let's read it to him.	(*no se lo leamos*)
*sentémonos***	Let's sit down.	(*no nos sentemos*)

Exception: *Vámonos* = Let's go. *No nos vayamos.* = Let's not go. The affirmative is not derived from the subjunctive, but from the indicative.

*   Because double *s* does not exist in Spanish, this verb form will eliminate one (*leámoselo*).

**   Before adding ***nos*** to the reflexive verb form, the final *–s* is dropped. An accent mark is needed.

"Have"/"Let"/"May" Statements

Que + third person singular/plural present subjunctive

Examples:		
	Have her go.	*Que vaya ella.*
	Let him read it.	*Que lo lea.*
	May they do it well.	*Que lo hagan bien.*
	Have them give it to me.	*Que me lo den.*

Note: Pronouns precede these verb forms because they are the conjugated verb of the noun clause.

Dejar is also used to express **let**, with direct object pronouns.

Déjame ver.	Let me see.
Déjanos salir.	Let us leave.

☞ **Drill 5**

1. No te...en el cuarto de Felipe.

    (A) acueste   (C) acuesten

    (B) acostéis   (D) acuestes

2. ¡No...Ud., por favor!

    (A) me hable   (C) me habla

    (B) hábleme   (D) me hables

3. ¡Que lo...Ud. bien!

    (A) pasar   (C) pases

    (B) pase   (D) pasa

4. Hola, mis amigos. ¡...para hablar conmigo!

    (A) Siéntense   (C) Sentados

    (B) Siéntese   (D) Sentaos

5. La madre le dijo a su hijo, –¡...al supermercado!

    (A) vete   (C) no vaya

    (B) váyase   (D) no va

6. Antes de salir mi madre me dijo, –¡...el abrigo, hijo!

    (A) póngase   (C) pónete

    (B) póngate   (D) ponte

7. Hijos, no...mientras estoy hablando.

    (A) os reís   (C) os reíais

    (B) os riáis   (D) reíos

8. Juanito, cuando salgas,... la luz.

   (A) apaga   (C) apagues

   (B) apague   (D) apagaste

9. ...aquí para poder ver mejor.

   (A) Nos sentamos   (C) Sentémosnos

   (B) Sentémonos   (D) Sentámonos

10. No... con vuestros amigos esta noche.

   (A) os vayáis   (C) os vais

   (B) se vayan   (D) idos

Drill 5—Detailed Explanations of Answers

1.   **(D)**   This item tests your knowledge of the various forms of the imperative. The choices given are all command forms. We know that we are searching for the "tú" command, i.e., the second person singular imperative, because of the second person singular reflexive pronoun, "te," which is given in the sentence. Furthermore, we know that we must choose a negative imperative from the list because of the "No" in the sentence. Negative familiar singular commands in Spanish correspond to the second person singular of the present subjunctive, which, for "acostarse" (ue) (to go to bed), is "No te acuestes." Choice (A), "acueste," will not work because it is the command form for the third person singular (the "Usted" command), but we are given the second person singular of the reflexive pronoun in the sentence, "te." Choice (B), "acostéis," is the negative command for the "vosotros" form of the verb. Being a negative command, it is also like the corresponding form of the subjunctive of "acostarse," i.e., the second person plural. "Vosotros" is used only in Spain. In all of Central and South America, the third person plural (the "Ustedes" form) is used in its place. "Acostéis" is an incorrect answer here because the reflexive pronoun "te" is not the second person plural form. For (B) to be correct, we would have to say "No os acostéis..." (C), "acuesten," is wrong also because the reflexive pronoun for it would have to be "se," the third person plural form.

2.   **(A)**   The negative formal singular command (Ud.) is required in this sentence. Object pronouns precede negative commands. Choice (B) is incorrect because the pronoun is after and attached to the positive command. Choice (C) is not in a command form, and (D) is the negative familiar command form.

3.   **(B)**   The exclamatory statement "May it go well for you!" requires the use of the present subjunctive which in this sample is the same as the formal command for "Ud." Choice (A), an infinitive, (C), the "tú" form of the verb, and (D), the present indicative form, are all incorrect.

4.   **(D)**   The familiar plural positive command is required in this statement ("amigos"). This is formed by removing the –**d** from the infinitive before attaching the reflexive pronoun **os** to the end. Choice (C) is incorrect because the –**d** has been retained. Choices (A) and (B) are both formal commands.

5. **(A)** Because the mother is speaking to her son, the familiar positive command is required in this sample. The familiar singular positive command of **irse** is irregular. Choice (B) is the formal command, (C) is the present subjunctive, and (D) is the present indicative.

6. **(D)** The mother is again addressing her son in this sentence which requires the use of the familiar positive singular command of **ponerse** (to put on). This is irregular. Both (A) and (B) are formal command forms but (B) also has the incorrect reflexive pronoun attached. Choice (C) is an incorrect verb form.

7. **(B)** Because the children are being asked **not** to laugh in this sentence, the negative familiar plural command form is required. This form comes from the second person plural of the present subjunctive. Choice (A) is the second plural of the present indicative. Choice (C) is the second plural of the conditional tense, and (D) is the familiar plural positive command form.

8. **(A)** Because Juanito is being addressed in the familiar ("salgas"), the familiar positive singular command is required. For regular verbs this comes from the third person singular of the present tense. Choice (B) is the formal command, (C) is the second person singular of the present subjunctive, and (D) is the preterite tense.

9. **(B)** One way to express **let's** in Spanish is by using the "nosotros" form of the present subjunctive. If the verb is reflexive, the pronoun **nos** is attached to the end of this form, after removing the –s. Choice (A) is the present indicative. Choice (C) has retained the –s of the verb, and (D) is not in the present subjunctive.

10. **(A)** Because "vuestros" indicates that the command should be familiar plural and because the sentence is negative, the command form here will come from the "vosotros" form of the present subjunctive. Pronouns precede negative commands. Choice (B) is the third plural of the present subjunctive, (C) is the second plural of the present indicative, and (D) is the familiar plural positive command form.

THE SUBJUNCTIVE–USES

Subjunctive vs. Indicative

The indicative mood tenses express certainty or factual knowledge. The subjunctive mode is used to convey ideas in the realm of all areas other than those of objective fact: concepts that are hypothetical, contrary to fact, those which embody the expression of feelings of the speaker toward a state or action. Because the subjunctive is a **subjoined, subordinate, dependent** verb form, it is logical that it will occur in the **dependent clause** of the sentence. There are four types of clauses that could contain the subjunctive: noun, adjective, adverb, and if.

The Noun Clause

The noun clause is a group of words that acts as the subject or object of the main clause. The subjunctive will occur in this clause if two conditions are met:

1. a change of subject between two clauses

2. a specific category of verb is used in the main clause: wishing/wanting, emotion, impersonal expression, doubt/denial, or indirect command

To join the independent clause to the dependent clause, the relative pronoun *que* (that) is required in Spanish. In English we often leave this word out. Note the two possible ways to express the following statement in English.

I hope he's here.   I hope **that** he's here.

Category I–Wishing/Wanting

querer (to want)   *Quiero **que Juan vaya**.*
                             I want Juan to go.

Others: *desear* (to want), *preferir* (to prefer), *me gusta* (I like), etc.

Category II–Emotion

temer (to fear)   *Temo **que Juan vaya**.*
                             I fear Juan (may, will) go.

Others: *tener miedo de* (to be afraid of), *lamentar* (to regret), *ojalá que* (if only), *sentir* (to regret/feel)

Category III–Impersonal Expression

An impersonal expression is a combination of **to be** with an adjective. The subject is always **it**. In Spanish **to be** will come from *ser*.

es importante   *Es importante **que Juan vaya**.*
                                                It's important for Juan to go.

Others: *Ser* + adjective (*necesario, natural, probable, posible, mejor, lástima, triste*, etc.)

Note: Some impersonal expressions will **not** prompt a subjunctive if they imply **no doubt**. See exceptions on the next page. These expressions will require subjunctive only if negative.

Category IV–Doubt/Denial

dudar (to doubt)   *Dudo **que Juan vaya**.*
                                                I doubt Juan will go/is going.

Others: *negar* (to deny), *suponer* (to suppose), *puede ser*, (it may be), *creer* (to believe)*, *pensar* (to think)*, *tal vez/quizás* (perhaps)

* *Creer/pensar* commonly take a subjunctive if they are negative or in a question. This is dependent upon the speaker's point of view. If he/she actually believes or thinks what he/she is saying, the indicative will be used.

Category V–Indirect Command

pedir (to ask for)*   *Le pido a **Juan que vaya**.*
                                                I ask Juan to go.

Others: *decir* (to tell), *sugerir* (to suggest), *exigir*, (to demand), *insistir en* (to insist on), *aconsejar* (to advise), *rogar* (to beg)

Note: Several verbs from this category may be used with the infinitive or the subjunctive.

permitir (to permit)   *dejar* (to allow)
hacer (to make)   *aconsejar* (to advise)
impedir (to prevent)   *mandar* (to command)
prohibir (to prohibit)   *recomendar* (to recommend)

*(Te) aconsejo que **vayas**.* or *Te aconsejo ir.*
I advise you to go.

*No (me) permiten que **fume**.* or *No me permiten fumar.*
They do not permit me to smoke.

* Many verbs in this category require the use of the indirect object pronoun in the independent clause used with the second subject: *rogar, pedir, decir, aconsejar*, etc.

Example: *Te ruego que (tú) hables con ella.*
I beg you to speak with her.

Exceptions

The following expressions are used with the **indicative unless** they are **negative**.

ocurre que	it happens that
sucede que	
es evidente que	it's evident that
es cierto que	it's certain that
es verdad que	it's true that
es seguro que	it's sure that
es obvio que	it's obvious that
es que	it's that
se sabe que	it's known that
parece que	it seems that
no es dudoso que	it's not doubtful that

Sequence of Tenses

Whether the present or past subjunctive is used in the dependent clause is based on the tense used in the independent or main clause. Sequence primarily means the present subjunctive will follow present tense forms while past subjunctive will follow past tense forms. Following is a list of tenses with sequence indicated.

Independent Clause (Indicative)		Dependent Clause (Subjunctive)
Present	*espero*	
Present Progressive	*estoy esperando*	**que vaya**
Future	*esperaré*	
Present Perfect	*he esperado*	**que haya ido**
Future Perfect	*habré esperado*	
Command	*espere/espera*	
Preterite	*esperé*	
Imperfect	*esperaba*	**que fuera**

Past Progressive	*estaba esperando*	**que hubiera ido**
Conditional	*esperaría*	**que hubiese ido**
Past Perfect	*había esperado*	
Conditional Perfect	*habría esperado*	

The Adjective Clause

An adjective clause is one that modifies or describes a preceding noun. This noun is called the antecedent and it will determine if the subjunctive will exist in the adjective clause itself. This antecedent must be (1) negative or (2) indefinite for the subjunctive to exist in the adjective clause.

To determine this one must focus not solely on the antecedent itself but the surrounding words (the verb and/or any articles used with that noun).

Compare these two adjective clauses:

Indicative:	Subjunctive:
Tengo *un coche que es nuevo.* (antecedent=*coche*) [exists because he **has** it]	**Busco** *un coche que sea nuevo.* [does not yet exist]
Busco **el** *libro que tiene la información.* (antecedent=*libro*) [a specific book exists with the information]	*Busco* **un** *libro que tenga la información.* [no specific book]
Hay **varios** *hombres que van con nosotros.* (antecedent=*hombres*) [these men exist]	*No hay* **ningún** *hombre que vaya con nosotros.* [a negative antecedent]

The Adverbial Clause

An adverbial clause answers the questions when? where? how? why? etc. These clauses are introduced by conjunctions. These conjunctions can be broken down into three separate types:

1. conjunctions **always** followed by the subjunctive

2. the *–quiera* group conjunctions (which are **always** followed by the subjunctive)

3. conjunctions **sometimes** followed by the subjunctive

Always Subjunctive

a fin de que/para que	so that
a menos que/salvo que	unless
con tal que	provided that
antes (de) que	before
en caso de que	in case (that)
sin que	without
a condición de que	on condition that

Examples: *Salió sin que yo lo supiera.*
He left without my knowing it.

Lo haré antes de que lleguen.
I'll do it before they arrive.

The –Quiera Group

dondequiera que	wherever
cualquier (a) que	whatever
quienquiera que	whoever
quienesquiera que	whoever (plural)
cuando quiera que	whenever
por + adj/adv + *que*	however, no matter how

Examples: *Dondequiera que vayas, serás feliz.*
Wherever you go, you'll be happy.

Por enferma que esté, ella asistirá.
No matter how sick she is, she'll attend.

Sometimes Subjunctive

Adverbial clauses begun with these conjunctions will be subjunctive only if there is speculation or doubt as to whether the action will take place in the future.

aunque	although
cuando	when
después (de) que	after
en cuanto	as soon as
luego que	
tan pronto como	
así que	
hasta que	until
mientras	while

Subjunctive	Indicative
*Aunque **cueste** mucho, lo quiero.*	*Aunque **costó** mucho, lo compré.*
Although it may cost a lot, I want it.	Although it cost a lot, I bought it.
*Léalo hasta que **llegue**.*	*Lo leí hasta que **llegó**.*
Read it until he arrives.	I read it until he **arrived**.
*Dijo que lo haría cuando **llegara**.*	*Lo hizo cuando **llegó**.*
He said he would do it when he arrived.	He did it when he arrived.
[hasn't gotten here yet]	

Normally, if the verb in the independent clause is in the future or command form, the subjunctive will be needed in the dependent clause. However, this is not always the case. One must always think in terms of "has this happened yet or not?" and use the subjunctive accordingly.

THE "IF" CLAUSE

The imperfect and pluperfect subjunctives are used in contrary-to-fact statements, as follows:

If Clause	Result Clause
Si yo estudiara/estudiase más,...	*recibiría (recibiera) buenas notas.*
If I studied more,...	I would get good grades.
Si yo hubiera/hubiese estudiado más,...	*habría (hubiera) recibido buenas notas.*
If I had studied more,...	I would have gotten good grades.

Note: The present subjunctive is **never** used in the **if** clause. Instead the proper sequence (present indicative with future) follows:

Si yo estudio más,...	*recibiré buenas notas.*
If I study more,...	I will get good grades.

"Como Si (as if)" Statements

"As if" statements are always followed by the imperfect or the pluperfect subjunctive.

Habla como si la conociera bien.
He speaks as if he knew her well.

Me castigó como si lo hubiera hecho.
He punished me as if I had done it.

The –ra Form as Polite Request

The *–ra* forms of the imperfect subjunctive of ***querer, poder***, and ***deber*** are often used instead of the conditional of these verbs to express a polite request or statement.

Quisiera hacerlo.	I would like to do it.
¿Pudieras pasarme la sal?	Could you pass me the salt?
Debieran comprarlos.	They should buy them.

☞ Drill 6

1. Mis padres no deseaban que yo...eso.

    (A) hiciera   (C) haría

    (B) hacía   (D) haga

2. Si estuviera aquí,...hablar con ella.

    (A) me gustará   (C) tratarían de

    (B) podemos   (D) me negué a

3. Te lo dirán cuando te...

    (A) ves.   (C) visitemos.

    (B) lo venden.   (D) ven.

4. Dijeron que nos enviarían el paquete tan pronto como...

    (A) lo recibieron.   (C) tengan tiempo.

    (B) llegara.   (D) sabrán nuestra dirección.

5. Me aconsejó que...

    (A) no siguiera la ruta de la costa.

    (B) duerma más.

    (C) voy al médico.

    (D) venga inmediatamente.

6. ¡Ojalá que me...un recuerdo de París!

    (A) traen   (C) enviarán

    (B) han comprado   (D) den

7. María le dio el periódico a Enrique para que él lo...

    (A) lee.   (C) lea.

    (B) leyeran.   (D) leyera.

8. Si yo fuera al centro, te ... algo.

   (A) compraría   (C) compre

   (B) compré   (D) compraré

9. Yo conozco a un señor que ... español muy bien.

   (A) hable   (C) hablando

   (B) habla   (D) hablara

10. Su madre le dijo que ... todo o no podría tener postre.

   (A) come   (C) comía

   (B) coma   (D) comiera

11. Lo harán cuando ...

   (A) llegas.   (C) puedan.

   (B) entran.   (D) tienen tiempo.

12. Si ... dinero, iría a Bolivia.

   (A) tenía   (C) tengo

   (B) tuviera   (D) tuve

13. ... que tienes razón.

   (A) Creo   (C) Niego

   (B) Dudo   (D) Me alegro de

14. Siento que ellos ... con Uds. ayer.

   (A) no estuvieron   (C) no estaban

   (B) no estuvieran   (D) no estarán

15. Si yo tuviera tiempo a Roma, te ...

   (A) visito.   (C) visitaré.

   (B) voy a visitar.   (D) visitaría.

16. No estoy seguro, pero tal vez él...

    (A) viniera.   (C) viene.

    (B) vendrá.   (D) venga.

17. Mi consejero me dijo que no dijera nada hasta que alguien me lo...

    (A) pide.   (C) ha pedido.

    (B) pidiera.   (D) va a pedir.

18. Se lo expliqué en detalle para que lo...

    (A) comprendiera.   (C) comprende.

    (B) comprenda.   (D) comprendió.

19. Mi madre dice que está bien que vaya mi hermano, con tal de que se lo...

    (A) cuida.   (C) cuidaba.

    (B) cuidara.   (D) cuide.

20. Le pedí que...temprano para acabar temprano.

    (A) venga   (C) venir

    (B) viniera   (D) venía

21. No quiere que su hijo...malas costumbres.

    (A) tenga   (C) tengan

    (B) tiene   (D) tienen

22. No creo que mis amigos me...abandonado.

    (A) han   (C) hayan

    (B) habían   (D) hubieran

23. Si él te...un beso, ¿cómo reaccionarías?

    (A) daba   (C) diera

    (B) da   (D) dar

24. No vendrías si...lo que te espera.

    (A) sabías   (C) sabes

    (B) supieras   (D) supiste

25. Mis padres me compraron un automóvil para que...a pasear.

    (A) salgo   (C) salga

    (B) salir   (D) saliera

26. Por bien que...Ana, no quiero jugar con ella.

    (A) juega   (C) está jugando

    (B) juegue   (D) jugara

27. Habla con ella como si la...bien.

    (A) conoce   (C) conociera

    (B) conozca   (D) conoció

28. Es evidente que los chicos no...en sus cuartos.

    (A) están   (C) son

    (B) estén   (D) sean

29. Mi mamá quería que...nuestra tarea a tiempo.

    (A) hagamos   (C) hiciéramos

    (B) hacemos   (D) hicimos

30. Si yo hubiera sabido la respuesta, se la...

    (A) diría.   (C) había dicho.

    (B) habría dicho.   (D) diga.

Drill 6—Detailed Explanations of Answers

1. **(A)** The verb "desear" can express volition, or desire that something happen. With verbs of this type, if there are two different subjects in the two clauses of the sentence, i.e., if someone is bringing his will to bear on someone or something else, then the subjunctive is required. In our sentence the two different subjects are "Mis padres" and "yo." My parents were exerting their will on me. The sentence, however, requires the imperfect subjunctive, "hiciera," rather than the present subjunctive "haga," because the first verb, "deseaban," is in a past tense, the imperfect. Spanish normally observes a logical tense sequence in sentences requiring the subjunctive. If the first verb, the one that **causes** the subjunctive (in this case, "deseaban"), is in a past tense or the conditional tense, a past subjunctive is required (in this case, the imperfect subjunctive). On the other hand, if the verb that causes the subjunctive is in a present tense or the future, a present subjunctive is used. Note that we would not use the subjunctive, but rather the infinitive, if there were not two separate subjects involved: "Yo no deseaba decir eso" (I didn't want to say that).

2. **(C)** Sentences with subordinate clauses beginning with "si" (if), which establish an unreal or hypothetical situation, contain a past tense of the subjunctive (imperfect of pluperfect subjunctive). Our statement begins with such a clause. In these cases, the other clause (the one which shows what would happen if the "si" clause were true) is in the conditional or conditional perfect tense. Since the "si" clause (the hypothesis) is given here in a simple imperfect subjunctive, rather than the pluperfect subjunctive, we also should use the simple conditional tense in the result clause, rather than the conditional perfect. Note that there are times when one might use the future tense in a result clause, but in those cases the verb of the "si" clause is in the simple present or the present perfect. In such instances, the situation is viewed as much less hypothetical and thus, holding a greater possibility of happening. Compare the following examples: "Si estudia, entonces sacará buenas notas" (If he studies...and it is possible he will..., then he will get good grades); "Si estudiara, entonces sacaría buenas notas" (If he were to study...but he doesn't..., then he would get good grades). Only choice (C) could be used in this sentence because it is the only one which appears in the conditional tense. Choice (A) is in the future, (B) is in the present, and (D) is in the preterite. Remember that "tratar de" + infinitive is an idiom meaning "to try to." The expression "negarse a" + infinitive signifies "to refuse to."

3.   **(C)**   The word "cuando" in our sentence is an adverb which pertains to time. When adverbs of time such as "cuando," "hasta que," "tan pronto como," "así que," "luego que," and "mientras" refer to the future, we are obliged to use the subjunctive following them. Of the four possible choices, the only verb form which is subjunctive is found in (C), "visitemos," the first person plural of the present subjunctive of "visitar" (to visit). In (A), "ves," we find the second person singular of the present indicative of "ver" (to see); (B) gives us the third person plural of the present indicative of "vender" (to sell); in choice (D), we find the third person plural of the present indicative of "ver." Remember that we do not always use the subjunctive after these adverbs of time. If the sentence does not refer to some future time, or if it expresses a customary or habitual situation, the indicative is used: "Siempre los veo cuando **vienen** a nuestro pueblo." (I always see them when they come to our town.) There are even situations in the **past** in which we may refer to some action that was **yet to happen** at some future time. In such instances, a subjunctive is also used following the adverb of time: "Iban a hablarles cuando **llegaran**" (They were going to speak to them whenever they arrived). Note that here we have had to use the imperfect subjunctive of "llegar," rather than the present subjunctive, because we are talking about something that was yet to happen in the past. This sentence implies that they had not yet arrived but were to arrive at some future time. Now, compare the following sentences: "Tratarán de hacerlo cuando tengan tiempo" (They will try to do it whenever they have time); "Dijeron que tratarían de hacerlo cuando tuvieran tiempo" (They said that they would try to do it whenever they had time). In the first example, the verb of the main clause, "tratarán," is future. If the verb of the main clause is future or some present form, then we use a form of present subjunctive. In the second example, the principal verb, "tratarían," is conditional. If the main verb is conditional or a past tense, we use a past form of the subjunctive, in this case, the imperfect subjunctive: "tuvieran."

4.   **(B)**   For a complete explanation of the use of the subjunctive following adverbs of time such as "tan pronto como" (as soon as), see the explanation for question 3. Also, pay particular attention to the example there which illustrates the use of the past subjunctive after these expressions if the main verb is in a past tense, as is the case in our sentence here. Choice (A) does not qualify because it is in the preterite tense of the indicative. Choice (C) is given in the present subjunctive, rather than the imperfect subjunctive. (D) appears in the future tense of the indicative.

5.   **(A)**   The verb "aconsejar" (to advise) embodies an expression of will or desire that someone else do something. It carries an implicit com-

mand. After such verbs it is necessary to use a subjunctive form in the dependent clause. Because the main clause of our sentence uses a past tense (preterite) of the verb "aconsejar," we must use a past tense of the subjunctive, the imperfect subjunctive. Choice (B) employs the present subjunctive of the verb; (C) offers us the present indicative; in (D), we once again find a present subjunctive.

6.   **(D)**   The noun "recuerdo" in our sentence means "souvenir." "Ojalá" and "Ojalá que" both mean "Oh, if only..." or "I wish or hope that..." They are expressions of desire. Unlike many such expressions, they do not require a change of subject to produce a subjunctive in the following verb. In fact, if there is a verb after them, the subjunctive is obligatory. For that reason choices (A), (B), and (C) are not useful to us. (A) is the third person plural of the present indicative of "traer" (to bring). (B) gives us the third person plural of the present perfect tense of "comprar" (to buy). (C) is the third person plural of the future of "enviar" (to send). Following "Ojalá" and "Ojalá que," if the present or present perfect subjunctive is used, the implication is that the situation is feasible and possible of happening. When we say "¡Ojalá que me den un recuerdo de París!," we mean "I hope that they will give me a souvenir from Paris!" (and it is **possible** that they will). On the other hand, we use a past subjunctive (imperfect or pluperfect) after these two expressions to show that the situation is highly hypothetical, unreal, or impossible: "¡Ojalá que **fuera** millonario!" (I wish I were a millionaire!...but I'm not, and probably never will be...).

7.   **(D)**   After the expression **para que,** the subjunctive must be used, and this sentence is in the past. The imperfect subjunctive is used after a principle clause containing the preterite, imperfect, or conditional tenses. Choice (D) is the only one in the imperfect subjunctive which is also singular.

8.   **(A)**   In an "if" clause in the past, using the subjunctive, the conditional is the appropriate form to follow.

9.   **(B)**   A known individual or thing does not require the subjunctive, but an unknown, i.e., an indefinite person or thing, does. In this case, it is known, present tense, and indicative. Therefore, choice (B) is correct.

10.   **(D)**   The imperfect subjunctive is necessary since the verb of the main clause is in the past and it requires the subjunctive following the rule of a verb of request (or similar meaning) directing an action of an object or person different from the subject.

11. **(C)**   In our sentence, the word "cuando" is what we term an adverb of time. We can tell from the verb "harán" that we are talking about the future. Whenever an adverb of time refers to the future, we are required to use a subjunctive form of the verb in the following clause. Generally, if the main verb appears in the future or present tenses, we use the present tense of the subjunctive. Among the verbs which are your possible choices, only "puedan" is a present subjunctive form. All of the other choices appear in the present indicative. Even sentences whose main verb is in a past tense may occasionally refer to some future time, e.g., "Dijeron que lo harían cuando **pudieran**" (They said that they would do it whenever they could). Observe that here we cannot use the present subjunctive. We must, on the other hand, use the imperfect subjunctive because we are referring to the past. When the verb does not refer to a future time or when it indicates a customary action, we use an indicative tense following adverbs of time: "Siempre me llaman cuando pueden" (They always call me when they can). Other common adverbs of time which have the same effect are: "hasta que," "tan pronto como," "mientras que," "así que," "luego que," and "en cuanto."

12. **(B)**   Dependent clauses beginning with "si" (if) require the use of the **imperfect subjunctive** if they set up an impossible, hypothetical, or unreal situation. Then, in the other clause, we use the **conditional** tense to show what would happen (what the result would be) if that hypothesis were true. The only imperfect subjunctive form appearing among the choices is (B) "tuviera." (A) "tenía" is the imperfect indicative; (C) "tengo" is the present indicative; (D) "tuve" is the preterite. When we say "Si tuviera dinero, iría a Bolivia," we mean "If I had money (but I don't), I would go to Bolivia." In other words, we are emphasizing the unreality or impossibility of my having enough money. If, on the other hand, we wanted to imply that it is not totally unfeasible that I will have the money, we would say in English, "If I have the money, I will go to Bolivia." Notice that here, in the "if" clause, we have used the **present indicative**, and in the result clause, the **future** tense. This pattern would be observed also in Spanish: "Si tengo dinero, iré a Bolivia." Suppose we were talking about a situation in the past and we wanted to set up an unfeasible hypothesis or assumption: "If I had had money, I would have gone to Bolivia" ("Si hubiera tenido dinero, habría ido a Bolivia"). Here we have used compound or perfect tenses: in the "si" clause, the **pluperfect subjunctive**; in the result clause, the **conditional perfect**. Remember this caution: we never use a present or a present perfect subjunctive immediately after the word "si."

13. **(A)** How much do you remember about the uses of the subjunctive as opposed to the indicative? A careful scrutiny of the possible choices reveals that (B) "Dudo" (I doubt), (C) "Niego," (I deny), and (D) "Me alegro de" (I am happy) would require a subjunctive following them if we were to use them in the sentence, but the sentence does not give the subjunctive form of "tener," "tengas," but rather the indicative, "tienes." Consequently, we must use (A) Creo (I believe), which does not cause a subjunctive following it if it is used affirmatively. There are only two possible times when we **may** use the subjunctive after "creer": (1) if "creer" is used negatively, e.g., "No creo que tengas razón" (I don't believe you are right) and (2) if "creer" is used in a question, e.g., "Crees que llueva mañana?" (Do you think it will rain tomorrow?). Even when "creer" is used negatively or interrogatively, the speaker has the **option** of using the indicative, rather than the subjunctive, following "creer" if he wishes to show that he himself feels no doubt about the situation. Earlier, we indicated that the verb "dudar" requires the subjunctive. That is because expressions which cast doubt on the second clause of the sentence bring about a subjunctive in the subordinate verb. The verb "negar" (to deny) produces a subjunctive in the following clause whenever it denies the validity or truth of the subordinate clause. Expressions of emotion, such as "alegrarse de" (to be happy), bring about a following subjunctive only if there is a change of subject between the two verbs. Otherwise, simply the infinitive is used.

14. **(B)** "Siento" is the first person singular of the present tense of "sentir" (ie, i) (to be sorry). "Sentir" is a verb of emotion. It requires a subjunctive in the second part of the sentence when we have two different subjects. For this reason, (A) "no estuvieron," the preterite of "estar" (to be), (C) "no estaban," the imperfect of "estar," and (D) "no estarán," the future of "estar," are all wrong. (B), however, "no estuvieran," the imperfect subjunctive of "estar," is correct. Notice that although "Siento" is given in the present tense, we must use a past tense of the subjunctive because the action of the subordinate clause took place in the past. The word "ayer" (yesterday) is our clue.

15. **(D)** In an "in" clause in the present tense, the independent clause is usually in the future and the dependent clause in the present subjunctive. If, however, the "if" clause is in the past, the independent clause is in the conditional. None of the other answers is correct.

16. **(D)** After the expression **tal vez** indicating a future idea, the present subjunctive is used. Choice (A) is past subjunctive. Only choice (D) is correct.

17. **(B)** The use of the subjunctive is required after **hasta que**. In this case, the sentence is in the past, so the imperfect subjunctive is required, even though the idea of the sentence indicates some action in the future.

18. **(A)** After the expression **para que** the subjunctive can be expected. The introductory sentence begins in the preterite, so the imperfect subjunctive should be chosen.

19. **(D)** After the expression **con tal de que** one expects the subjunctive. It should be noticed that this sentence is in the present tense. The only answer in the present subjunctive is (D). The reflexive in this answer is sometimes referred to as the dative of interest, or it could be considered as the indirect object meaning "for her."

20. **(B)** First you have to decide between the subjunctive and the indicative mood (choice (C), an infinitive, is ungrammatical in the context), and once you decide that the correct mood is the subjunctive (because it is governed by a verb—"pedir"—that always requires a subjunctive), then you have to opt between (A) and (B), that is, the present and the past. Since the main verb is in the past, the subjunctive form to follow must be in the same tense.

21. **(A)** You should first eliminate the last two choices as ungrammatical since they are plural and "hijo" is not. Then you must decide between subjunctive (the correct choice because "querer" always requires the subjunctive) and indicative.

22. **(C)** The four choices break down into two indicatives and two subjunctives. You must choose a subjunctive form at this point because when "creer" is preceded by a negative, it requires the subjunctive mood. Finally, this subjunctive verb must be (like "creo") in the present.

23. **(C)** Three of these choices—(A), (B), and (D)—are ungrammatical, the first two because there is no tense correlation between "daba" (an imperfect form) or "da" (a present) and "reaccionarías" (a conditional form), and the third one because the infinitive must be conjugated. You should also realize that the structure of the sentence is of the "if/then" type, which always requires a subjunctive in the "if" clause.

24. **(B)** This is also an "if/then" clause (inverted: "then/if"). Consequently, the "if" clause must contain a subjunctive form, the only one available being (B).

25. **(D)**   Your task in this question is easy if you know that "para que" always takes a subjunctive, though you still have to decide between (C) and (D). The key to this part of the answer is the main verb ("compraron"), which is in the past; therefore, the subjunctive verb that depends on it must also be in the past.

26. **(B)**   This adverbial phrase requires the use of the present subjunctive to follow sequence. Therefore, (A) the present tense, (C) the present progressive, and (D) the past subjunctive are incorrect.

27. **(C)**   "Como si" is always followed by the past subjunctive. Therefore, choice (A) the present indicative, (B) the present subjunctive, and (D) the preterite are incorrect.

28. **(A)**   Although this sentence begins with an impersonal expression and there is a change in subject (i.e., a second clause follows), the subjunctive is not required in the noun clause because there is no doubt implied. Other expressions of this type are "es verdad," "es cierto," "no es dudoso," and "es obvio que." This will eliminate choices (B) and (D) which are both in the present subjunctive. Choice (C) is incorrect because this sentence points out location for which the verb **estar** is used.

29. **(C)**   This sentence requires the use of the subjunctive because it begins with a verb of volition and there is a change in subject (from "mamá" to "we"). Because the verb in the independent clause (quería) is in the imperfect tense, to maintain proper sequencing, the past subjunctive is required in the dependent clause. Choice (A) is present subjunctive. Choice (B) the present indicative and (D) the preterite are incorrect since this sentence requires the use of the subjunctive.

30. **(B)**   An "if" clause containing a compound verb form (the perfect tense) in the past subjunctive requires the use of a compound tense in the other clause, commonly written in the conditional tense. Choice (A), although it is in the conditional tense, is not compound. Choice (D) is in the present subjunctive and is, therefore, incorrect in this context. Choice (C) is a compound tense but in the pluperfect, not in the conditional perfect tense.

CONJUGATION OF *SER*

Indicative

	Present	Imperfect	Preterite	Future	Condit.
yo	*soy*	*era*	*fui*	*seré*	*sería*
tú	*eres*	*eras*	*fuiste*	*serás*	*serías*
él/ella/Ud.	*es*	*era*	*fue*	*será*	*sería*
nosotros, –as	*somos*	*éramos*	*fuimos*	*seremos*	*seríamos*
vosotros, –as	*sois*	*erais*	*fuisteis*	*seréis*	*seríais*
ellos/ellas/ Uds.	*son*	*eran*	*fueron*	*serán*	*serían*

Subjunctive

	Present	Imperfect
yo	*sea*	*fuera/fuese*
tú	*seas*	*fueras/fueses*
él/ella/Ud.	*sea*	*fuera/fuese*
nosotros, –as	*seamos*	*fuéramos/fuésemos*
vosotros, –as	*seáis*	*fuerais/fueseis*
ellos/ellas/Uds.	*sean*	*fueran/fuesen*

Imperative

Singular	Plural
sé (tú)	*sed (vosotros)*
no seas (tú)	*no seáis (vosotros)*
(no) sea (Ud.)	*(no) sean (Uds.)*

Participles

Past Participle: *sido*
Present Participle: *siendo*

CONJUGATION OF *ESTAR*

Indicative

	Present	Imperfect	Preterite	Future	Condit.
yo	estoy	estaba	estuve	estaré	estaría
tú	estás	estabas	estuviste	estarás	estarías
él/ella/Ud.	está	estaba	estuvo	estará	estaría
nosotros, –as	estamos	estábamos	estuvimos	estaremos	estaríamos
vosotros, –as	estáis	estabais	estuvisteis	estaréis	estaríais
ellos/ellas/ Uds.	están	estaban	estuvieron	estarán	estarían

Subjunctive

	Present	Imperfect
yo	esté	estuviera/estuviese
tú	estés	estuvieras/estuvieses
él/ella/Ud.	esté	estuviera/estuviese
nosotros, –as	estemos	estuviéramos/ estuviésemos
vosotros, –as	estéis	estuvierais/estuvieseis
ellos/ellas/Uds.	estén	estuvieran/estuviesen

Imperative

Present	Imperfect
está (tú)	estad (vosotros)
no estés (tú)	no estéis (vosotros)
(no) esté (Ud.)	(no) estén (Uds.)

Participles

Past Participle: *estado*
Present Participle: *estando*

Uses of *Ser*

"To be" followed by a predicate noun (a noun that is the same person as the subject) is always *ser*.

*Él **es** médico.*
He **is** a doctor.

Somos hombres con una misión.
We **are** men on a mission.

To express origin, ownership, or material consistency.

¿Es Ud. de Atlanta?
Are you from Atlanta?

Ese libro es de la biblioteca.
That book **is** the library's.

Esta mesa es de madera.
This table **is** (made) of wood.

Ser is used to mean "to take place."

La fiesta fue ayer.
The party **was** yesterday.

La reunión es mañana.
The meeting **is** tomorrow.

The use of *ser* with an adjective denotes that the speaker considers the quality signified by the adjective an essential or permanent component of the noun.

El agua es clara.
Water **is** clear.

La madera es dura.
Wood **is** hard.

Mi hermano es alto.
My brother **is** tall.

To tell time/dates/seasons:

Son las dos y media.	It **is** 2:30.
Es verano.	It **is** summer.
Es el primero de enero.	It **is** January 1.
Será tarde.	It **will be** late.

With "impersonal expressions"—these are expressions with adjectives whose subject is "it."

Es posible.	**It's** possible.
Será imposible.	It **will be** impossible.
Ha sido necesario.	It **has been** necessary.

To express religion or occupation:

Soy católica.   I **am** Catholic.
Son doctores.   They **are** doctors.

With the adjective *feliz:*

Ella es feliz.   She **is** happy.

To express "passive voice"—when the agent (doer) is expressed:

La información fue leída por el profesor.
The information **was** read by the teacher.

With personal pronouns:

Soy yo.   It **is** I.
Es ella.   It **is** she.

Uses of *Estar*

Estar is used to express location.

El estadio está a dos cuadras.
The stadium **is** two blocks away.

Los pañuelos están en el cajón.
The handkerchiefs **are** in the drawer.

Estar is used with the present participle of other verbs to form the progressive tense.

Está lloviendo.
It **is** raining.

Están comprando los boletos.
They **are** buying the tickets.

Estar is used with adjectives to indicate a change from the norm, a temporary state of the subject, or a subjective reaction.

Estaba gordo cuando lo vi.
He **was** fat when I saw him.

El postre está rico.
The dessert **is** good.

To express the result of a previous action:

La tarea está hecha.
The homework **is** done.

*La casa **está** bien construida.*
The house **is** well built.

With certain idiomatic expressions:

*Mi primo **está de** médico allí.*
My cousin **"acts as"** a doctor there.

***Estamos** por salir ahora.*
We are in favor of leaving now.

***Estoy por** llorar.*
I am about to cry.

Adjectives that Change Meaning with *Ser* or *Estar*

*Mi tío **es** bueno.* — My uncle is **good**.
*Mi tío **está** bueno.* — My uncle is **in good health**.

*Tu perro **es** malo.* — Your dog is **bad**.
*Tu perro **está** malo.* — Your dog is **sick**.

*La función **es** aburrida.* — The show is **boring**.
*Mi esposa **está** aburrida.* — My wife is **bored**.

*Mi hijo **es** listo.* — My son is **smart**.
*Mi hijo **está** listo.* — My son is **ready**.

*Este edificio **es** seguro.* — This building is **safe**.
*El portero **está** seguro.* — The porter is **sure**.

*Ese hombre **es** cerrado.* — That man is **narrow-minded**.
*La puerta **está** cerrada.* — The door is **closed**.

*Su hija **es** callada.* — His daughter is **taciturn**.
*La noche **está** callada.* — The night is **silent**.

Use of *Lo* with *Estar/Ser*

In Spanish, when a question with a form of *ser* or *estar* is followed by an adjective, the neuter object pronoun *lo* replaces that adjective in the reply.

¿Estás enfermo? — Are you ill?
*Sí, **lo** estoy.* — Yes, I am.

¿Son ricos los Garcías? — Are the Garcías rich?
*Sí, **lo** son.* — Yes, they are.

☞ Drill 7

1. ¿De dónde...Uds.?

   (A) van

   (B) se dirigen

   (C) son

   (D) están

2. Esos cocos...de Cuba, ¿verdad?

   (A) están

   (B) estarán

   (C) son

   (D) sean

3. La boda...en la iglesia.

   (A) estuvo

   (B) fueron

   (C) fue

   (D) estando

4. Yo...dos noches en la selva.

   (A) esté

   (B) era

   (C) estuve

   (D) fui

5. El padre de Alicia...médico.

   (A) está

   (B) es

   (C) estaba

   (D) estará

6. Tú...equivocado cuando dijiste que yo no iría a la fiesta.

   (A) eres

   (B) estás

   (C) eras

   (D) estabas

7. Los niños han...tristes desde que sus padres les prohibieron ver televisión.

   (A) sido

   (B) sidos

   (C) estado

   (D) estados

8. El accidente...en la esquina, cerca de la tienda.

   (A) estuvo   (C) está

   (B) fue   (D) estaría

9. Los deportistas...débiles porque no han comido en tres días.

   (A) son   (C) eran

   (B) están   (D) habían sido

10. ...posible hacer la tarea.

    (A) Serán   (C) Está

    (B) Ha sido   (D) Estaría

Drill 7—Detailed Explanations of Answers

1. **(C)** The question we most likely want to ask is "Where are you from?" The verb "ser" is used when we are talking about origin; for example, "Soy de los Estados Unidos" (I am from the United States). In our question we are not talking about where these people are, i.e., what their location is. Consequently, "están" (D) would be wrong here. "Estar" does not refer to origin but to location. "Van" (A), and "se dirigen" (B) are normally followed by the preposition "a" (to), because people "go" or "direct themselves" **to** a place, not **from** a place, as "de" would mean.

2. **(C)** The origin of people and things is expressed in the verb **ser**. The subjunctive form is not needed here.

3. **(C)** **Ser** is used for an event or time, and in this case it is singular and in the past.

4. **(C)** To answer correctly, you must understand the differences between the two verbs in Spanish which mean "to be": "ser" and "estar." Only the latter is used to refer to position or location. This immediately eliminates choice (B) "era" (the imperfect of "ser") and (D) "fui" (the preterite of "ser"). (A) "esté" is a form of "estar" but not the right one. It is the first person present of the subjunctive, and there is no reason to use a subjunctive form in this sentence. On the other hand, (C) "estuve" (I was), the first person preterite of "estar," works fine. We have used the preterite of "estar" rather than the imperfect because we know that the action came to an end. The expression "dos noches" puts a limit on the duration of my stay in the jungle ("selva"). Therefore, "estaba" (the imperfect) should not be used here. This particular use of the preterite of "estar" means the same as "pasé" (I spent).

5. **(B)** The only correct way to translate the verb "to be" when the complement is a noun is by means of "ser" and not "estar."

6. **(D)** The primary choice is between "ser" and "estar." In the expression "to be wrong," only "estar" can be used. In addition, you have to realize that the blank has to be filled with a verb in the past to correlate with "dijiste." This eliminates (B).

7. **(C)** The first thing you should notice here is that a form of "haber" is to be followed by some form of "to be." If you analyze the problem in

this way, you'll immediately eliminate (B) and (D), provided you remember that a past participle is invariable in gender and number. Now you are left with the choice between "ser" and "estar," which should go in favor of "estar" because the action (or description "to be sad") began at a certain point and is thus a deviation from the norm (not to be sad).

8. **(B)** If you chose any of the forms of "estar" you might be confusing the sense of location with the notion of occurrence or happening that is translated into Spanish with "ser." To take place ("ser") is not the same as "to be located."

9. **(B)** Now an anomalous element (not eating in three days) has been introduced in the picture of normality described in the previous question, which explains why the right choice is "están" and not any of the other forms of "ser."

10. **(B)** Impersonal expressions (the subject of the verb **to be** is **it** followed by an adjective) require the third person singular of the verb **ser** in Spanish. This would eliminate (C) and (D) since they are both derived from **estar** and (A) because it is plural.

PERSONAL PRONOUNS

Personal Pronoun Chart

Subject		Prepositional		Direct		Indirect	
yo	I	*mí*	me	*me*	me	*me*	to me
tú	you	*ti*	you	*te*	you	*te*	to you
él	he	*él*	him, it–m	*le**	him, you	*le–a él*	to him
ella	she	*ella*	her, it–f	*lo*	him, it–m	*le–a ella*	to her
ello	it–neutral	*ello*	it–neutral	*la*	her, it–f	*le–a Ud.*	to you
Ud.	you	*Ud.*	you		you	*(se)*	
		sí	("self")				

Subject		Prepositional		Direct		Indirect	
nosotros, –as	we	*nosotros, –as*	us	*nos*	us	*nos*	to us
vosotros, –as	you	*vosotros, –as*	you	*os*	you	*os*	to you
ellos	they–m	*ellos*	them–m	*los*	them–m	*les–a ellos*	to them–m
ellas	they–f	*ellas*	them–f	*las*	them–f	*les–a ellas*	to them–f
Uds.	you	*Uds.*	you			*les–a Uds.*	to you
		sí	("self")			*(se)*	

*   *Le* is used to translate **him** or **you**. In Spain the direct object pronouns *lo* and *los* are often replaced by *le* and *les* when the pronoun relates to a person or to a thing personified. For the AP exam one should follow the Latin American usage and avoid this substitution.

Subject Pronouns

These pronouns are usually omitted in Spanish as the verbal form by itself indicates person and number. (For the sake of clarity, *Ud.* and *Uds.* are usually not omitted.) Naturally, subject pronouns are used when confusion would result otherwise and in order to emphasize a statement. Often the particle *mismo (misma, mismos, mismas)* is used to add emphasis.

> *Fue a comprar vino.*
> **He went** to buy wine.

> *Ud. fue a comprar vino.*
> **You went** to buy wine.

> *Ud. mismo fue a comprar vino.*
> **You yourself went** to buy wine.

Second-Person Subject Pronouns

Tú (you, singular) differs from *usted* in terms of familiarity. *Tú* is more intimate; *usted* is more formal. As a rule of thumb, *tú* is used with those people with whom the speaker is on a first-name basis.

In certain parts of Latin America (Argentina, Uruguay, Paraguay, Central America), the form *vosotros* is often used instead of *tú*.

Vos comes with its own verbal forms: *Vos venís a la hora que queréis (Tú vienes a la hora que quieres)*. You come at whatever time it pleases you.

Vosotros (you, plural) differs from *ustedes* regionally. In Latin America and in southern Spain, *vosotros* has been replaced by *ustedes*.

Ser Followed by a Subject Pronoun

In Spanish, the subject pronoun follows "to be."

*Soy **yo**.*
It is **I**.

*Fue **ella** quien me envió el regalo.*
It was **she** that sent me the present.

OBJECT PRONOUNS

The direct object pronouns answer the question "whom" or "what"; the indirect object pronouns answer the question "to (for) whom" or "to (for) what."

*Ella **me** dio un regalo.*
She gave **me** a present. (**To whom** did she give a present?)

*Nosotros **lo** vimos.*
We saw **him**. (**Whom** did we see?)

Prepositional Complement with Indirect Object Pronoun

The indirect object pronoun can be clarified or emphasized by the addition of a prepositional complement (*a* + prepositional pronoun).

*Yo **le** hablé ayer.*
Yesterday I spoke to **him/her/you**.

*Yo **le** hablé **a ella** ayer.*
Yesterday I spoke to **her**.

Special Uses of the Indirect Object Pronoun

a) **Redundant Indirect Object Pronoun.** An indirect object pronoun is used in Spanish even when the indirect object noun is present in the sentence. The latter, however, must designate a person.

Les dije a los empleados que trabajaran más.
I told the employees to work harder.

   Common verbs of this type are: *pedir* (to ask for), *preguntar* (to ask), *dar* (to give), *decir* (to tell), *gustar* (to like), and *regalar* (to give).

   ¡Pídaselo a Jorge!   Ask George for it!

b) **Dative of Interest.** Indirect object pronouns are also used to represent the interested party involved in the action designated by the verb. (In these cases English uses a possessive adjective or pronoun.)

   Also, when the action results in some disadvantage or loss to the person directly concerned with the action, the indirect object is used. These are usually expressed with **from + person** in English.

Me robaron la billetera.
They stole my wallet from me.

Ella siempre le esconde la torta al chico.
She always hides the cake from the boy.

c) **for + person** is often expressed in Spanish by an indirect object rather than by *para + person*, particularly when a service is rendered.

Le lavé la ropa a ella.
I washed the clothes for her.

Ella me cocinó la comida.
She cooked the meal for me.

Juan nos arregló la puerta.
Juan fixed the door for us.

Exceptions: With *ser–*   *Este té es para ti.*
                              This tea is for you.

Where the indirect object is receiving a concrete object, either way is acceptable.

> *Te traje flores.* **or**
> *Traje flores para ti.*

d) **Use the definite article** and indirect object pronoun if the subject of the sentence performs an action on a part of someone else's body.

*Ella **le** lavará la cara a María.*
She will wash Mary's face (for her).

*Julio **le** cortó el pelo a su hijo.*
Julio cut his son's hair (for him).

e) **After *ser* used impersonally**, the indirect object pronoun may be employed to denote the person **to** whom the impersonal expression is applicable.

***Le** será fácil hacerlo.*
It will be easy **for him** to do it.

When Not to Use the Indirect Object Pronoun

In the following two instances, the indirect object pronoun should be avoided and the prepositional phrase used in its place.

a) **After verbs of motion** (*ir, venir, correr,* etc.)

*¡Ven **a mí**, Paco!*	Come to me, Paco!
*El niño corrió **a ellos**.*	The boy ran to them.
*¡No se acerque **a él**!*	Don't approach him!

b) **When the direct object is in the first or second person** (that is, when it is *me, te, nos, os*), Spanish uses the prepositional phrase instead of the indirect object pronoun.

*Me presentaron **a él**.*
They presented **me** (D.O.) to him (prepositional phrase).

*Nos mandó **a ellos**.*
He sent **us** (D.O.) to them (prepositional phrase).

Special Uses of the Direct Object Pronoun

a) **Neuter Direct Object Pronoun.** In English the verb "to be" does not require a direct object pronoun, but in some cases both *estar* and *ser* need a **neuter** direct object pronoun to make the sentence grammatical. In these cases *lo* refers back to the whole idea expressed in the previous sentence.

*¿Es Ud. médico? Sí, **lo** soy.*
Are you a doctor? Yes, I am.

*¿Estáis enfermos? No, no **lo** estamos.*
Are you sick? No, we are not.

The neuter direct object pronoun may also be used with the verb "to know."

*¿Sabes que Catalina se casó ayer? Sí, **lo** sé.*
Do you know that Catalina got married yesterday? Yes, I know.

*¿Tienes dinero que prestarme? ¡Ya **lo** creo!*
Do you have money to lend me? You bet!

b) ***Haber* with Direct Object Pronoun.** The verb *haber* sometimes requires the use of a direct object pronoun unknown in English. Note that the direct object pronoun in the following example is no longer neuter.

*¿Hay chicas en la fiesta? Sí, **las** hay.*
Are there girls at the party? Yes, there are.

c) ***Todo* with Direct Object Pronoun.** A direct object pronoun is required before the verb when the object of the verb is *todo*. Note that the object pronoun agrees in number and gender with *todo*.

Lo *he visto todo.*
I have seen everything.

Las *aprendí todas.*
I learned them all.

d) **Verbs that contain prepositions in their meaning** (*esperar*–to wait **for**, *mirar*–to look **at**, *buscar*–to look **for**, *escuchar*–to listen **to**, etc.) will use the direct object pronouns.

La *miré.*
I looked at her.

Los *buscaré para siempre.*
I'll look for them always.

e) **Verbs used with D.O. + infinitive** = *dejar* (to let), *hacer* (to make), *ver* (to see), and *oír* (to hear).

No lo dejen jugar.
Don't let him play.

Lo hizo recitar.
He made him recite.

La vi entrar.
I saw her enter.

f) **Redundant direct object pronouns** are needed as follows:

1. With the noun when the object is a person or proper name.

   Conociéndola a Eloisa...
   Knowing Eloisa...

   Ojalá que lo cojan al ladrón.
   I hope they catch the thief.

2. When the object precedes rather than follows the verb.

   La salida (D.O.) *la encontrará a su derecha.*
   The exit, you'll find it to your right.

Position of Object Pronouns in the Sentence

Unlike English, object pronouns in Spanish precede the conjugated verb (see examples below). However, they are attached at the end of the verb when the verbal form is an affirmative command, an infinitive, or a present participle.

Ud. le escribe. You write **to him.**	conjugated—present tense
¡Escríbale! Write **to him!**	positive command
Uds. la perdonaron. You forgave **her.**	conjugated—preterite tense
Hubo que perdonarla. It was necessary to forgive **her.**	infinitive
Los dejó sobre la mesa. He left **them** on the table.	conjugated—preterite tense
Salió dejándolos sobre la mesa. He went out leaving **them** on the table.	present participle

Note: When the infinitive or the present participle is subordinated to an auxiliary verb such as *querer, ir, poder,* or *estar,* the direct object pronoun can go before these verbs or after, attached to the infinitive or present participle:

I'm going to see **him**.	*Voy a ver**lo**.*
I'm going to see **him**.	***Lo** voy a ver.*
I am looking at **her**.	***La** estoy mirando.*
I'm looking at **her**.	*Estoy mirándo**la**.*

Syntactic Order of Object Pronouns

When a verb has two object pronouns, the indirect object pronoun precedes the direct object pronoun.

Envían una carta.	They send a letter.
***Nos** envían una carta.*	They send a letter **to us**.
***Nos la** envían.*	They send **it to us**.
*¡Enví**enosla**!*	Send **it to us**!
*¡No **nos la** envíen!*	Don't send **it to us**!

But when the two object pronouns in the sentence are third person pronouns, the **indirect** object pronoun (*le* or *les*) is replaced by *se*.

Escribes una carta.	You write a letter.
***Les** escribes una carta.*	You write a letter **to them**.
***Se la** escribes.*	You write **it to them**.
*¡Escríbe**sela**!*	Write **it to them**!

Prepositional Pronouns

Prepositions are words or phrases that relate words to one another. They may be followed by nouns, pronouns, or verbs (in the infinitive form in Spanish).

Here is a basic list of prepositions:

a	to, at	*excepto**	except
bajo	under	*hacia*	toward
*como**	like	*hasta*	until, as far as, to
*con***	with	*menos**	except
contra	against	*para*	for
de	from, of	*por*	for
desde	from, since	*salvo**	except
durante	during	*según**	according to
en	in, at, on	*sin*	without
*entre**	between, among	*sobre*	on, upon, over, above

* These prepositions are used with **subject** pronouns, not the prepositional group.

según él y yo   according to him and me

** With this preposition the prepositional pronouns *mí, ti*, and *sí* combine to form *conmigo, contigo, consigo*. These combinations are invariable; there are no plural or feminine forms.

Here is a basic list of compound prepositions:

además de	besides	*encima de*	on top of
alrededor de	around	*en cuanto a*	in regard to
antes de	before	*enfrente de*	in front of
a pesar de	in spite of	*en lugar de*	instead of
cerca de	near	*en vez de*	instead of
debajo de	under	*frente a*	in front of
delante de	in front of	*fuera de*	outside of
dentro de	within	*lejos de*	far from
después de	after (time)	*para con**	toward
detrás de	behind	*por + inf.*	because of

* To show an attitude towards, as in "*Es muy cariñoso (para) con su mujer.*" He is very affectionate toward his wife.

Use of *Sí, Consigo*

Sí is a special prepositional form of the pronoun *se*. It is often combined with a form of *mismo (–a, –os, –as)* to express "self." Note the difference between these two examples.

Ella no se refiere a sí misma.
She is not referring to herself.

vs.

Ella no se refiere a ella.
She is not referring to her (someone else).

Están disgustados consigo mismos.
They are disgusted with themselves.

vs.

Están disgustados con ellos.
They are disgusted with them (others).

Use of *Ello*

Ello means **it** when referring to situations or statements, but not to nouns.

Todo fue horrible; prefiero no hablar de ello.
It was all horrible; I prefer not to talk about it.

Por vs. *Para*

In general, *por* expresses the ideas contained in "for the sake of," "through," "exchange"; whereas *para* expresses destination, purpose, end, intention.

a) *Por* means "through"; *para* refers to destination.

*Iba **por** el parque.*   I was walking **through** the park.
*Iba **para** el parque.*   I was **on** my **way to** the park.

b) *Por* refers to motive; *para* to purpose or end.

*Lo hizo **por** mí.*
He did it **for** me (for my sake, on my behalf).

*El artesano hizo una vasija **para** mí.*
The artisan made a vase **for** me.

c) *Por* expresses the idea of exchange.

*Lo cambié **por** una camisa.*   I exchanged it **for** a shirt.

d) *Por* denotes a span of time; *para* designates an endpoint in time.

*Los exiliados caminaron **por** tres días y tres noches.*
The exiles walked **for** (during, for the space of) three days and three nights.

*El traje estará listo **para** el lunes.*
The suit will be ready by Monday.

e) *Para* translates "in order to."

*Fui a su casa **para** hablar con él.*
I went to his house **in order to** speak to him.

f) *Por* and *para* have set meanings in certain idiomatic constructions.

por *ejemplo*	**for** example
por lo menos	at least
para *siempre*	**for**ever
No es **para** *tanto.*	It's not that serious.

g) Other expressions using *por*.

por ahora	for now
por avión	by plane
por consiguiente	consequently
por desgracia	unfortunately
por ejemplo	for example
por escrito	in writing
por eso	therefore
por fin	finally
por lo común	generally
por lo contrario	on the contrary
por lo general	generally
por regla general	as a general rule
por lo tanto	consequently
por lo visto	apparently
por otra parte	on the other hand
por poco	almost
por si acaso	in case
por supuesto	of course
por teléfono	by phone
por todas partes	everywhere

Idioms with *A*, *En*, *De*, *Sin*

a) Idioms with *a*

a caballo	on horseback
a casa/en casa	at home
a causa de	because of
a eso de	at about (with time)
a fines de	at the end of
a fondo	thoroughly
a fuerza de	by dint of
a la derecha	to the right
a la izquierda	to the left
a la vez	at the same time

a lo largo de	along
a lo lejos	in the distance
a lo menos (al menos)	at least
a mano	by hand
a menudo	often
a mi parecer	in my opinion
a pie	on foot
a pierna suelta	without a care
a principios de	at the beginning of
a saltos	by leaps and bounds
a solas	alone
a tiempo	on time
a través de	across
a veces	at times
a la española (francesa, etc.)	in the Spanish/French way
a la larga	in the long run
a la semana	per week
al aire libre	outside
al amanecer	at dawn
al anochecer	at nightfall
al cabo	finally
al contrario	on the contrary
al día	up to date
al fin	finally
al lado de	next to
al parecer	apparently
al por mayor	wholesale
al por menor	retail
al principio	at first

b) Idioms with *de*

de antemano	ahead of time
de arriba	upstairs
de balde	free
de broma	jokingly
de buena gana	willingly
de cuando (vez) en cuando	from time to time
de día (noche)	by day, at night
de día en día	from day to day
de esta (esa) manera	in this (that) way
de este (ese) modo	in this (that) way
de hoy (ahora) en adelante	from today (now) on

de mala gana	unwillingly
de mal humor	in a bad mood
de manera que/de modo que	so that
de memoria	by heart
de moda	in style
de nada	you're welcome
de ninguna manera/de ningún modo	by no means
de nuevo	again
de otro modo	otherwise
(abrir) de par en par	(to open) wide
de pie	standing
de prisa	in a hurry
de pronto/de repente	suddenly
de rodillas	kneeling
de todos modos	anyway
de uno en uno	one by one
de veras	really

c) Idioms with *en*

en bicicleta	by bike
en broma	jokingly
en cambio	on the other hand
en caso de	in case of
en contra de	against
en cuanto	as soon as
en cuanto a	as for, in regard to
en efecto	in effect
en este momento	at this time
en lugar (vez) de	instead of
en marcha	under way, on the way
en medio de	in the middle of
en ninguna parte	nowhere
en punto	sharp (telling time)
en seguida	at once
en suma	in short, in a word
en todas partes	everywhere
en vano	in vain
en voz alta (baja)	in a loud (low) voice

d) Idioms with *sin*

sin aliento	out of breath
sin cuento	endless
sin cuidado	carelessly
sin duda	without a doubt
sin ejemplo	unparalleled
sin embargo	nevertheless
sin falta	without fail
sin fondo	bottomless
sin novedad	same as usual

Verbs with Prepositions

a) Verbs with *con*

amenazar con	to threaten to
casarse con	to get married to
contar (ue) con	to rely on
cumplir con	to keep (one's word)
encontrarse (ue) con	to run into by chance
enojarse con	to get angry with
estar de acuerdo con	to agree with
meterse con	to pick a quarrel with
quedarse con	to keep
soñar (ue) con	to dream about
tropezar (ie) con	to meet by chance with

b) Verbs with *en*

apoyarse en	to lean on
confiar (í) en	to trust in
consentir (ie, i) en	to consent to
consistir en	to consist of
convenir en	to agree to/on
convertirse (ie, i) en	to become, change into
empeñarse en	to insist on
especializarse en	to major in
fijarse en	to notice, stare at
influir en	to influence
insistir en	to insist on
meterse en	to get involved in
pensar (ie) en	to think about
reparar en	to notice

quedar en	to agree to
tardar en	to delay in

c) Verbs with *de*

acabar de + inf	*Acabo de comer.*	I just ate.
	Acababa de comer.	I'd just eaten.
	Acabé de comer.	I finished eating.

acordarse (ue) de	to remember
alegrarse de	to be glad
alejarse de	to go away from
apoderarse de	to take possession of
aprovecharse de	to take advantage of
arrepentirse (ie, i) de	to repent
avergonzarse (ue)* de	to be ashamed
burlarse de	to make fun of
carecer de	to lack
constar de	to consist of
cuidar de	to take care of
darse cuenta de	to realize
dejar de	to stop (doing something)
depender de	to depend on
despedirse (i, i) de	to say goodbye to
disfrutar de	to enjoy
enamorarse de	to fall in love with
encargarse de	to take charge of
enterarse de	to find out about
fiarse (í) de	to trust
gozar de	to enjoy
olvidarse de	to forget about
oír hablar de	to hear about
pensar (ie) de	to think about (have an opinion)
preocuparse de	to be worried about
quejarse de	to complain about
reírse (í, i)** de	to laugh at
servir (i, i) de	to serve as
servirse (i, i) de	to make use of
tratar de	to try to + inf.
tratarse de	to be a question of

*   This verb will have a dieresis mark over the *ü* in the present indicative and sub-
    junctive, in all forms except *nosotros* and *vosotros*: *me avergüenzo* but *nos aver-*
    gonzamos.
** This verb is conjugated as follows: *reírse*   to laugh at

Present Indicative	Present Subjunctive	Preterite	Imperfect Subjunctive
me río	me ría	me reí	me riera/se
te ríes	te rías	te reíste	te rieras/ses
se ríe	se ría	se rió	se riera/se
nos reímos	nos riamos	nos reímos	nos riéramos/semos
os reís	os riáis	os reísteis	os rierais/seis
se ríen	se rían	se rieron	se rieran/sen

Present Participle: *riendo*

Past Participle: *reído*

Formal Commands: *ríase, no se ría   ríanse, no se rían*

Familiar Commands: *ríete, no te rías   reíos, no os riáis*

d) Verbs with *por*

acabar por	to end up by
dar por	to consider, to regard as
esforzarse (ue) por	to make an effort
interesarse por	to be interested in
preguntar por + person	to ask for (a person)
tomar por	to take (someone) for

e) Verbs with *a*

Verbs of beginning, learning, and motion are followed by an *a* in Spanish.

Beginning

comenzar (ie) a
empezar (ie) a
ponerse a
principiar a

Learning

aprender a	to learn
enseñar a	to teach

Motion

acercarse a	to approach
apresurarse a	to hurry to
dirigirse a	to go toward

ir a	to go to
regresar a	to return to
salir a	to leave to
subir a	to go up
venir a	to come to
volver a (ue)	to return to

Other verbs followed by *a*:

acertar (ie) a	to happen to
acostumbrarse a	to become used to
alcanzar a	to succeed in (doing something)
asistir a	to attend
asomarse a	to appear at
aspirar a	to aspire to
atreverse a	to dare to
ayudar a	to help
condenar a	to condemn to
convidar a	to invite to
cuidar a	to take care of (person)
decidirse a	to decide to
dedicarse a	to devote oneself to
detenerse a	to pause to
disponerse a	to get ready to
exponerse a	to run the risk of
invitar a	to invite to
jugar (ue) a	to play (game)
negarse (ie) a	to refuse to
obligar a	to obligate to
oler (ue) a*	to smell like
parecerse a	to resemble
querer (ie) a	to love
resignarse a	to resign oneself to
saber a	to taste like
ser aficionado, –a a	to be fond (a fan) of
someter a	to submit to
sonar a	to sound like
volver (ue) a + verb	to (do something) again

---

*   This verb in the present indicative and subjunctive (except for *nosotros* and *vosotros*) will begin with "*h*." *Él huele a ajo.* He smells like garlic.

Conjunctions

Conjunctions are words or phrases that connect clauses to one another. The following is a basic list of conjunctions:

o (u)	or
y (e)	and
pero, mas, sino que	but
ni	nor, neither
que	that
si	if, whether

Uses of the Basic Conjunctions

a) *O* changes to *u* in front of words beginning with *o* or *ho:*

*No sé si lo dijo Roberto **u** Horacio.*
I don't know whether Roberto **or** Horacio said it.

b) *Y* changes to *e* in front of words beginning with *i* or *hi:*

*Padre **e** hijo viajaban juntos.*
Father **and** son were traveling together.

Note: *Y* does not change in front of *y* or *hie:*

*fuego **y** hielo*	fire **and** ice.
*Tú **y** yo.*	You **and** I.

c) *Ni* is the counterpart of *y.* It is often repeated in a sentence to mean "neither ... nor":

***ni** chicha **ni** limonada*	**neither** fish **nor** fowl

Pero vs. *Sino*

Pero, mas, and *sino* mean "but." (*Mas* with an accent mark, however, is an adverb meaning "more.") *Pero* and *mas* are interchangeable, but *pero* and *sino* have different uses. *Sino* (or *sino que*) has the sense of "rather" or "on the contrary." For *sino* or *sino que* to be used, the first part of the sentence must be negative.

*No dije roca **sino** foca.*
I didn't say "rock" **but** "seal."

*No vino para quedarse **sino que** vino y se fue.**
She didn't come to stay **but** came and left.

*Mi abuelo ya murió **pero** me dejó un buen recuerdo.*
My grandfather already died **but** he left me good memories.

* When the contrast is between clauses with different verb forms, *que* is introduced.

Correlative Conjunctions

Conjunctions such as *ni...ni* above are not uncommon in Spanish. Other pairs are:

o...o	either...or
ya...ya	whether...or, sometimes...sometimes
no sólo...sino también	not only...but also

*Decídete. **O** te vas **o** haces lo que te digo.*
Make up your mind. **Either** you leave **or** you do as I say.

Ella no sólo gana el dinero sino que también lo gasta.
She not only earns the money but also spends it.

Conjunctive Phrases

Some conjunctions may require the use of the subjunctive. (See subjunctive–the adverbial clause.) The others follow:

apenas...cuando	hardly...when
a pesar de que	in spite of
conque	so then, and so, then
desde que	since
empero	however
entretanto que	meanwhile
más bien que	rather than
mientras tanto	meanwhile
no bien...cuando	no sooner...than
no obstante	notwithstanding

☞ Drill 8

1. Mi viejo amigo Fernando trabaja…la Compañía Equis.

   (A) por   (C) cerca

   (B) a   (D) para

2. Miguelín…trajo café de Colombia.

   (A) ti   (C) mí

   (B) nos   (D) ella

3. …a él, no a ella.

   (A) Le parecen   (C) Se negaron

   (B) Se lo enseñaron   (D) Los vieron

4. Ayer compré unas sillas nuevas; son muy elegantes y juegan bien con los otros muebles. Son nuevecitas y no quiero que la gente se siente en…

   (A) las.   (C) les.

   (B) ellas.   (D) ella.

5. María me dijo un secreto. …dijo el otro día.

   (A) Me lo   (C) Me los

   (B) Lo me   (D) No me lo

6. Cuando entramos en el dormitorio, nos dimos cuenta de que los ladrones sólo habían robado nuestras corbatas nuevas. …llevaron toditas.

   (A) Las nos   (C) Se las

   (B) Nos la   (D) Me la

7. Invité a Carmela a que fuera…

   (A) conmigo.   (C) con yo.

   (B) con mi.   (D) conmiga.

8. Siempre al comer me gusta el pan con mucha mantequilla. A la mesa tengo que decirles a los otros que...

   (A) me pasen.   (C) me la pasen.

   (B) pásenmela.   (D) se la pasen.

9. —Mamá, prepáreme la comida. Ella me dice,...

   (A) «Te lo estoy preparando.»

   (B) «Estoy preparándotela.»

   (C) «La te preparo.»

   (D) «Prepárotela.»

10. Como era natural, el perro salió...la puerta.

    (A) para   (C) a

    (B) por   (D) de

11. Raúl no entendía el subjuntivo; el profesor...

    (A) se lo explicó.   (C) lo explica.

    (B) se los explica.   (D) los explicó.

12. Nuestros enemigos están trabajando...

    (A) con nos.   (C) contra nosotros.

    (B) contra nos.   (D) connos.

13. La silla estaba...la mesa.

    (A) antes de   (C) en cuanto a

    (B) detrás de   (D) después de

14. Mi novia quería casarse conmigo pero nunca...dijo.

    (A) se le   (C) me lo

    (B) se lo   (D) lo me

15. Al presidente...trataron de asesinar hace varios años.

    (A) se   (C) ello

    (B) lo   (D) les

16. Carmen es muy bella. Ayer...vi.

    (A) la   (C) les

    (B) lo   (D) se

17. Me pidieron que...entregara el informe directamente al jefe.

    (A) lo   (C) se

    (B) le   (D) la

18. El fugitivo ha regresado; yo mismo...vi.

    (A) lo   (C) les

    (B) te   (D) se

19. Él...dio un beso al despedirse.

    (A) lo   (C) le

    (B) la   (D) se

20. Este político sabe mucho...la poca educación que tiene.

    (A) a causa de   (C) por

    (B) para   (D) porque

21. Todos mis amigos van al mercado menos...

    (A) mí.   (C) conmigo.

    (B) mi.   (D) yo.

22. Ella no es alta...baja.

    (A) pero   (C) también

    (B) sino   (D) sino que

23. Yo no conozco al niño…me gusta su coche nuevo.

    (A) pero   (C) pero que

    (B) sino   (D) sino que

24. Ella siempre…esconde su dinero a mi madre y a mí.

    (A) nos   (C) les

    (B) le   (D) los

25. No puedo ver a mis amigas; tengo que…

    (A) buscarles.   (C) buscarlas.

    (B) las buscar.   (D) las busco.

26. Fue horrible; prefiero no pensar en…

    (A) lo.   (C) ella.

    (B) él.   (D) ello.

27. Esta taza es…café. ¡Démela, por favor!

    (A) por   (C) en

    (B) para   (D) con

28. La semana pasada me quedé en casa…tres días.

    (A) por   (C) en

    (B) para   (D) de

29. ¿Cuánto dinero me dará Ud.…mi trabajo?

    (A) por   (C) de

    (B) en   (D) para

30. …el viernes tenemos esta lección.

    (A) En   (C) Para

    (B) Por   (D) De

Drill 8—Detailed Explanations of Answers

1. **(D)** To work **for**, in the sense of "to be employed by," requires the use of "para" rather than "por." For this reason, (A) is wrong, but (D) is right. Thinking that you wanted to say "at," you might have mistakenly chosen answer (B), but the word "a" normally means "at" only when it follows verbs of motion: "Tiró la pelota a la pared" (He threw the ball at the wall). When motion is not involved, we use the preposition "en" to mean "at": "Mi madre está en el mercado" (My mother is at the market). Choice (C) is wrong because "near to" is "cerca **de**" and not simply "cerca."

2. **(B)** In the sentence, the verb "trajo" is the third person preterite of "traer" (to bring). We know that Miguelín brought someone coffee, i.e., Miguelín brought coffee **to** someone. The indirect object pronouns, which mean "to" or "for," are "me" (to or for me), "te" (to or for you, familiar singular), "le" (to or for him, her, you, polite singular), "nos" (to or for us), "os" (to or for you, familiar plural), and "les" (to or for them, you, polite plural). In the list of possible answers, we encounter only one pronoun from this list, "nos." In (A), we see the second person singular familiar form of the prepositional pronoun, i.e., a pronoun which is used following a preposition. Since there is no preposition this choice is incorrect.

3. **(B)** Choice (A) is incorrect because "parecerse a" (to resemble) requires a reflexive pronoun, but we are given the third person singular indirect object pronoun. In (C), we find the reflexive form of "negar," which is used in the idiomatic expression "negarse a" + infinitive (to refuse to). The "a" in our sentence, however, is not followed by an infinitive, but rather by a prepositional pronoun, "él." In (D), we have used the third person plural masculine form of the direct object pronoun. Since we are referring to "él" (him), for this to be correct, we would have to use the masculine singular form of that pronoun, "lo." (B) is correct. It says, "Se lo enseñaron" (They showed or taught it to him). Observe the two object pronouns at the beginning of this answer. Remember that if we have two third person object pronouns (the first indirect, the second direct), the first of these automatically changes to "se." In our sentence, then, the "Se" would actually stand for the word "le." English speakers might question why the indirect object pronoun appears here since later in the sentence we find the prepositional phrase "a él," which means "to him." Nevertheless, the redundant use of the indirect object pronoun is typical of Spanish style, even though there

may be a prepositional phrase later in the sentence which explicitly states the same idea.

4.   **(B)**   After a preposition, the object pronoun is expressed by the subject pronoun with the exception of the first and second persons singular. In this case, **ellas** is plural and would be the only correct answer because it refers to "chairs."

5.   **(A)**   The indirect object pronoun always precedes the direct. Both precede the verb unless this is in the infinitive. **Me lo** is the only correct answer because **lo** refers to **secreto**. Choice (D), although grammatically correct, does not follow the train of information given in the first sentence.

6.   **(C)**   The passive voice in Spanish can be translated by the reflexive **se**, and choice (C) is the only possible one because **las** refers to **corbatas**. (A) has the plural **las**, but the indirect object does not precede the direct.

7.   **(A)**   The first and second persons singular with the preposition **con** are always **conmigo** and **contigo**. Occasionally **consigo** is used, meaning **con él, con ella,** or **con usted**. The verb **invitar** is one of the verbs which when followed by a change in subject requires the subjunctive, and in this case, it is in the past. **Fuera** is the imperfect subjunctive form of **ir**. (D) is incorrect because **conmigo** is invariable and has no feminine form.

8.   **(C)**   The indirect object pronoun always precedes the direct. In this case, the subjunctive is required because of the verb **decir**, as a request with a change of subject. The **la** refers to **mantequilla**. (A), (B), and (C) have **me**, but only (C) includes both the indirect and the direct objects in their proper position.

9.   **(B)**   The use of the auxiliary **estar** is correct with the present participle. The indirect and direct objects are joined in that order following the present participle. **Te** is used because the familiar form is appropriate, and the **la** refers to **comida**.

10.   **(B)**   **Por** is correct. It is the correct word for "through" in this context.

11.   **(A)**   The indirect object pronoun **le** is changed to **se** when used in conjunction with a direct object pronoun. **Lo**, in this sentence, refers to the subjunctive in the sentence. Choice (C) is a remote possibility, but is not totally correct grammatically.

12. **(C)** After a preposition, the subject pronoun should be used except for the first and second persons singular. Our enemies are supposedly working "against us," so choice (C) is the only correct answer.

13. **(B)** The preposition "antes de," in (A), means "before." It refers to time, not location. The sentence is talking about the position of the "chair" ("silla"). If we meant "before" in the sense of "in front of," we would have to use the preposition "delante de." The contrary of "delante de" is "detrás de" (behind, in back of), which fits well in our sentence. In (D) "después de" (after), we have another preposition which refers to time, not location. In (C) "en cuanto a" means "about" in the sense of "concerning."

14. **(C)** Neither of the first two choices can be the correct answer because in both "se" refers to a third person not to be found in the question. Choice (D) has the right object pronouns but in the wrong order. Choice (C) is the right answer because it contains the appropriate indirect object pronoun ("she said **to me**") and direct object pronoun ("she said **it** to me") in the correct sequence.

15. **(B)** The correct answer is the only direct object pronoun available. This is a peculiar but common use of the pronoun, which wouldn't be necessary if the sentence were in the normal syntactic order, namely, with the subject in front (an implicit "ellos") and the direct object ("presidente") in back. When the usual order is inverted, then a redundant object pronoun must be introduced.

16. **(A)** The question calls for a direct object pronoun. Of the two available, you need to choose the feminine form to go with "Carmen."

17. **(B)** This question calls for the indirect object pronoun, which you have to identify (there is only one) from the choices offered. The reason for this type of pronoun is that Spanish tends to reinforce the indirect object ("jefe") when it refers to a person.

18. **(A)** Here you need a direct object pronoun that refers to "el fugitivo" and the only possibility among the four choices is "lo."

19. **(C)** The direct object in this sentence is "un beso" and since it is present in the phrase there is no need for a direct object pronoun (such as "lo" or "la"). What the sentence does need is an indirect object pronoun referring to the implicit person (or pet, or whatever) in the statement.

20. **(B)** Para is used whenever the idea of "considering" is implied.

21. **(D)** After certain prepositions (menos, excepto, salvo, entre, como, and según), subject pronouns are used in Spanish. Therefore, choice (A), which is prepositional, is incorrect. Choice (B) means "my" and choice (C) means "with me."

22. **(B)** "Sino" has the sense of "rather" or "on the contrary" and is used as the conjunction in a negative sentence where the second part directly contradicts the first. It is important to note that direct contradictions must be between equal parts of speech, in this case, between the adjectives "alta" and "baja." Choice (A) is incorrect because it cannot be used where a direct contradiction is implied. Choice (C) "also" makes no sense in this context. Choice (D) is used when the direct contradiction is between two conjugated verbs, (i.e., Ella no quiere sentarse sino que quiere levantarse.)

23. **(A)** Even though the first part of this sentence is negative, the second part is not a direct contradiction of the first. Therefore, choice (B) and (D) are incorrect. Choice (C) "pero que" (but that) makes no sense.

24. **(A)** When the action results in some disadvantage or loss ("hides") to the person directly concerned with the action, the indirect object pronoun is used. In English these statements are commonly expressed with **from + person**. Choice (A) is correct because the indirect object must correlate with the phrase "a mi madre y a mí," which is equivalent to **us**. Choices (B) "to him," (C) "to them," and (D) "to you" are also indirect object pronouns but do not correlate with the previously mentioned phrase.

25. **(C)** Verbs which include a preposition in their meaning (buscar–to look for, esperar–to wait for, mirar–to look at) are used with direct object pronouns. Choice (A) is incorrect because it has an indirect object pronoun. Choice (C) has the correct direct object pronoun but it is incorrectly placed. Choice (D) is incorrect because the conjugated verb "busco" cannot follow "tengo que," which requires the use of the infinitive.

26. **(D)** The neuter pronoun "ello" (it) is used to refer to entire happenings, events, or occurrences previously alluded to. Choice (A) is a direct object pronoun and cannot be used after a preposition. Choices (B) "he/it (m)" and (C) "she/it (f)" are incorrect since there is no reference to anything specific that is either masculine or feminine in gender.

27. **(B)** To indicate what something is intended for, use **para**. The intended use of the cup is for coffee.

28. **(A)** **Por** is used to express a length of time. In this example, the length of time is three days.

29. **(A)** **Por** is used when "in exchange for" is intended. In this sample it is money in exchange for work.

30. **(C)** **Para** is used to express some point in future time. In this sample the future time indicated is Friday.

GUSTAR

Gustar and verbs like it follow a certain pattern that is unlike English. These verbs are commonly used in the third person singular and plural in conjunction with the indirect object pronoun group.

Pattern of *Gustar*

Because *gustar* means "to be pleasing to," its translation into Spanish from the English "to like" will require setting the verb up according to the following pattern:

I like cars.   = Cars **are pleasing** to me.
            = *Me gustan los coches.*

In the example given, after rearranging the sentence to fit the Spanish pattern, the indirect object surfaces (to me). In addition, one can see that the new subject (cars) will require using the verb in the third person plural. The following chart shows the indirect object pronoun group with **all** six persons "explained" with the prepositional phrase.

me	*– a mí*	*nos*	*– a nosotros*
te	*– a ti*	*os*	*– a vosotros*
le	*– a él*	*les*	*– a ellos*
le	*– a ella*	*les*	*– a ellas*
le	*– a Ud.*	*les*	*– a Uds.*

This additional prepositional phrase that can accompany each of the indirect object pronouns can be used to:

1. further emphasize the indirect pronoun itself.

    *A **mí** me gusta la música clásica.*
    I **really** like classical music.

2. further clarify the meaning of le/les.

    A ella le gustaban las películas de horror.
    She liked horror movies.

3. provide a place to put names/nouns/proper nouns.

    *A **Juan** le gustará ir al cine conmigo.*
    Juan will like to go to the movies with me.

    *A **los chicos** les gustan los coches.*
    Boys like cars.

"Gustar" Types

Verbs that follow the *"gustar* pattern":

agradar	to be pleasing	*Nos agrada ir.* It pleases us to go.
bastar	to be enough	*Me basta un traje.* One suit is enough for me.
doler (ue)	to be painful	*Me duele la cabeza.* My head aches.
parecer	to seem	*A él le parece imposible.* It seems impossible to him.
placer	to be pleasing	*Nos place verte.* It pleases us to see you.
quedar	to have left	*Me quedó un buen libro.* I had one good book left.
sobrar	to be left over	*Les sobran tres dólares.* They have $3.00 left over.
tocar	to be one's turn	*A María le toca.* It's Mary's turn.

To Need

To need can be expressed three ways: *falter, hacer falta,* and *necesitar.*

I need a car.	*Me falta un coche.* *Me hace falta un coche.* *Necesito un coche.*
I needed a car.	*Me faltó/faltaba un coche.* *Me hizo/hacía falta un coche.* *Necesité/Necesitaba un coche.*

Note: The verb *"faltar/hacer falta"* is commonly used in the present, preterite, and imperfect tenses. If one needs to express "need" in other tenses, use *necesitar.*

☞ Drill 9

1.   A Roberto...gusta ir a la playa todos los días durante el verano.

    (A) se   (C) le

    (B) os   (D) te

2.   ...chico le gusta jugar al tenis.

    (A) El   (C) A

    (B) Al   (D) nothing needed

3.   A Rob y a mí...el helado.

    (A) les gusta   (C) nos gusta

    (B) les gustan   (D) nos gustan

4.   Me encanta...dinero.

    (A) gastar   (C) gastaré

    (B) gastando   (D) pasar

5.   ...falta dos dólares.

    (A) Me hace   (C) Me haces

    (B) Me hacen   (D) Me hago

6.   ¿A quiénes...toca?

    (A) lo   (C) les

    (B) le   (D) los

7.   A mis amigos...el chocolate.

    (A) les gustó   (C) le gustó

    (B) les gustaron   (D) nos gustó

8.   …nos encantó la cuidad.

   (A) A María

   (B) A las mujeres

   (C) A vosotros

   (D) A los niños y a mí

9.   A José…dos cursos difíciles.

   (A) le bastará   (C) se bastarán

   (B) le bastarán   (D) bastarán

10.   A Juan no le importaba…

   (A) los coches.   (C) estudiando.

   (B) ir al cine.   (D) a trabajar.

Drill 9—Detailed Explanations of Answers

1. **(C)** Normally, with the verb "gustar" and similar verbs, we use indirect object pronouns (me, te, le, nos, os, les). Although we usually translate "gustar" to mean "to like," we should remember that it literally means "to be pleasing **to**." This explains the use of "A" before "Roberto" in the sentence. It is pleasing "**to** Roberto." The indirect object pronoun can mean "to" or "for." It is for this reason that the indirect object pronoun is required here. Because "Roberto" is a singular noun, we must then use the third person singular indirect object pronoun "le."

2. **(B)** "Gustar" type verbs use indirect object pronouns which can be further clarified by using prepositional phrases. These phrases begin with "a" and normally precede the indirect object pronoun that they go with. Choice (A) is incorrect because the preposition "a" is required. Choice (C) is missing the article "el" which is needed before the noun "chico."

3. **(C)** The "a" phrase contains the hint as to which indirect object pronoun to select. By including "me" with "Rob" the corresponding pronoun is "we" (nos). The verb is singular because the noun "helado" is singular. Choices (A) and (B) have the incorrect object pronoun. Choice (D) has the incorrect form of "gustar."

4. **(A)** If a verb follows any verb used like "gustar," it must be in the gerund form (infinitive) since it is acting as the actual subject of the statement. Choices (B) the present participle and (C) the future tense are both in the incorrect form. Choice (D), although it is an infinitive, is incorrect because this verb means to spend "time," not "money."

5. **(B)** The main verb in this expression (hacer), which means "to need," must match the item(s) needed. In this case two dollars are needed, which is plural. Answer (A) is singular and will not match the subject. Answer (C) the "tú" form of the verb and answer (D) the "yo" form of the verb **hacer** are not acceptable forms of this verb when used in this manner. It must either be third singular or third plural.

6. **(C)** This "gustar" type means "to be one's turn." The prepositional phrase ("a quiénes") contains the hint as to which indirect object pronoun to select. Choices (A) and (D) are direct object pronouns and are not used with "gustar" types. Choice (B) is singular and will not match "a quiénes."

7.   **(A)**   Because the noun "chocolate" is singular, a singular form of **gustar** is required. The prepositional phrase "A mis amigos" corresponds to the indirect object pronoun "les," Choice (B) is incorrect because the verb is plural. Choices (C) and (D) have the incorrect I.O. pronouns.

8.   **(D)**   Because the indirect object pronoun "nos" has been used in this sentence, the corresponding prepositional phrase must match it. "A María" (A) would require "le," "A las mujeres" (B) would require "les," and "A vosotros" (C) would require using "os."

9.   **(B)**   The verb must be plural to match "dos cursos difíciles," and the indirect object pronoun must correspond to the prepositional phrase "A José." Choice (A) has the incorrect verb form. Choice (C) has a reflexive pronoun, and (D) is missing the indirect object pronoun entirely.

10. **(B)**   After the verb "importaba" either an infinitive or a singular noun may be used. Choice (A) has a plural noun, and (C) is the present participle of "estudiar." Choice (D) has an additional "a" before the infinitive, which is unnecessary.

DEMONSTRATIVES: ADJECTIVES/PRONOUNS

These two groups share identical forms except that the accent mark is used over the pronouns.

Adjective		Pronoun	
this	*este, esta*	this one	*éste, ésta*
that	*ese, esa*	that one	*ése, ésa*
that*	*aquel, aquella*	that one*	*aquél, aquélla*
these	*estos, estas*	these	*éstos, éstas*
those	*esos, esas*	those	*ésos, ésas*
those*	*aquellos, aquellas*	those*	aquéllos, aquéllas

* These demonstratives are used to indicate greater distance from the speaker as well as distance in time. *Ése* (etc.) refers to something near the listener but removed from the speaker, whereas *aquél* (etc.) refers to something far from **both** the speaker and listener.

En aquella época...	At that time...
Aquellas montañas...	Those mountains...

Note: The definite article (*el, la, los, las*) followed by *de* or *que* is often translated as a pronoun.

*mi corbata y **la de** mi hermano*
my tie and **that of** my brother

*Este libro y **el que** tiene Juan son interesantes.*
This book and **the one that** Juan has are interesting.

NEUTER FORMS

The neuter forms (*eso, esto, aquello*) are used when the gender is not determined or when referring to vague or general ideas. These words do not vary in gender or number, and no accent is required.

¿Qué es esto?
What is this?

Estoy enfermo y esto me enoja.
I'm ill and this makes me angry.

Former and Latter

The pronoun *éste* (*–a, –os, –as*) is used to translate **the latter** (the latest or most recently mentioned), while *aquél* (*–la, –los, –las*) expresses **the former** (the most remotely mentioned).

Juana and Pablo are siblings; the former is a doctor, the latter is a dentist.

Juana y Pablo son hermanos; éste es dentista, aquélla es doctora.

Note: In English we say "the former and the latter," but in Spanish this order is reversed.

☞ Drill 10

1. Querida, ¿no crees que...anillo es tan lindo como los otros?

    (A) esto   (C) este

    (B) aquello   (D) esa

2. Mis nietos me regalaron...televisor.

    (A) eso   (C) aquel

    (B) esto   (D) esté

3. Muéstreme otro apartamento, no me gusta...

    (A) esto.   (C) esté.

    (B) este.   (D) éste.

4. ...problemas son fáciles de resolver.

    (A) Estos   (C) Estas

    (B) Estes   (D) Esas

5. Llegó tarde y...me hace enojada.

    (A) eso   (C) esta

    (B) ésta   (D) aquel

6. ¿Qué es...?

    (A) éste   (C) ésto

    (B) esto   (D) ésta

7. Estas camisas y...a lo lejos son caras.

    (A) ésos   (C) aquellas

    (B) aquéllas   (D) ésas

8. Rolando y Antonia son hermanos; ésta es alta y... es inteligente.

   (A) este   (C) aquél

   (B) aquel   (D) ése

9. Me gustan...guantes porque son de cuero.

   (A) estos   (C) estas

   (B) éstos   (D) éstas

10. Mi corbata y...Juan son de seda.

   (A) ella de   (C) éste de

   (B) ésa de   (D) la de

Drill 10—Detailed Explanations of Answers

1. **(C)** The masculine demonstrative adjective "este" means "this" and should be used to modify a masculine singular noun, just as is required by the sentence. "Esto" (this) in (A) and "aquello" (that) in (B) are pronouns, not adjectives, and they are neuter, i.e., they are neither masculine nor feminine. The neuter pronouns "esto," "eso" (that), and "aquello" (that) are used to refer to ideas or concepts (not specific nouns), for example "Llueve mucho aquí. **Eso** no me gusta." Here the word "eso" does not refer to any particular word, nor does it modify anything. Rather, as a pronoun, it stands for or takes the place of the whole idea which was previously expressed. "Llueve mucho aquí." "Esa" in (D) is clearly wrong because we cannot use a feminine form of the adjective to modify a masculine noun.

2. **(C)** The verb "regalar" means "to give a gift." A "televisor" is a "television set." Choice (D) is inappropriate because it is a form of the present tense of the subjunctive "estar." The syntax of the sentence does not require a verb in the blank. All of the remaining choices are demonstratives, but only one, "aquel" (that), may function as an adjective, which is what we need in the blank in order to modify the word "televisor." (A) "eso" (that) and (B) "esto" (this), are not adjectives, but rather **neuter demonstrative** pronouns. Because they are neuter (neither masculine nor feminine), they cannot be used to refer to any specific noun. Instead, they are used to refer to whole concepts or ideas which have previously been mentioned: Hace mucho calor en esta región y **esto** no me gusta" (It's very hot in this region, and I don't like this). The word "esto" in this sentence refers to no specific noun, but rather to the whole idea previously stated, "Hace mucho calor en esta región..."

3. **(D)** The demonstrative adjective form for "this" is converted into a pronoun by using the orthographic accent. (A) **Esto** is considered neuter, since it does not refer to a masculine or feminine noun. Choice (B) is the correct form for the masculine, but it needs the accent. Choice (C) is the correct form for the imperative. Only choice (D) is the proper form.

4. **(A)** "Problema" is masculine, which eliminates (C) and (D). The plural form of este (B) is estos.

5. **(A)** When referring to an entire event, happening, or occurrence, the neuter form "eso" is used. Choice (B) is the feminine singular demon-

strative pronoun meaning "this one." Choice (C) is the feminine singular demonstrative adjective meaning "this." Choice (D) is the masculine singular demonstrative adjective meaning "that" (in the distance).

6. **(B)**   The neuter demonstrative is used when one doesn't know the gender of the item asked about. Choice (A) is the masculine singular demonstrative meaning "this one." Choice (C) is incorrect because the neuter forms do not require accent marks. Choice (D) is the feminine singular demonstrative pronoun meaning "this one."

7. **(B)**   Because this demonstrative is replacing "camisas," it is being used as a pronoun and must, therefore, have the accent mark to differentiate it from the adjective. Also, "a lo lejos" (in the distance) requires some form of "aquél." Although (A) and (D) are pronouns, neither one is used for distance and (A) is the wrong gender. (C) is the demonstrative adjective meaning "that" and must precede a noun, *not* replace it.

8. **(C)**   Latter (a form of "éste") and former (a form of "aquél") are expressed using the demonstrative pronouns. Whereas we say "the former…the latter," in Spanish this is reversed. In this sentence the former, Rolando, is being referred to by the statement "…es inteligente." Therefore, the masculine singular form "aquél" is needed to express "former." Choices (A) and (B) are incorrect because they are demonstrative adjectives. Choice (D) means "that one" and is not used to express "former or latter" in Spanish.

9. **(A)**   "Guantes" (gloves) is the masculine noun requiring the demonstrative adjective. Choice (C) is incorrect because it is feminine. Choices (B) and (D) are demonstrative pronouns and cannot be used to modify nouns.

10. **(D)**   Before the preposition **de,** the demonstrative is replaced by the definite article which will have the same gender as the noun referred to, in this case "corbata." Choices (B) and (C) are still in the demonstrative forms. Choice (C) also has the incorrect gender. Choice (A) makes no sense when translated ("she of").

RELATIVE PRONOUNS

Relative pronouns come in both a long and short form as follows:

que   who, that, which, whom   *el que/el cual, los que/los cuales*
                                     la que/la cual , las que/las cuales

quien   who, whom
quienes who, whom (plural)

El hombre que vi es médico.
The man that I saw is a doctor.

La mujer con quien hablé es mi hermana.
The woman with whom I spoke is my sister.

Las chicas con quienes ando son estudiantes.
The girls with whom I walk are students.

Note: When referring to people, after a preposition only *quien* or *quienes* may be used.

La madre de Juan, la que/la cual está allí, llegó tarde.
Juan's mom, who is there, arrived late.

La madre de Juan, que/quien es médica, llegó.
Juan's mom, who is a doctor, arrived.

Aquí está la mesa, sobre la que/la cual, está la caja.
Here's the table upon which is the box.

Note: The difference between *el que/el cual* is one of formality, *el cual* being more formal and less idiomatic than *el que*.

Use of the Long Forms

With reference to the samples above, the long form of the relative pronoun is preferred when:

1. introducing a parenthetical clause whose antecedent is ambiguous; the long form always refers to the antecedent farthest away from that clause.

    Note: When referring to the closest of the double antecedent, use the shorter form.

2. using a long preposition followed by a relative pronoun.

    Note: *por, sin,* and *para* must be included since putting *que* after these words will result in a change in meaning.

por qué = why	*por la que* = through which
sin que = without + subj.	*sin la que* = without which
para que = so that + subj.	*para la que* = for which

The Neuter Pronouns

1. ***lo que***   that which, what
Lo que dijo es verdad.   What you said is true.

2. ***lo que/lo cual***
"which" when referring to an entire idea, event, etc.

   *Todos los estudiantes salieron bien, **lo que/lo cual** le gustó a la maestra.*
   Everyone passed, which the teacher liked.

3. ***Todo lo que*** means "all that."

Note: ***Lo que/lo cual*** are only interchangeable when used as in (2) above. ***Que*** standing alone cannot be used.

Idiomatic Uses of the Pronouns

el que/quien	he who
la que/quien	she who
los que/quienes	those who
las que/quienes	those who (f)

Note: There are **no** accent marks. ***Quien*** is most commonly used in proverbs.

Whose = Cuyo vs. De Quien

Cuyo (*–a, –os, –as*) acts as an adjective and will agree with the noun following it.

El hombre cuya hija acaba de graduarse…
The man whose daughter has just graduated…

Note: When referring to parts of the body, use ***a quien*** instead of *cuyo*.

La niña, a quien la madre lavó las manos, es bonita.
The girl, whose hands her mother washed, is pretty.

De quién/de quiénes is an interrogative and is followed by a verb.

¿De quién es este libro?	Whose is this book?
No sé de quién es.	I don't know whose it is.

☞ **Drill 11**

1. Los señores de...te hablo son extranjeros aquí.

   (A) que   (C) cuyos

   (B) cuales   (D) quienes

2. Marta,...hijo es ingeniero, vive en Buenos Aires.

   (A) quien   (C) de quien

   (B) cuya   (D) cuyo

3. ...que no puedo entender es por qué se fue sin decir adiós.

   (A) Lo   (C) El

   (B) Ello   (D) Esto

4. ¿Conoces a los hombres con...el jefe acaba de hablar?

   (A) quien   (C) las cuales

   (B) quienes   (D) que

5. ...estudia, aprende.

   (A) Quienes   (C) El que

   (B) Lo que   (D) Él que

6. La chica,...la madre cortó el pelo, es mi amiga.

   (A) a que   (C) de quién

   (B) a quien   (D) cuya

7. El padre de Anita,...es profesora, acaba de morir.

   (A) quien   (C) el cual

   (B) la cual   (D) a quien

8. La puerta, por... entró la reina, es del siglo IX.

   (A) quien   (C) qué

   (B) cual   (D) la cual

9. Mi hija Anita juega bien al tenis,... es bueno.

   (A) que   (C) cual

   (B) lo cual   (D) quien

10. En este edificio hay una gran ventana,... se ve las montañas.

    (A) por la cual   (C) por que

    (B) por cual   (D) por el que

Drill 11—Detailed Explanations of Answers

1. **(D)**   We need a relative pronoun to complete the sentence correctly. A relative pronoun is one that relates back to a specific noun, pronoun, or idea stated earlier in the sentence (in this case, "señores"). The most common relative pronoun for both people and things is "que," but **following a preposition** (in this case, "de"), if we are referring to people, we may **not** use "que." On the contrary, we use "quien" (if we are referring back to a singular noun) or "quienes" (if we are referring back to a plural noun, as is the case in our sentence). The longer forms of the relative pronoun, "los que" and "los cuales," may also be used in this same situation, but are perhaps less frequent. Note that these must agree in number and gender with the noun to which they refer. Choices (A) and (B) could be correct only if we placed "los" in front of them.

2. **(D)**   In our sentence, the word "ingeniero" means "engineer." "Cuyo" is a relative adjective which means "whose." By "relative" we mean a word which relates back to a noun which is previously mentioned in the sentence. In this instance, "cuyo" relates back to "Marta." It is she whose son is an engineer. Since "cuyo" is an adjective, it must agree in number and gender with the noun which follows it. In this case, then, "cuyo" agrees with "hijo," not with "Marta," and must be masculine singular. "Cuyo" and its other forms ("cuya," "cuyos," and "cuyas") are not used as interrogatives, i.e., to ask questions. If we want to ask "Whose is this book?", we would have to inquire "¿De quién es este libro?" Choice (A) "quien" is incorrect, for it is not the masculine form and cannot modify "hijo." (C) "de quien" will not fit because it cannot be followed immediately by a noun. It means "of whom."

3. **(A)**   For this answer you need to remember that "que" is preceded by "lo" (a particle that never varies regardless of the context) when the construction can be translated as "that which."

4. **(B)**   After a preposition when referring to a person or persons, a form of "quien" or "quienes" is needed. Because the antecedent (hombres) is plural, choice (B) is correct. Choice (C) could have qualified if it were masculine and choice (D) cannot refer to people.

5. **(C)**   Although this sentence translates as "he who" studies, learns, the relative pronoun without the accent is the correct answer. Choice (A)

does not qualify because it is plural. Choice (B) means "that which" and choice (D) has an accent and is, therefore, incorrect.

6.   **(B)**   When referring to parts of the body, use **a quien** instead of a form of **cuyo**, which eliminates choice (D). Choice (C) is incorrect because it means "whose" as an interrogative and would be followed by a verb. Choice (A) means "to which" and makes no sense in this sentence. Also, after a preposition, when referring to people use quien or quienes.

7.   **(A)**   When referring to the last person mentioned in the double antecedent, a form of "quien" is used. Because it is stated that this person is a "profesora," we know the clause refers to Anita. Choice (C) would be correct if referring to the "padre." Choice (B) is the long form and would need to refer to "padre" which is the wrong gender, and choice (D) means "whom" or "to whom," which is not grammatically correct.

8.   **(D)**   The longer forms of the relative pronouns follow long prepositions or, as in this case, ones that would change meaning if used with the short form. In this case the translation "through which" cannot be stated using choice (C) "por qué" since that would mean "why." Choice (A) refers to people and choice (B) requires a definite article (in this case **la**) to be correct.

9.   **(B)**   The neuter form **lo cual** is correct since the second part of the sentence ("which is good") refers to the entire event or occurrence (the fact that Anita plays tennis well) stated in the first part of this sentence Choices (A) and (C) would each need "lo" to be correct. Choice (D) would refer to people.

10.   **(A)**   Choices (A) and (D) each mean "through which"; however, because the antecedent is feminine (ventana), choice (A) is correct. Choice (B) would need the definite article "la" to be correct. Choice (C) is confusing since it could be "why" if it had an accent.

AFFIRMATIVES AND NEGATIVES

The Affirmative and Negative Words

no	no	*sí*	yes
nadie	nobody, no one	*alguien*	someone
nada	nothing	*algo*	something
tampoco	neither	*también*	also
sin	without	*con*	with
ni...ni	neither...nor	*o...o*	either...or
jamás	never, not ever	*siempre*	always
nunca	never		
ninguno*	no, none	*alguno**	some, any

* See explanation that follows.

Negative Expressions

ni (yo, Juan, ella) tampoco	nor (I, Juan, she) either
ni siquiera	not even
ya no	no longer
todavía no	not yet
sin novedad	nothing new
no...más que	only
no...más de	no more than
ahora no	not now
más que	more than
mejor que	better than
peor que	worse than
antes de	before
de ningún modo	by no means
de ninguna manera	by no means
apenas	hardly
no sólo...sino también	not only...but also

The Rules for Usage

Unlike English, statements with double (or more) negatives are correct. A negative sentence in Spanish, whether it has only one negative word or many, **must have** one negative **before** the verb. If there is more than **one** negative, the Spanish sentence may be written two ways.

*No tengo **nada**.*	*Nada tengo.*
*No veo a **nadie**.**	*A nadie veo.*
*No como **ni** pan **ni** queso.*	*Ni pan **ni** queso como.*

Sentences with multiple negatives are common.

*No dije **nunca nada a nadie***.
I **never** said **anything to anyone**.

*If a personal *a* is required, it must accompany the negative.

Use of *Ninguno*

The plural forms of ***ninguno**, – **a*** are no longer used. This word may be used with the noun or to replace the noun. *Ninguno, –a* and alguno, –a, –os, –as have shortened forms before masculine, singular nouns: *ningún, algún*.

Ningún** libro . . . no tengo **ninguno.
No book . . . I don't have any.

***Ninguna** pluma . . . no hay **ninguna** aquí*.
No pen . . . there isn't any here.

***Ninguno** de ellos salió*.
None of them left.

***Ninguna** de ellas irá*.
None of them will go.

¿Tiene amigos Juan?
Does Juan have friends?

*No tiene **ninguno***.
He hasn't any.

Use of *Alguno*

When *alguno, –a* follows a noun in Spanish, it makes the negative more emphatic (= at all). This happens with singular nouns only.

*Juan **no** tiene **ninguna** amiga*.
Juan doesn't have **any** girlfriend.

*Juan **no** tiene amiga **alguna***.
Juan doesn't have a girlfriend **at all**.

Uses of *Jamás* and *Nunca*

The English **"never"** is normally expressed by ***nunca*** and **"never again"** by ***nunca más***. In modern Spanish, ***jamás*** is a learned form mainly in literature. In spoken Spanish it is used to give great emphasis to **never**. In that case it means **absolutely never**.

*No volvió **jamás** a ver a su novia.*
He never again saw his fiancée.

***Jamás** lo sabrás.*
You'll absolutely never know it.

¡Nunca jamás!
Never again!

Jamás also means **ever** in a question expecting a negative answer.

*¿Ha visto Ud. **jamás** nada que iguale a esto? ¡**Nunca**!*
Have you **ever** seen anything to equal this? **Never**!

Nada as Intensifier

Nada may be used adverbially with the meaning "not at all."

Manuel no trabaja nada.
Manuel does absolutely no work.

No hemos dormido nada.
We haven't slept a wink.

No ha sido nada cómodo el cuarto.
The room wasn't comfortable at all.

Algo to Mean "Somewhat"

Algo may be placed before an adjective to express the meaning "somewhat."

Este curso es algo fácil.
This course is somewhat easy.

Estamos algo inquietos.
We are somewhat worried.

Note: *¿Sabes una cosa?*
Do you know something?

¿Sabes algo?
Do you know anything?

Pero vs. *Sino/Sino Que*

Pero, sino, and *sino que* all mean **but**. However, *sino* and *sino que* are used:

(a) when the first clause is negative **and**

(b) the second clause contradicts the first—this contrast must be between two equivalent parts of speech (noun–noun, adjective–adjective, infinitive–infinitive). ***Sino que*** connects the same way but must be followed by a **conjugated** verb.

*No habla español, **sino** inglés.* He doesn't speak Spanish, but English.	noun–noun
*No le gusta blanco, **sino** azul.* He doesn't like white, but blue.	adjective–adjective
*No quiere estudiar, **sino** jugar.* He doesn't want to study, but to play.	infinitive–infinitive
*No cerró la puerta, **sino que** la dejó abierta.* He didn't leave the door open, but left it closed.	conjugated verb– conjugated verb

But: *No habla bien, **pero** me gusta su traje.*
       He doesn't speak well, but I like his suit.

Note: *Pero* = "but nevertheless"
       Sino = "but on the contrary"

☞ Drill 12

1. Viene a vernos...

   (A) nunca.   (C) nadie.

   (B) alguien.   (D) jamás.

2. No me dijo...sobre el asunto

   (A) nadie   (C) algo

   (B) nada   (D) ninguno

3. ¿Tienes algunos amigos íntimos? No, no tengo...

   (A) ningunos.   (C) ningún.

   (B) nadie.   (D) ninguno.

4. ...día voy a hacerme médico.

   (A) Alguna   (C) Ninguno

   (B) Algún   (D) Alguno

5. Nunca hace nada por nadie. No tiene...

   (A) amigo alguno.   (C) algún amigo.

   (B) ningunos amigos.   (D) amigos algunos.

6. Él juega mejor que...

   (A) algo.   (C) alguien.

   (B) ninguno.   (D) nadie.

7. Nadie va con ellos, ni con Juan...

   (A) ni.   (C) nadie.

   (B) tampoco.   (D) también.

8. . . . de las camisas me queda bien.

    (A) Nada   (C) Ningún

    (B) Ninguna   (D) Ningunas

9. . . . veo en el estadio.

    (A) Nadie   (C) A nada

    (B) Ningún   (D) A nadie

10. Sin decirme . . . , se fue para siempre.

    (A) algo   (C) nada

    (B) alguna cosa   (D) ninguno

Drill 12—Detailed Explanations of Answers

1. **(B)** Choices (A), (C), and (D) are all negatives. None of them can be used in the blank because, if a negative word such as "nunca" (never), "nadie" (no one), "ninguno" (none, not any, no one), or "jamás" (never) come after the verb, then there must be a "no" in front of the verb. In other words, we must use a double negative. This does not happen in this sentence. Of the four choices, only the indefinite "alguien" (someone) is acceptable.

2. **(B)** In Spanish the double negative is required when "no" is at the beginning of the sentence, which eliminates (C) because "algo" is a positive particle. Choice (A) is not appropriate because "nadie" refers to persons, and (D) is equally inappropriate because there is no specific antecedent in the question to which "ninguno" could refer.

3. **(D)** "Ninguno" is used exclusively in the singular forms either to modify or refer to previously mentioned nouns. Choice (A) is incorrect because it is plural. Choice (B) means "nobody" and cannot be used to replace the noun "amigos." Choice (C) is apocopated which is not necessary since it does not precede a masculine noun.

4. **(B)** Both "alguno" and "ninguno" have apocopated forms (drop the –o) before masculine singular nouns. "Día" is a masculine singular noun which makes (A) incorrect because it is feminine. Choice (C) and (D) would need to be apocopated to be used correctly before "día."

5. **(A)** When a form of "alguno" is used **after** the noun, it makes the statement more negative and is commonly translated with "at all." Because it is being used like "ninguno" in this type of statement, it will only be correct in the singular forms. Because both (B) and (D) are plural, neither is correct. Although (C) is singular, because "algún" precedes the noun it no longer is a negative and would only be correct in this statement written as "ningún."

6. **(D)** Comparative expressions like "mejor que" (better than), "peor que" (worse than), and "más que" (more than), for example, are negative. Therefore, (A) and (C), which are both affirmative cannot follow this expression. Choice (B), although negative, is incorrect since there is no noun to which it refers.

7.   **(B)**   The expression "ni...tampoco" (nor...neither) is used in statements such as this one. "Tampoco" is the negative form of "también" (also). Choice (A) cannot be used because "ni" must be followed by something, a noun, pronoun, verb, etc., to be used. It cannot stand alone. Choice (C) which means "no one or nobody" makes no sense in this statement. "También" (also) is affirmative and cannot be used after the negative "ni."

8.   **(B)**   Forms of "ninguno" are used only in the singular and modify or refer to nouns. In this statement, this word refers to "camisas" which is feminine. "Ninguna" in this sample is also the subject of "queda." Choice (A), "nada," can not be used to modify nouns. Choice (C) is incorrect because it is apocopated and this can only occur before a masculine singular noun. Choice (D) is incorrect because it is plural.

9.   **(D)**   Because "nadie" is the direct object of the verb "veo" in this example and also refers to a person, the personal "a" is required before it whether it precedes or follows the verb. Choice (A) needs a personal "a." Choice (B) can only be used before masculine singular nouns. Choice (C) means "to nothing" and makes no sense in this context.

10.   **(C)**   "Sin" is a preposition that is considered negative. Choices (A) and (B) are both affirmative forms. Choice (D) must have a noun either to modify or to refer to.

INTERROGATIVES

Interrogative Words

qué	what, which, what a + noun
quién, quiénes	who, which one(s)
cuál, cuáles	which, what, which one(s)
cuánto, –a, –os, –as	how much, how many
cuándo	when
dónde	where
adónde	(to) where
por qué	why (answer uses porque)
para qué	why (answer uses para)
cómo	how
a quién, a quiénes	whom
de quién, de quiénes	whose

Note: **All** interrogatives have accent marks.

Uses of *Qué*

a) To ask a definition:

¿Qué es el amor?
What is love?

b) To ask about things not yet mentioned (choice involved):

¿Qué prefieres, manzanas o peras?
Which ones do you prefer, apples or pears?

c) To express **what a**!:

¡Qué día (tan/más) hermoso!
What a beautiful day!

d) To precede a noun:

¿Qué clases te gustan?
What/which classes do you like?

Uses of *Cuál/Cuáles*

a) Followed by *de* = which one(s) of several:

*¿**Cuál** de los libros es más necesario?*
Which of the books is most necessary?

b) Refers to a definite object already mentioned (choice involved):

Hay dos vestidos, ¿cuál prefieres?
There are two dresses, **which** do you prefer?

c) Followed by *ser*– when there are a number of possibilities:

¿Cuál es la fecha?
What is the date?

¿Cuál es la capital?
What is the capital?

Por Qué, Para Qué, and Porque

Por qué and *para qué* both mean *why*. The former is used if the expected answer will begin with *porque* (because). The latter starts a question where the expected answer will begin with *para* (in order to).

¿Por qué vas al cine?
Why do you go to the movies?

Porque me gusta la película.
Because I like the film.

¿Para qué vas al cine?
Why do you go to the movies?

Para ver a mi actor favorito.
In order to see my favorite actor.

Dónde/Adónde vs. Donde

a) *Adónde* is used with verbs of motion.

¿Adónde vas?
Where are you going?

b) *Donde* (without the accent) requires a noun to refer to.

La casa donde vivo es vieja.
The house **where** (in which) I live is old.

c) *Dónde* (with accent) is the interrogative.

¿Dónde está la casa?
Where is the house?

Note: There are other combinations with *dónde...de dónde*, *por dónde*, etc.

Cuándo vs. Cuando

a) *Cuando* (without accent) can be replaced by **as** and not change the meaning drastically.

   *Te lo diré **cuando** venga Julio.*
   I'll tell you **when/as** Julio arrives.

b) *Cuándo* (with accent) is the interrogative.

   *¿**Cuándo** vas a salir?*
   When are you going to leave?

Quién/Quiénes

a) With prepositions to refer to people:

   *¿**Con quién** hablas?*
   With whom do you speak?

b) With *de* to express **whose**:

   *¿**De quién** es el carro?*
   Whose is the car?   (Whose car is it?)

Note: The word order must be changed to express the Spanish sentence correctly: **Of whom** is the car?

A Quién/A Quiénes

Whom is often misused in English. It is used as the object of the verb. **Who**, on the other hand, can only be the subject of the verb. Note the differences below.

   Who is the subject of "is."

   Who is going with me?   *¿**Quién** va conmigo?*

   Whom is the object of "see"; the subject is **you.**

   Whom do you see?   *¿**A quién** ves?*

In Spanish the **whom** statements are actually a combination of the **personal "a"** and the words *quién/quiénes*. In some sentences, the *"a"* may act as an actual preposition and have a translation.

   *¿**A quién** escribiste?*
   To **whom** did you write?

   *¿**A quiénes** enviaron el paquete?*
   To **whom** did they send the package?

☞ Drill 13

1. ¿...es tu número de teléfono?

   (A) Qué   (C) Que

   (B) Cual   (D) Cuál

2. ¿...día es hoy?

   (A) Cuál   (C) Cómo

   (B) Qué   (D) A cuál

3. ¿...de los libros es mejor?

   (A) Cuáles   (C) Qué

   (B) Cuál   (D) Quiénes

4. Mama, ¿...sirven los anteojos?

   (A) porque   (C) para que

   (B) por qué   (D) para

5. ¿...vestidos quieres comprar?

   (A) Cuál   (C) Cuáles

   (B) Qué   (D) Cómo

6. El pueblo...vivo es viejo.

   (A) donde   (C) a donde

   (B) dónde   (D) que

7. No sé...es ese carro.

   (A) quién   (C) que

   (B) de quien   (D) de quién

8. ¡ ... día más hermoso!

    (A) Qué un   (C) Qué

    (B) Cuál   (D) Qué una

9. ¿ ... es la astronomía?

    (A) Qué   (C) Quién

    (B) Cuál   (D) A quién

10. ¿ ... son los meses del año?

    (A) Cuál   (C) Qué

    (B) Cuáles   (D) De quién

Drill 13—Detailed Explanations of Answers

1. **(D)** From the question marks in our sentence we can tell that we need an interrogative pronoun, a pronoun which asks a question, in the blank. There are only two of these given in the list of possible answers: (A) "Qué" and (D) "Cuál." How do we know that these two are interrogative pronouns? Because this type of pronoun always bears an accent mark. The word "Que," in (C), is a relative pronoun, one that relates back to a previous noun in a sentence: "Los turistas **que** hablan francés…" Here the "que" refers back to "turistas." In (B), the word "Cual" is part of another relative pronoun, "el cual," "la cual," "lo cual," which is designed to show gender and is used for the sake of clarity when we have previously been talking about two nouns: "La madre de José, la cual tiene dos hermanos, viaja por España." If we did not use this longer, feminine form ("la cual"), i.e., if we were to say instead "que" or "quien," we would be referring to the noun immediately preceding the relative pronoun ("José"). But since we want to show that it is José's mother, and not José, who has two brothers, then we must use this longer pronoun or its alternate form, "la que." In English, we say "What is your telephone number?" In Spanish, the interrogative word "qué" asks for a definition. If we ask "¿Qué es la física?", we are asking for a definition of what physics is. In our sentence, we do not want to ask for a definition of what one's telephone number is, which is what (A) "Qué" would imply. Instead, we must ask, "Which one" ("Cuál"), out of all the possible numbers in the directory, is your phone number. In other words, "cuál" asks for a choice or selection from a number of possibilities.

2. **(B)** Before a noun "qué" means what/which. Choice (A) is not correct because it cannot modify a noun. Choice (C) means "how" and (D) means "to which."

3. **(B)** "Cuál" is used with a form of **ser** to mean "which." It is also the subject of the verb, which is singular. Choice (A) is incorrect because it is plural. Choice (D) means who and choice (C), which can also mean what/which, cannot be used before a "de" phrase where there is an indication of choice.

4. **(C)** "Para qué" is used when the question intimates "for what purpose/use." Choice (A) "because" and (D) "in order to" are not interrogatives and make no sense. Choice (B) means "why" and does not fit within the intended meaning of this question.

5. **(B)** "Qué" is used before a noun to mean what/which. Therefore, choices (A) and (C) are incorrect since neither can precede a noun. Choice (D) means "how."

6. **(A)** "Donde" without an accent requires a noun to refer to, in this case "pueblo." Because an indirect question is not being asked, choice (B) is incorrect since all interrogatives have accent marks. Choice (C) is used in questions with verbs of motion (i.e., Where are you going?). Choice (D) is the relative pronoun meaning "that."

7. **(D)** Because an indirect question is being asked, the accented form of "whose" is required. This would make choice (B) incorrect. Choice (A) means "who" and choice (C) is a relative pronoun meaning "that."

8. **(C)** Because "¡qué!" in this context means "What a!" and the indefinite article (a) is included in its translation, choices (A) and (D) would be incorrect. Choice (B) is never used to mean "What a!" and again a form of "cuál" is not correct before a noun.

9. **(A)** "Qué" is used before a form of **ser** when asking for a definition, as in this example. Choices (C) "who" and (D) "whom" make no sense. "Cual" precedes a form of **ser** when there are a number of possibilities, which makes choice (B) incorrect.

10. **(B)** A form of "cuál" will precede a form of **ser** when a number of possibilities are given to choose from (i.e., months). Because it is the subject of the verb and because the verb is plural, choice (A) is incorrect. Answer (D) means "whose" and makes no sense in this context. Choice (C) can only be used before a form of **ser** when asking a definition.

THE PERSONAL *A*

Normally the preposition *a* means **to** or **at** in Spanish. There are instances when this preposition will appear in the sentence with **no** apparent translation into English. In this case this preposition is called the Personal A. This *a* will appear in the Spanish sentence if the **direct object** of the verb:

a) refers to a person in some way:

No veo a Juan/a su amigo/al ejército/a nadie.
I don't see Juan/his friend/the army/anyone.

b) refers to a domestic animal:

Juan ama mucho a su perro, Spot.
Juan loves his dog, Spot.

c) refers to a specific geographical location (if **it does not** have an article):

Visito a España/a Barcelona/a México.
I visit Spain/Barcelona/Mexico.

But: *Visito el Perú.*   I visit Peru.

Omission of the Personal *A*

a) After the verb *tener*, unless it means "keep/hold":

Tengo dos hermanos.   I have two brothers.

But: *Tengo al culpable*   I have the guilty
     en la cárcel.   one in jail.

b) Before an indefinite personal direct object (usually modified by a numeral or an indefinite article):

*Vi **tres** hombres en el bosque.*   (numeral)
I saw three men in the forest.

*Oí **un** ladrón dentro del banco.*   (indefinite article)
I heard a thief inside the bank.

c) When the Personal A would be in close proximity to another *a* (such as one meaning to, at, toward or the *a* preceding an indirect object):

Presenté mi esposo a mis amigos.
I introduced my husband to my friends.

POSSESSIVES: ADJECTIVES/PRONOUNS

The Possessive Adjectives:

my	*mi, mis*	our	*nuestro, –a, –os, –as*
your	*tu, tus*	your	*vuestro, –a, –os, –as*
his/her/your	*su, sus*	their/your	*su, sus*

The possessive adjectives precede the noun they modify and match it as closely as possible in gender and number.

mi casa, mis casas	my house, my houses
nuestra pluma, nuestras plumas	our pen, our pens

Because the third person adjective has several possible translations, the following may be done for clarification:

su casa =	his house	*la casa **de él***
	her house	*la casa **de ella***
	your house (s)	*la casa **de Ud.***
	their house (f)	*la casa **de ellas***
	their house (m)	*la casa **de ellos***
	your house (pl)	*la casa **de Uds.***

The Possessive Pronouns

The pronoun group is used **to replace** the noun already stated and, therefore, takes on the properties of that noun. This includes retention of the definite article. Also note the difference in translation.

mine	el mío, la mía
	los míos, las mías
yours	el tuyo, la tuya
	los tuyos, las tuyas
his/hers/yours	el suyo, la suya
	los suyos, las suyas
ours	el nuestro, la nuestra
	los nuestros, las nuestras
yours	el vuestro, la vuestra
	los vuestros, las vuestras
theirs/yours	el suyo, la suya
	los suyos, las suyas

Again, because the third person pronouns have several possible meanings, clarification with the prepositional phrase is also possible. With the pronouns, however, the definite article must be retained.

mi coche y el suyo	my car and his	*y el de él*
	my car and hers	*y el de ella*
	my car and yours	*y el de Ud.*
	my car and theirs (f)	*y el de ellas*
	my car and theirs (m)	*y el de ellos*
	my car and yours	*y el de Uds.*

Uses of the Pronouns

The possessive pronouns are used primarily in three areas:

a) As the replacement for the noun:

my house and **ours**   *mi casa y **la nuestra***

b) As an "adjective" with nouns as follows:

several friends of **mine**   *unos amigos **míos***

Note: "of" is **not** expressed.

c) As the possessive used after *ser*:

¿Este vestido?	This dress?
*Es **tuyo**.*	It is **yours**.
¿Estos carros?	These cars?
*Son **nuestros**.*	They are **ours**.

Note: The definite article is normally omitted after *ser*.

Possessives with Clothing/Body Parts

Normally with parts of the body and clothing, the possessive adjective is replaced by the definite article. However, in the following instances, the possessive is correct.

a) With body parts:

1. When ambiguity would result without it.

2. When the body part is modified.

Ella levantó sus grandes ojos azules.

3. When the body part is the subject.

Tus manos tienen callos.

b) With clothing:

1. When the article worn is the subject.

   Su camisa está allí.

2. When the article is **not** being worn by the subject.

   *Encontré **mis** calcetines allí.*

☞ **Drill 14**

1. Ayer vimos...señorita Corrales.

    (A) a la   (C) a

    (B) la   (D) la a

2. Mi hermana es más alta que...

    (A) la suya.   (C) su.

    (B) el suyo.   (D) mía.

3. ¿Conoce Ud....padres?

    (A) mi   (C) a mis

    (B) mis   (D) míos

4. Su amigo es más inteligente que...

    (A) la nuestra.   (C) los míos.

    (B) el nuestro.   (D) la mía.

5. Los hombres se pusieron...antes de salir.

    (A) el sombrero   (C) su sombrero

    (B) sus sombreros   (D) sombreros

6. Se quitaron...al entrar en la casa.

    (A) sus abrigos   (C) sus guantes

    (B) su abrigo   (D) el abrigo

7. ¿De quién es este lápiz? –Es...

    (A) mío.   (C) de mi.

    (B) el mío.   (D) de mí.

8. Mis hermanas y…Isabel son bellas.

   (A) las que   (C) las

   (B) las de   (D) aquellas

9. Tu casa es más grande que…

   (A) el mío.   (C) mío.

   (B) mi.   (D) la mía.

10. Sus pirámides y…vienen de épocas distintas.

    (A) los nuestros   (C) las nuestras

    (B) nuestros   (D) nuestras

11. Tengo…padre en el hospital.

    (A) mi   (C) a mi

    (B) a mí   (D) el

Drill 14—Detailed Explanations of Answers

1.   **(A)**   The personal **a** must be used when speaking about a person, and the article should accompany a title when not in direct address. The answer (A) is the only one fulfilling these requirements.

2.   **(A)**   The long form of the possessive is used when the noun is replaced. Because the possessive is now being used as a pronoun, it will take on the properties of the noun it has replaced, including the definite article. The noun in this example is "hermana." Choice (B) is incorrect because it is the wrong gender. Choice (C) is a possessive adjective and must be used with a noun. Choice (D) is the possessive pronoun but needs an article.

3.   **(C)**   The possessive adjective is required to match the noun "padres." Also, because "padres" is the direct object of the verb and refers to a person, the personal **a** is also required. Choice (A) needs to be plural and have a personal **a**. Choice (B) needs the personal **a** and choice (D) is the possessive pronoun which cannot precede the noun.

4.   **(B)**   All choices are possessive pronouns but only (B) is the correct gender for "amigo."

5.   **(A)**   With parts of the body and clothing in Spanish, the possessive is replaced by the definite article. The ownership is established by the reflexive pronoun. In addition, in Spanish, each person wears only **one** hat at a time and even if the subject is plural, the article of clothing remains singular. Answer (C) has the possessive and is incorrect. Choice (B) is plural and has the possessive and choice (D) needs to be singular with a definite article to be correct.

6.   **(D)**   For the same reason given in number 5 above, each person wears only one coat and the possessive must be replaced by the definite article. Choice (A), therefore, is incorrect because it is plural and has retained the possessive. Choice (B) needs to replace the possessive with the article "el." Choice (C) would be correct if "sus" were replaced with "los" since gloves are worn in pairs.

7.   **(A)**   The long form of the possessive is used to replace a noun previously referred to. In this example, the noun is "lápiz." Normally, the long form has a definite article. However, after **ser** the article is omitted. Choice

(B) is incorrect because it has the article. Choice (C) means "of my" and choice (D) is incorrect because in spoken Spanish "of me" is not used in this manner. Forms of "mío" are used instead.

8. **(B)** To eliminate 's in Spanish, an **of** phrase is used. When replacing a possessive such as this one (Isabel's) wherein there is a name to deal with, the definite article is retained followed by **de**. Because the noun here is "hermanas," the feminine plural article is needed. Neither (C) nor (D) makes sense when placed directly before Isabel. Choice (A) can be translated "those that or those who" but neither makes sense in front of Isabel.

9. **(D)** The long form of the possessive with the definite article is needed to replace the noun previously mentioned ("casa"). Choice (A) is the wrong gender. Choice (B) is the possessive adjective which means "my" and must precede a noun, and choice (C) needs to be feminine with an article to be correct.

10. **(C)** Again, the long form of the possessive with the definite article is needed to replace the noun previously mentioned ("pirámides") which is feminine plural. Choice (A) is the wrong gender. Choice (B) is the wrong gender and needs an article, and choice (D) needs a definite article to be correct.

11. **(C)** The personal **a** is used after **tener** when it means "keep or hold" as it does in this sample. Also, the possessive adjective "mi" has no accent. Choice (A) needs a personal **a**. In choice (B) the accented "mí" means me and is prepositional, not possessive. Choice (D) needs a personal **a**.

THE PASSIVE VOICE

The passive voice is the "mirror image" of the active voice. In passive voice statements the subject receives the action of the verb instead of actually doing it.

Active: I built the house.
Construí la casa.

Passive: The house was built by me.
La casa fue construida por mí.

The combination of *ser* with the **past participle** of the transitive verb constitutes the "true passive" in Spanish. The past participle is used as an adjective and must agree with the subject in number and gender. The formula follows:

ser + **past participle** + *por* + **agent** (doer)

Whenever the agent is expressed, this formula is used.

Agent Expressed by *De*

By is normally translated by *por*. If, however, the past participle expresses feelings or emotion, **by** is translated by *de*.

Juana es amada (respetada, odiada, admirada) de todos.
Juana is loved (respected, hated, admired) by all.

Reflexive Substitute for the Passive Voice

Commonly when the agent is **not** expressed and the subject is a thing, the passive "Spanish" statement will be written using the third person singular or plural of the verb with the pronoun *se*.

Aquí se habla español.   Spanish is spoken here.
Se vendieron guantes allí.   Gloves were sold there.

Note: The subject follows the verb.

Third-Person Plural Active Equivalent for Passive Voice

The best way to avoid using a passive construction is to convert the passive statement to an active one by using the subject **they**.

The house was sold.   =   They sold the house.
Se vendió la casa.   =   *Vendieron la casa.*

No Agent Expressed, Person Acted Upon

In sentences where the agent is indefinite (not mentioned or implied) and a person is acted upon, the indefinite *se* is coupled with the **third singular** of the verb.

The man was killed.	He was killed.
*Se **mató** al hombre.*	*Se le **mató**.*
The girls will be punished.	They will be punished.
*Se **castigará** a las chicas.*	*Se las **castigará**.*

Note: The person acted upon is the direct object of the Spanish sentence. Therefore, direct object pronouns are used to replace it, with one exception—*les* is used instead of *los* for the masculine plural.

The men will be killed.	They will be killed.
*Se **matará** a los hombres.*	*Se les **matará**.*

Idiomatic Expressions with *Se*

Se plus the third person singular of the verb will render "impersonal" subject statements. In English we say **people, one, they, you** and the like. This type of statement may also be translated as a passive construction.

se dice =	it is said	*se cree* =	it is believed
[dicen]	people say	*[creen]*	people believe
	they say		they believe
	one says		one believes
	you say		you believe

This may also be rendered with the third plural of the verb.

The Apparent Passive: *Estar* Plus the Past Participle

The true passive in Spanish is formed with *ser* and a past participle. Constructions formed with *estar* and a past participle are different. Instead of expressing an action carried out by an explicit or implicit agent, the apparent passive denotes a state or a condition resulting from a previous action. The past participle becomes an adjective. Compare the following examples:

Apparent Passive

*La puerta **está** abierta.*
The door **is** open. (The action of opening it happened earlier.)

True Passive

> *La puerta es abierta (por el niño).*
> The door **is opened** (by the boy). (We see the action happening now.)

Apparent Passive

> *La pieza estaba reservada.*
> The room **was** reserved. (Someone reserved it earlier.)

True Passive

> *La pieza había sido reservada (por el turista).*
> The room had **been reserved** (by the tourist).

☞ **Drill 15**

1. ...la mujer.

    (A) Asesinaron a   (C) Asesinamos

    (B) Se asesinaron a   (D) Fue asesinado

2. La universidad...por el presidente Juárez.

    (A) fundó   (C) fue establecida

    (B) estaba fundado   (D) se estableció

3. El asesino fue...por el policía.

    (A) muerto   (C) morido

    (B) matado   (D) muriendo

4. La ventana...abierta por el viento.

    (A) sido   (C) estaba

    (B) estuvo   (D) fue

5. La señora García es respetada...todos los alumnos.

    (A) de   (C) a

    (B) por   (D) con

6. ...que va a mejorar la economía.

    (A) Se dicen   (C) Se dice

    (B) Es dicho   (D) Está dicho

7. Aquí...español e inglés.

    (A) es hablado   (C) son hablados

    (B) se habla   (D) se hablan

8.   ¿Los traidores?...matará mañana.

   (A) Se les   (C) Se

   (B) Se los   (D) Los

9.   Al entrar, vi que las ventanas...abiertas.

   (A) fueron   (C) han sido

   (B) estaban   (D) han estado

10. Esas casas fueron...por un arquitecto famoso.

   (A) construida   (C) construidos

   (B) construido   (D) construidas

Drill 15—Detailed Explanations of Answers

1.   **(A)**   When a person is acted upon in a passive voice sentence, the statement may be expressed three ways: by using true passive (ser + past participle) which matches the noun (thus eliminating answer choice (D)), by using an active voice statement requiring the personal **a** (thus eliminating choice (C)), or by using the third singular of the verb preceded by the reflexive **se** followed by the personal **a** (thus eliminating choice (B)). (A) is correct in the active voice with the personal **a**.

2.   **(C)**   Choice (A) "fundó" means "founded," but it will not function in the sentence because the "university" ("universidad") did not found anything. On the contrary, it was founded "**by** President Juárez." This gets us into what is called the passive voice. In a passive sentence, the subject is acted upon by someone or something. In our sentence, the subject, "universidad," is acted upon by "el presidente Juárez." To form the passive voice in Spanish, we follow this pattern: the proper tense and form of the verb "ser" + past participle. Look at the correct answer: "fue establecida." You will see that we have followed this pattern. One other thing you will notice is that in the passive voice the past participle always agrees in number and gender with the subject. In our sentence, "establecida" is feminine singular to agree with "universidad." Observe also that the verb "fue" is third person singular since the subject, "universidad," is a singular noun. The passive voice must always be used when the subject is acted upon and the doer of the action is expressed by a "por" phrase ("por el presidente Juárez"). (B) "estaba fundado" is incorrect because (1) we have not used the verb "ser," but rather "estar" (therefore, we are not indicating an action; we are merely describing a state), and (2) the past participle does not agree with the subject "universidad." Now look at (D), "se estableció." Sometimes the reflexive form of the verb can be used as a substitute for the true passive voice, but never when we have a "por" phrase which indicates who did the action, as is the case in our sentence.

3.   **(A)**   The last two choices are ungrammatical. In order to identify the correct answer, you have to know that the past participle of the verb "matar" is "muerto" when the sentence refers to people.

4.   **(D)**   To get the right answer you must recognize that this construction is in the passive voice, which means that it's always formed with the

appropriate form of "ser"—but not with the past participle (as in choice (A)) because this particular form needs the support of "haber."

5.   **(A)**   In a passive voice statement **by** is usually translated by **por**. If the past participle expresses feeling or emotion, rather than action, **by** is translated by **de**. Therefore, choice (B) is incorrect. Because **de** is the only choice to complete this passive statement, (C) and (D) are both incorrect.

6.   **(C)**   The pronoun **se** used with the third singular of the verb expresses an indefinite subject. This can be translated a number of ways: it is said, people say, they say, one says, etc. Choice (A) is incorrect because the verb is plural. Both (B) and (D) appear to have the literal translation needed but this type of statement is done with **se** + third singular of the verb.

7.   **(D)**   If the agent (doer) is not mentioned and the subject of the statement is a thing, the reflexive construction is used for the passive. The verb will, in these cases, match the noun. In this case the actual subject ("español e inglés") is plural. Choices (A) and (C) are written in the true passive formula (**ser** + past participle) but cannot be used when the subject is a thing. Choice (B) is incorrect because the verb is singular.

8.   **(A)**   The indefinite **se** is used when the agent (doer) is indefinite (not mentioned or implied) and a person is being acted upon. In this case the verb is always third singular and the person acted upon becomes the direct object. "Los," however, is the only direct object pronoun not used and is replaced by "les." Therefore, choice (B) is incorrect because "los" has been used. Choice (C) needs the pronoun "les" and choice (D) is simply the direct object pronoun by itself.

9.   **(B)**   When there is a focus on the "resultant state of a previous action" and **not** on the action itself, a form of **estar** will precede the past participle. The past participle will still be used as an adjective. Therefore, choices (A) and (C) are incorrect because **ser** has been used. Choice (D) when translated (Upon entering, I saw that the windows have been opened.) is incorrect usage of the perfect tense.

10. **(D)**   The focus is on the past participle and its function as an adjective in the passive voice statement. It must agree in this sample with "casas." All other answers use incorrect gender or number.

MEASURES OF TIME

The word *tiempo* in Spanish designates both "time" and "weather," as in the following examples:

*Ha pasado tanto **tiempo** desde que nos vimos.*
So much **time** has passed since we saw each other.

*¿Cómo está el **tiempo** hoy?*
How is the **weather** today?

The following are some of the expressions Spanish uses to measure or divide time.

Seasons of the Year

las estaciones – the seasons
el verano – summer   *el otoño* – fall
el invierno – winter   *la primavera* – spring

Months of the Year

el mes – the month
enero – January   *febrero* – February
marzo – March   *abril* – April
mayo – May   *junio* – June
julio – July   *agosto* – August
septiembre – September   *octubre* – October
noviembre – November   *diciembre* – December

Note: In Spanish the names of the months are not capitalized.

Days of the Week

el día – the day   *la semana* – the week
el lunes – Monday   *el martes* – Tuesday
el miércoles – Wednesday   *el jueves* – Thursday
el viernes – Friday   *el sábado* – Saturday
el domingo – Sunday

Note: The days of the week (which are not capitalized in Spanish) are preceded by the definite article except after a form of *ser*:

el lunes – Monday; on Monday   *los lunes* – Mondays; on Mondays
Es lunes. – It is Monday.

Other Expressions of Time

hoy – today	*ayer* – yesterday
mañana – tomorrow*	*anoche* – last night
anteanoche – the night before last	*anteayer* – the day before yesterday
pasado mañana – the day after tomorrow	*el día siguiente* – the following day
la madrugada – dawn	*la mañana* – the morning*
el mediodía – noon	*la tarde* – afternoon
la noche – night (time)	*la medianoche* – midnight

* Be sure to distinguish between *mañana* (tomorrow) and *la mañana* (the morning).

TELLING TIME

When telling the time of day, the word "time" is rendered as *hora*.

*¿Qué **hora** es?*	What **time** is it?

When telling the hours of the day, Spanish uses the feminine definite article before the time expression.

*Es **la** una.*	It's one o'clock.
*Son **las** dos*	It's two o'clock.

Note: To specify A.M. Spanish uses *de la mañana* or *de la madrugada*. (The hours after midnight but before dawn). P.M. is expressed with either *de la tarde* or *de la noche*.

*Son las tres **de la mañana**.*	It's three A.M.
*Son las cinco **de la tarde**.*	It's five P.M.

To render the half-hour, Spanish uses *media*. To render the quarter-hour, *cuarto* or *quince* are used.

*Son las diez y **cuarto**. Son las diez y **quince**.*
It's a **quarter** past ten. It's ten **fifteen**.

*Son las diez y **media**.*
It's **10:30**. It's **half past** ten.

*Son las once menos **cuarto**. Son las once menos **quince**.*
It's a **quarter** of eleven.

Falta un **cuarto** (Faltan **quince**) para las once.*
It's a **quarter** of eleven.

*Faltar means "to be wanting, lacking."

Note: *y* is used through the half-hour and *menos* is used after the half-hour.

Portions of time other than the half- or quarter-hour are expressed thus:

Son las seis y diez.	It's 6:10.
Son las seis y veinte.	It's 6:20.

Son las siete menos veinte. (Faltan veinte para las siete.)
It's 6:40. (It's twenty of seven.)

At plus the hour is expressed with *a* + *la/las.*

A la una/A las dos salí.	At one/at two I left.

To tell time in the past, use the imperfect tense.

Era la una/Eran las dos.	It was 1:00/2:00.

To express "a little after" the hour, use ***y pico***.

Llegó a las cinco y pico.	He arrived a little after 5:00.

To express "at about," use ***a eso de*** + the hour.

Salió a eso de las seis.	He left about 6:00.

When **no** exact hour is indicated, "in the morning/afternoon/evening" is expressed with ***por la mañana, por la tarde, por la noche***.
If using the 24-hour clock, the following applies:

1:00 p.m.	*trece horas*
2:00 p.m.	*catorce horas*
8:00 p.m.	*veinte horas*
15:30 (3:30 p.m.)	*quince horas treinta*
20:42 (8:42 p.m.)	*veinte horas cuarenta y dos*
9:10 (9:10 a.m.)	*nueve horas diez*

Note: ***Cuarto, media,*** and *y* are not used.

HACER WITH EXPRESSIONS OF TIME

With expressions of time, *hacer* is an impersonal verb. Only the third person singular is used.

Hace (Tiempo) Que + Present Indicative of Main Verb

This formula shows that the action is still going on in the present. Note that Spanish uses the simple present where English uses the present perfect.

Hace una semana que los equipos no juegan.
The teams have not played for a week.

Hace muchos días que llueve.
It has been raining for many days.

Note: By turning the sentence around, the conjunction *que* can be suppressed. (In negative sentences, it is possible to use a compound tense.)

Los equipos no juegan hace una semana.
(Los equipos no han jugado hace una semana.)
The teams have not played for a week.

Llueve hace muchos días.
It has been raining for many days.

Hace (Tiempo) Que + Preterite of Main Verb

This formula designates the sense of time expressed by the English particle "ago."

Hace tres días que la vi. (La vi hace tres días.)
I saw her three days ago.

Hace años que nos dejaron. (Nos dejaron hace años.)
They left us years ago.

Hacía (Tiempo) Que + Imperfect of Main Verb

This formula shows that the action was still going on in the past.

Hacía tres días que llovía. (Llovía hacía tres días.)
It had been raining for three days.

Hacía tiempo que te esperaba. (Te esperaba hacía tiempo.)
I had been waiting for you for a while.

AGE

Cumplir años and *tener años* are the expressions most commonly used to indicate age:

Mi padre tiene cuarenta y dos años.
My father is 42 (years of age).

Hoy es mi cumpleaños. Cumplo ocho.
Today is my birthday. I turn eight.

To express "at the age of 40 (or any number)," one says "*a los cuarenta años*."

WEATHER EXPRESSIONS

In English these weather expressions are formed with the verb "to be," in Spanish they are formed with the verb *hacer* used impersonally.

Hace calor.	It **is** hot.
Hizo frío.	It **was** cold.
Hará buen tiempo.	The weather **will be** good.
Hace sol.	It **is** sunny.
Hacía viento.	It **was** windy.
¿Qué tiempo hace?	What's the weather like?
Hace mal tiempo.	The weather **is** bad.

With *Tener*

When the sentence is personal, Spanish uses *tener* where English uses "to be."

Tengo calor.	I **am** hot.
Teníamos frío.	We **were** cold.

With *Haber* Used Impersonally

Notice that the third person singular of the present indicative changes from *ha* to *hay* when *haber* is impersonal.

Hay neblina.	It **is** misty (foggy).
Hubo humedad.	It **was** damp.
Habrá tempestad.	It **will be** stormy.

With *Nevar* and *Llover*

"To snow" and "to rain" are rendered by the impersonal verbs *nevar* and *llover*, respectively:

Ayer nevó.	**It snowed** yesterday.
Mañana lloverá.	Tomorrow **it will rain**.

CARDINAL AND ORDINAL NUMBERS

The cardinal and ordinal forms of numbers in Spanish are as follows:

Cardinal Numbers

1	*uno/a*	11	*once*
2	*dos*	12	*doce*
3	*tres*	13	*trece*
4	*cuatro*	14	*catorce*
5	*cinco*	15	*quince*
6	*seis*	16	*diez y seis*
7	*siete*	17	*diez y siete*
8	*ocho*	18	*diez y ocho*
9	*nueve*	19	*diez y nueve*
10	*diez*	20	*veinte*

21	*veinte y uno, –a*	300	*trescientos, –as*
22	*veinte y dos*	400	*cuatrocientos, –as*
30	*treinta*	500	*quinientos, –as*
40	*cuarenta*	600	*seiscientos, –as*
50	*cincuenta*	700	*setecientos, –as*
60	*sesenta*	800	*ochocientos, –as*
70	*setenta*	900	*novecientos, –as*
80	*ochenta*	1,000	*mil*
90	*noventa*	1,100	*mil ciento*
100	*cien(to)/a*	2,000	*dos mil*
101	*ciento uno, –a*	1,000,000	*un millón (de)*
200	*doscientos, –as*	2,000,000	*dos millones (de)*

Note: The cardinal numbers from 16 to 29 may be written together: *dieciséis, diecisiete, dieciocho, diecinueve, veintiuno, veintinueve.* Beyond 30, cardinal numbers are written: *treinta y uno, treinta y dos,* etc.

Ordinal Numbers

First	*primero*	Sixth	*sexto*
Second	*segundo*	Seventh	*séptimo*
Third	*tercero*	Eighth	*octavo*
Fourth	*cuarto*	Ninth	*noveno (nono)*
Fifth	*quinto*	Tenth	*décimo*

a) Ordinal numbers are variable in gender and number:

*Eres la **cuarta** persona que me pregunta lo mismo.*
You are the **fourth** person to ask me the same thing.

*Los **primeros** en irse fueron los últimos en llegar.*
The **first** to leave were the last to arrive.

b) *Primero* and *tercero* drop their final *"o"* in front of masculine singular nouns:

*el **tercer** ojo*   the **third** eye

c) Ordinal numbers precede the noun except when referring to kings, dukes, popes, or some other kind of succession:

*Juan Carlos **Primero** es el rey de España.*
Juan Carlos I is the king of Spain.

*Juan Pablo **Segundo** es el papa.*
John Paul II is the pope.

d) Usage dictates that after *décimo* no more ordinal numbers are used; they are replaced by cardinal numbers situated after the noun:

*La **décima** carrera fue más emocionante que la (carrera) **once**.*
The **tenth** race was more exciting than the **eleventh** (race).

*España no tuvo un rey llamado Pedro **Quince**.*
Spain did not have a king named Pedro the Fifteenth.

Un, Una or Uno

Un and ***una*** (like the indefinite articles they resemble) are used according to the gender of the noun they precede. ***Uno*** is used alone (i.e., not before a noun).

un** libro, **una** mujer, veinte y **uno

Note: ***un*** will precede a noun that begins with a stressed ***a–*** *or* ***ha–*** *for pronunciation.*

el águila = ***un*** *águila*   *el* hacha = ***un*** *hacha*
the eagle = an eagle   the hatchet = a hatchet

Ciento vs. Cien

a) ***Ciento*** will apocopate to ***cien*** before any noun or a number larger than itself (i.e., mil, millones).

cien casas	*cien soldados*	*cien mil*	*cien millones*
100 houses	100 soldiers	100,000	100 million

But: *ciento once, ciento veinte y tres, ciento sesenta*

Note: After 100 an **y** is not placed between it and the next number.

b) *Ciento* and *mil,* when used as collective nouns, may be plural

muchos miles de dólares   *cientos (centenares) de leguas*
many thousands of dollars   hundreds of leagues

Note: *Centenar* is preferred to *ciento* as a collective noun.

c) The multiples of 100 (200–900) have both masculine and feminine forms.

doscientas una mujeres   *quinientos un hombres*
201 women   501 men

d) Although *ciento* should be used when the number stands alone, in everyday speech it is apocopated as follows:

Hemos comprado cien.   *Yo vivo en el cien.*
We have bought 100.   I live in number 100.

Expressing Millions

Millón is considered a noun and therefore takes the indefinite article and is followed by the preposition *de:*

un millón de dólares   *doscientos millones de aves*
one million dollars   200 million birds

DATES

Contrary to English usage, **cardinal** numbers are used to indicate dates **except in the case of the first of the month:**

*el **primero** de mayo*	the first of May
*el **dos** de mayo*	the second of May
*el **tres** de mayo*	the third of May
*el **diez** de mayo*	the tenth of May
*el **treinta** de mayo*	the thirtieth of May

The year may be added to these dates by inserting the preposition *de:*

*el tres de octubre **de** 1951*   October 3, 1951
*el veinte de abril **de** este año*   April 20 of this year

In dating letters the definite article is omitted.

It's common to replace *de este año* by *del corriente* (of the current year):

el veintiocho de febrero del corriente
February 28 of this year

What day is today? may be rendered literally as *¿Qué día es hoy?* or idiomatically as *¿A cómo estamos (hoy)?* The latter expression implies a date as an answer, not just the day of the week:

¿A cómo estamos? Estamos a trece de junio.
What's the date? It is June 13.

¿Qué día es hoy? Hoy es lunes.
What day is today? Today is Monday.

Arithmetical Signs

+	*más*
−	*menos*
×	*por*
÷	*dividido por*

2 + 2 is dos **más** dos
10 ÷ 5 is *diez* **dividido por** *cinco*
3 × 3 is *tres* **por** *tres*

Collective Numerals

un par	a pair
una decena	ten
una docena	a dozen
una quincena	fifteen, two weeks
una veintena	twenty
una centena (un centenar)	hundred
un millar	thousand

Pagan cada **quincena.**
They pay every two weeks.

El libro tiene una **centena** *de poemas.*
The book has **one hundred** poems.

Un **millar** *de personas*
A **thousand** people

Note: *Quincenal* is an adjective made from *quincena.* Other similar numerical adjectives are *semanal* (weekly), *mensual* (monthly), *semestral* (half-yearly), and *anual* (yearly).

Una publicación quincenal
A **bi-weekly** publication

Una revista semestral
A **half-yearly** magazine

Fractions

1/2	*un medio*	1/3	*un tercio*
1/4	*un cuarto*	1/5	*un quinto*
1/6	*un sexto*	1/7	*un séptimo*
1/8	*un octavo*	1/9	*un noveno*
1/10	*un décimo*		

Two-thirds is either *dos tercios* or *las dos terceras partes*; three-fourths is either *tres cuartos* or *las tres cuartas partes*.

Un medio is only used in arithmetical calculations; the adjective meaning "half" is *medio/a;* the noun meaning "half" is *la mitad:*

*Trabajamos sólo **medio** día hoy.*
Today we only worked **half** a day.

***La mitad** del electorado no votó.*
Half of the electorate did not vote.

☞ **Drill 16**

1. ¿Cuánto tiempo...que esperaban el tren?

   (A) hace   (C) hacían

   (B) hizo   (D) hacía

2. ...tres horas que regresó de su viaje.

   (A) Hacen   (C) Hace

   (B) Ha   (D) Desde

3. Mis botas están sucias porque...lodo afuera.

   (A) hay   (C) es

   (B) hace   (D) está

4. No puedo conducir bien porque...neblina.

   (A) está   (C) hace

   (B) es   (D) hay

5. Había (231)...mujeres en el estadio.

   (A) doscientos treinta y uno

   (B) doscientas treinta y uno

   (C) doscientas treinta y una

   (D) doscientas treinta y unas

6. Ganó (100 million)...dólares en la lotería.

   (A) cien millón de

   (B) ciento millón de

   (C) ciento millones de

   (D) cien millones de

7. (The first)...de mayo es mi cumpleaños.

    (A) El primero

    (C) El uno

    (B) El primer

    (D) Primero

8. Había (hundreds)...de pájaros en San Juan Capistrano.

    (A) cien

    (C) centenares

    (B) cientos

    (D) un cien

9. Juan llegó un poco después de las cinco, o sea,...

    (A) a las cinco en punto.

    (B) a eso de las cinco.

    (C) a las cinco y pico.

    (D) hace las cinco.

10. Durante el invierno mi mamá siempre...

    (A) está fría.

    (C) hace frío.

    (B) tiene frío.

    (D) es fría.

Drill 16—Detailed Explanations of Answers

1. **(D)**   In time expressions involving the verb "hacer," the form of this verb will be third singular. To balance with "esperaban" in the other part of the sentence, "hacer" will be expressed in the imperfect tense also. This renders the translation "had been + ing." Therefore, (A) the present tense and (B) the preterite are incorrect. (C) is incorrect because it is plural.

2. **(C)**   The formula for this kind of expression is **hace** (never in the plural) + **time** + **que** + **preterite** (or **preterite** + **hace** + **time**). In English, this formula translates the particle "ago."

3. **(A)**   Weather conditions used with **haber** are "lodo" (muddy), "neblina" (foggy), "polvo" (dusty), "luna" (moonlight), and "nieve" (snow). A good way to remember is that these conditions are visible whereas hot and cold are not. Forms of "estar/ser" (to be) are never used to express weather.

4. **(D)**   See the explanation given in number 3 above.

5. **(C)**   Because "doscientos" and "uno" have gender and can be feminine, and because they precede a feminine plural noun in this sample, each must also be feminine. It should be noted that "uno" cannot be plural and still mean "one."

6. **(D)**   "Ciento" apocopates to "cien" before nouns or numbers larger than itself. "Millón" also has a plural form. It will remain "millón" when accompanied by "un." Whenever a noun follows this number **de** is needed.

7. **(A)**   The first of the month is expressed with the ordinal number "primero." All other days of the month use cardinal numbers. "Primero" apocopates to "primer" before a masculine singular noun. In this case it precedes **de** (a preposition) and apocopation is not needed.

8. **(C)**   Forms of "centenar" are preferred to forms of "ciento" when used as collective nouns.

9. **(C)**   To express "a little after the hour," use **y pico**. "En punto" means "exactly," "A eso de" means "at about," with the hour.

10. **(B)** To express warm or cold personally, **tener** is used. Because "frío" and "calor" are nouns, they do not change in gender to match the subject. "Hace frío" expresses the weather condition itself. Forms of **estar** with "frío/caliente" refer to the warmth or coolness of things (such as soup, tea, coffee, etc.).

VOCABULARY/IDIOMS

Idioms with *Dar*

dar a	to face, to look out upon
dar con	to come upon, to find
dar cuerda (a)	to wind
dar de beber (comer) a	to give a drink to, to feed
dar en	to strike against, to hit
dar gritos (voces)	to shout
dar la bienvenida	to welcome
dar la hora	to strike the hour
darse la mano	to shake hands
dar las gracias (a)	to thank
dar por + past part.	to consider
darse por + past part.	to consider oneself
dar recuerdos (a)	to give regards to
darse cuenta de	to realize
dar prisa	to hurry
dar un abrazo	to embrace
dar un paseo	to take a walk
dar un paseo en coche	to take a ride
dar una vuelta	to take a stroll
dar unas palmadas	to clap one's hands

Idioms with *Haber*

hay	there is, are
había	there was, were
hubo	there was, were (took place)
habrá	there will be
habría	there would be
ha habido	there has been
había habido	there had been
haya	there may be
hubiera	there might be
va a haber	there is going to be
iba a haber	there was going to be
tiene que haber	there has to be
puede haber	there can be
debe haber	there should be
haber de + infinitive	to be (supposed) to
haber sol	to be sunny

haber (mucho) polvo	to be (very) dusty
haber (mucho) lodo	to be (very) muddy
haber (mucha) neblina	to be (very) cloudy, foggy
hay luna	there is moonlight
hay que + infinitive	one must, it is necessary
hay + noun + *que* + inf.	there is/are + noun + inf.

Idioms with *Hacer*

hace poco	a little while ago
hacer buen (mal) tiempo	to be good (bad) weather
hacer (mucho) frío (calor)	to be (very) cold (hot)
hacer (mucho) viento	to be (very) windy
hacer caso de (a)	to pay attention to, to heed
hacer de	to act as, to work as
hacer falta	to be lacking
hacerle falta	to need
hacer el favor de	please + infinitive
hacer el papel de	to play the role of
hacer pedazos	to tear (to shreds)
hacer una broma	to play a joke
hacer una maleta	to pack a suitcase
hacer una pregunta	to ask a question
hacer una visita	to pay a visit
hacer un viaje	to take (make) a trip
hacerse	to become (through effort)
hacerse tarde	to become (grow) late
hacer daño (a)	to harm, to damage
hacerse daño	to hurt oneself

Idioms with *Tener*

tener (mucho) calor (frío)	to be (very) warm (cold)
tener cuidado	to be careful

tener dolor de cabeza
   (de estómago, etc.)
	to have a headache
	   (stomach ache, etc.)

tener éxito	to be successful
tener ganas de	to feel like doing something
tener gusto en	to be glad to
tener (mucha) hambre (sed)	to be (very) hungry (thirsty)
tener la bondad de	please + infinitive
tener la culpa (de)	to be to blame (for)
tener lugar	to take place

tener miedo de	to be afraid of
tener por + adj.	to consider
tener prisa	to be in a hurry
tener que	to have to, must
tener que ver con	to have to do with
tener razón (no tener razón)	to be right (wrong)
tener (mucho) sueño	to be (very) sleepy
tener (mucha) suerte	to be (very) lucky
tener vergüenza (de)	to be ashamed (of)

Miscellaneous Verbal Idioms

dejar caer	to drop
echar al correo	to mail
echar de menos	to miss (people)
echar la culpa (a)	to blame
encogerse de hombros	to shrug one's shoulders
estar a las anchas	to be comfortable
estar a punto de + inf.	to be about to
estar conforme (con)	to be in agreement (with)
estar de acuerdo (con)	to agree (with)
estar de pie	to be standing
estar de vuelta	to be back
estar para + inf.	to be about to
guardar cama	to stay in bed
llegar a ser	to become (through effort)
llevar a cabo	to carry out (plans, etc.)
pensar + inf.	to intend
perder cuidado	not to worry
perder de vista	to lose sight of
ponerse + adj.	to become (involuntarily)
ponerse de acuerdo	to come to an agreement
querer decir	to mean
(saber) de memoria	(to know) by heart
tocarle a uno	to be one's turn (uses I.O.)
valer la pena	to be worthwhile
volver en sí	to regain consciousness

Words with the Same English Translation

The following pairs of words cause problems because they share the same translation in English but are not interchangeable in Spanish.

To Know

a) *Conocer* is to know the sense of "being acquainted with" a person, place, or thing.

¿Conoce Ud. a María?	Do you know Mary?
¿Conoces bien a España?	Do you know Spain well?
¿Conoce Ud. esta novela?	Do you know this novel?

Note: In the preterite, *conocer* means **met** for the first time.

La conocí ayer.	I met her yesterday.

b) *Saber* means to know a fact, know something thoroughly, or to know how (with infinitive).

¿Sabe Ud. la dirección?	Do you know the address?
¿Sabes la lección?	Do you know the lesson?
¿Sabes nadar?	Do you know how to swim?

Note: In the preterite, *saber* means **found out**.

Supiste la verdad.	You found out the truth.

To Leave

a) *Dejar* is used when you leave someone or something behind.

Dejé a María en el cine.	I left Mary at the movies.
Dejó sus libros en casa.	He left his books at home.

b) *Salir* is used in the sense of physically departing.

Salió del cuarto.	He left the room.

To Spend

Gastar refers to spending money. *Pasar* refers to spending time.

Me gusta gastar dinero.	I like to spend money.
Pasé mucho tiempo allí.	I spent a lot of time there.

To Play

Jugar refers to playing a game; *tocar* to playing an instrument.

Juego bien al tenis.	I play tennis well.
Juana toca el piano.	Juana plays the piano.

Note: *Tocar* has other uses as well:

Le toca a Juan.	It's Juan's turn.
Toqué la flor.	I touched the flower.
Alguien tocó a la puerta.	Someone knocked.

To Take

a) *Llevar* means to take in the sense of carry or transport from place to place or to take someone somewhere. It also means to wear.

José llevó la mesa a la sala.	Joe took the table to the living room.
Llevé a María al cine.	I took Mary to the movies.
¿Por qué no llevas camisa?	Why aren't you wearing a shirt?

b) *Tomar* means to grab, catch, take transportation or take medication.

Ella tomó el libro y comenzó a leerlo.
She took the book and began to read it.

Tomé el tren hoy.
I took the train today.

¡Tome esta aspirina!
Take this aspirin!

To Ask

a) *Pedir* means to request or to ask for something. (If there is a change in subject, it will require the use of the subjunctive.)

Pedí el menú al entrar.	Upon entering I asked for the menu.
Le pido a Juan que vaya.	I ask Juan to go.

b) *Preguntar* means to inquire or ask a question.

Ella le preguntó a dónde fue. She asked him where he went.

To Return

Volver (ue) means to come back; *devolver (ue)* to give back.

Volví (Regresé) tarde.   I came back late.
Devuelve el libro.   He returns the book.

To Realize

Realizar means to "make real" one's dreams, ambitions, or desires. *Darse cuenta de* means to "take note."

Juan realizó su sueño de ser doctor.
Juan realized his dream to be a doctor.

Me di cuenta de que no tenía mis apuntes.
I realized that I didn't have my notes.

To Become

a) *Llegar a ser* + noun/adj. means to become something through natural developments of time/circumstance.

Llegó a ser capitán/poderoso.
He became a captain/powerful.

b) *Hacerse* + noun/adj. means to become something through personal will or effort.

Se hizo abogado/indispensable.
He became a lawyer/indispensable.

c) *Ponerse* + adj. indicates a sudden change of emotional state or change in physical appearance.

Ella se puso triste/gorda.
She became sad/fat.

d) *Convertirse (ie, i)* + noun often indicates a somewhat unexpected change (not a profession).

Hitler se convirtió en un verdadero tirano.
Hitler became a real tyrant.

e) *Volverse (ue)* + adj. indicates a sudden or gradual change of personality. [Only adjectives that can be used with **both** *ser* and *estar* may follow *volverse*.]

Ella se volvió loca/alegre/sarcástica.
She became mad/happy/sarcastic.

To Enjoy

a) *Gustar, gozar de, disfrutar de* = to get pleasure from.

   Me gusta viajar.
   Gozo de viajar/Gozo viajando.   I like (enjoy) traveling.
   Disfruto de viajar/Disfruto viajando.

b) *Divetirse (ie, i)* = have a good time, enjoy oneself.

   Nos divertimos mucho aquí.   We enjoy ourselves a lot here.

To Save

a) *Salvar* means to rescue from destruction.

   Ellos le salvaron la vida a ella.
   They saved her life.

b) *Guardar* means to keep or put aside.

   Voy a guardar mis cuentas.
   I am going to keep my bills.

c) *Ahorrar* means **not** to spend or waste.

   Vamos a ahorrar agua/dinero.
   We are going to save water/money.

d) *Conservar* means to preserve, maintain.

   Los indios conservan sus tradiciones.
   The Indians preserve their traditions.

To Miss

a) *Extrañar* or *echar de menos* are used when miss = feel the absence of.

   ¡Cuánto lo extraño/echo de menos!
   How much I miss you!

b) *Perder (ie)* means to miss an opportunity, deadline, or transportation.

   Perdí el autobús/la última parte de la película.
   I missed the bus/the last part of the movie.

c) *Faltar a* means to miss an appointment or fail to attend (as in a class, etc.).

Yo perdí/falté a la clase ayer.
I missed class yesterday.

To Move

a) *Mudarse* or *trasladarse* means to move from place to place (city to city, office to office, etc.)

Cuando era joven, me mudaba mucho.
When I was young, I moved a lot.

La compañía le trasladó a Nueva York.
The company transferred him to New York.

b) *Mover (ue)* means to physically move something.

Voy a mover el sofá cerca de la ventana.
I'm going to move the sofa near the window.

To Work

a) *Trabajar* means to work, labor, or toil.

Juan trabaja cada día en la oficina.
Juan works everyday in the office.

b) *Funcionar* means to work, operate, or function.

El coche/tocadiscos no funciona.
The car/record player doesn't work.

To Keep

a) *Quedarse con* means to keep something in one's possession.

Me quedo con la tarea hasta mañana.
I'll keep the homework until tomorrow.

b) *Guardar* means to hold or put away for safekeeping.

Voy a guardar mi dinero en la caja fuerte.
I'm going to keep my money in the safe.

False Cognates

Cognates are words found in different languages, which share the same linguistic origins, and therefore share similar spellings, pronunciations, and meanings. The false cognates, however, cause the most problems, particularly in the reading comprehension passages.

actual	of the present time
antiguo, –a	former, old, ancient
la apología	eulogy, defense
la arena	sand
asistir a	to attend
atender	to take care of
el auditorio	audience
bizarro, –a	brave, generous
el campo	field, country(side)
el cargo	duty, burden, responsibility
la carta	letter
el colegio	(high) school
el collar	necklace
la complexión	temperament
la conferencia	lecture
la confidencia	secret, trust
constipado, –a	sick with a cold
la consulta	conference
la chanza	joke, fun
la decepción	disappointment
el delito	crime
la desgracia	misfortune
el desmayo	fainting
embarazada	pregnant
el éxito	success
la fábrica	factory
la firma	signature
el idioma	language
ignorar	to be unaware
intoxicar	to poison
largo, –a	long
la lectura	reading
la librería	book store
la maleta	suitcase
el mantel	tablecloth
mayor	older, greater

molestar	to bother
el oficio	trade, occupation
la pala	shovel
el partido	game (sports)
pinchar	to puncture
pretender	to attempt
recordar (ue)	to remember
ropa	clothing
sano, –a	healthy
sensible	sensitive
soportar	to tolerate
el suceso	event, happening

☞ Drill 17

1. El tiempo ya había pasado, pero él no...

   (A) los realizaba   (C) daba cuenta

   (B) lo realizó   (D) se daba cuenta

2. Me gusta juntar dinero para las necesidades del futuro, por eso tengo una cuenta de...

   (A) ahorros   (C) guarda

   (B) salvos   (D) salvar

3. Ramón no...a los padres de su novia.

   (A) muerde   (C) conoce

   (B) toca   (D) sabe

4. Ramón no...que los padres de su novia son inmigrantes.

   (A) conoce   (C) responde

   (B) sabe   (D) pregunta

5. Quiso abrir la puerta del auto pero en ese momento...de que había perdido la llave.

   (A) realizó   (C) se encerró

   (B) se repuso   (D) se dio cuenta

6. En el estadio...muchos espectadores ayer.

   (A) tenían   (C) hay

   (B) habían   (D) había

7. La mujer...su bolsa en su coche.

   (A) dejó   (C) salió

   (B) partió   (D) se quitó

8. Elena...los apuntes al profesor.

   (A) preguntó   (C) pidió

   (B) preguntó para   (D) pidió por

9. Juan...la silla de la sala a la cocina.

   (A) llevó   (C) tomó

   (B) levantó   (D) arrancó

10. Cuando vi el huracán,...pálida.

    (A) llegué a ser   (C) me hice

    (B) volví   (D) me puse

11. Yo sé jugar al golf y mi mejor amigo sabe...piano.

    (A) jugar el   (C) tocar el

    (B) jugar al   (D) tocar al

12. Este alumno no...estudiar bien.

    (A) conoce   (C) sabe de

    (B) sabe a   (D) sabe

13. Basta que los turistas...la ciudad antes de salir.

    (A) conozcan   (C) saben

    (B) sepan   (D) conocen

14. Los estudiantes...a la profesora cómo estaba.

    (A) pidieron   (C) preguntaron

    (B) pusieron   (D) pudieron

15. La señora Gómez...el cheque y se fue al banco.

    (A) vendió   (C) llevó

    (B) compró   (D) tomó

16. Mi hermano quiere...doctor.

    (A) llegar a ser

    (C) ponerse

    (B) volverse

    (D) convertirse en

17. No me encanta...mucho tiempo en la cárcel.

    (A) gastar

    (C) pasar

    (B) gastando

    (D) pasando

18. Mis amigas han...traer los refrescos.

    (A) de

    (C) por

    (B) a

    (D) nothing needed

19. Nuestro cuarto da...patio.

    (A) por el

    (C) al

    (B) para el

    (D) en el

20. Juan y María hablan de ganar el premio gordo y esperan tener...

    (A) lugar

    (C) hambre

    (B) el tiempo

    (D) éxito

21. Ese actor sabe bien...de Sancho Panza.

    (A) hacer caso

    (C) hacer el papel

    (B) hacer falta

    (D) hacer un viaje

22. Tengo que...los libros a la biblioteca hoy.

    (A) regresar

    (C) devolver

    (B) dejar

    (D) volver

23. Yo quiero que los chicos...en la playa.

    (A) se diviertan

    (C) gozan

    (B) gocen

    (D) se divierten

24. Cuando me levanto tarde, siempre...el autobús.

    (A) falto a   (C) echo de menos

    (B) pierdo   (D) extraño

25. ...de Los Ángeles hace cinco años.

    (A) Moví   (C) Me mudé

    (B) Movía   (D) Me mudaría

26. Por ser tan viejo mi coche rehusa...

    (A) trabajar   (C) empezar

    (B) tejer   (D) funcionar

27. La profesora me dijo, −¡...la tarea para mañana!

    (A) quédese con   (C) salve

    (B) guarde   (D) gaste

28. Murió sin...su sueño de ser doctor famoso.

    (A) darse cuenta de   (C) saber

    (B) realizar   (D) ponerse

29. ...mucha tarea...hacer esta noche.

    (A) Hay...para   (C) Hay...que

    (B) Hay...nothing needed   (D) Hay...por

30. Tiene que...una razón por sus acciones.

    (A) haber   (C) ser

    (B) estar   (D) pensar

Drill 17—Detailed Explanations of Answers

1. **(D)** **Darse cuenta** must be used here for "to realize." **Realizar** means "to realize" in the sense of gaining or resulting in. (C) would be correct if it were reflexive.

2. **(A)** A "savings account" (**ahorros**) is the only correct answer. None of the other answers indicates this. **Salvar** is "to save," but in the sense of rescuing, not in the banking sense, and **guardar** might mean "to save," but only in the sense "to keep from harm" or "to keep back."

3. **(C)** The correct answer comes down to a choice between "conoce" and "sabe," both modalities of "to know." (The first two choices don't make much sense.)

4. **(B)** Again, an exercise to distinguish between "saber" and "conocer" (and again, the last two choices don't fit semantically or grammatically). When it's a matter of knowing information (as in this case), the correct choice is "saber."

5. **(D)** Choices (B) and (C) simply make no sense in the context. You may think that (A) is the obvious choice since it sounds like it means "realized." It does, but not in the sense demanded by the question, which can only be rendered by (D). ("Realizar" means "to realize" a project or a plan, to make something real.)

6. **(D)** Choice (B) is incorrect because the verb "haber" is impersonal when it translates "there is," "there are," etc. (i.e., when not used in an auxiliary capacity). Choice (C) contradicts the adverb of time in the question ("ayer"), and choice (A) could only be the product of confusion between the meaning and use of "haber" and "tener."

7. **(A)** "Dejar" means to leave something behind. "Salir" means to physically leave a place. "Partir" means to depart, and "quitarse" means to remove (as in clothing).

8. **(C)** "Pedir" means to ask for something or to request, while "preguntar" means to inquire or ask a question. Neither needs "por" nor "para" in this sample.

9. **(A)** "Llevar" means to carry or transport from one place to another or to take someone somewhere. "Tomar" means to take, in the sense of grab or catch. "Levantar" means to lift and "arrancar" means to start, as in an engine.

10. **(D)** "Ponerse" is used with adjectives to indicate a sudden change of emotional state or physical appearance. "Llegar a ser" is used with adjectives/nouns and means to become something through natural developments of time/circumstance. "Harcerse" also used with adjectives/nouns means to become something through effort. "Volverse" is used with adjectives to indicate a sudden or gradual change of personality.

11. **(C)** "Jugar a" is used in connection with sports. "Tocar" is used in connection with instruments.

12. **(D)** "Conocer" means to know or be acquainted with people, places, or things. "Saber" is to know facts or know "how" to do something (when followed by an infinitive).

13. **(A)** The difference betweeen "saber" and "conocer" is given in number 12. One also needs to recognize that the subjunctive is required in this sample. The sentence begins with an impersonal expression ("it is enough") and there is a change in subject.

14. **(C)** "Preguntar" is used to inquire or ask a question. "Pusieron" from "poner" means "they put" and "pudieron" from "poder" means "they were able/managed."

15. **(D)** "Tomar" means to take in the sense of grab or catch. In this sample Mrs. Gomez is "grabbing" the check to take it to the bank. "Vendió" from "vender" means "she sold," and "compró" from "comprar" means "she bought."

16. **(A)** To become something through the natural development of time/circumstance is "llegar a ser." "Ponerse" and "volverse" must be followed by adjectives. "Convertirse en" is used with nouns but indicates a somewhat unexpected change (not a profession).

17. **(C)** To spend **time** is "pasar." "Gastar" means to spend money. Because this verb is the subject of "me encanta," it is a gerund and must be in the infinitive form in Spanish. In Spanish a present participle may not be treated as a noun.

18. **(A)**   The idiom "haber de" means to be (supposed) to. Neither "a" nor "por" is used with this verb. "Han" cannot be used alone.

19. **(C)**   "Dar a" means to face. "Dar en" means to hit or strike against, which makes no sense in this sentence.

20. **(D)**   "Tener éxito" means to be successful. "Tener lugar" means to take place. "Tener el tiempo" means to have the time, and "tener hambre" means to be hungry.

21. **(C)**   "Hacer el papel de" means to play a part or role. "Hacer caso de" means to notice. "Hacer falta" means to need and is used like gustar. "Hacer un viaje" means to take a trip.

22. **(C)**   To return objects/things one uses the verb "devolver." Both "regresar" and "volver" are intransitive verbs (cannot take direct objects) and are used to indicate a physical return. "Dejar" means to allow/let.

23. **(A)**   "Divertirse" means to enjoy oneself. "Gozar" followed by a present participle or "gozar de" followed by a noun means to get pleasure from. Also, one needs the subjunctive here since there is a verb of volition and a change in subject.

24. **(B)**   "Perder" means to miss a deadline or transportation. "Echar de menos" and "extrañar" mean to feel the absence of (as in people). "Faltar a" means to miss an appointment or a class, for example.

25. **(C)**   To move from place to place is "mudarse." "Mover" is to move objects. The preterite is needed here since this is an "hace" statement meaning **ago**.

26. **(D)**   "Funcionar" means to work/operate/function (as in things). "Trabajar" is for people. "Tejer" means to weave, and "empezar" means to begin or start. To start a car, however, is "arrancar."

27. **(A)**   "Quédese con" means to keep in one's possession. "Guardar" means to put away for safe keeping (as in money or jewelry). "Salvar" means to save lives and "gastar" means to spend money.

28. **(B)**   "Realizar" means to realize one's dreams, hopes, or ambitions. "Darse cuenta de" means to take note. "Saber" is to know facts or how to do something and "ponerse" means to become something unexpectedly (as in pale, sick, angry, etc.).

29. **(C)** These are the missing parts of the idiom "hay + noun + que + infinitive" which is translated: There is a lot of homework to do tonight.

30. **(A)** Through translation "haber" is the logical choice: There has to be a reason for his actions.

PRACTICE EXAM 1

AP Spanish Language

AP Spanish Language
Practice Exam 1

1. A B C D	24. A B C D	47. A B C D
2. A B C D	25. A B C D	48. A B C D
3. A B C D	26. A B C D	49. A B C D
4. A B C D	27. A B C D	50. A B C D
5. A B C D	28. A B C D	51. A B C D
6. A B C D	29. A B C D	52. A B C D
7. A B C D	30. A B C D	53. A B C D
8. A B C D	31. A B C D	54. A B C D
9. A B C D	32. A B C D	55. A B C D
10. A B C D	33. A B C D	56. A B C D
11. A B C D	34. A B C D	57. A B C D
12. A B C D	35. A B C D	58. A B C D
13. A B C D	36. A B C D	59. A B C D
14. A B C D	37. A B C D	60. A B C D
15. A B C D	38. A B C D	61. A B C D
16. A B C D	39. A B C D	62. A B C D
17. A B C D	40. A B C D	63. A B C D
18. A B C D	41. A B C D	64. A B C D
19. A B C D	42. A B C D	65. A B C D
20. A B C D	43. A B C D	66. A B C D
21. A B C D	44. A B C D	67. A B C D
22. A B C D	45. A B C D	68. A B C D
23. A B C D	46. A B C D	

PRACTICE EXAM 1

AP Spanish Language

Total Test Time—2 hours and 50 minutes

SECTION I: Multiple Choice (Listening)
Time—1 hour and 30 minutes

Part A
(Approximate time—30 minutes)

(Listen to the audio recording on the accompanying CD—Audio Track 1.)

Get ready for the first dialogue.

Dialogue Number 1

1. (A) En una tienda de ropa para caballeros.

    (B) En una tienda de ropa para mujeres.

    (C) En una tintorería.

    (D) En un mercado al aire libre.

2.　(A)　El cliente.

　　　(B)　El hermano del cliente.

　　　(C)　El amigo del cliente.

　　　(D)　El hijo del cliente.

3.　(A)　Porque es producto nacional.

　　　(B)　Porque es de una tela especial.

　　　(C)　Porque es la última moda importada.

　　　(D)　Porque es la última de ese estilo.

Dialogue Number 2

4.　(A)　La hermana de Rosa.

　　　(B)　La tía de Rosa.

　　　(C)　La hermana de Chepe.

　　　(D)　La mamá de Rosa.

5.　(A)　Porque su tía no tiene teléfono.

　　　(B)　Porque a Chepe no le interesa su problema.

　　　(C)　Porque no quiere a su hermana.

　　　(D)　Porque no quiere que su mamá se preocupe por ella.

6.　(A)　Que le encargue un recado a Paula.

　　　(B)　Que le escriba una carta a su mamá.

　　　(C)　Que habla con su mamá por teléfono.

　　　(D)　Que vuelva a su casa de inmediato.

7.　(A)　Es simpática.

　　　(B)　Es responsable.

　　　(C)　Es mentirosa.

　　　(D)　Es rencorosa.

> **Dialogue Number 3**

8. (A) A Florencio Varela.

    (B) A Morón.

    (C) A la casa de Carlos.

    (D) A Moreno.

9. (A) Porque no quiere perder el tren.

    (B) Porque no quiere equivocarse de tren.

    (C) Porque Juan siempre anda atrasado.

    (D) Porque no quiere perderse por el camino.

10. (A) El rápido a Once.

    (B) El tren de las Once.

    (C) El tren a Florencio Varela.

    (D) El rápido a Morón a las tres.

11. (A) De Once.

    (B) De Constitución.

    (C) De Florencio Varela.

    (D) De Retiro.

12. (A) Subieron al tren a la hora equivocada.

    (B) Subieron al tren en la estación equivocada.

    (C) Subieron al rápido en el día equivocado.

    (D) Bajaron del tren en la estación equivocada.

INSTRUCCIONES: Escucha los narrativos siguientes. Después, escucha las preguntas basadas en los que acabas de oír, y escoge la mejor respuesta de las que siguen. Llena el óvalo que corresponde en la hoja de respuestas.	DIRECTIONS: Listen to the following short narratives. Afterwards, listen to the questions based on the narratives you have just heard, and choose the best answer from the choices that follow. Color in the corresponding oval on your answer sheet.

Get ready for the first narrative.

Narrative Number 1

13. (A) Regresaba su casa.

(B) Le gustaba mucho viajar.

(C) Era Navidad.

(D) No pudo bajar.

14. (A) Que no subiera más gente al tren.

(B) Encontrar un asiento desocupado en el tren.

(C) Conocer a Carmela.

(D) Ganar la lotería.

15. (A) Porque comprar lotería era un vicio para él.

(B) Porque lo consideraba su número de la suerte.

(C) Porque su esposa le dijo que lo comprara.

(D) Porque siempre ganaba con ese número.

16. (A) A ella le parecía muy bien que Juan jugara.

(B) Tenía muchos celos porque ella también quería jugar.

(C) Permanecía indiferente a los hábitos de su esposo.

(D) Pensaba que era un derroche de dinero.

Narrative Number 2

17. (A) Él ha hablado con el ejército.

    (B) Él ha hablado con unos actores.

    (C) Él ha hablado con unos antifemenistas.

    (D) Él ha hablado con los periodistas.

18. (A) Tiene que pagar una multa.

    (B) Tiene un estilo elegante.

    (C) Tiene la mente cerrada.

    (D) Tiene prejuicios sobre la mujer.

19. (A) El escritor se ha puesto unos pantalones nuevos.

    (B) El novelista es filósofo.

    (C) En casa de Requetemacho manda la mujer.

    (D) La esposa de Requetemacho se ha fugado.

20. (A) Es sobre las alabanzas de la sociedad.

    (B) Es para destacar la progresión de la mujer.

    (C) Es para criticar a los hombres.

    (D) Es para delatar a su propia mujer.

INSTRUCCIONES: Escucha las conferencias siguientes. Cada una durará aproximadamente cinco minutos. Es una buena idea tomar apuntes mientras escuchas las conferencias. En el examen habrá espacio para tus apuntes; usa tu propio papel para este examen de práctica. Al terminar cada conferencia, habrá pre-guntas basadas en la que acabas de oír. Escoge la mejor respuesta de las que siguen. Llena el óvalo que corresponde en la hoja de respuestas.

DIRECTIONS: Listen to the following lectures. Each will be approximately five minutes in length. It would be a good idea to jot down some notes while you are listening to the lectures. On the actual exam you will be provided a space for your notes; please use your own paper for this practice exam. At the end of each lecture, you will be presented with questions based on the lecture you have just heard. Choose the best answer from the choices that follow. Color in the corresponding oval on your answer sheet.

Get ready for the first lecture.

Lecture Number 1

21. Un "santo popular"

    (A) cuenta con la plena aprobación de la Iglesia Católica.

    (B) es un santo creado por la imaginación colectiva de la gente.

    (C) es un fenómeno que existe solamente en la América Latina.

    (D) es la persona más bondadosa de la vecindad.

22. El culto a Maximón es un ejemplo de

    (A) una mezcla de leyendas paganas y elementos cristianos.

    (B) la veneración de un santo reconocido oficialmente por la Iglesia Católica.

    (C) un fenómeno puramente cristiano.

    (D) un homenaje a un personaje histórico que se destacó por sus buenas obras.

23. Según la leyenda, ¿qué le pasó a Deolinda Correa?

    (A) Huyó de su casa porque su esposo la maltrataba.

    (B) Se casó con Facundo Quiroga en La Rioja.

    (C) Se murió de sed entre San Juan y La Rioja.

    (D) Abrió un negocio donde vendía agua embotellada.

24. ¿Cuál es la actitud del Obispado Argentina con respecto al culto a la Difunta Correa?

    (A) Ha aprobado por completo el culto a la Difunta Correa.

    (B) Ha adoptado una política de tolerancia al respecto.

    (C) Ha condenado el culto como profano.

    (D) Ha buscado maneras de incorporar el culto al dogma oficial de la Iglesia.

25. ¿Qué significa una botella de agua colocada en un santuario de la Difunta Correa?

    (A) Indica que la persona que la depositó allí pide la protección de la Difunta Correa en un viaje que piensa hacer.

    (B) Significa que el devoto quiere que la Difunta Correa le ayude a encontrar trabajo.

    (C) Significa que a la persona que la colocó allí le sobra agua potable.

    (D) Demuestra que la persona ha cambiado la botella de agua por un repuesto para su auto.

Lecture Number 2

---

26. El Día de los Muertos

    (A) es una celebración que carece de elementos de origen pagano.

    (B) es celebrada el 2 de noviembre.

(C) fue establecido para rendir homenaje a los que murieron en la revolución de 1910.

(D) no se celebra en la actualidad.

27. Los aztecas creían que cuando un familiar falleció

(A) se convirtió en un miembro invisible del clan.

(B) dejó de existir para siempre.

(C) se convirtió en un cempazúchil.

(D) se trasladó a la capital en busca de una vida mejor.

28. ¿Por qué mucha gente ya no celebra el Día de los Muertos como antes?

(A) Porque la gente moderna ya no cree en esas cosas.

(B) Porque la Iglesia Católica ha prohibido que los fieles lo celebren.

(C) Porque hoy en día a nadie le gusta el pan de muerto.

(D) Porque muchas personas se han trasladado del campo a la ciudad.

29. ¿Cuál fue la actitud de los misioneros católicos con respecto a las prácticas paganas entre los aztecas que se convirtieron al cristianismo?

(A) Los animaban a conservar su religión indígena.

(B) Quisieron aniquilar el paganismo por completo.

(C) Nada más los regañaban cuando los pescaban en algún rito pagano.

(D) Aceptaron la mezcla de lo pagano con el cristianismo sin discutir.

30. El propósito principal de la celebración actual del Día de los Muertos es

    (A) adorar a Coatlicue, la diosa de la tierra y de la muerte.

    (B) mezclar elementos paganos con el cristianismo.

    (C) rendirles homenaje a los seres queridos que han fallecido.

    (D) renovar la religión de los aztecas.

STOP.
This is the end of Part A. You may check your answers to the lecture questions, or you may go on to Part B.

Part B: Multiple Choice (Reading)

(Approximate time—60 minutes)

Passage Number 1

La casita de Lencho estaba en el cerro. Desde allí se veía el campo de maíz y el frijol en flor. Todo prometía una buena cosecha. Pero para ello se necesitaba mucha lluvia.

Linea

(5) Desde temprano por la mañana Lencho examinaba el cielo hacia el noreste.

—¡Ahora sí que lloverá!

Su esposa asintió:

—Lloverá si Dios quiere.

Al mediodía, mientras la familia comía, grandes gotas de lluvia

(10) comenzaron a caer. Enormes nubes negras avanzaban hacia el noreste. El aire estaba cada vez más fresco y dulce, y Lencho observaba sus campos con placer. Pero, de pronto, sopló un viento fuerte y comenzó a granizar.

Durante una hora cayó el granizo sobre todo el valle. Lencho se iba angustiando cada vez más y cuando la tempestad pasó dijo con voz triste a

(15) sus hijos:

—Esto fue peor que las langostas; el granizo no ha dejado nada. No tendremos ni maíz ni frijoles este año.

Sólo guardaban una esperanza en el corazón los habitantes del valle: la ayuda de Dios.

(20) Lencho pensaba en el futuro. Aunque era un hombre rudo, él sabía escribir. Así es que decidió escribir una carta a Dios:

"Dios, si no me ayudas, pasaré hambre con toda mi familia durante este año. Necesito cien pesos para volver a sembrar y vivir mientras viene la cosecha, porque el granizo..."

(25)   Escribió "A DIOS" en el sobre. Le puso un sello a la cara y la echó en el buzón.

Un empleado de correo la recogió más tarde, la abrió y la leyó, y, riéndose, se la mostró al jefe de correos. El jefe también se rió al leerla, pero muy pronto se puso serio y exclamó:

(30)   —¡La fe! ¡Qué fe tan pura! Este hombre cree de veras y por eso le escribe a Dios.

Y para no desilusionar a un hombre tan puro, el jefe de correos decidió contestar la carta.

El jefe pudo reunir sólo un poco más de la mitad del dinero pedido por

(35) Lencho. Metió los billetes en un sobre dirigido a Lencho y con ellos una carta que consistía en una palabra: DIOS.

Una semana más tarde Lencho entró en el correo y preguntó si había carta para él. Sí, había, pero Lencho no mostró la menor sorpresa. Tampoco se sorprendió al ver los billetes, pues él tenía fe en Dios y los esperaba.

(40) Pero al contar el dinero se enfadó. En seguida se acercó a la ventanilla, pidió papel y tinta, y se fue a una mesa a escribir:

"Dios, del dinero que te pedí sólo llegaron a mis manos sesenta pesos. Mándame el resto, porque lo necesito mucho, pero no me lo mandes por correo porque todos los empleados de correo son ladrones. Tuyo,

(45)   LENCHO."

[Adapted from: "Carta a Dios," by Gregorio López y Fuentes, in Selecciones Españoles, A Basic Spanish Reader, *ed. Angel Flores (1967: Bantam Books, Inc., 271 Madison Ave., New York, NY 10016), pp. 26–30.]*

31. ¿Cuál fue el motivo del jefe en darle a Lencho el dinero?

(A) Conocía a Lencho y no quería verle tener hambre.

(B) Le conmovía la confianza que tenía Lencho en Dios.

(C) También había comunicado con Dios y había recibido dinero.

(D) Quería demostrarles a sus empleados su propia fe en Dios.

32. ¿Qué habilidad tenía Lencho que compartió con sólo unos pocos otros campesinos?

(A) La de pronosticar el tiempo

(B) La de cosechar sin lluvia

(C) La de comunicar con Dios

(D) La de leer y escribir

33. ¿Por qué se entristeció Lencho?

    (A) Sus hijos se murieron.

    (B) Llovió demasiado.

    (C) Las langostas destruyeron su sembrado.

    (D) El granizo arrasó su cultivo.

34. ¿Qué trabajo hacía Lencho?

    (A) Era cura.

    (B) Era agricultor.

    (C) Era cartero.

    (D) Era escribano.

35. ¿Por qué escribió Lencho su primera carta a Dios?

    (A) Para pedirle que le ayudara

    (B) Para quejarse de su mala suerte

    (C) Para denunciar irregularidades en el correo

    (D) Para rogarle que le diera una buena cosecha

36. Luego de leer la carta de Lencho, ¿qué hizo el jefe de correos?

    (A) Se rió nada más.

    (B) Regañó al empleado por abrir una carta ajena.

    (C) Juntó dinero para ayudarle a Lencho.

    (D) Le devolvió la carta a Lencho sin dinero.

37. ¿Cómo reaccionó Lencho al recibir la respuesta a su carta?

    (A) Se sorprendió.

    (B) Se rió a carcajadas.

    (C) Perdió la esperanza.

    (D) No mostró ninguna sorpresa.

38. ¿Qué pensaba Lencho de los empleados de correo?

    (A) Que eran hombres honrados

    (B) Que eran deshonestos

    (C) Que eran muy generosos

    (D) Que eran muy bondadosos

39. ¿Qué sintió Lencho al ver la lluvia en sus campos?

(A) Placer

(C) Enojo

(B) Desesperación

(D) Angustia

Passage Number 2

El cacao no debe confundirse ni con el coco ni con la coca, fuente de la cocaína. Los árboles crecen en los trópicos, y por eso no pueden ser cultivados en los Estados Unidos. El cacao y su derivado, el chocolate,

Linea pueden ser auxiliares digestivos, estimular el flujo sanguíneo al corazón y

(5) ayudar a las personas con pecho congestionado a respirar mejor.

Una vez recolectados los granos del cacao, se tuestan y muelen para producir el licor de cacao. A ese líquido se le agrega cantidades minúsculas de lejía para intensificar su sabor. Se continúa el proceso para eliminar su grasa, conocida como manteca de cacao. El producto final, el chocolate, es

(10) una combinación del polvo de cacao desgrasado con un poco de su misma manteca que se le vuelve a añadir.

El polvo al que llamamos cocoa es simplemente licor de cacao seco, quizá con un poco de azúcar. El chocolate de pasterlería es licor de cacao procesado sin azúcar. Al chocolate amargo se le añade un poco de azúcar;

(15) al chocolate semidulce un poco más, y al chocolate de leche todavía más— además de leche para hacerlo cremoso.

Los europeos desconocían la existencia del cacao hasta 1519, cuando el conquistador español Hernán Cortés vio al emperador azteca Moctezuma tomar una bebida llamada *chocolatl* en un tazón de oro. Cortés se interesó

(20) más en el tazón que en su contenido, hasta que los aztecas le informaran que la bebida se elaboraba de granos tan valiosos que cien podían comprar un esclavo en buen estado de salud.

Cortés introdujo el agasajo azteca a la corte española, donde resultó una sensación. Los españoles trataron de mantener el chocolate en secreto y

(25) lo lograron por más de cien años, pero para 1660 se había extendido por toda Europa. El chocolate adquirió especial popularidad en Inglaterra y Holanda, donde la amarga bebida se enriqueció y endulzó con leche y azúcar. Por extraño que parezca, hasta el siglo XIX el chocloate era sólo una bebida, en ocasiones amarga, a veces dulce, pero siempre líquida. No

(30) fue hasta hace uno 150 años que se elaboró en las barras y dulces que nos gustan tanto.

[Adapted from: Las Hierbas que Curan, *por Michael Castleman (1991, Rodale Press, 33 East Minor St., Emmaus, PA), pp. 123, 124, 127.]*

40. ¿A qué se refiere "el agasajo azteca"?

    (A) A la actitud del emperador Moctezuma con respecto a los conquistadores

    (B) Al tazón de oro del cual bebía Moctezuma

    (C) A la bebida *chocolatl* que Cortés llevó a España

    (D) A la destrucción del Imperio Azteca por los expañoles

41. ¿Dónde se cultivan los árboles de cacao?

    (A) En los Estados Unidos

    (B) En las zonas tropicales

    (C) En España

    (D) En Inglaterra y Holanda

42. ¿Qué hizo la corte española cuando supo del cacao?

    (A) Difundió las noticias de inmediato al resto de Europa.

    (B) Armó un escándalo, pues no le gustó la bebida amarga.

    (C) Empezó a hacer chocolate en barra para exportar.

    (D) Procuró que nadie más se enterara.

43. ¿De qué forma mejoraron la bebida de cacao los ingleses y los holandeses?

    (A) Le echaron azúcar y leche.

    (B) La sirvieron helada en vez de caliente.

    (C) Le agregaron lejía para intensificar su sabor.

    (D) Le quitaron toda la grasa.

44. Además de molerlos para elaborar una bebida, ¿qué otro uso les daban a los granos de cacao los aztecas?

    (A) Los usaban como armas para hacer la guerra.

    (B) Los echaban al mar para tener buena suerte.

    (C) Los utilizaban para envenenar a sus enemigos.

    (D) Los empleaban como dinero.

45. Según este pasaje, el cacao

(A) no tuvo mucho éxito fuera de México.

(B) tiene cierto valor medicinal.

(C) carece de valor nutritivo.

(D) se asemeja al coco y la coca.

Passage Number 3

En 1810 los fundadores de la Biblioteca Nacional tuvieron el sueño de que fuera un lugar que preservará la memoria de los argentinos. Ya es hora de actuar con decisión para convertir ese sueño en realidad de una vez por

Linea todas.

(5) La nueva Biblioteca Nacional fue inaugurada hace dos años, pero por falta de fondos, el edificio sigue sin terminar y no se puede llevar a cabo la clasificación de unos 200.000 libros. El Sr. Héctor Yannover, el director actual, sigue esperando el dinero para abrir dos salas más, y para poder incorporar más bibliotecarios, ya que por el momento cuenta sólo con dos.

(10) Alrededor de 8.500 personas visitan la Biblioteca Nacional todos los meses. Sin embargo, no todos quedan satisfechos con lo que encuentran en el enorme edificio ubicado en Agüero y Libertador, y se van decepcionados. Aunque los archivos cuentan con algo más de un millón de ejemplares, casi todos son libros editados hace más de una década. Por

(15) eso, los que buscan información actualizada se ven totalmente frustrados. Por ejemplo, si alguien quiere consultar obras sobre el conflicto por las Islas Malvinas, no hay nada.

Además de los problemas con el fichero, puede haber otros inconvenientes: un cartel al costado de los ascensores indica que en el

(20) quinto piso hay dos salas de lectura que nunca existieron.

Una sombra de incertidumbre envuelve los 45.000 metros cuadrados y siete pisos del inmenso edificio. El Sr. Yannover, un librero de profesión que anteriormente servía de Director de Bibliotecas Municipales, comenta: "Acepté el cargo por el desafío de modificar algo. Pero me trajeron

(25) engañado. No hay un centavo y un proyecto así, sin plata, es imposible."

Según Yannover, no es posible efectuar combios ni aprovecharse de los últimos avances tecnológicos si los fondos nunca llegan. "Los mecanismos para conseguir dinero son eternos, puede pasar más de un año, y para ese tiempo ya se acabó el entusiasmo." Aunque no sea completamente justo

(30) comparar la biblioteca local con otras, vale la pena echar un vistazo a la

de Madrid, cuyo director tiene la dicha de manejar directamente un presu-
puesto anual de 30 millones de dólares.

    Los libros, anteriormente albergados en el edificio de la calle México,
han luchado perpetuamente contra la humedad y los insectos. Centenares
(35) de tomos se estropearon debido a las inundaciones, el moho y el descuido.

*[Adapted from: Clarín, Edición Internacional, Año XX–No 1030, Semana del 6 al 12
de septiembre de 1994, "Biblioteca Nacional: un gigante que no logra ponerse de pie,"
p. 12. Address: Diario Clarín (Edición Internacional), Piedras 1743, 1140 Buenos Aires,
Argentina.]*

46. ¿Cuál sería el mejor título para este pasaje?

    (A) "Nueva sede de la Biblioteca Nacional: un sueño hecho realidad"

    (B) "Biblioteca Nacional clausurada: fuertes protestas en la Capital"

    (C) "Biblioteca Nacional: un gigante que no logra ponerse de pie"

    (D) "Superávit tributaria: recibirá beneficios la Biblioteca Nacional"

47. Seqún el Director, ¿cuál es el problema principal que encara la
Biblioteca Nacional?

    (A) La falta de dinero para funcionar debidamente

    (B) No hay suficiente espacio para acomodar todos los libros

    (C) Que la humedad y el moho destruyen los libros

    (D) El hecho de que casi nadie se aprovecha de las instalaciones

48. ¿Cuál fue el propósito original de la Biblioteca Nacional?

    (A) Ser la colección de libros más extensa de la Argentina

    (B) Ser un modelo para otras bibliotecas por todo el mundo

    (C) Ser un centro de investigación para todo el mundo hispano

    (D) Ser un sitio donde fuera protegida la memoria de los argentinos

49. ¿Qué otro factor mencionado en el pasaje causa problemas en la
nueva Biblioteca Nacional?

    (A) Muchos libros están en malas condiciones.

    (B) Hay insuficiente estantería para acomodar la extensa colección.

    (C) Los usuarios no respetan las reglas de la biblioteca.

(D) Hay demasiados bibliotecarios para una colección de ese tamaño.

50. ¿Cuánto hace que la nueva Biblioteca Nacional empezó a atender al público?

(A) Hace más de 185 años.

(B) Hace 2 años.

(C) Hace casi 2 meses.

(D) Hace como 20 años.

51. ¿Qué le podría ser motivo de frustración para un investigador en la nueva Biblioteca Nacional?

(A) Tener que subir al séptimo piso por las escaleras porque no funcionan los ascensores

(B) Verse obilgado a usar la sala de lectura en el sexto piso

(C) Quedar abrumado por la superabundancia de materiales sobre el conflicto por las Islas Malvinas

(D) Enterarse de que la colección carece casi por completo de títulos recientes

---

Passage Number 4

Una tarde de lluvias primaverales, cuando viajaba sola hacia Barcelona conduciendo un automóvil alquilado, María de la Luz Cervantes sufrió una avería en el desierto de los Monegros. Era una mexicana de veintisiete

Linea años, bonita y seria, que años antes había tenido un cierto nombre como

(5) actriz de variedades. Estaba casada con un prestidigitador de salón, con quien iba a reunirse aquel día después de visitar a unos parientes en Zaragoza. Al cabo de una hora de señas desesperadas a los automóviles y camiones de carga que pasaban raudos en la tormenta, el conductor de un autobús destartalado se compadeció de ella. Le advirtió, eso sí, que no iba

(10) muy lejos.

—No importa—dijo María—. Lo único que necesito es un teléfono.

Era cierto, y sólo lo necesitaba para prevenir a su marido de que no llegaría antes de las siete de la noche. Parecía un pajarito ensopado, con un abrigo de estudiante y los zapatos de playa en abril, y estaba tan aturdida

(15) por el percance que olvidó llevarse las llaves del automóvil. Una mujer que

viajaba junto al conductor, de aspecto militar pero de maneras dulces, le dio una toalla y una manta, y le hizo un sitio a su lado. Después de secarse a medias, María se sentó, se envolvió en la manta y trató de encender un cigarrillo, pero los fósforos estaban mojados. La vecina de asiento le dio
(20) fuego y le pidió un cigarrillo de los pocos que quedaban secos. Mientras fumaban, María cedió a las ansias de desahogarse, y su voz resonó más que la lluvia y el traqueteo del autobús. La mujer le interrumpió con el índice en los labios.

—Están dormidas—murmuró.

[From «Sólo vine a hablar por teléfono», Doce Cuentos Peregrinos, Gabriel García Márquez, pp. 99–100 (1992, Editorial Oveja Negra, Carrera 14, No 79–17, Bogotá Colombia.]

52. ¿Qué le sucedió a la protagonista en el desierto de los Monegros?

   (A) Se perdió.

   (B) Sufrió un paro cardiáco en su auto.

   (C) Se le descompuso el carro.

   (D) Se puso muy enferma.

53. ¿Qué fue lo que más le hacía falta a María?

   (A) Un paquete de cigarrillos

   (B) Un médico

   (C) Un cajita de cerillos

   (D) Un teléfono

54. ¿Cuál es el tema central de este pasaje?

   (A) Las condiciones climáticas del desierto Monegros en la primavera

   (B) La escasez de teléfonos públicos en España

   (C) Un contratiempo imprevisto por la carretera

   (D) Los efectos tranquilizantes del tabaco

55. ¿Qué se le olvidó a María?

   (A) Llamar por teléfono a su esposo

   (B) Sacar las llaves del carro

   (C) Visitar a sus parientes en Zaragoza

   (D) Desahogarse en el autobús

56.   ¿Quién se apiadó de María?

   (A) El conductor de un autobús

   (B) Un militar

   (C) Su esposo

   (D) Su compañero de viaje

Passage Number 5

Don Quijote va al espacio, para defender la Tierra. Así se denomina el proyecto de la agencia espacial europea elegido para desviar asteroides que amenacen al planeta. El Caballero de la Triste Figura cabalga de nuevo, esta vez en el cosmos y en lugar de molinos convertidos en gigantes deberá arremeter contra los asteroides que pueden chocar contra la Tierra. Y a su lado, estará como siempre el inseparable Sancho Panza. Así lo imagina la Agencia Espacial Europea (ESA), que acaba de elegir al proyecto Don Quijote, de la empresa española Doimes, para defender a nuestro planeta. Se trata de enviar dos naves—bautizadas Hidalgo y Sancho Panza— contra la roca espacial a la que sea necesario desviar de una eventual colisión con la Tierra.

La "lanza" principal es el Hidalgo, que impactaría contra el asteroide y, al chocar, lo desviaría de su peligroso curso. El "escudero", la aeronave Sancho Panza, estaría encargado de controlar "a prudente distancia" toda la operación y enviar información a la ESA. La BBC de Londres, que informa del proyecto Don Quijote, también explica que "podrían pasar varias semanas y hasta meses antes de que los científicos puedan calcular con precisión si el asteroide 2002 NT7 chocará o no con la Tierra a principios de 2019."

"Cuando contemos con mejores observaciones, quizá descubramos que pasará muy cerca pero no chocará con el planeta", afirmó Mark Bailey, director del Observatorio de Armagh en Irlanda del Norte. En el poco probable caso de que 2002 NT7 sí vaya a colisionar, "los astrónomos tendrán suficiente tiempo para hacer predicciones más exactas de la hora y el lugar de impacto y, de ser posible, establecer un plan para evitar el desastre", señala la BBC."

El proyecto Don Quijote tiene como socios a las universidades de Pisa, París y Berna y a la Fundación de Vigilancia Espacial de Roma. El director general de Doimes, Miguel Belló Mora, explicó que esta iniciativa primero fue seleccionada junto a otros 20 trabajos similares. Después

Linea (5) (10) (15) (20) (25) (30)

"ganó" la semifinal a otros seis y finalmente obtuvo el primer puesto." El proyecto Don Quijote es relativamente barato: "apenas" sale 160 millones de euros. Y por eso fue elegido por la ESA, además de por sus virtudes técnicas. La clave es encontrar fuentes de financiación.

(35)   "Es bastante improbable que un asteroide mayor de 10 metros choque con la Tierra en los próximos centenares de años, pero es necesario estar preparados", dijo Belló Mora. "Si es de 100 metros de diámetro provocará al chocar un efecto similar al de la mayor explosión nuclear registrada en nuestro planeta. Si tiene un kilómetro de diámetro provocará la (40) desaparición de un continente, y si tiene 10 kilómetros, los efectos será tan catastróficos como los que provocaron la desaparición de los dinosaurios", agregó el científico.

[Adapted from: Clarín, 18 julio de 2004, "Don Quijote al espacio, para defender la Tierra," por Juan Carlos Algañaraz, Buenos Aires, Argentina.]

57. ¿Para qué sirve el proyecto Don Quijote?

(A) Para calcular si el asteroide 2002 NT7 chocará con la Tierra.

(B) Para desviar los asteroides de su trayectoria hacia la Tierra.

(C) Para comunicar con las universidades de Pisa, París y Berna.

(D) Para controlar las naves Hidalgo y Sancho Panza.

58. Según el autor, ¿por qué se denomina el proyecto Don Quijote?

(A) Porque son parecidos los asteroides en el espacio y los molinos que el personaje Don Quijote atacó en la novela.

(B) Porque la Agencia Espacial Europea escogió el nombre.

(C) Porque las dos naves se llaman Hidalgo y Sancho Panza.

(D) Porque la novela *Don Quijote* tuvo lugar en el año 2019 del futuro.

59. ¿Cuál es la meta principal de la nave Hidalgo?

(A) Chocar contra los asteroides.

(B) Enviar información a la Agencia Espacial Europea.

(C) Asegurar la precisión del punto de impacto.

(D) Buscar fuentes de financiación para el proyecto.

60. ¿Cuál es el papel de los científicos del Observatorio de Armagh, Irlanda en el proyecto Don Quijote?

    (A) Hacer observaciones del espacio en 2019.

    (B) Predecir el lugar y la hora de la colisión del asteroide 2002 NT7.

    (C) Manejar los movimientos de las naves Hidalgo y Sancho Panza.

    (D) Comunicar con la Agencia Espacial Europea.

61. ¿Cuál es la razón principal por la cual fue seleccionado el proyecto Don Quijote a los otros trabajos similares?

    (A) Porque tiene socios en las mejores universidades de Europa.

    (B) Por sus virtudes técnicas.

    (C) Por su formidable fuerza de impacto.

    (D) Porque sólo cuesta 160 millones de euros.

62. ¿Qué advierte Miguel Bolló Mora?

    (A) Un asteroide probablemente va a chocar con la Tierra.

    (B) Un asteroide probablemente no va a chocar con la Tierra.

    (C) Un asteroide provocará la desaparición de un continente.

    (D) Un asteroide causará una explosión nuclear.

Passage Number 6

El día que lo iban a matar, Santiago Nasar se levantó a las 5.30 de la mañana para esperar el buque en que llegaba el obispo. Había dormido poco y mal, sin quitarse la ropa, y se despertó con dolor de cabeza y con un
Linea sedimento de estribo de cobre en el paladar, y los interpretó como estragos
(5) naturales de la parranda de bodas que se había prolongado hasta después de la medianoche.

Santiago Nasar se puso un pantalón y una camisa de lino blanco, ambas piezas sin almidón, iguales a las que se había puesto el día anterior para la boda. Era un atuendo de ocasión. De no haber sido por la llegada del
(10) obispo se habría puesto el vestido de caqui y las botas de montar con que se iba los lunes a *El Divino Rostro*, la hacienda de ganado que heredó de su padre, y que él administraba con muy buen juicio aunque sin mucha fortuna.

(15) Había cumplido 21 años la última semana de enero, y era esbelto y pálido, y tenía los párpados árabes y los cabellos rizados de su padre. Era el hijo único de un matrimonio de conveniencia que no tuvo un solo instante de felicidad, pero él parecía feliz con su padre hasta que éste murió de repente, tres años antes, y siguió pareciéndolo con la madre solitaria hasta el lunes de su muerte. De ella heredó el instinto. De su padre (20) aprendió desde muy niño el dominio de las armas de fuego, el amor por los caballos y la maestranza de las aves de presas altas, pero de él aprendió también las buenas artes del valor y la prudencia. Hablaban en árabe entre ellos.

El día en que lo iban a matar, su madre creyó que él se había equivocado (25) de fecha cuando lo vio vestido de blanco. Pero él le explicó que se había vestido de pontifical por si tenía ocasión de besarle el anillo al obispo. Ella no dio ninguna muestra de interés.

A su madre, en cambio, lo único que le interesaba de la llegada del obispo era que el hijo no se fuera a mojar en la lluvia, pues lo había oído (30) estornudar mientras dormía. Le aconsejó que llevara un paraguas, pero él le hizo un signo de adiós con la mano y salió del cuarto. Fue la última vez que lo vio.

[*Adapted from «Crónica de una muerte anunciada», Gabriel García Márquez, (1981: Vintage Books, New York, United Status of America) pp.3-8]*

63. ¿Por qué se despertó tan temprano Santiago Nasar esa mañana?

   (A) Porque sabía que lo iban a matar.

   (B) Porque iba a ver al obispo.

   (C) Porque quería llegar temprano a su trabajo.

   (D) Porque iba de viaje en un buque.

64. ¿Qué había hecho Santiago la noche anterior?

   (A) Había asistido a una boda hasta muy tarde.

   (B) Había dormido bien toda la noche.

   (C) Había trabajado en la hacienda de su papá.

   (D) Había celebrado su cumpleaños.

65. ¿Qué hacía Santiago normalmente los lunes?

    (A) Se vestía de pantalones y una camisa de lino blanco.

    (B) Se despertaba con un dolor de cabeza.

    (C) Montaba a caballo.

    (D) Trabajaba en una hacienda de ganado.

66. ¿Cómo era el papá de Santiago?

    (A) No tenía muy buena fortuna.

    (B) Era esbelto y pálido.

    (C) Tenía los párpados árabes y los cabellos rizados.

    (D) Tenía el instinto muy bueno.

67. ¿Qué nos dice el autor que no sabía Santiago Nasar ni su mamá?

    (A) Los padres de Santiago nunca tuvieron un instante de felicidad.

    (B) El papá de Santiago hablaba árabe.

    (C) Santiago se puso el mismo vestido que había llevado la noche anterior.

    (D) Alguien iba a matar a Santiago ese mismo día.

68. ¿Qué le aconsejó su mamá a Santiago antes de salir de su casa?

    (A) Le aconsejó que cambriarse de ropa.

    (B) Le aconsejó que no se mojara en la lluvia.

    (C) Le aconsejó que tuviera cuidado.

    (D) Le aconsejó que se quedara en casa.

STOP.
This is the end of Section I. If you finish before the first hour
and 30 minutes are up, you may check your work on this
section only.

SECTION II

Total Time — Approximately 1 hour and 40 minutes

Part A—Free Response (Writing)

Time — Approximately 80 minutes

INSTRUCCIONES: Hay varios espacios en blanco en el párrafo siguiente. A la derecha del párrafo, después de cada número hay un espacio en blanco y una palabra entre paréntesis. Primero lee el párrafo, entonces en la línea que sigue cada número, escribe la forma apropiada de la palabra entre paréntesis que complete la oración de una manera correcta y lógica. Para recibir todo el crédito posible, se debe deletrear todas las palabras correctamente y tener los acentos apropiados. Sólo se puede usar UNA palabra en cualquier espacio, y en unos casos, la palabra entre paréntesis NO cambiará de la forma original.

DIRECTIONS: There are several numbered blanks in the following passage. To the right of the passage, each number is followed by a blank and a word in parenthesis. Read the entire passage first, then on the line following each number, write the form that the word in parenthesis should take to make the sentence logical and grammatically correct. To receive full credit, all words must be spelled correctly and have the appropriate accents. Only ONE word may be inserted in any given spot, and in some cases, the word in parenthesis will not change from the suggested form.

(Approximate time—7 minutes)

Martín llegó a __(1)__ universidad lleno de las esperanzas. __(2)__ llegado allí por los esfuerzos de sus padres __(3)__ finca les proporcionaba nada más que las necesidades. La tierra no __(4)__ muy buena y su padre trabajaba en las __(5)__ condiciones. Para __(6)__ a su hijo una educación universitaria, tenía que trabajar mucho. Martín sentía una __(7)__ responsabilidad de salir bien en __(8)__ cursos y siempre __(9)__ en lo que su padre le había dicho: __(10)__ tienen una educación, tienen el poder.

1. _____ (el)
2. _____ (Haber)
3. _____ (cuyo)
4. _____ (ser)
5. _____ (peor)
6. _____ (dar)
7. _____ (grande)
8. _____ (su)
9. _____ (pensar)
10. _____ (El que)

INSTRUCCIONES: Hay varios espacios en blanco en los párrafos a continuación. A la derecha de estos párrafos, después de cada número hay un espacio en blanco. Lee primero cada pasaje luego completa las oraciones de una manera correcta y lógica, escribiendo una palabra lógica y correcta en cada espacio en blanco. Para recibir todo el crédito posible, se debe deletrear todas las palabras correctamente y tener los acentos apropiados. Sólo se puede usar UNA palabra en cualquier espacio.

DIRECTIONS: There are several blanks in the following paragraphs. To the right of the paragraphs, after each number there is a blank space. First read each passage then complete the sentences in a correct and logical way, writing the logical word in the blank. To receive all the possible credit, you should spell all the words correctly and have proper accents. You can only use ONE word in each space.

(Approximate time—10 minutes)

¡Qué susto!

Félix se despertó experimentando cierta inquietud por los sonidos extraños rodeándolo. En pleno verano solía dormir __(11)__ las ventanas abiertas y esa noche las había dejado así. Por todas __(12)__ de su vecindario había varios animales domésticos pero en esta ocasión se oía otra clase de ruido. Por mucho __(13)__ intentara hacerlo, Félix no pudo relajarse sin identificar el origen de esos sonidos. Se puso la bata luego salió a la calle con su linterna para investigar este misterio. Dentro de un minuto se __(14)__ cuenta de que sus vecinos habían llevado a casa su bebé recién nacido del hospital y __(15)__ que le parecía un animal salvaje en la oscuridad de hecho fue el llanto del niño.

11. _____

12. _____

13. _____

14. _____

15. _____

La guitarra

Cuando (16) pedimos la última vez, Lupe no quiso prestarnos su guitarra. Nos explicó que preferiría guardar el instrumento en la seguridad de su (17) casa. Según ella (18) diseñada por su abuelo hace cuarenta años entonces desde su muerte el año (19), ha sido un recuerdo constante de su querido abuelito. (20) vez que la toca piensa en él y Lupe sonríe pensando en los momentos que pasaban juntos.

16. _____

17. _____

18. _____

19. _____

20. _____

Informal Writing Task

INSTRUCCIONES: Para contestar la siguiente pregunta, escribirás un mensaje. Tendrás diez minutos para leer la pregunta y escribir tu respuesta. Debes incluir un mínimo de 60 palabras en tu mensaje.

DIRECTIONS: For the question given, you will write a short message. You will be given 10 minutes to read the question and write a response. Your message should contain at least 60 words.

—Escribe una tarjeta postal. Imagina que acabas de pasar una semana visitando a tus primos lejos de tu pueblo o ciudad. Saluda a tus padres y

- descríbeles lo que hiciste esta semana
- expresa por qué te ha gustado la visita
- despídete.

Formal Writing Task

<table>
<tr>
<td>

INSTRUCCIONES: La siguiente pregunta se basa en las Fuentes 1–3 incluidas aquí. Estas fuentes incluyen lo escrito y lo auditivo. Primero, tendrás 7 minutos para leer lo escrito. Luego, oirás la grabación auditiva que durará unos tres minutos, y se recomienda tomar apuntes al escucharla. Por fin, tendrás 5 minutos para organizar y planear tu ensayo y 40 minutos para escribirlo. Tu ensayo debe tener una extensión mínima de 200 palabras.

    Tu respuesta a la pregunta debe reflejar tu capacidad de interpretar y sintetizar unas fuentes. Debes utilizar la información de CADA UNA de las fuentes en tu ensayo para apoyar tu argumento. Asegúrate de citar las fuentes apropiadamente al referirte a cada una. Tu ensayo no debe ser un simple resumen de las fuentes individuales.

</td>
<td>

DIRECTIONS: The following question is based on Sources 1–3 included here. These sources are written and audio material. You will be given 7 minutes to read the written material. Then, you will hear the audio recording of approximately 3 minutes in length, and it is recommended you take notes as you listen. Finally, you will have 5 minutes to plan your essay and 40 minutes to write it. Your essay should be at least 200 words in length.

    Your answer to this question should reflect your ability to interpret and synthesize several sources. You should use information from EACH source in your essay to support your argument. Be sure to cite the sources appropriately as you refer to them. Your essay should not be a simple summary of the individual sources.

</td>
</tr>
</table>

¿Cuál es la importancia de mantener la buena salud?

Fuente No. 1

FUENTE: Este artículo apareció en el suplemento de salud en el periódico *El mundo* en febrero de 2006.

Fruta y verdura para prevenir el infarto cerebral

ALEJANDRA RODRÍGUEZ

    Las recomendaciones dietéticas actuales aconsejan ingerir cinco raciones diarias de fruta y verdura. Sin embargo, la mayoría de la población no cumple con la cifra y, en muchas ocasiones, se queda a bastante distancia.

Sin embargo, un trabajo recogido la semana pasada en 'The Lancet' ha aportado nuevos datos acerca de la conveniencia de tratar de cumplir esta pauta. Sus autores, pertenecientes a la Universidad de Londres (Reino unido) revisaron ocho estudios previos y llegaron a la conclusión de que los individuos que consumían una media de cinco raciones diarias de vegetales tenían hasta un 26% menos de riesgo de sufrir un infarto cerebral, tanto isquémico como hemorrágico. «Sabíamos que estos productos reducen la probabilidad de tener un ictus, pero desconocíamos hasta qué punto. Nuestro trabajo corrobora la relación y la cuantifica», explican los autores. Éstos insisten en que la población del mundo desarrollado toma, por término medio, sólo tres raciones de estos alimentos y que añadir otras dos contribuiría a bajar la mortalidad cardiovascular y la incidencia de algunos tumores.

> ## Fuente No. 2

FUENTE: Este artículo apareció en el suplemento de salud en el periódico *El mundo* en abril de 2006.

El estrés, no el edificio, enferma la trabajador

Una nueva investigación sostiene que los síntomas que se asocian al 'síndrome del edificio enfermo' responden más al estrés que sufre el propio trabajador que a las condiciones físicas del lugar donde desarrolla su actividad laboral. Esa es la conclusión a la que ha llegado un trabajo británico que ha analizado el problema en una muestra de 4.000 funcionarios del Gobierno. Los autores concluyen que las elevadas exigencias del trabajo y la percepción de que se recibe un escaso apoyo se asocian más a la aparición de los síntomas definitorios del citado síndrome, que incluyen dolor de cabeza, congestión nasal, irritación ocular y fatiga y se suelen dar con mayor frecuencia en las personas que trabajan en espacios cerrados. Estudios previos no habían logrado demostrar la relación entre este tipo de molestias y las características de los centros de trabajo. El publicado ahora en la revista 'Occupational and Environmental Medicine' considera que el término 'síndrome del edificio enfermo' es erróneo y que las molestias, que sí son reales y cuestan millones a las empresas en bajas laborales y pérdidas de productividad, responden realmente al estrés.

Fuente No. 3

(Listen to the audio recording on the accompanying CD—Audio Track 2.)

FUENTE: Este informe, basado en un artículo en la revista *Club de corredores* apareció en el número de agosto de 2006 (reprinted with permission).

PART B—Free Response (Speaking)

Informal Speaking

Read the following outline of the conversation.

A. (El anuncio) [You will hear the announcement you are asked to imagine on the recording.
Escucharás el anuncio que te piden imaginar en la grabación.]

B. (La conversación) [The darkened lines represent what Gloria will say.
Las líneas en gris representan lo que Gloria te dice.]

Te saluda y te dice su reacción al anuncio.

Tú — Salúdala y reacciona al anuncio.

Continúa la conversación.

Tú — Reacciona a la pregunta.
　　 Sugiere otra opción.

Continúa la conversación.

Tú — Reacciona y justifica tu reacción.

Continúa la conversación.

Tú — Reacciona.

Continúa la conversación.

Tú — Concluye la conversación y despídete.

(On the accompanying CD, play Audio Track 3. Record your answers on your recording device in the time allowed.)

Formal Oral Presentation

<table>
<tr>
<td>

INSTRUCCIONES: La siguiente pregunta se basa en el artículo impreso y una grabación. Primero, tendrás 5 minutos para leer el artículo impreso. Después escucharás una grabación; debes tomar apuntes mientras escuches. Entonces, tendrás 2 minutos para preparar tu respuesta y 2 minutos para grabar tu respuesta.

</td>
<td>

DIRECTIONS: The following question is based on the accompanying printed article and audio recording. First, you will have 5 minutes to read the printed article. Afterward, you will hear the audio recording; you should take notes while you listen. Then, you will have 2 minutes to plan your answer and 2 minutes to record your answer.

</td>
</tr>
</table>

Imagina que tienes que dar una presentación formal ante una clase de español sobre el siguiente tema:

El artículo que vas a leer es sobre la tienda de ropa Zara y su fundador Amancio Ortega; el informe que vas a escuchar habla sobre la doctora Juliet Villareal García. En una presentación formal, compara el éxito de las dos personas.

> Fuente No. 1

FUENTE: Este reportaje apareció en la revista educativa *Puerta del Sol, Año XI, Número 2. www.puerta-del-sol.com* (reprinted with permission)

Hace unos años surgieron, como de la nada, unas tiendas de ropa llamadas Zara. Vendían los últimos diseños de *prêt à porter* a precios muy económicos y cambiaba los escaparates cada 15 días. Era una nueva manera de vender moda. Si, de media, una mujer visitaba una tienda tres veces al año, a Zara acudía[n] en 17 ocasiones. De forma que, en pocos años se multiplicó un negocio que no tenía rostro. Nadie conocía el nombre del fundador de ese pequeño imperio en emergencia. Hoy se sabe que se llama Amancio Ortega. Preside Inditex, empresa propietaria de las siguientes marcas: Zara, Máximo Tutti, Stradivarius, Bershka, Oysho. Posee más de 1.100 tiendas en todo el mundo. Gracias al uso de tecnología punta, consigue reponer prendas nuevas dos veces por semana en Nueva York, París o Tokio. Sólo la marca Zara mueve más de 11.000 modelos diferentes al año. Y todo comenzó hace poco más de 25 años.

El reportaje es de Matilde Suárez.

Para muchas personas en el mundo, Zara es su segunda piel.

—Bueno, yo me visto de arriba abajo. La verdad es que yo voy entera vestida de Zara.

Hace 27 años, el artífice de este fenómeno empresarial, Amancio Ortega, abre la primera tienda de Zara en A Coruña. Desde entonces ofrece lo que ninguna empresa textil había dado hasta el momento: moda actual, diseño de calidad, precios razonables y respuesta ágil a las demandas del mercado. Hoy está presente en 30 países de América, Europa y Asia, y tiene más de 500 tiendas ubicadas en las mejores calles y centros comerciales de las principales ciudades del mundo. Lola Carretero, periodista especializada en moda, destaca de su éxito haber enseñado a miles de personas una misma cultura de vestir:

—Ha enseñado a vestir, a, a, bueno, a la sociedad española, la ha modernizado en la moda Zara. Te puedes comprar una chaqueta espléndida y durante tres temporadas [y] ir muy bien con ella. Los pantalones, eh, son yo creo uno de los mejores patrones que hay en el mundo hoy en esa, en esa calidad y en ese precio, sin duda, con, y te duran dos y tres temporadas. Y, eh, y bueno, ha enseñado a vestir para enseñar a que ni hay que ir de una determinada cara marca ni de un determinado diseño caro, y que, bueno, y sí, se puede vestir muy bien y con estilo sabiendo mezclar y sabiendo buscar en Zara.

Fuente No. 2

**(Listen to the audio recording on the accompanying
CD—Audio Track 4.)**

FUENTE: El siguiente informe, basado en un artículo que apareció en el periódico *Diario Las Américas* en septiembre de 2006, tiene que ver con la doctora Juliet Villareal García. (reprinted with permission)

PRACTICE EXAM 1

AP Spanish Language

Answer Key

Section I

Part A

1.	(A)	9.	(A)	17.	(D)	25.	(A)
2.	(B)	10.	(D)	18.	(B)	26.	(B)
3.	(C)	11.	(A)	19.	(D)	27.	(A)
4.	(A)	12.	(B)	20.	(B)	28.	(D)
5.	(D)	13.	(A)	21.	(B)	29.	(B)
6.	(C)	14.	(D)	22.	(A)	30.	(C)
7.	(D)	15.	(B)	23.	(C)		
8.	(B)	16.	(D)	24.	(C)		

Part B

31.	(B)	41.	(B)	51.	(D)	61.	(D)
32.	(D)	42.	(D)	52.	(C)	62.	(B)
33.	(D)	43.	(A)	53.	(D)	63.	(B)
34.	(B)	44.	(D)	54.	(C)	64.	(A)
35.	(A)	45.	(B)	55.	(B)	65.	(D)
36.	(C)	46.	(C)	56.	(A)	66.	(C)
37.	(D)	47.	(A)	57.	(B)	67.	(D)
38.	(B)	48.	(D)	58.	(A)	68.	(B)
39.	(A)	49.	(A)	59.	(A)		
40.	(C)	50.	(B)	60.	(B)		

Section II

Part A

1. la
2. Había
3. cuya
4. era
5. peores
6. dar
7. gran
8. sus
9. pensaba
10. Los que

11. con
12. partes
13. que
14. dio
15. lo
16. le
17. propia
18. fue
19. pasado
20. Cada

Note: Please see "Detailed Explanations of Answers" for examples of responses to the essay and Part B.

PRACTICE EXAM 1

AP Spanish Language

Detailed Explanations of Answers

Section I

Part A

1.   **(A)**   Choice (A) is the correct answer. The question asks: "Where is the man?" The dialogue is set in a men's clothing store, and the information given makes it clear that the customer is buying a shirt for his brother. This would preclude (B) as a possible answer, since one would not buy a man's shirt in a women's clothing store. (C) cannot be correct, because the clothes are not sold at the dry cleaner's shop (la tintorería). In the dialogue the customer asks to see the shirt in the shop window (el escaparate), and since you would not find one of those in an open air market, (D) cannot be the correct response.

2.   **(B)**   Choice (B) must be the correct response to the question: "Who is going to have a birthday tomorrow?" In the dialogue the customer says that he is buying the shirt for his brother (hermano). This eliminates (A) the customer, (C) the customer's friend, and (D) the customer's son from being correct answers.

3.   **(C)**   Choice (C) correctly answers the question. When the customer asks the saleswoman why the shirt is so expensive, she replies that it is the latest fashion imported from Paris (la última moda importada de París). Because of this (A) is automatically ruled out, since "producto nacional" refers to something made in the country, not imported. (B) is not correct, because the type of cloth from which the shirt is made is never even mentioned in the conversation, and (D) "la última de ese estilo" (the last one of that style) refers to information not contained in the dialogue, making it incorrect.

4. **(A)** Choice (A) correctly answers the question: "Who is Paula?" In the dialogue Rosa has left a message for her mother with her sister, Paula. Chepe first mentions her by name, then Rosa clarifies that she is her sister. (B) is incorrect, because the information given in the dialogue makes it clear that Rosa and Chepe are going to Rosa's aunt's house. The aunt is mentioned near the end of the conversation and her name is not given. (C) Chepe addresses Rosa as "mi vida" (my darling), and she calls him "mi amor" (my love) which is a fair indication that they are not brother and sister. Since Paula is identified as Rosa's sister, she cannot be Chepe's. (D) According to the conversation, Rosa has given Paula (her sister) a message for their mother, making it impossible for Paula and "la mamá de Rosa" (Rosa's mother) to be the same person.

5. **(D)** Choice (D) is the correct response. The question asks why Rosa is worried, and out of these four choices, this is the only one that is plausible according to the information given in the dialogue. Rosa states at the beginning of the conversation that she does not want her mother to worry on account of her. (A) Rosa is going to call her mother from her aunt's house, so the statement that her aunt doesn't have a phone cannot be correct. (B) The conversation is between Chepe and Rosa, and it is he who ultimately suggests that she use her aunt's phone to call her mother. The assertion that he does not care about her problem (no le interesa su problema) is false. (C) Although it might be true that Rosa does not love her sister, it is not an appropriate response because the dialogue makes it clear that she is worried about something else.

6. **(C)** Choice (C) is the correct response, because Chepe does suggest that Rosa use her aunt's telephone to call her mother. (A) is incorrect, because in the conversation Chepe asks Rosa if she left a message with Paula, but he never suggests that is what she should do. (B) Given Rosa's level of anxiety that her mother know her whereabouts and not worry about her, it is unlikely that Chepe would suggest that she write her mother a letter. (D) is not correct, because Chepe does not suggest Rosa return home immediately. He proposes that she call her mom from her aunt's house.

7. **(D)** Choice (D) is correct. Of these four possible responses, "rencorosa" (resentful, bitter) is the only one mentioned by Chepe, which precludes (A) "nice," (B) "responsible," and (C) "deceptive" from being correct responses. Also, neither (A), (B), nor (C) are mentioned by either Rosa or Chepe as being indicative of Paula's character.

8. **(B)**   Choice (B) correctly answers the question: "Where did Juan and Carlos want to go?" Carlos' cousin is getting married in Morón, and they are going to the wedding. (A) Florencio Varela is the destination of the train that they got on by mistake. (C) According to the information conveyed in the conversation, it is not logical that they would be headed to Carlos' house. (D) The dialogue indicates that Juan and Carlos should be on their way to Morón, not Moreno.

9. **(A)**   Choice (A) is the correct response. In the dialogue Carlos wants Juan to hurry up, because he does not want to miss the train. (B) Although they do get on the wrong train, that is not why Carlos is hurrying Juan. (C) We do not know from the dialogue if Juan is always running late, so this response is not appropriate. (D) This response is illogical, since it is unlikely that Carlos would hurry Juan because he did not want to get lost along the way.

10. **(D)**   Choice (D) is correct. The train they were supposed to take was the 3 o'clock "rápido" (express) to Morón, which was their destination. (A) The express to Once cannot be correct, because the dialogue reveals that the express to Morón leaves from Once. (B) There is no "11 o'clock train" in the dialogue. (C) They got on the wrong train, which was an express to Florencio Varela.

11. **(A)**   Choice (A) is correct. The dialogue indicates that the express train to Morón leaves from Once. (B) Constitución is the station where Carlos and Juan got on the wrong train to (C) Florencio Varela, where they did not want to go. (D) is not an appropriate response, since Retiro is a station that is not mentioned in the conversation.

12. **(B)**   Choice (B) is correct. They managed to get on the wrong train by taking the express that left at 3 o'clock from Constitución, the wrong station. (A) is not correct, because they did get on the train at the right time, they were just at the wrong station. (C) As far as we know, they had the right day and the right time, just the wrong train from the wrong station. (D) The dialogue deals with getting on the wrong train, so getting off the train at the wrong station does not fit into the context.

13. **(A)**   Choice (A) is correct. Juan Carlos was going home, which is explicitly stated in the narrative. He had to stand up on the train all the way home. Since it is also revealed that he made this trip daily, except Sundays and holidays, we can reasonably infer that he was returning from work. (B) The narrative does not mention if Juan Carlos likes to travel or

not, but the overcrowded condition of the train suggests that he might not be too fond of it. (C) is incorrect, because the narrative informs us that the following day was Christmas. (D) That he was on the train because he could not get off is an unlikely situation, especially on a train trip that he was accustomed to taking almost every day.

14. **(D)**   Answer choice (D) is the correct response. Juan Carlos wished with all his soul that the lottery ticket he had bought would win the big prize this year. (A) The conditions on the train were rather uncomfortable, but the narrative does not indicate that Juan Carlos wished that no one else would get on. (B) Juan Carlos would have felt fortunate to have been able to make the train trip home sitting down, but his heart was set on winning the lottery. (C) Juan Carlos was married to Carmela, so hoping to meet (get to know) her would be anachronistic.

15. **(B)**   Choice (B) is correct. We can infer that he considered 16 to be his lucky number, first because he always bought it, and second because it was his age when he met Carmela, which he considered to be the single most fortunate event in his life. (A) The narrative specifically states that playing the lottery was not a vice to him. (C) cannot be correct; Carmela was opposed to him buying lottery tickets, so it is unlikely that she would have told him which number to buy. (D) He always bought that number, but so far he had never been lucky enough to win anything.

16. **(D)**   Choice (D) correctly tells us that Carmela thought that playing the lottery was a waste of money. (A) The statement that she thought it was perfectly alright for Juan to play the lottery is false. (B) Given what the narrative reveals about Carmela's attitude toward Juan Carlos playing the lottery, it is highly unlikely that she was very jealous because she wanted to play too. (C) The idea that she was indifferent to her husband's habits is not supported by the narrative. He was thinking about how she was going to scold him for wasting money, and how she practically assured him a place in Hell because he spent it on the lottery.

17. **(D)**   Choice (D) is correct because the reading tells us that the novelist held a press conference following the ceremony, at which time he made certain statements. This was obviously before a group of journalists. (A) You should be careful not to allow the similarity between "ejército" (army) and the verb "ejercer" (to exercise or carry out) to confuse you. (B) Likewise, Requetemacho did not speak before a group of actors just because of the similarity between this word and the word "acta" (minutes or official record). (C) Requetemacho did not address any antifeminists.

18. **(B)** Choice (B) correctly tells us that one of the reasons the judges have awarded the prize to Requetemacho is because of the sublime literary quality of his novel. Therefore, we might conclude that it has an elegant style. (A) cannot be correct because he was awarded a prize, not required to pay a fine. Though (C) and (D) may be true, they are not the opinion of the judges and certainly would not have earned Requetemacho the prize.

19. **(D)** Choice (D) correctly tells us that Requetemacho's wife has fled their home, evidently because her husband is a tyrant. (A) There is no mention in the reading that the writer has put on new pants. (B) Although the novelist teaches in the "Facultad de Filosofía y Letras," this does not mean that he necessarily teaches philosophy since there are many subjects in the liberal arts department of a university. Choice (C) is totally contradictory to what Requetemacho himself declares because if he wears the pants in his family, then we cannot conclude that the female is the boss in his house.

20. **(B)** Choice (B) is correct because Requetemacho tried in his speech to emphasize how women have progressed. This was evident when he stressed the rapidity with which females have been occupying the positions which before were only reserved for men. (A) would have us think that he praised society, but he did not. (C) Requetemacho did not directly criticize men. (D) He did not accuse his wife of anything.

21. **(B)** Choice (B) best completes the sentence concerning a "folk saint," which is actually created by the collective imagination of the people. (A) is obviously incorrect, because folk saints are condemned by official Catholic dogma. (C) The statement that folk saints are phenomena that exist only in Latin America is inaccurate, and the narration mentions that they are also present in other places in the world. (D) The kindest person in the neighborhood is not a folk saint as described in the narrative.

22. **(A)** Choice (A) correctly describes the cult of Maximón in Guatemala as a mixture of pagan legends and Christian elements. In the narrative he is mentioned as an example of the combining of Christian and pagan elements. (C) is false; the cult of Maximón is not a purely Christian phenomenon, but rather a syncretism between pagan and Christian beliefs. (B) is not a true statement since the Catholic Church not only does not recognize folk saints, but officially condemns them. (D) The narration does not supply information that would indicate that Maximón was a historical figure who stood out because of his good deeds. La Difunta Correa is

the illustration given of a folk saint whose origin goes back to an actual person.

23. **(C)** Choice (C) correctly describes what happened to Deolinda Correa. She was fleeing San Juan and on her way to La Rioja when she got lost and eventually died of thirst. (A) The story provides no indication that she was running away because her husband mistreated her, and to the contrary, tells us she was going to look for her husband in La Rioja because other men were harrassing her in San Juan. (B) She was already married, and her husband had gone to join the forces of Facundo Quiroga in La Rioja, so this is not a good choice. (D) Although bottles of water are piled up around shrines dedicated to her, according to the legend she died of thirst, so it would be impossible for her to open a business that sold bottled water.

24. **(C)** Response (C) accurately states the attitude of the Argentine Bishopric concerning the cult of la Difunta Correa as one of condemnation, which immediately precludes (A) which suggests that the Bishopric has given its complete approval to the cult, and (B) which states that the Bishopric has adopted a policy of tolerance in relation to it. (D) Since the Catholic church has officially condemned the cult as profane, the statement that it has looked for ways to incorporate it in its official dogma cannot be the correct answer.

25. **(A)** Choice (A) gives the correct significance of a bottle of water placed at a shrine dedicated to La Difunta Correa, according to the information given in the narrative. It means that the person has asked her protection during a trip he or she is planning to make. (B) The narrative does not indicate that people ask La Difunta Correa to help them find work. It does, however, explicitly state that they offer her a bottle of water in exchange for a safe trip. (C) The placing of a bottle of water at one of La Difunta Correa's shrines has a much deeper meaning than a mere surplus of potable water. (D) The bottle of water is a symbol of goodwill, asking La Difunta Correa for a favor, or thanking her for one; it does not mean that the person has traded the bottle of water for a replacement part for his car.

26. **(B)** Choice (B) correctly indicates that the Day of the Dead is celebrated on November 2. (A) According to the information given, the statement that the celebration lacks any pagan elements is obviously false. (C) The celebration of the Day of the Dead existed long before the Revolution of 1910, so it could not have been established to pay tribute to

those who died in it. (D) is incorrect because it states that the Day of the Dead is not celebrated these days.

27. **(A)** Response (A) is correct. The Aztecs believed that when a member of the family died he became an invisible member of the clan. That rules out (B) which states that he ceased to exist forever, (C) which says he changed into a cepazúchil, the bright yellow flowers common in Day of the Dead celebrations, and (D) which indicates that he moved to the capital in search of a better life.

28. **(D)** Response (D) is the best answer because, as the narrative reveals, fewer people are participating in traditional celebrations, like the Day of the Dead, due in part to large numbers of people moving to the urban centers and leaving many of their traditional practices behind. (A) The statement that modern people no longer believe in those things implies that no one celebrates it, which is not true. (B) The narrative indicates that the Catholic church does not oppose certain aspects of the celebration, and has never prohibited its parishioners from observing it. (C) The assertion that nowadays nobody likes "pan de muerto" is false, so it cannot be given as a reason for the declining participation in the Day of the Dead festivities.

29. **(B)** Choice (B) correctly states the position that the Catholic missionaries took concerning pagan practices among their converts, as one of intolerance which sought to annihilate pagan rites and to replace them with Christian ones. (A) is false; the Catholic priests never encouraged the Aztecs to preserve their pagan religion. (C) The assertion that they just scolded them if they caught them in some pagan ritual implies a level of tolerance which did not exist, according to the information given. (D) The statement that the priests simply accepted the mixture of pagan rites with Christianity without raising any objection contradicts the information communicated in the narrative. They tore down the Aztecs' idols, destroyed their religious writings, and took special pains to replace pagan rituals with Christian practices.

30. **(C)** Choice (C) correctly captures the essence of the main purpose of the current Day of the Dead celebrations: to pay tribute to those loved ones who have died. (A) In pre-Columbian days, it was a celebration in which Coatlicue, goddess of earth and death, was worshiped, and while certain ancient rites persist, worship of Coatlicue is no longer the prime objective. (B) The celebration's purpose is not for the intentional mixing of Christianity with pagan elements. (D) The purpose of the Day of the Dead festivities is not to renew the religion of the Aztecs.

Part B

31. **(B)** "He was moved by the confidence that Lencho had in God" is the best answer. The text reads *"Este hombre cree de veras"* (this man really believes) and "para no desilusionar a un hombre tan puro" (in order not to disillusion a man so pure), the postal chief decided to respond to the letter. (A) and (C) are not good choices since no mention was ever made of his being acquainted with Lencho, nor of his ever having written a letter to God. (D) is a poor choice because although the postal chief referred to "la fe" (the faith) upon reading the letter, it was in reference to Lencho's, not his own.

32. **(D)** "That of reading and writing" is the best choice. In the text it is indicated that *"aunque era un hombre rudo, el sabía escribir"* (although he was an unpolished man, he knew how to write). (A) is a poor choice because although Lencho seemed to predict the weather by looking at the sky that morning, no reference was made to this being an ability shared with any other farmer. (B) would not be logical since harvesting without rain is not feasible. (C) is a poor choice because although the reader knows that Lencho did indeed write to God, again no reference was made to this being an ability shared by other farmers.

33. **(D)** Choice (D) is the correct answer. Lencho became sad because a hailstorm had destroyed his crop of beans and corn. The story tells us: *"...cuando la tempestad pasó dijo con voz triste a sus hijos:...el granizo no ha dejado nada"* (when the hailstorm was over he told his children with a sad voice:...the hail has left nothing). (A) is not a good choice, since nothing is said in the narrative about his children dying. (B) is not correct; we are told that a lot of rain was needed to ensure a good harvest. What saddened Lencho was not too much rain, but that the storm also brought hail. (C) is not the best choice. Lencho mentions the locusts (*langostas*) only to say that the damage done by the hail was much worse than what a cloud of locusts might have caused.

34. **(B)** Choice (B) is the best answer. In the letter he wrote to God he said, *"Necesito cien pesos para volver a sembrar y vivir mientras viene la cosecha"* (I need 100 pesos to sow again and to live on while the harvest comes). This as well as other statements in the text make it clear that he was a farmer (*agricultor*). That means (A) priest (*cura*), (C) postman (*cartero*), and (D) notary, court clerk (*escribano*) are all incorrect.

35. **(A)** Choice (A) is the correct answer. The story tells us that Lencho had faith in God, so he wrote him a letter asking for 100 pesos to replant his crop and to live on until harvest time. (B) is incorrect, because Lencho never complained about his bad luck. (C) is not the best answer, because in his first letter to God, he does not mention any irregularities in the Post Office. In his second letter, at the end of the narrative, he indicates that he thinks the postal workers stole part of the money God sent him. (D) is not a good choice; in his letter Lencho does not ask God to give him a good harvest.

36. **(C)** Choice (C) is correct. After reading Lencho's letter, the postmaster was impressed by Lencho's faith, so he decided to collect some money to help him. (A) is not a good choice; while the postmaster's initial reaction to the letter was laughter, he did not "just laugh," but rather took steps to help Lencho. (B) is not right, because in the story the postmaster does not scold the employee for opening someone else's mail. (D) cannot be correct, because we are told that the postmaster collected money and answered Lencho's letter; he did not simply give the letter back to him without any money.

37. **(D)** Choice (D) is the best choice. The story tells us that Lencho showed no surprise at all when he received the letter from God. He was not surprised to see the money either, because he had faith and was expecting it. (A) is not correct, since we are told that he was not surprised in the least (*no mostró la menor sorpresa*). (B) is not a good choice; he did not "roar with laughter." (C) is incorrect, because he did not "lose hope" when he received the letter.

38. **(B)** Choice (B), "dishonest," is the correct answer. When Lencho got the money "from God," there was only 60 pesos in the envelope, and he had asked for 100. Lencho assumed God had sent the 100 pesos as requested, and that the postal workers had stolen some of it. In his second letter, he asks God to send the rest of the money, but advises him not to send it through the post office, because "all the postal employees are thieves" (*todos los empleados de correo son ladrones*). (A) is incorrect, because Lencho did not believe the postal workers were "honest" (*honrados*), but rather dishonest. (C) is not a good choice; although the postmaster was very generous, Lencho did not know it, and in fact suspected that the postal workers had stolen part of the money God had sent for him. (D) is not the best choice, since there is no information in the narrative that would indicate that Lencho thought the post office employees were "*bondadosos*" (kind, good-natured).

39. **(A)** Choice (A) is the best answer. Since a lot of rain was necessary for a good harvest, Lencho was pleased that it was raining. The story tells us: "...*Lencho observaba sus campos con placer*" (Lencho watched his fields with pleasure). (B) is not a good choice, because his reaction to the rain was not "despair (or desperation)." (C) "Anger" does not accurately express what Lencho felt when he saw the rain falling on his crops, so it is not the best choice. (D) cannot be correct; Lencho did not feel "anxiety" (*angustia*) when the rain came. The story indicates that he began to feel that way when it started hailing.

40. **(C)** (C) is the correct answer. In the context in which it is used in the passage, *agasajo* means "gift" or "present," and clearly refers to *chocolatl*, the drink the aztecs made from ground cacao beans. (A) is not an appropriate answer, since Moctezuma's attitude toward the Conquistadors is not mentioned in the selection. Although (B) fits in with the concept of a gift, the *tazón de oro* (large golden cup) from which Moctezuma drank the *chocolatl* is only mentioned in passing, and the context excludes it as the antecedent of *agasajo*. Since the destruction of the Aztec Empire by the Spaniards is not dealt with in this passage, (D) is not a good choice.

41. **(B)** Choice (B) correctly answers the question, "Where are the cacao trees cultivated?" The text states that they grow in the tropics. (A) is not a good choice, because the information given in the passage indicates that cacao trees do not grow in the U.S. (C) is incorrect; since cacao was unknown in Europe until Cortés brought it from Mexico, and Spain is not in the tropics, it is logical to conclude that cacao trees are not cultivated in Spain. (D) is not a logical choice; while England and Holland are mentioned as having made improvements on the cacao drink, the European climate precludes the cultivation of cacao trees in those countries.

42. **(D)** Choice (D) is the best answer, since the passage reveals that the Spanish court tried to keep cacao, and the drink made from it, a secret, and managed to for more than 100 years. (A) is not a good choice, since Spain did not immediately spread the news to the rest of Europe. (B) is not correct, because although the passage relates that *chocolatl* caused a sensation in the Spanish court, it mentions nothing of the members of the court kicking up a scandal because they did not like the bitter drink. Choice (C) cannot be right; we are told in the reading that chocolate was only a drink up until 150 years ago when the process for making solid bar chocolate was developed.

43. **(A)** Choice (A) is correct, since the passage tells us that they sweetened it and made it richer by adding sugar and milk to it. (B) is not a good choice, since the text mentions nothing at all about whether the cacao drink was served hot or cold. (C) is incorrect; the passage states that a miniscule amount of lye (*lejía*) is added to the liquid cacao during processing to intensify its flavor, but that has nothing to do with making the drink. (D) makes reference to another step in the refining process, the removal of cocoa butter, which has no connection with the early improvements made on the cacao drink by the English and Dutch.

44. **(D)** Choice (D) is the correct answer. Besides grinding the cacao beans to make the drink *chocolatl*, the Aztecs used them as a form of money. The passage reveals that 100 beans could buy a healthy slave. (A) is not a good choice, because nothing is said in the reading about the beans being used as weapons to wage war. Since the text does not mention throwing beans into the sea for good luck, (B) is eliminated as a correct response. (C) cannot be right; since the Aztecs themselves make *chocolatl* from the cacao beans, it is not logical that they would use the same beans to poison their enemies.

45. **(B)** Choice (B) is the best answer. The first paragraph of the passage tells us that "cacao and its derivative, chocolate, can aid in digestion, stimulate blood flow to the heart, and help people with chest colds breathe better," all of which would come under the heading of "medicinal value" (*valor medicinal*). (A) is incorrect, since the information given in the text indicates that cacao became very popular in Europe, making the statement that it "was not very successful outside of Mexico" false. (C) is not the best response; the passage does not take up cacao's nutritional value. (D) is not a good choice; in the first sentence of the passage we are told that "cacao should not be confused with coconut (*coco*) or coca, the source of cocaine," so the assertion that cacao "resembles coconut and coca" cannot be right.

46. **(C)** Choice (C) is the best answer. Although the National Library is housed in a beautiful and spacious new building, there is not enough money to operate it properly, which is the main thrust of the article. It is like "a giant that cannot manage to stand up." (A) is not a good choice, because according to the passage, the new building is a far cry from "a dream come true" (*un sueño hecho realidad*). (B) is not the best choice, since nothing is said in the article about the library having been closed down, causing strong protests in the Capital. (D) cannot be correct; nothing is mentioned in the passage about the library receiving the benefits of a "tax surplus" (*superávit tributaria*).

47. **(A)** Choice (A) correctly answers the question: "According to the Director, what is the main problem facing the National Library?" The Director indicates in the article that insufficient funding is the main thing that is keeping the library from functioning properly. (B) is not a good choice, because nothing is said about the building being too small to accommodate all the books. (C) is not the best choice; the article mentions humidity and mildew as problems, but they are secondary to the shortage of operating funds. (D) is not the best choice, since the article says that every month the library receives around 8,500 visitors, making the statement that "hardly anyone takes advantage of the facilities" incorrect.

48. **(D)** Choice (D) is the best choice, because in the article we are told that its founders wanted the National Library to be "a place that would protect the memory of the Argentines" (*un lugar que preservara la memoria de los argentinos*). (A) is incorrect; in the passage nothing is said about its original purpose being "to be the most extensive collection of books in Argentina." (B) is also incorrect, since it was not originally intended "to be a model for other libraries all over the world." (C) is not right; the initial objective of the National Library was not "to be a research center for all the Hispanic world."

49. **(A)** Choice (A) is the best choice, because the last paragraph of the article mentions insects, humidity, floods, mildew, and neglect as factors that have damaged and destroyed many books. (B) is not a good choice; nothing is said in the passage about a shortage of shelves. (C) is incorrect, because the article does not mention people not respecting library rules as being a problem. (D) The statement that "there are too many librarians for a collection of that size" is inaccurate. We are told in the article that the Director needs money to hire more librarians, since there are only two. (*El Sr. Héctor Yannover . . . sigue esperando el dinero . . . para poder incorporar más bibliotecarios, ya que por el momento cuenta sólo con dos.*)

50. **(B)** Choice (B) correctly answers the question: How long ago did the new National Library begin to serve the public? The second sentence of the article indicates that it was inaugurated two years ago. (A) is not a good choice, because no mention is made of the creation of the National Library "more than 185 years ago." (C) is incorrect, since the new library opened two years ago, not "almost two months ago." (D) is not correct; the new National Library was set up two years ago, instead of "about 20 years ago."

51. **(D)** Choice (D) is the best answer. The passage indicates that almost all of the National Library's one million-plus volumes are books that were edited more than a decade ago (*Aunque los archivos cuentan con algo más de un millón de ejemplares, casi todos son libros editados hace más de una década*). (A) is not a good choice, because the article does not address "having to take the stairs up to the seventh floor because the elevators do not work." (B) is incorrect; the passage says that the reading room on the sixth floor never existed, so one could hardly be upset about having to use it. (C) is also wrong, since we are told that the library has no information at all about the Falkland Islands conflict.

52. **(C)** Choice (C) is the correct answer; the passage says: *"sufrió una avería en el desierto de Monegros,"* which means "her car broke down in the Monegros desert." *"Se le descompuso el carro"* is another way to say that her car broke down. (A) is not a good choice, since the text does not indicate that she got lost. (B) cannot be correct, because the narrative never mentions her having a heart attack in her car. (D) is not right; she did not "get very sick."

53. **(D)** Choice (D) is the best answer, since María clearly states: *"Lo único que necesito es un teléfono,"* which means "All I need is a telephone." Since she had cigarettes that were dry enough to smoke, (A) is not a good choice, and although she was soaked to the bone, no indication is given that she needed a doctor, making (B) also incorrect. (C) is not the best choice; her matches were wet, but since another lady on the bus gave her a light, "a box of matches" was not what she needed most.

54. **(C)** Choice (C) is the best of all these choices, because the passage deals with a young woman whose rented car unexpectedly breaks down on the road between Zaragoza and Barcelona. Although the writer makes much of the fact that she is caught in a spring rainstorm, the bad weather is not the central concern. The heavy rain simply serves to accentuate the discomfort of her situation, making (A) an incorrect response. (B) is not a good choice, because although she needs the telephone to call her husband, nothing is said about a shortage of public telephones in Spain. (D) is also incorrect; when María finally manages to get a ride, she does settle down and smoke a cigarette, but the "tranquilizing effects of tobacco" is not the main idea of the passage.

55. **(B)** Choice (B) is correct. The text indicates that she was so upset about her mishap that she forgot to take the car keys (*"estaba tan aturdida*

por el percance que olvidó llevarse las llaves del automóvil"). (A) is not correct, because getting to a phone to call her husband was her primary objective, not something she would be likely to forget. (C) is not a good choice; we can deduce that she had already paid her relatives in Zaragoza a visit, since we are told that she was travelling toward Barcelona (Zaragoza is west of Barcelona). (D) is incorrect; in the passage we see that on the bus she gave in to a desire to vent her feelings ("*cedió a las ansias de desahogarse*"), which precludes her forgetting to do it.

56. **(A)** Choice (A) is the best answer, since the narrative tells us that a bus driver took pity on her ("*el conductor de un autobús destartalado se compadeció de ella*"). (B) is incorrect, because there is no soldier in the passage, only a woman with a "military air" ("*aspecto militar*"). (C) is not a good response; "her husband" could not take pity on her, because he was not even aware of her situation. (D) cannot be right; we are told in the first sentence of the passage that she was travelling alone ("*viajaba sola*"), so she did not have a "travel companion" ("*compañero de viaje*").

57. **(B)** The correct answer is (B). The Don Quijote project's main purpose is to cause any asteroid headed for Earth to go off course. Choice (A) is incorrect because scientists will be making that calculation. Choice (C) is incorrect because these universities have faculty working on the project. Choice (D) is incorrect because it is the ship called Sancho Panza that controls the ship called Hidalgo.

58. **(A)** is the correct choice. The author draws a comparison between attacking an asteroid in space and the character Don Quijote attacking the wind mills in the novel. Choice (B) is incorrect because the Spanish company Doimes chose the name. Choices (C) and (D) are incorrect as well.

59. **(A)** Hidalgo is the name of the ship that will impact with the asteroid, making (A) the correct answer. Choices (B) and (C) are incorrect because they refer to the tasks of the ship Sancho Panza. Choice (D) is incorrect because the financing of the project is the task of the ESA.

60. **(B)** The correct answer is (B). This is stated in the third paragraph. Choice (A) is incorrect because the Observatory is looking for the asteroid now. Choices (C) and (D) are incorrect because Sancho Panza will control the movements of the ships and send information to ESA.

61. **(D)** The correct answer is (D). All of the other choices were mentioned as virtues of Don Quijote, but the principal reason it was chosen was its relatively low cost.

62. **(B)** is the correct answer and is stated in the quote in paragraph six. Choice (A) is incorrect because it states the opposite. Choices (C) and (D) are incorrect because these are both improbable results.

63. **(B)** is the correct response. This is stated in the first paragraph. Choice (A) is incorrect because he did not know he was going to be killed. Choice (C) is incorrect because he was not going to work, and choice (D) is incorrect because there is no mention of his traveling anywhere by boat.

64. **(A)** The correct answer is (A). The first paragraph explains that he went to a wedding until very late. Choice (B) is incorrect because the author explains the Santiago slept poorly. Choice (C) is incorrect because there is no mention of his working the previous day, and choice (D) is incorrect because he had celebrated his birthday before.

65. **(D)** is the correct response. Normally he worked on Mondays at the cattle farm. Choice (A) is incorrect because he only dressed in white linen for the sake of the bishop. Choices (B) and (C) are incorrect because he normally did not wake up with a headache, nor is it mentioned that he normally goes horseback riding.

66. **(C)** The correct answer is (C), as these qualities are mentioned in the third paragraph. The other characteristics were mentioned in the description of Santiago, not his father.

67. **(D)** Santiago and his mother did not know that he was to be killed that day. Santiago and his mother knew of the other facts. Thus, (D) is the correct answer.

68. **(B)** Santiago's mother says that she does not want him to get wet in the rain in paragraph five, making (B) the correct answer. Choices (A), (B), and (C) are incorrect because she did not ask him to change clothes, be careful, or stay at home.

Section II

Part A—Writing

1. **(la)**
    The definitive article agrees in gender with the noun it modifies; all words that end in -dad (universidad) in Spanish are feminine.

2. **(Había)**
    The past perfect (había llegado) is used here because the previous sentence established that we are talking about the past.

3. **(cuya)**
    This relative pronoun agrees with the noun it modifies (finca), not with the person who possesses it (el padre).

4. **(era)**
    The imperfect is used because a description, not a completed action, is being expressed.

5. **(peores)**
    The comparative adjective agrees in number with the noun it modifies (condiciones).

6. **(dar)**
    The infinitive form of the verb is used after a preposition (para).

7. **(gran)**
    The adjective "grande" shortens to "gran" before all singular nouns.

8. **(sus)**
    Possessive adjectives agree in number and gender with the nouns they modify (cursos).

9. **(pensaba)**
    The imperfect is used because a repeated action is being described, as indicated by the adverb "siempre."

10. **(Los que)**
    The relative pronoun should be plural to agree with the verb form in this sentence (tienen).

11. **(con)**

The preposition properly completes the description of the condition of the windows.

12. **(partes)**

This is part of an expression describing "everywhere."

13. **(que)**

The "que" connects the two independent clauses.

14. **(dio)**

The preterite of "dar" used in this idiomatic expression indicates a completed, not habitual, action.

15. **(lo)**

This word completes the relative pronoun "lo que" (what / that which).

16. **(le)**

The indirect object pronoun is used with the verb "pedir" to refer to the question asked of Lupe.

17. **(propia)**

The adjective agrees in number and gender with the noun modified and logically completes the expression.

18. **(fue)**

The preterite of "ser" is used in this passive voice construction, describing a completed action in the past.

19. **(pasado)**

The preterite verb used in this sentence indicates a past action.

20. **(Cada)**

This sentence indicates a repeated or habitual action, and the word agrees in number with the singular "vez."

SAMPLE INFORMAL WRITING SCORING HIGH

Querida familia,

Esta semana ha sido fantástica. Mis primos y yo hemos ido a muchos lugares muy interesantes. Visitamos Sacramento, la capital de su estado, California. Compramos ropa en un centro comercial muy grande llamado La Galería luego nadamos en un parque acuático donde hay olas muy grandes y unos ríos. Recogimos manzanas en el pueblo en que ellos viven e hicimos una torta de las.

Me he divertido mucho durante mi visita a causa de las numerosas actividades que hicimos juntos. Nos reímos un montón y la verdad es que me gustaría volver a la casa de mis primos el próximo verano.

Bueno, ¡los veré en el aeropuerto pronto!

Cariños,
Cristina

*This message is very well-organized and well-written. Though not perfect (una torta de **ellas**), it expresses ideas clearly and in relatively accurate Spanish. There is a good variety of vocabulary and verb tenses used.*

SAMPLE INFORMAL WRITING SCORING MID-RANGE

¡Hola mamá y papá!

¿Cómo estás? Este viaje con mis primos en Texas sería ocupado pero divertido. Porque es verano en Texas, hace mucho calor pero a mis primos no molestan.

Durante la semana, me llevaron al San Antonio y visitamos el Álamo y el río San Antonio con sus talleres y vendedores cerca del río. Los otros días, nadamos en su piscina y vemos películas de horror en el cine porque la temperatura fue caliente. A mí me gustó la visita porque Texas es una nueva experiencia para mí y mis primos planearon actividades interesantes.

¡Quiero dormir en mi cama mañana! Hasta luego.

un beso,
Teo

*This message is organized and addresses the stated question, but there are more than a few errors (¿Cómo **están**, no **les molesta**, **vimos**, etc.). Agreement of nouns and adjectives, articles, etc., is generally correct, and there are sufficient details to answer the question.*

SAMPLE INFORMAL WRITING SCORING LOW

Querido mis padres,

Tengo un buen semana en Chicago. Este semana hacimos muchos cosas y exploramos la cultura de Chicago. Fuimos a un partido de los Cubs en Wrigley Field. También cambiamos por el museo aquatico. Comimos mucha comida italiana a una pizzería. A mi me gusta pasando un rato con mis primos. Ellos conocen este ciudad muy bien y saben sus secretos. Espero que yo puedo volver a Chicago y visita mis primas en el futuro. En dos días ellos me llegan al aeropuerto Midway.

Hasta luego,
Carlos

*Though this student tries to address the topic, there are many grammatical mistakes (**Queridos** padres, me gusta **pasar** and Espero **poder** volver) and errors in use of vocabulary (**cambiamos** instead of **caminamos** and **llegan** instead of **llevan**). The agreement of nouns and adjectives is inconsistent (**una buena** semana, **muchas** cosas, and **esta ciudad**) with misspelled words included as well (**acuático**). Many other grammatical errors contribute to making this essay weak.*

SAMPLE FORMAL WRITING SCORING HIGH

Todo el mundo quiere una vida larga, cómoda y alegre. Para vivir de esta manera, es muy importante mantener la buena salud de día a día. Como muestran estos artículos, el bienestar depende del ejercicio, la salud mental y la nutrición.

La tercera fuente, basada en un artículo en *Club de corredores*, mantiene que el ejercicio aeróbico, como el correr, es muy importante para la salud. Dice que correr ayuda a desarrollar una mejor circulación de sangre y una mejor mobilidad. Si uno corre veinte minutos o más cada día puede mantener un corazón más fuerte y mejor tono muscular también. Todos sabemos que el ejercicio contribuye a un mejor estado físico pero este artículo describe específicamente por qué. Un corredor puede bombear más sangre por más energía pero este artículo menciona la salud mental además de lo físico.

Para mantener la buena salud, se necesita bajar el estrés. El correr puede aumentar un hormona que puede tranquilizarle a alguien. La segunda fuente menciona que "el síndrome del edificio enfermo" responde más al estrés que a las condiciones física del lugar donde desarrolla su actividad laboral. Si uno trata de mantenerse sano y relajarse más, se puede trabajar en espacios cerrados sin sentir los síntomas del citado síndrome. De todos modos, hay que comer alimentos nutritivos y no sólo descansar.

La primera fuente menciona la relación entre la dieta y la salud. Dice que cinco raciones diarias de fruta y verdura puede prevenir un infarto cerebral o un ictus. Comentan los autores, "Nuestro trabajo corrobora la relación y la cuantifica." Ellos insisten que dos o tres raciones no son suficientes y que el añadir otras dos contribuiría a bajar la mortalidad cardiovascular y la incidencia de algunos tumores. Lo que se come es una parte esencial de su salud.

En nuestras vidas, hay que mantener la buena salud diariamente para mejorar el bienestar. Estas fuentes muestran que el ejercicio como el correr, la nutrición con raciones apropiadas de frutas y verduras, y la buena salud mental nos ayudarán a vivir contentamente por mucho tiempo.

Citing each of the three sources, this essay is well structured and well presented. It clearly addresses the question using relatively accurate Spanish.

Content: This essay has nice opening and closing paragraphs and presents many clear ideas.

Grammar: Though predominantly narrated in the present tense, the structures are used accurately with few exceptions (cinco raciones . . . pueden . . .). Agreement of nouns and adjectives, articles, etc. is maintained throughout the sample. The sentence structure is varied and correctly used.

Vocabulary: This essay contains advanced vocabulary, correctly used. The use of idiomatic expressions (depender de, de esta manera) adds sophistication to the essay, demonstrating command of the language.

SAMPLE FORMAL WRITING SCORING MID-RANGE

Según estos artículos, hay varias maneras de mejorar la salud. Una mescla de todos es la manera ideal de vivir como una persona feliz con buen salud. Ejercicio, frutas y verduras, y el control del estrés son las tres maneras importantes de mantenerse en control de su propia vida.

En el primer artículo, describe un estudio sobre las raciones de frutas y verduras que se deben comer. Aunque muchos estudios han dicho que todos necesitan cinco raciones diarias de tal comidas, este artículo muestra que la media de eso puede mejorar o mantener la buena salud. Dice que con solo tres raciones diarias, puede tener "un 26% menos riesgo de sufrir un infarto cerebral."

El estrés es una enfermedad que es difícil de entender. En una investigación encontraron que cuando hay enfermos en el trabajo no es el edificio que le enferma al trabajador sino el estrés. El artículo no incluye maneras de evitar el estrés pero explica que el estrés acuenta para muchas enfermedades.

El ejercicio es algo necesario para la salud. Ayuda el área skeletal, músculo, emocional, y la respiración. También ayuda a la circulación de sangre en el cuerpo. Correr es el mejor ejercicio para la salud y puede mejorar la vida personal también.

Con respecto al estrés, el ejercicio ayuda a quitar la depressión y puede funcionar como un tranquilisante emocional. El comer y el ejercicio funcionan juntos para prolongar la vida. Lo hace más feliz también.

En conclusión, si comes correctamente y comes mucho, tendres una vida mejor.

Content: This essay deals with the topic well, referring to the three sources and even commenting on what was left out that would have been helpful (no incluye maneras de evitar el estrés). The misunderstanding of the "sick building" (not a building of sick people) causes some confusion in the writing.

Grammar: Though generally correct verb use, there is a shift from the impersonal third person use to the specific personal "you" in the conclusion (si comes). The student uses the third person form without "se/uno" to try to express a general sense unsuccessfully (En el primer artículo, **se** describe). As the essay progresses, there are several mistakes made in spelling (skeletal instead of **esqueletal**, depression instead of **depresión**, and tranquilisante instead of **tranquilizante**). Seeming rushed in the end, the one attempt at the future tense results in an incorrect form (tendres instead of **tendrás**).

Vocabulary: In general, the use of vocabulary here is pretty good. Occasionally, a misused word interrupts the flow (la media instead of **la mitad**).

SAMPLE FORMAL WRITING SCORING LOW

La buena salud es muy importante para todos. Si se tiene mal salud, esto causa muchos problemas por todos sus parientes y amigos por que ellos le necesitan cuidar a usted. Por eso, es un buen idea mantener la buena salud por usted y su familia. Hay tres cosas que se puede hacer para hace salud mejor.

Comida es una factora más grande con su salud. Es necesario que se coma tres tiempos todos las días, pero es más importante que se coma frutas y verduras. Estas bajan el gordo en tu cuerpo. Alimento es el primer parte en se hace la buena salud.

Estrés lleva estrés en todo su cuerpo. Estudias primeras sostuven que el espacio en su edificio de trabajador causa estrés. Pero una nueva investigación sostiene que la causa más probable es estrés. Se desarolla enferma por estrés y se estás más vunerable cuando sufre estrés. Eliminando estrés en tu vida es el segundo parte en se hace la buena salud.

Finalmente el ejercicio es el más importante de las causas de la buena salud. Su corazón necesito más circulación de sangre y ejercicio se lo da. Tambien el ejercicio puede eliminar estrés y depreción. Cuando se está haciendo ejercicio, su cuerpo produce endofinas que ayuda tu cuerpo mucho. Personas que hace ejercicio, vive vidas beneficias.

La salud es muy importante y manteniendo la buena salud es más importante. Dieta, estrés, y ejercicio es causas grandes en su salud. Sí se come la comida correcta, elimine estrés, y hace ejercicio, se vivirá una vida más alegre con menos depresión.

Content: The content tends to be too general and repetitive. Some ideas are presented without any supporting evidence or direct reference to the sources given.

Grammar: There are some correct uses of the present subjunctive yet at times it is used without the proper subject/verb agreement (es más importante que se **coman** frutas y verduras). Throughout the essay, gender agreement is an issue (**mala** salud, **una buena** idea, **la primera** parte) because of its inconsistency. The impersonal "se" with the present tense is not controlled (se come la comida correcta, **se elimina** estrés y **se** hace ejercicio). The gerund is improperly used as a subject (**Eliminar** estrés en **la** vida es, **mantener** la buena salud es importante). Many other grammatical errors combine to make this essay weak.

Vocabulary: Several verbs are used improperly (se desarolla enferma instead of **uno se enferma**, se hace to mean "to become" when inappropriate). Misspelled words, few vocabulary resources, and repetition make this essay weak.

Part B—Speaking

SAMPLE INFORMAL SPEAKING SCORING HIGH

—Sí, será muy increíble. Habrá muchas personas compitiendo para un espacio en el espectáculo y será muy interesante.

—Tal vez pero a mí me tocan muchos nervios cuando voy enfrente de tantas personas criticándome. No sé qué voy a hacer. Tal vez sí, tal vez no.

—Bueno, yo no creo que bailo tan bien pero tal vez, ...Todavía tengo mucho miedo de hacerlo. Yo no sé si me van a escoger para estar en el evento. Vamos a ver.

—Sí, creo que voy a hacerlo entonces. Va a ser una experiencia muy divertida. Bueno, sí, lo voy a hacer.

—Sí, claro. Voy a prepararme muy bien este fin de semana. Voy a tratar de hacer un buen trabajo. Deséame suerte.

*There is a good variety of gramatical structures and verb tenses. Though not completely free of errors (no creo que **baile**, compitiendo **por**), this shows an excellent control of the language.*

SAMPLE INFORMAL SPEAKING SCORING MID-RANGE

—Sí, sí, pero yo no sé si quiero participar en este espectáculo. Es muy . . . tengo mucho miedo de performar a una audiencia.

—No sé si toda la gente.. a toda la gente les gustará oír cantar yo. Porque nunca he tocado mi voz a una audiencia.

—Sí sí a mí me gusta bailar con mis amigos pero toda la gente no se portan como Uds. en un grupo y . . .

—Sí y gracias para tu apoyo. Yo creo que sería muy divertido y me gustaría tratar si la otra gente de la escuela le gusta.

—Sí tenemos la clase de historia justos en la mañana y nos vemos por la mañana y hablar más de esta cosa.

*This sample shows that the student can follow the idea of the conversation with fair vocabulary (should say **actuar/presenter** instead of **performar**). The grammar is relatively accurate, but some errors (a toda la gente **le gusta**, la gente se **porta**, gracias **por**, y **hablaremos**) weaken the overall flow.*

SAMPLE INFORMAL SPEAKING SCORING LOW

—Sí, estoy muy espectáculo. ¿Y tú?

—No pienso porque no tengo mucho tiempo para participar en esta oportunidad. Me quiero que participar pero no sé . . .

—Sí, me amo cantar y bailar también. Sí, bailo hace . . . hace 15 años que bailar y cantar en mi vida.

—Sí, crees. Me encanta acompañar al teatro ese día y me apoyo totalmente. Me creo que es muy divertido.

—Ojalá que vea por la mañana. Voy a la escuela pero posiblemente me veas por la mañana. Adiós.

*The first question is misunderstood (el espectáculo, not espectacular). The use of too many reflexives (**quiero**, **amo**, **creo**) is awkward, and the verb forms are incorrectly used (hace 15 años que **bailo y canto**, creo que **será**). Object pronouns are misued or absent (acompañar**me**, **te** vea). The fourth response is confusing and leaves one wondering if the student understands who the subject is. Overall, this sample is weak.*

SAMPLE FORMAL ORAL PRESENTATION SCORING HIGH

Para comparar el éxito de una persona en el sistema educativo con un hombre de negocios, hay que buscar un elemento en común. La Sra. García trabajó duro durante toda su vida, ganando el respeto de sus colegas. Siendo una educadora extraordinaria, la doctora Villareal García tiene gran fama en el estado de Texas, más que nada por ser una mujer latina y llegar a un nivel bastante alto como administradora universitaria en los Estados Unidos. Aunque empezó su empresa en España, el Sr. Ortega y sus tiendas de ropa Zara tienen fama mundial. El hecho de que hay más de mil tiendas por todas partes del mundo reflejan que el Sr. Ortega ha tenido tremendo éxito en su carrera durante más de veinte años. Cuando los diseños de ropa cambian, así cambia la ropa en venta. La creatividad y constante cambio de mercancía muestra que el fundador de esta cadena de tiendas entiende bien su mercado. La Sra. García ha ganado premios en su campo y sigue contribuyendo a organizaciones influyentes en éste y otros países. Parece que el éxito de las tiendas Zara y el de esta educadora van a continuar desarrollándose por años.

Content: This has a nice opening and closing and presents a number of fine points.

Grammar: Verb tenses are used accurately with few exceptions. Agreement of nouns and adjectives, articles, etc. is correctly maintained. The correct use of the gerund (**Siendo** una educadora . . .) and other more difficult structures adds to the sophistication of the sample.

Vocabulary: This selection has a wide variety of advanced vocabulary, correctly used with few errors. There is very little repetition of ideas.

SAMPLE FORMAL ORAL PRESENTATION SCORING MID-RANGE

Es claro que las dos personas tienen tipos de éxito diferente. El Sr. Ortega fundó una compañía que da ropa a muchas personas. Tiene muchas tiendas internacionales y en muchos países. La Sra. García se hace en una mujer latina muy importante. Combate los esteriotípicos de la mujer latina y se considera muy importante con mucha influencia. Ella también es muy educada y se graduó de una de las universidades más grandes del Estados Unidos. El Sr. Ortega se fundó una compañía que ha criado en una de los más grandes de ropa en muchos países del mundo. En conclusión, pienso que el Sr. Ortega tiene más éxito porque ha hecho algo que nadie ha hecho con su compañía. Es fenomenal que su compañía puede criar en una manera que se hace tan grande y pienso que este tipo de éxito es mucho más raro de la educación de la Sra. García y pienso que debe ser uno de los hombres más influencias del mundo.

Content: This sample shows a number of ideas related to the topic. Though stated simply, there is a clear introduction and a conclusion.

Grammar: The verb tenses are generally correct and properly used with one missed use of the present subjunctive (. . . que . . . **pueda** criar . . .). The overuse of reflexives (**fundó**) does not interfere with understanding.

Vocabulary: A few of these verbs are misued ("criar" instead of "**crear**", "se hace" instead of "se **ha convertido**"), but most of the vocabulary is appropriate.

SAMPLE FORMAL ORAL PRESENTATION SCORING LOW

Pienso que las tiendas de ropa Zara y Juliet Villareal García no tienen mucho en común sin su éxito en el mundo en su especialidad. La doctora Juliet Villareal García es la primera españa doctora en los EEUU. Ella nació en 1949 en Texas. Ella era la presidente de Texas Southmost College. Ella era uno de los 100 Hispanos más Influencias en los EEUU y una de las mujeres más importantes de Texas. Ella gradúa de University of Texas at Austin en un doctorado lingüista. Las tiendas de ropa llamada Zara comenzan en España, un poco más de 25 años. Las tiendas son . . . tienen muy éxito en el mundo de la moda hoy . . . eh, um . . . Posee más de un milas y ciento tiendas en todo el mundo. Hay tiendas en NY, París y Tokio y en las ciudades en Europa y en América. El hombre quien comenzió las tiendas se llama Amancio Ortega y él abrió la primer tienda de Zara en A Coruña, España. Pienso que los dos personas son muy importantes en la moda y la educación.

Content: There is an introduction and conclusion, but the vast majority is a simple restatement of the information presented.

Grammar: The missed reflexive (**se** gradúa) and a few improperly formed simple verbs (**comienzan, comenzó**) make this difficult to read. There are errors of gender agreement (la **primera** tienda, **las** dos personas) and use of numbers (**mil cien**). The relative pronoun is used improperly ("quien" instead of "**que**"), and many other errors contribute to making this sample weak.

Vocabulary: The word "**hispana/latina**" should have been used instead of "españa" and "**Influyentes**" instead of "**Influencias**". When talking about one of the doctor's degrees, it sould have been called "un doctorado en **lingüística**". There are many other errors present.

PRACTICE EXAM 2

AP Spanish Language

AP Spanish Language
Practice Exam 2

1. Ⓐ Ⓑ Ⓒ Ⓓ	24. Ⓐ Ⓑ Ⓒ Ⓓ	47. Ⓐ Ⓑ Ⓒ Ⓓ
2. Ⓐ Ⓑ Ⓒ Ⓓ	25. Ⓐ Ⓑ Ⓒ Ⓓ	48. Ⓐ Ⓑ Ⓒ Ⓓ
3. Ⓐ Ⓑ Ⓒ Ⓓ	26. Ⓐ Ⓑ Ⓒ Ⓓ	49. Ⓐ Ⓑ Ⓒ Ⓓ
4. Ⓐ Ⓑ Ⓒ Ⓓ	27. Ⓐ Ⓑ Ⓒ Ⓓ	50. Ⓐ Ⓑ Ⓒ Ⓓ
5. Ⓐ Ⓑ Ⓒ Ⓓ	28. Ⓐ Ⓑ Ⓒ Ⓓ	51. Ⓐ Ⓑ Ⓒ Ⓓ
6. Ⓐ Ⓑ Ⓒ Ⓓ	29. Ⓐ Ⓑ Ⓒ Ⓓ	52. Ⓐ Ⓑ Ⓒ Ⓓ
7. Ⓐ Ⓑ Ⓒ Ⓓ	30. Ⓐ Ⓑ Ⓒ Ⓓ	53. Ⓐ Ⓑ Ⓒ Ⓓ
8. Ⓐ Ⓑ Ⓒ Ⓓ	31. Ⓐ Ⓑ Ⓒ Ⓓ	54. Ⓐ Ⓑ Ⓒ Ⓓ
9. Ⓐ Ⓑ Ⓒ Ⓓ	32. Ⓐ Ⓑ Ⓒ Ⓓ	55. Ⓐ Ⓑ Ⓒ Ⓓ
10. Ⓐ Ⓑ Ⓒ Ⓓ	33. Ⓐ Ⓑ Ⓒ Ⓓ	56. Ⓐ Ⓑ Ⓒ Ⓓ
11. Ⓐ Ⓑ Ⓒ Ⓓ	34. Ⓐ Ⓑ Ⓒ Ⓓ	57. Ⓐ Ⓑ Ⓒ Ⓓ
12. Ⓐ Ⓑ Ⓒ Ⓓ	35. Ⓐ Ⓑ Ⓒ Ⓓ	58. Ⓐ Ⓑ Ⓒ Ⓓ
13. Ⓐ Ⓑ Ⓒ Ⓓ	36. Ⓐ Ⓑ Ⓒ Ⓓ	59. Ⓐ Ⓑ Ⓒ Ⓓ
14. Ⓐ Ⓑ Ⓒ Ⓓ	37. Ⓐ Ⓑ Ⓒ Ⓓ	60. Ⓐ Ⓑ Ⓒ Ⓓ
15. Ⓐ Ⓑ Ⓒ Ⓓ	38. Ⓐ Ⓑ Ⓒ Ⓓ	61. Ⓐ Ⓑ Ⓒ Ⓓ
16. Ⓐ Ⓑ Ⓒ Ⓓ	39. Ⓐ Ⓑ Ⓒ Ⓓ	62. Ⓐ Ⓑ Ⓒ Ⓓ
17. Ⓐ Ⓑ Ⓒ Ⓓ	40. Ⓐ Ⓑ Ⓒ Ⓓ	63. Ⓐ Ⓑ Ⓒ Ⓓ
18. Ⓐ Ⓑ Ⓒ Ⓓ	41. Ⓐ Ⓑ Ⓒ Ⓓ	64. Ⓐ Ⓑ Ⓒ Ⓓ
19. Ⓐ Ⓑ Ⓒ Ⓓ	42. Ⓐ Ⓑ Ⓒ Ⓓ	65. Ⓐ Ⓑ Ⓒ Ⓓ
20. Ⓐ Ⓑ Ⓒ Ⓓ	43. Ⓐ Ⓑ Ⓒ Ⓓ	66. Ⓐ Ⓑ Ⓒ Ⓓ
21. Ⓐ Ⓑ Ⓒ Ⓓ	44. Ⓐ Ⓑ Ⓒ Ⓓ	67. Ⓐ Ⓑ Ⓒ Ⓓ
22. Ⓐ Ⓑ Ⓒ Ⓓ	45. Ⓐ Ⓑ Ⓒ Ⓓ	68. Ⓐ Ⓑ Ⓒ Ⓓ
23. Ⓐ Ⓑ Ⓒ Ⓓ	46. Ⓐ Ⓑ Ⓒ Ⓓ	

PRACTICE EXAM 2

AP Spanish Language

Total Test Time—2 hours and 50 minutes

SECTION I: Multiple Choice (Listening)
Time—1 hour and 30 minutes

Part A
(Approximate time—30 minutes)

(Listen to the audio recording on the accompanying CD—Audio Track 5.)

INSTRUCCIONES: Escucha los diálogos siguientes. Después, escucha las preguntas basadas en los diálogos que acabas de oír, y escoge la mejor respuesta de las que siguen. Llena el óvalo que corresponde en la hoja de respuestas.	**DIRECTIONS:** Listen to the following dialogues. Afterwards, listen to the questions based on the dialogues you have just heard, and choose the best answer from the choices that follow. Color in the corresponding oval on your answer sheet.

Get ready for the first dialogue.

Dialogue Number 1

1. (A) Porque se había olvidado de llamarlo.

   (B) Porque la amiga no quería hablar con él.

   (C) Porque había cambiado de número telefónico.

   (D) Porque no tenía teléfono.

2. (A) Que se fue de vacaciones.

 (B) Que hizo un crucero.

 (C) Que se ha casado.

 (D) Que está en Wellington.

3. (A) Que se casará.

 (B) Que irá al mar Báltico.

 (C) Que hará un crucero.

 (D) Que irá a visitar a su amiga a Nueva Zelandia.

Dialogue Number 2

4. (A) Quiere comprar un ratón para su apartamento.

 (B) No sabe cómo eliminar al ratón que hay en su apartamento.

 (C) No tiene nada que hacer.

 (D) No quiere matar al ratón de su apartamento.

5. (A) Porque prefiere usar papel encolado.

 (B) Porque no quiere malgastar queso.

 (C) Porque no se cree capaz de usarla.

 (D) Porque no sabe dónde comprarla.

6. (A) Que atrapa al ratón.

 (B) Que el ratón se muere.

 (C) Que hay que eliminar al ratón posteriormente.

 (D) Que hay que utilizar una escoba.

7. (A) La mujer.

 (B) El hombre.

 (C) Nadie.

 (D) Un exterminador.

Dialogue Number 3

8. (A) El horno no funciona.

    (B) Los pilotos de la cocina no funcionan.

    (C) Ni el horno ni los pilotos funcionan bien.

    (D) Tiene un escape de gas.

9. (A) El día anterior.

    (B) Hace ya tiempo.

    (C) En ese mismo momento.

    (D) Esa mañana.

10. (A) Sucio.

    (B) Viejo y con un agujero.

    (C) Bloqueado.

    (D) Agujereado.

11. (A) Porque están sucios.

    (B) Porque están llenos de agujeros.

    (C) Porque son viejos.

    (D) Porque hay un escape de gas.

12. (A) Limpiar el horno.

    (B) Limpiar los pilotos.

    (C) Cambiar de cocina.

    (D) Cambiar los fogones.

Get ready for the first narrative.

Narrative Number 1

13. (A) En las costas de la Península Ibérica.

    (B) En el desierto del Sáhara.

    (C) Junto a las costas africanas.

    (D) Muy lejos de España.

14. (A) Altos, rubios y de ojos claros.

    (B) Bajitos, morenos y de ojos oscuros.

    (C) De características físicas similares a las de pueblos cercanos.

    (D) Como la imagen prototipo que el mundo tiene de los españoles.

15. (A) Que los guanches vienen del desierto del Sáhara.

    (B) Que proceden de la Península Ibérica.

    (C) Que son descendientes de los habitantes de la Atlántida.

    (D) Que son descendientes de pueblos africanos.

16. (A) Que son un pico que el agua nunca llegó a cubrir.

    (B) Que son los picos que sobresalen de la Atlántida que se hundió en el mar.

    (C) Que son un archipiélago español.

    (D) Que son un archipiélago del Sáhara.

17. (A) Demasiado grande.

    (B) Muy pequeño.

    (C) Aproximadamente, como Texas.

    (D) Aproximadamente, como la Comunidad Europea.

18. (A) Porque se habla en Latinoamérica.

    (B) Porque está muy extendido.

    (C) Porque los otros idiomas que se hablan en España también son "españoles."

    (D) Porque se habla en toda España.

19. (A) Castellano.

    (B) Catalán.

    (C) Vasco.

    (D) Gallego.

20. (A) Los distintos idiomas que hay en España.

    (B) La diferencia entre castellano y español.

    (C) El desarrollo histórico de España.

    (D) El catalán, el gallego y el vasco.

INSTRUCCIONES: Escucha las conferencias siguientes. Cada una durará aproximadamente cinco minutos. Es una buena idea tomar apuntes mientras escuchas las conferencias. En el examen habrá espacio para tus apuntes; usa tu propio papel para este examen de práctica. Al terminar cada conferencia, habrá pre-guntas basadas en la que acabaa de oír. Escoge la mejor respuesta de las que siguen. Llena el óvalo que corresponde en la hoja de respuestas.

DIRECTIONS: Listen to the following lectures. Each will be approximately five minutes in length. It would be a good idea to jot down some notes while you are listening to the lectures. On the actual exam you will be provided a space for your notes; please use your own paper for this practice exam. At the end of each lecture, you will be presented with questions based on the lecture you have just heard. Choose the best answer from the choices that follow. Color in the corresponding oval on your answer sheet.

Get ready for the first lecture.

Lecture Number 1

21. ¿Cuál es la obra más importante de Miguel de Cervantes?

(A) Rinconete y Cortadillo.

(B) El ingenioso hidalgo Don Quijote de la Mancha.

(C) Novelas Ejemplares.

(D) La Galatea.

22. ¿Cuál fue la principal ocupación de Cervantes en su juventud?

(A) Soldado.

(B) Poeta.

(C) Recaudador de impuestos.

(D) Prisionero.

23. ¿Cuáles se consideran las más famosas obras del teatro cervantino?

(A) Entremeses.

(B) Novelas Ejemplares.

(C) Los baños de Argel.

(D) Viaje al Parnaso.

24. ¿Cuál es la principal característica de la segunda etapa teatro de Cervantes?

(A) Se adapta a las reglas de Lope de Vega.

(B) Se adapta a las reglas de Lope de Vega, pero conservando un tono personal.

(C) Exalta el espíritu heroico nacional.

(D) Es de inspiración clásica.

25. ¿En general, se puede decir que Cervantes...?

(A) Fue un famoso dramaturgo.

(B) Destacó por su poesía.

(C) Fue un literato precoz.

(D) Empezó a escribir tarde pero alcanzó fama con "El Quijote."

Lecture Number 2

26. ¿Cuánto tiempo estuverion los musulmanes en la Península Ibérica?

(A) Siete siglos

(B) Siete años

(C) Treinta años

(D) Tres siglos

27. ¿Cuál fue la capitál en la época del Califato independiente?

(A) Córdoba

(B) Granada

(C) Toledo

(D) Almería

28. ¿Qué aportaron los musulmanes a la agricultura del Al-Andalus?

    (A) El cultivo del olivo

    (B) El cultivo de los frutales

    (C) Innovaciones en las técnicas agrícolas

    (D) El sistema del regadío

29. ¿Cuál era el centro del comercio interior?

    (A) El mercado o zoco

    (B) Los puertos

    (C) Las calzadas romanas

    (D) Las comunidades judías

30. ¿Qué se utilizaba como objeto de canje para el comercio?

    (A) Moneda musulmana

    (B) El dirhem

    (C) Oro

    (D) Plata

STOP.

This is the end of Part A. You may check your answers to the
lecture questions, or you may go on to Part B.

Part B: Multiple Choice (Reading)

(Approximate time–60 minutes)

<table>
<tr>
<td>

INSTRUCCIONES: Lee con cuidado las lecturas siguientes. Después de cada una habrá varias oraciones o preguntas incompletas. Escoge la mejor respuesta basada en la lectura que acabas de leer. Llena el óvalo que corresponde en la hoja de respuestas.

</td>
<td>

DIRECTIONS: Carefully read the following passages for comprehension. After each passage there will be several incomplete statements or questions. Select the completion or answer that is the best, based on the passage you have just read. Color in the corresponding oval on your answer sheet.

</td>
</tr>
</table>

Passage Number 1

El 9 de diciembre, 1531, Juan Diego madrugó y se encaminó a la capilla de una aldea cercana para oír misa. Era sábado, y Juan se valió de un atajo por el cerro Tepeyac, unos 19 kilómetros al norte del centro de la Ciudad de México. Encima del cerro se le apareció la Virgen María. Le dijo en náhuatl que era la Madre de Dios, y que ella quería que los indios tuvieran un lugar donde acudir a ella. Le envió a Juan Diego a la Ciudad de México para decirle al Obispo Juan de Zumárraga que ella quería que le contruyera una iglesia en Tepeyac.

Juan complió con lo que le encargó la Virgen, y le comunicó el mensaje al Obispo, quien parecía no creer. Juan volvió a Tepeyac y le informó a la Virgen con respecto a la actitud del Obispo. La Virgen le dijo que volviera a la ciudad para insistir con el Obispo.

Al día siguiente Juan volvió a hablar con el Obispo, y éste le dijo que le trajera alguna evidencia de la aparición. Juan le comunicó eso a la Señora, quien le dijo que regresara por la mañana y le daría evidencias que convincieran al Obispo.

Por la mañana siguiente, Juan no fue a Tepeyac porque su tío estaba agónico. Decidió ir a buscar un cura de una población cercana, pero evitó pasar por Tepeyac, porque le daba mucha pena haberle fallado a la Señora. No obstante, ella se le apareció por el otro camino y le dijo que no se preocupara de su tío, pues no iba a morir. Le mandó a Tepeyac para conseguir las pruebas que exigía el Obispo.

Juan obedeció, y al llegar a Tepeyac vio que la cima del cerro estéril estaba cubierta de rosas castellanas, florecidas fuera de temporada.

Linea (5)

(10)

(15)

(20)

(25) Recogió algunas y la Señora las arregló. Las envovió en su capa y fue a ver al Obispo. Cuando el Obispo Zumárraga lo recibió, Juan abrió su capa y las rosas cayeron al suelo. El Obispo se arrodilló, maravillado, y Juan sintió alivio al ver que por fin le creyó. Juan no sabía que la imagen de la Virgen, tal como la había visto en Tepeyac quedaba grabada en su capa.

(30) Fue el 12 de diciembre, fecha que se conmemora todos los años con las fiestas guadalupanas.

Un santuario fue construido de inmediato en Tepeyac, y con el paso de los años una basílica llegó a ocupar el lugar, donde la capa fue expuesta públicamente. El Vaticano le confirió el título de "Patrona y Protectora de

(35) la Américas," y finalmente la imagen fue coronada. Entre otros nombres, los mexicanos la llaman "La Morenita," porque apareció en forma de una campesina indígena.

En 1976 se construyó una nueva basílica cerca del sitio original para albergar la capa grabada con la imagen de Nuestra Señora de Guadalupe.

(40) La antigua basílica, que sufrió daños estructurales extensos porque se hundía en el suelo, fue restaurada e inaugurada como museo religioso.

31. ¿Por qué no pudo regresar Juan a Tepeyac para conseguir las pruebas exigidas por el Obispo?

    (A) Otro cura le prohibió salir de la Cuidad de México.

    (B) La Virgen rehusó aparecer otra vez.

    (C) Cayó enfermo su tío.

    (D) Temía que muriera su tío si fuera a Tepeyac.

32. ¿Cómo adquirió la Virgen el nombre "La Morenita"?

    (A) Por haber aparecido ante los campesinos

    (B) Por haberse comunicado en español con los indios

    (C) Por haberse vestido de campesina mexicana

    (D) Por haberse parecido a las indias mexicanas

33. ¿Qué aconteció encima de Tepeyac el 9 de diciembre, 1531?

    (A) Juan Diego recogió rosas castellanas.

    (B) Fue construido un santuario.

    (C) Juan Diego vio una aparición de la Madre de Dios.

    (D) El Obispo vio la imagen milagrosa de la Virgen.

34. ¿Cuántas veces fue Juan Diego a hablar con el Obispo?

    (A) Siete veces   (C) Dos veces

    (B) Tres veces   (D) Cuatro veces

35. Cuando Juan Diego fue a hablar con el Obispo por primera vez, ¿cómo reaccionó el Obispo al mensaje que Juan le comunicó?

    (A) No le quiso escuchar.

    (B) Le escuchó pero no entendió nada.

    (C) Creyó todo lo que le dijo.

    (D) No le creyó.

36. ¿Qué encontró Juan Diego en Tepeyac, que por fin convenció al Obispo?

    (A) Rosas florecidas fuera de temporada

    (B) Una basílica construida milagrosamente

    (C) Un remedio que curó a su tío

    (D) Una nueva capa hecha de una tela desconocida

37. ¿Por qué se arrodilló el Obispo ante Juan Diego?

    (A) Quería mostrarle el respeto que merecía.

    (B) Estaba agobiado por la insistencia de Juan Diego.

    (C) Quería ver las rosas más de cerca.

    (D) Vio la imagen de la Virgen grabada en la capa.

38. ¿Qué fue construido en Tepeyac?

    (A) Una mansión para Juan Diego

    (B) Un santuario para la Virgen

    (C) Una casa de campo para el Obispo

    (D) Una tienda: "La Morenita"

39. ¿Qué le exigió el Obispo a Juan Diego?

    (A) Que le trajera evidencias que respaldaran lo que decía

    (B) Que se fuera y no volviera jamás

    (C) Que le regalara una capa nueva

    (D) Que no le hablara en náhuatl

Passage Number 2

Blas de Santillana, mi padre, después de haber servido muchos años en los ejércitos de España, se volvió al pueblo donde había nacido. Allí se casó con una aldeana, y yo nací al mundo diez meses después que se
Linea habían casado.

(5) De Santillana pasaron mis padres a vivir a Oviedo donde ambos encontraron trabajo. En Oviedo vivía un hermano mayor de mi madre, llamado Gil Pérez, el cual era sacerdote. Éste me llevó a su casa cuando yo era niño, y me enseñó a leer; más tarde me envió a la escuela del doctor Godínez, el maestro más hábil que había en Oviedo, para estudiar la lengua
(10) latina.

Aprendí tanto en esta escuela, que al cabo de cinco o seis años entendía un poco los autores griegos, y bastante bien los autores latinos. Estudié, además, la lógica, que me enseñó a pensar y argumentar sin término. Me gustaban mucho las disputas, y dentenía a los que encontraba por la calle,
(15) conocidos o desconocidos, para proponerles cuestiones y argumentos.

De esta manera me hice famoso en toda la ciudad, y mi tío estaba muy orgulloso de mí. Un día me dijo:

—Gil Blas, ya no eres niño; tienes diecisiete años, y Dios te ha dado habilidad. Voy a enviarte a la universidad de Salamanca, donde con tu clara
(20) inteligencia llegarás a ser un hombre de importancia. Para tu viaje te daré dinero y una buena mula que podrás vender en Salamanca.

Mi tío no podía porponerme cosa más de mi gusto, porque yo tenía ganas de ver el mundo; pero no mostré mi gran alegría. Al contrario, cuando llegó la hora de partir, puse una cara tan triste que mi tío me dio
(25) más dinero del que me habría dado si hubiese mostrado alegría.

Antes de montar en mi mula fui a dar un abrazo a mi padre y a mi madre, los cuales me dieron no pocos consejos. Me repitieron muchas veces que viviese cristanamente, y sobre todo no tomase jamás lo ajeno contra la voluntad de su dueño, y que no engañase a nadie. Después de
(30) haberme hablado largamente, me dieron la única cosa que podía esperar de ellos: su bendición. Inmediatamente monté en mi mula y salí de la ciudad.

[From: *Aventuras de Gil Blas*, retold and edited by Carlos Castillo and Colley F. Sparkman, *Graded Spanish Readers, Book Four*, (New York: D.C. Heath and Company, 1936 and 1937), pp. 1–2.]

40. ¿Cómo se llama el narrador del relato?

(A) Blas de Santillana

(B) Gil Blas

(C) Gil Pérez

(D) El doctor Godínez

41. ¿Cómo aprendió a leer Gil Blas?

(A) Su tío se lo enseño.

(B) Lo aprendió en la escuela del doctor Godínez.

(C) Se lo enseñaron en la universidad.

(D) Sus padres se lo enseñaron.

42. ¿Por qué Gil Blas abandonó Oviedo?

(A) Quería ir a vivir con su tío.

(B) Pensaba volver a su pueblo natal.

(C) Sus padres lo echaron de la casa.

(D) Iba a estudiar en la universidad.

43. ¿De quién fue la idea de que Gil Blas fuera a Salamanca?

(A) Gil Pérez   (C) Sus padres

(B) El doctor Godínez   (D) Gil Blas

44. Antes de que Gil Blas se fuera a Salamanca, sus padres le dieron

(A) una mula y dinero para el viaje.

(B) un abrazo y muchos consejos.

(C) un caballo negro y una espada.

(D) un traje nuevo y varios libros.

45. ¿Cómo reaccionó Gil Blas a la idea de ir a Salamanca?

(A) No le gustó para nada.

(B) Se encolerizó.

(C) Le gustó mucho.

(D) Empezó a llorar.

Passage Number 3

El héroe de estas aventuras nació en una aldea de la provinicia de Salamanca un poco después del descubrimiento de América.

Carlos V reinaba en España, la cual era la nación más poderosa del mundo. Sus navegantes habían descubierto el Nuevo Mundo, y sus soldados estaban peleando en Europa, en Africa, y en América.

No obstante, el país no era rico, porque perdió el mejor de sus tesoros, que es el hombre. Pocos de los hombres que fueron a pelear en la América, en Europa o en Africa volvieron a España.

Por eso, en la época de tanto esplendor para las armas españolas había pobreza y miserias en España.

Los padres de Lazarillo se llamaron Tomé González y Antoña Pérez. Como Lazarillo nació cerca del río Tormes, tomó el nombre de Lazarillo de Tormes cuando fue al mundo en busca de aventuras.

Cuando Lazarillo era todavía muy joven, su padre fue encarcelado. Un poco más tarde el gobierno lo puso en libertad para que fuera a pelear contra los moros. Se murió en la guerra, y su mujer tuvo que buscarse la vida para sí misma y su niño.

Antoña fue a trabajar en la ciudad de Salamanca, donde estaba la universidad que en el siglo XVI era la más famosa del mundo.

Alquiló una casa y alojó a varios estudiantes, que le pagaban mal, porque los estudiantes nunca han tenido mucho dinero. Antoña ganaba tan poco que decidió casarse otra vez. Se casó con un negro, Zaydé, que ganaba mucho dinero y ahora Lazarillo estaba contento.

Después de pocos años Zaydé perdió todo su dinero, abandonó a su familia, y jamás volvió.

Antoña obtuvo un puesto de criada en un mesón pero le pagaban tan poco dinero que tuvo que encontrar otro puesto para su niño.

Un viejo ciego que estaba por unos días en el mesón dijo a Antoña que él quería que el niño lo acompañara como su guía.

La pobre consintió y pronto después el ciego y Lazarillo se fueron juntos del mesón. Así empezaron las aventuras de las que Lazarillo iba a ser famoso.

Linea (5), (10), (15), (20), (25), (30)

[Adapted from *Easy Spanish Reader*, New and Enlarged Edition, William T. Tardy, M.A. (Dallas: Banks Upshaw and Company, 1947, 1942) pp. 167–168, 170.]

46. ¿Qué le pasó al padre de Lazarillo?

   (A) Su esposa lo envenenó.

   (B) Murió en la guerra.

(C) Falleció en la cárcel.

(D) Se ahogó en el río Tormes.

47. ¿Por qué decidió volver a casarse la madre de Lazarillo?

(A) Porque ella no ganaba suficiente dinero

(B) Porque estaba enloquecidamente enamorada

(C) Porque era todavía muy joven y hermosa

(D) Porque Lazarillo le daba muchos problemas

48. ¿Quién era Zaydé?

(A) El padre de Lazarillo

(B) Un ciego que pasó por Salamanca

(C) El padrastro de Lazarillo

(D) El hermano de Antoña

49. ¿Qué trabajo consiguió Antoña para su hijo?

(A) Un puesto en el mesón

(B) Un trabajo como guía de un ciego

(C) Lo alistó en el ejército

(D) Un trabajo en la universidad

50. Cuando Lazarillo nació

(A) todavía no se había descubierto el Nuevo Mundo.

(B) España era muy poderosa.

(C) Tomé y Antoña tenían mucho dinero.

(D) su padre ya había muerto en la guerra.

51. ¿Por qué tuvo que trabajar como criada la madre de Lazarillo?

(A) Tomé González la obligó a que lo hiciera.

(B) Zaydé no ganaba mucho dinero.

(C) Lazarillo gastó todo el dinero.

(D) Zaydé se fue y no regresó.

Passage Number 4

José Suárez es el auténtico campesino mexicano: tez morena, sombrero campero y ropa humilde, y de pocas palabras. Nunca ha salido de su pueblo en el estado de Querétero, en el centro de la república, y no conoce
Linea las tendencias del arte moderno. Pero tiene una pasión, la naturaleza, y con
(5) ella pasa sus horas, sus días, sus años, realizando un trabajo poco común, entre el arte y la técnica. Es el "escultor de la naturaleza."

La Hacienda de Jurica tiene hermosos jardines que don José cuida, pero su arte no se limita sólo a eso. También planta árboles y arbustos que vigila con amor. Cuando han alcanzado la altura necesaria comienza a
(10) podar cuidadosamente cada rama, a nivelar o desnivelar, a redondear, hasta alcanzar la forma deseada. Realiza esculturas de gran variedad: el escudo nacional, un campesino sentado en un burro, una divertida pareja de monos jugando...

Don José, joven a sus casi sesenta años, piensa sus esculturas lenta-
(15) mente. No tiene prisa nunca, pues no vive al ritmo de la ciudad moderna. Lo más difícil para él es encontrar la forma que corresponde al carácter y estructura de cada árbol o arbusto. Pero él los conoce bien, después de muchos años, viéndolos crecer día a día, cuidándolos, quizás incluso hablando con ellos.
(20) El trabajo de Don José, más que un arte, es una meditación sobre la naturaleza. Parece que ha comprendido algo que muchos no entienden: que no se puede hacer una distinción entre el arte y la vida de todos los días.

[Adaptación de un artículo de *Tiempo* (México), by Claudio de la Cadena, México D.F., taken from *Sol y Sombra*, 3rd ed., Paul Pimsleur, Beverly Pimsleur, Frederick Suárez-Rich-ard (New York: Harcourt Brace Jovanovich, Inc., 1983), pp. 86–88.]

52. El Sr. José Suárez

   (A) es un terrateniente adinerado de Querétaro.

   (B) es un jardinero humilde.

   (C) saca fotos de árboles y arbustos.

   (D) es muy hablador.

53. En su trabajo Don José

   (A) ha viajado a muchos países extranjeros.

   (B) ha viajado solamente a las ciudades grandes de México.

(C) ha llegado a ser perito en el arte moderno.

(D) se ha quedado siempre en su pueblo en Querétaro.

54. A Don José le encanta

(A) la naturaleza.

(B) la escultura del arte moderno.

(C) cuidar los animales de la hacienda.

(D) el ajetreo de la vida urbana.

55. ¿Qué es lo que hace insólito el trabajo de José Suárez?

(A) Sólo planta árboles y arbustos.

(B) Convierte los árboles y arbustos en obras de arte.

(C) Tiene que hacer su trabajo a un ritmo acelerado.

(D) Hace una clara distinción entre el arte y la vida cotidiana.

56. ¿Qué es lo más difícil para Don José?

(A) Meditar por muchas horas en la naturaleza

(B) Caminar todo el día en la hacienda

(C) Acostumbrarse al ritmo febril de la ciudad moderna

(D) Descubrir la forma ideal para cada árbol y arbusto

Passage Number 5

La delegación argentina que viajará a Atenas para los Juegos Olímpicos ha incorporado a una nueva integrante, Jimena Florit, quien representará al país en una modalidad del ciclismo: el mountain bike. La argentina, que
Linea reside en los Estados Unidos y ganó el oro en los Juegos Panamericanos de
(5) 2003, recibió una invitación especial.

Florit vive en la ciudad estadounidense de San Diego y corre para el equipo RLX Polo Sport de ese país. Hasta ayer pensaba que no podría competir en los Juegos Olímpicos ya que el año pasado, luego de contraer un virus estomacal en los Panamericanos de Santo Domingo que la
(10) mantuvo dos meses fuera de competencia, terminó en el 32º puesto del ranking de la Unión Ciclista Internacional (UCI) y sólo había pasaje hasta el 30º lugar. "Fue entonces cuando Gabriel Curuchet (presidente de la Unión Ciclista de la República Argentina) me dijo que pediría un wild card (invitación especial) y envió una carta a la UCI junto al coronel Rodríguez
(15) (presidente del Comité Olímpico Argentino (COA)", explicó Florit.

"Florit consiguió la invitación a Atenas gracias a sus antecedentes", indicó Oscar Santos, dirigente del COA. Y no fue para menos. La argentina consiguió la medalla de oro en los Panamericanos, se coronó en el Campeonato de los Estados Unidos en 2002 y 2003 y terminó sexta en dos
(20) oportunidades en la Copa del Mundo de 2002.

"Hoy tuve la buena noticia de que voy a los Juegos", comentó Florit, que tuvo la oportunidad de representar a Estados Unidos en Atenas —y recibiendo la tan ansiada nacionalidad estadounidense—, pero la rechazó: "Cuando fui a Santo Domingo y me puse la celeste y blanca, los colores de
(25) Argentina, me olvidé de todo y pensé: 'Correré siempre por Argentina.'"

[*Adapted from*: *Clarín, 21 julio de 2004, "Una ilusión para Florit," Buenos Aires, Argentina.*]

57. ¿De qué nacionalidad es Jimena Florit?

   (A) Es estadounidense.

   (B) Es dominicana.

   (C) Es griega.

   (D) Es argentina.

58. Según el pasaje, ¿en qué país trabaja Florit ahora?

   (A) La Argentina.

(B) Los Estados Unidos.

(C) Grecia.

(D) La República Dominicana.

59. ¿Por qué pensaba Florit que no podría competir en los Juegos Olímpicos?

(A) Porque es una ciudadana de los Estados Unidos.

(B) Porque no consiguió el puesto mínimo en la Unión Ciclista Internacional.

(C) Porque sufrió de un virus estomacal.

(D) Porque el Comité Olímpico Argentino no la permitió.

60. ¿Qué podría indicar el uso del inglés en este pasaje?

(A) Se trata de un deporte que empezó en un país que habla inglés.

(B) El autor no sabe español.

(C) El pasaje aparece en el Internet.

(D) Al autor no le gusta el español.

61. ¿En qué competencia no ha participado Florit?

(A) Los Panamericanos.

(B) La Copa del Mundo.

(C) Los Juegos Olímpicos.

(D) El campeonato de los Estados Unidos.

62. ¿Qué indica el uso de la frase "la tan ansiada nacionalidad estadounidense" en el último párrafo?

(A) El autor es estadounidense.

(B) Al autor le chocan los estadounidenses.

(C) Mucha gente espera tener la ciudadanía estadounidense.

(D) El autor cree que Jimena Florit debe recibir la ciudadanía estadounidense.

Passage Number 6

Aquella tarde, cuando tintinearon las campanillas de los teletipos y fue repartida la noticia como un milagro, los hombres de todas las latitudes se confundieron en un solo grito de triunfo. Tal como había sido

Linea predicho doscientos años antes, finalmente el hombre había conquistado la
(5)   inmortalidad en 2168.

Todos los altavoces del mundo, todos los transmisores de imágenes, todos los boletines destacaron esta gran revolución biológica. También yo me alegré, naturalmente, en un primer instante.

¡Cuánto habíamos esperado este día!

(10)   Una sola inyección, de cien centímetros cúbicos, era todo lo que hacía falta para no morir jamás. Una sola inyección, aplicada cada cien años, garantizaba que ningún cuerpo humano se descompondría nunca.

Hasta que vino la segunda noticia, complementaria de la primera. La inyección sólo surtiría efecto entre los menores de veinte años. Ningún ser

(15)   humano que hubiera traspasado la edad de crecimiento podría detener su descomposición interna a tiempo. Sólo los jóvenes serían inmortales.

Todos los muchachos sobrevivirían para siempre. Serían inmortales y de hecho animales de otra especie. Ya no seres humanos, su sicología, su visión, su perspectiva, eran radicalmente diferentes a las nuestras. Todos

(20)   serían inmortales. Dueños del universo para siempre. Libres. Fecundos. Dioses.

Nosotros, no. Nosotros, los hombres y las mujeres de más de veinte años, éramos la última generación mortal. Éramos la despedida, el adiós, el pañuelo de huesos y sangre que ondeaba, por última vez, sobre la faz de la

(25)   tierra.

Desde ese día éramos otra cosa, una cosa repulsiva y enferma, ilógica y monstruosa. Estos jóvenes derramarían lágrimas, ocultando su desprecio, mezclándolo con su alegría. Con esa alegría ingenua con la cual expresaban su certeza de que ahora, ahora sí, todo tendría que ir bien.

(30)   ¡Ahora cuánto nos costaría dejar la tierra! ¡Cómo nos iría carcomiendo una dolorosa envidia! ¡Cuántas ganas de asesinar nos llenaría el alma, desde hoy y hasta el día de nuestra muerte!

Hasta ayer. Cuando el primer chico de quince años, con su inyección en el organismo, decidió suicidarse. Cuando llegó esa noticia, nosotros,

(35)   los mortales, comenzamos recientemente a amar y a comprender a los inmortales.

[*Adapted from: "Nosotros, no," by José Bernardo Adolph, in"*Abriendo Paso: Lectura, *(2000: Heinle & Heinle Publishers, Boston, Massachussets), pp. 34-35.*]

63. ¿Cuál fue la noticia milagrosa del año 2168?

    (A) Los hombres del mundo se confundieron.

    (B) Los teletipos hicieron mucho ruido.

    (C) Inventaron transmisores de imágenes.

    (D) La gente del mundo nunca morirá.

64. ¿Cómo reaccionó el narrador a la noticia al principio?

    (A) Se desesperó.

    (B) Se alegró.

    (C) Se confundió.

    (D) Se puso enfermo.

65. ¿Quiénes recibieron la inyección?

    (A) Los menores de veinte años.

    (B) Los seres humanos enfermos.

    (C) Los mayores de veinte años.

    (D) Las jóvenes de quince años.

66. ¿Con qué están comparados los inmortales por el narrador?

    (A) Con huesos y sangre.

    (B) Con los abuelos.

    (C) Con los animales.

    (D) Con Dioses.

67. ¿Cómo veían los jóvenes a sus padres?

    (A) Los veían como monstruos.

    (B) Los veían con envidia.

    (C) Los veían como ancianos.

    (D) Los veían como titanes.

68. ¿Cómo cambió la perspectiva del narrador hacia el final?

    (A) En vez de tener celos, tiene miedo.

    (B) En vez de confundirse, se pone enojado.

    (C) En vez de sentirse marginado, entiende a los inmortales.

    (D) En vez de estar alegre, está decepcionado.

STOP.
This is the end of Section I. If you finish before the first hour and 30 minutes are up, you may check your work on this section only.

SECTION II
Total Time—Approximately 1 hour and 40 minutes

Part A—Free Response (Writing)
Time—Approximately 80 minutes

INSTRUCCIONES: Hay varios espacios en blanco en el párrafo siguiente. A la derecha del párrafo, después de cada número hay un espacio en blanco y una palabra entre paréntesis. Primero lee el párrafo, entonces en la línea que sigue cada número, escribe la forma apropiada de la palabra entre paréntesis que complete la oración de una manera correcta y lógica. Para recibir todo el crédito posible, se debe deletrear todas las palabras correctamente y tener los acentos apropiados. Sólo se puede usar UNA palabra en cualquier espacio, y en unos casos, la palabra entre paréntesis NO cambiará de la forma original.

DIRECTIONS: There are several numbered blanks in the following passage. To the right of the passage, each number is followed by a blank and a word in parenthesis. Read the entire passage first, then on the line following each number, write the form that the word in parenthesis should take to make the sentence logical and grammatically correct. To receive full credit, all words must be spelled correctly and have the appropriate accents. Only ONE word may be inserted in any given spot, and in some cases, the word in parenthesis will not change from the suggested form.

(Approximate time—7 minutes)

Hace dos meses, Antonio y su esposa Carmen recibieron las noticias de que tenían que mudarse. La idea les __(1)__ mucho. __(2)__ problemas de encontrar otro apartamento les parecían __(3)__. El __(4)__ apartamento que vieron era pequeño y no muy limpio. Luego, el agente __(5)__ mostró un apartamento encantador pero muy caro. Antonio se __(6)__ cuenta de que no tenían con qué alquilarlo. Los padres de Carmen y __(7)__ de Antonio __(8)__ querían ayudar, pero no podían.

Finalmente, la hermana de Antonio, __(9)__ tenía más recursos, ofreció prestarles el dinero que __(10)__.

1. _____ (fastidiar)
2. _____ (El)
3. _____ (enorme)
4. _____ (primero)
5. _____ (le)
6. _____ (dar)
7. _____ (el)
8. _____ (lo)
9. _____ (el cual)
10. _____ (necesitar)

(Approximate time—10 minutes)

El robo

(11) viernes mucha gente suele ir de compras a la Plaza de la Constitución y ayer no fue nada diferente. Con todas las personas presentes en el lugar, el ladrón se escapó (12) que nadie lo viera.. Huyó pensando en (13) le hubiera gustado pasar más tiempo en aquella (14) llena de mercancía valiosa. Iba a quedarse un rato más (15) sentía los ojos sospechosos de algunos clientes.

(16) salir a la calle, el ladrón no pudo contener su alegría. Dentro de un par de minutos podría encerrarse seguramente en su apartamento (17) poder empezar a contar su botín. Nadie (18) encontraría en ese lugar tan escondido jamás. Distraído con sus pensamientos, el hombre (19) deslizó en la acera y todas las joyas robadas del almacén se cayeron de sus bolsillos. Cuando el policía que (20) estado vigilando un banco cercano se le acercó, el joven delincuente no tuvo otro remedio que rendirse.

11. _____
12. _____
13. _____
14. _____
15. _____
16. _____
17. _____
18. _____
19. _____
20. _____

Informal Writing Task

—Escribe un mensaje electrónico. Imagina que acabas de ganar un premio. Saluda a tu amigo(a) y

- explícale cómo ganaste el premio
- descríbele cómo te sientes ahora
- despídete.

Formal Writing Task

¿Cuál es la importancia de proteger el medio ambiente?

Fuente No. 1

FUENTE: Este artículo apareció en Internet en una página de las Naciones Unidas. (reprinted with permission)

Océanos más limpios: Organización Marítima Internacional (OMI) *Contaminación con hidrocarburos*

La OMI se creó justo antes de la gran expansión del comercio internacional de petróleo. En menos de dos decenios, la flota mundial de buques petroleros decuplicó su tonelaje y los barcos aumentaron su tamaño en igual proporción. Una de las consecuencias de esto fue un alarmante incremento de la contaminación de los mares, en especial la contaminación con hidrocarburos. Tal contaminación no sólo fue causada por accidentes de los buques petroleros sino también como resultado de las operaciones de rutina, como la limpieza de los tanques de estos buques. Desde su creación, la OMI ha estado a la vanguardia de la lucha contra la contaminación, y como resultado de varias convenciones internacionales que promovió, ha disminuido el número de derrames accidentales de petróleo. Más recientemente, ha comenzado a estudiar con mayor atención la contaminación causada por operaciones terrestres y no marítimas. En un informe publicado recientemente por las Naciones Unidas se sugirió, por ejemplo, que los aceites lubricantes son una fuente importante de contaminación marítima, tal que el agua de sentina que contiene restos de aceite del cárter de los motores. Una de las tareas más importantes realizadas por la OMI es el establecimiento de normas que se incorporaron más tarde a convenciones internacionales. Los derrames de hidrocarburos aumentaron con el auge del comercio internacional del petróleo, pero disminuyeron tras la firma de una serie de convenciones internacionales, gracias a la labor desarrollada por la OMI.

Fuente No. 2

FUENTE: Este artículo apareció en el Internet en el sitio de las Naciones Unidas. (reprinted with permission)

Hay que salvar al mundo del mañana

Nuestro medio ambiente es frágil y necesita cuidado. El problema estriba en que hay más de 5.000 millones de personas en nuestro planeta y todas necesitan vivienda, combustible, alimentos, ropa y agua. El medio ambiente puede darles todo lo que necesitan, pero tenemos que cuidarlo.

Algunos países toman del medio ambiente más de lo que les corresponde. Su población quiere tener automóviles, alimentos bien envasados, casas grandes, toda clase de materias primas y otros muchos alicientes. Afortunadamente, si en el mundo hay unos 200 países, los países que quieren todos esos alicientes no pasan de 50.

El medio ambiente sufre incluso en los países más pobres, porque la gente lo utiliza sencillamente para seguir viviendo. Cortan los árboles para hacer leña y cultivan el suelo muy intensamente. Sus gobiernos procuran obtener dinero para poder construir escuelas y hospitales, pero a menudo no pueden hacerlo sin dejar que las industrias contaminen el agua y la atmósfera. Cuesta dinero mantener un medio ambiente limpio. El uso excesivo de recursos aumenta la contaminación.

$$\boxed{\text{Fuente No. 3}}$$

(Listen to the audio recording on the accompanying CD—CD #2, Audio Track 1.)

FUENTE: Este informe, basado en el artículo "El problema del agua" por José Galindo Gómez, apareció en el Internet en febrero de 2000.

PART B—Free Response (Speaking)

Informal Speaking

Read the following outline of the conversation.

A. (La conversación) [You will hear the situation you are asked to imagine on the recording.
   Escucharás la situación que te piden imaginar en la grabación.]

B. (La conversación) [The darkened lines represent what Fernando will say. Las líneas en gris representan lo que Fernando te dice.]

Te saluda y te hace una pregunta.

Tú — Salúdalo y responde a la pregunta.

Continúa la conversación.

Tú — Reacciona a la situación.
      Pídele más información.

Continúa la conversación.

Tú — Reacciona y justifica tu reacción.

Continúa la conversación.

Tú — Reacciona.

Continúa la conversación.

Tú — Reacciona.

Continúa la conversación.

Tú — Responde a la pregunta y despídete.

(On the accompanying CD #2, play Audio Track 2. Record your answers on your recording device in the time allowed.)

Formal Oral Presentation

INSTRUCCIONES: La siguiente pregunta se basa en el artículo impreso y una grabación. Primero, tendrás 5 minutos para leer el artículo impreso. Después escucharás una grabación; debes tomar apuntes mientras escuches. Entonces, tendrás 2 minutos para preparar tu respuesta y 2 minutos para grabar tu respuesta.

DIRECTIONS: The following question is based on the accompanying printed article and audio recording. First, you will have 5 minutes to read the printed article. Afterward, you will hear the audio recording; you should take notes while you listen. Then, you will have 2 minutes to plan your answer and 2 minutes to record your answer.

Imagina que tienes que dar una presentación formal ante una clase de español sobre el siguiente tema:

El artículo que vas a leer es sobre la ciudad de San Pedro, la Argentina; el informe que vas a escuchar habla sobre la Costa Norte de la República Dominicana. En una presentación formal, compara su atracción turística.

Fuente No. 1

FUENTE: Este artículo "San Pedro, una tradición argentina" por Graciela Mabel Fernández, apareció en el periódico *Diario Las Américas el 9 de septiembre de 2006.*

San Pedro, una tradición argentina

Dicen los sampedrinos, que no hay pueblo que los iguale. También afirman que el mejor río es el Paraná. Cuentan que la luna y el sol en ningún lado se disfrutan como allí. Aseguran que Dios creó el Cielo y la Tierra, pero en ese momento pensó que San Pedro sería el mejor lugar para desarrollar los cítricos, que el mundo entero puede saborear.

No es que sean fanáticos de su tierra, sino que la riqueza de ésta merece el respeto.

Se encuentra a 184 kilómetros de la ciudad de Buenos Aires, directo por la Panamericana, en el kilómetro 154, se dobla a la derecha y allí comienza a divisarse el arte de la siembra y la cosecha, la elección de las semillas y el trabajo incansable de los entendidos.

Con toda la abundancia natural y el esfuerzo humano se convirtió en la mayor productora de frutas, como cítricos, duraznos, ciruelas, kiwis y también hortalizas y miel.

PESCA Y FRUTALES

Los cargueros con toneladas de cereales y oleaginosas que recorrerán los lugares más remotos del mundo, parten orgullosos de su trabajo diario.

Pero la tierra no es la única abundancia, el río Paraná y la laguna San Pedro, tienen lo suyo y la pesca y los deportes náuticos lo convirtieron en el centro de la escena.

Todo el año se puede sacar mojarrita y patí bagre. Según la temporada también se pueden pescar armados, bogas, madubás, bagre de las piedras, surubí dorado, tarucha, pejerrey, anchoas y Carpas.

Para los más fanáticos se organiza pesca embarcada, con guías que conocen los lugares donde se obtienen las mejores piezas.

A sus atractivos naturales se suman, los recorridos más comunes. Desde el bulevar Almirante Brown, allí están los cuatro miradores sobre las barrancas brindando una vista panorámica hacia el río. A pocos metros se encuentra el Vía Crucis.

La iglesia Nuestra Señora del Socorro, reconocida como una de las más bellas arquitecturas de Buenos Aires, fue construida en 1860 y finalizaron su obra doce años después. El nombre se debe a la imagen de Nuestra Señora, cedida por los frailes franciscanos, con el compromiso que sería la patrona del pueblo.

Frente a ella está la plaza Provincia de Constitución, junto a un extremo de la plaza, una de las casas más antiguas de esta localidad construida en 1830, actualmente funciona un negocio de muebles antiguos y también una pulpería donde se puede tomar mate con tortas fritas o comer una picada con vino.

Por ser una zona con mucho campo, es posible realizar cabalgatas, visitas a galpones de empaque, viveros, donde se venden todo tipo de árboles, pero los mejores son los frutales de la zona. Mucha gente viaja exclusivamente para comprarlos.

Otro producto tradicional es el mimbre, gran cantidad de negocios ofrecen sus artesanías elaboradas por los nativos.

La variedad gastronómica con sus productos típicos permite conocer la cultura de un país, sumamente generoso con la naturaleza y a la hora del té, la famosa ensaimada de San Pedro.

El aburrimiento no tiene espacio, hay atractivos para todas las edades, se puede elegir entre paracaidismo en el Aero club, cabalgatas y todo tipo de deportes náuticos.

A orillas del río y de la laguna hay variedad de camping con todos los servicios. También se encuentra una gran oferta de hotelería y cabañas para alquilar, por día o por semana.

Fuente No. 2

(Listen to the audio recording on the accompanying CD—CD #2, Audio Track 3.)

FUENTE: Este informe, basado en el artículo "Costa Norte, el interminable paraíso dominicano" por Jesús Hernández, apareció en el periódico *Diario Las Américas el 23 de septiembre de 2006.*

PRACTICE EXAM 2

AP Spanish Language

Answer Key

Section I

Part A

1. (C)	9. (D)	17. (C)	25. (D)
2. (C)	10. (B)	18. (C)	26. (A)
3. (D)	11. (D)	19. (A)	27. (A)
4. (B)	12. (C)	20. (A)	28. (C)
5. (C)	13. (C)	21. (B)	29. (A)
6. (C)	14. (A)	22. (A)	30. (A)
7. (D)	15. (C)	23. (A)	
8. (C)	16. (B)	24. (B)	

Part B

31. (C)	41. (A)	51. (D)	61. (C)
32. (D)	42. (D)	52. (B)	62. (C)
33. (C)	43. (A)	53. (D)	63. (D)
34. (B)	44. (B)	54. (A)	64. (B)
35. (D)	45. (C)	55. (B)	65. (A)
36. (A)	46. (B)	56. (D)	66. (D)
37. (D)	47. (A)	57. (D)	67. (A)
38. (B)	48. (C)	58. (B)	68. (C)
39. (A)	49. (B)	59. (B)	
40. (B)	50. (B)	60. (A)	

Section II

Part A

1. fastidiaba
2. Los
3. enormes
4. primer
5. les
6. dio
7. los
8. los
9. la cual
10. necesitaban

11. Los
12. sin/para
13. cuánto/cómo
14. tienda
15. pero
16. al
17. para
18. lo/le
19. se
20. había

Note: Please see "Detailed Explanations of Answers" for examples of responses to the essay and Part B.

PRACTICE EXAM 2

AP Spanish Language

Detailed Explanations of Answers

Section I

Part A

1.   **(C)**   The correct answer is (C), *Porque había cambiado de número telefónico*. (A), *Porque se había olvidado de llamarlo*, is not true because she says she wanted to talk to him. (B), *Porque la amiga no quería hablar con él*, is not true. And (D), *Porque no tenía teléfono*, is false, too. She had a phone, but the wrong phone number.

2.   **(C)**   The correct answer is (C), *Que se ha casado*. That is what Luis means when he explains he has changed his life-style. (A), *Que se fue de vacaciones*, (B), *Que hizo un crucero*, and (D), *Que está en Wellington*, are news, but not the most important, so they would not be the appropriate answers to the question.

3.   **(D)**   The correct answer is (D), *Que irá a visitar a su amiga a Nueva Zelandia*. She insinuates she already has a place to stay in New Zealand, now that her friend is living there. All the other options are incorrect. She never says she will get married, go to the Baltic Sea or take a cruise.

4.   **(B)**   The correct answer is (B), *No sabe cómo eliminar al ratón que hay en su apartamento*. (A), *Quiere comprar un ratón para su apartamento*, and (C), *No tiene nada que hacer*, are false, because she has something to do: get rid of a mouse in her apartment. And (D), *No quiere matar al ratón de su apartamento*, is false, according to the dialogue. She wants to get rid of it, even if she has to kill it.

5.   **(C)**   The correct answer is (C), *Porque no se cree capaz de usarla*. (A), *Porque prefiere usar papel encolado*, is the option her friend suggests

later, but she's not going to use it. (B) is false. She never mentions any objection about the cheese she'd have to use in this kind of trap. (D) is incorrect, too. She doesn't say she doesn't know where to get this kind of trap, so this is not the reason she doesn't want to use it.

6.   **(C)**   The correct answer is (C). The inconvenience of the glue paper is, according to the woman, (C), *Que hay que eliminar al ratón posteriormente*. (A), *Que atrapa al ratón*, is true but it is not the inconvenience the woman explains to her friend, so it is not the appropriate answer. (D), *Que hay que utilizar una escoba*, is only partially correct, as one of the possibilities the man suggests to kill the mouse once it has been trapped. (B), *Que el ratón se muere*, is false, because the dialog establishes clearly that the mouse would get trapped, but would not die.

7.   **(D)**   The only possible answer is (D), *Un exterminador.* All the other options are false. (A), *La mujer*, is not correct because she would find someone to kill it for her. (C), *Nadie*, is incorrect because from the context of the dialogue we know someone is going to kill the mouse for sure. Finally, (B), *El hombre*, is not correct either because he only suggested how the woman could get rid of it.

8.   **(C)**   The correct answer is (C), *Ni el horno ni los pilotos funcionan bien*. Options (A) and (B) are only partially correct, because the most accurate answer is the combination of both of them. (D), *Tiene un escape de gas*, is the real problem, but at the time she noticed her stove was broken, she did not know it.

9.   **(D)**   The correct answer is (D), *Esa mañana*. (A) is not true. (B) is false too because, even though the woman says she noticed her oven was broken a long time ago, the technician was not notified until that morning. (C) is obviously wrong, too, because if he goes to the apartment, he already knows there is something to fix.

10.   **(B)**   The correct answer is (B), *Viejo y con un agujero*. Choices (A) and (D) are true, but they would be only partial answers because the exact one is the combination of both of them. Finally, (C) is totally false. The man never says it's blocked.

11.   **(D)**   The correct answer is (D), *Porque hay un escape de gas*. Option (A) is false. They never say that dirt causes the problem. (B), *Porque están llenos de agujeros*, is not true. There is only one little hole and the reason is the gas that escapes through it, not the hole itself. (C), *Porque son viejos*, is only the reason behind the correct answer.

12. **(C)** The solution is (C), *Cambiar de cocina*. All the other answers are false. Changing the pilots would not be enough, and cleaning the oven or the pilots wouldn't solve the problem either.

13. **(C)** The correct answer is (C), *Junto a las costas africanas*. (A), *En las costas de la Península Ibérica*, and (B), *En el desierto del Sáhara*, are wrong. (D), *Muy lejos de España*, is not correct, either, because the narrator explains that the Canary Islands are part of Spain.

14. **(A)** The guanches were tall, blonde and with blue or green eyes, so the correct answer is (A). (B) and (D) are exactly the opposite image of the guanches, according to the narrator. (C), *De características físicas similares a las de pueblos cercanos*, is wrong, too, because it is said in the text that no other people nearby looked like them.

15. **(C)** The explanation is (C), *Que son descendientes de los habitantes de la Atlántida*. The rest of the options are false, according to the narrator. (A) is false because the Canary Islands are near the Sahara desert, but the guanches didn't come from there. (B) is false, too, because the Canary Islands are far from the Iberian Peninsula and the guanches didn't come from there either. And (D) is incorrect too because the Canary Islands are near the African coast, but the narrator doesn't mention that the guanches are descended from African tribes.

16. **(B)** The correct answer is (B), *Que son los picos que sobresalen de la Atlántida que se hundió en el mar*. (A), *Que son un pico que el agua nunca llegó a cubrir*, is partially true, but it's not as complete as (B). (C), *Que son un archipiélago español*, is true, but it is not the correct answer to this specific question. Finally, (D), *Que son un archipiélago del Sáhara*, is false.

17. **(C)** The correct answer is (C), *Aproximadamente, como Texas*. The other options are incorrect, according to the narrative.

18. **(C)** The correct answer is (C), *Porque los otros idiomas que se hablan en España también son "españoles."* (A), *Porque se habla en Latinoamérica*, (B), *Porque está muy extendido*, and (D), *Porque se habla en toda España*, are true, but not the answer to the question asked.

19. **(A)** The only possible answer is (A), *Castellano*. (B), *Catalán*, is only spoken in Catalonia. (C), *Vasco*, is only spoken in the Basque Country. And (D), *Gallego*, is only spoken in Galicia.

20. **(A)** The main topic of this narrative is (A), *Los distintos idiomas que hay en España*. (B), *La diferencia entre castellano y español*, is only one of the explanations given in the main topic, as is (D), *El catalán, el gallego y el vasco*. Finally, (C), *El desarrollo histórico de España*, is mentioned briefly in the introduction to the main topic, but it is not the main topic.

21. **(B)** The correct answer is (B), *El ingenioso hidalgo Don Quijote de la Mancha*. The other options are also works by Cervantes, but none of them have the importance of "El Quijote."

22. **(A)** The correct answer is (A), *Soldado*. (B), *Poeta*, is not adequate because he began to write when he was a mature man. (C), *Recaudador de impuestos*, is not appropriate either because it was his occupation after his youth. Finally, (D), *Prisionero*, is incorrect, because it is not an occupation, but a situation.

23. **(A)** The most famous Cervantes play is (A) *Entremeses*. (C), *Los baños de Argel,* is another play by him, but not the most important. Options (B), *Novelas Ejemplares*, and (D), *Viaje al Parnaso*, are incorrect, because they are not plays, but novels and a poem.

24. **(B)** The correct answer is (B), *Se adapta a las reglas de Lope de Vega, pero conservando un tono personal*. (A) is not the most appropriate choice, because it is not as complete as (B). (C) and (D) are incorrect because they are characteristics of the plays of his first period.

25. **(D)** The correct answer is (D), *Empezó a escribir tarde pero alcanzó fama con "El Quijote."* (A) would not be the most correct answer because he was a popular dramatist, but he was more famous for his novels. Options (B) and (C) are false according to the text.

26. **(A)** The correct answer is (A), *Siete siglos*. All the other options are incorrect.

27. **(A)** The capital was (A), *Córdoba*. (B), *Granada,* was one of the Taifas, (C), *Toledo,* was an important industrial city, and (D), *Almería,* was the main harbor, but none of them are correct.

28. **(C)** The correct answer is (C), *Innovaciones en las técnicas agrícolas*. They extended the harvest of olive (A) and fruit trees (B), so they are not correct choices for this question. Option (D), *El sistema de regadío*, is

incorrect too because the system already existed and the Muslims only perfected it.

29. **(A)** The correct answer is (A), *El mercado o zoco*. Option (B), *Los puertos*, is the center for the international trade, so it is not the appropriate answer. (C), *Las calzadas romanas*, are the roads they used to go from one village to another, but no business was done there. Option (D), *Las comunidades judías*, is false. They were only part of the traders.

30. **(A)** The appropriate answer is (A), *Moneda musulmana*. (B), *El dirhem*, is only one of the two Islamic coins used. (C), *Oro*, and (D), *Plata*, are the metals the coins were made of, but they are not as correct as (A).

Part B

31. **(C)** "His uncle fell ill" is the best answer to the question. Although another priest "de una población cercana" (from a nearby town) is mentioned, it is in reference to Juan's decision to look for him, which makes (A) incorrect. (B) is not a good choice since the "Virgen" did appear "por el otro camino" (on the other road). (D) is not correct. Juan did not fear that his uncle would die if he went to Tepeyac since the "Virgen" indicated that "no iba a morir" (he was not going to die) before sending Juan to Tepeyac.

32. **(D)** "For having resembled the Mexican Indian women" is the best choice. The text reads "porque apareció en forma de una campesina indígena" (because she appeared in the form of an Indian country woman). (A) is not correct since she only appeared before Juan. (B) is not a good choice since she communicated in náhuatl. While she may have dressed as an Indian woman, the text states more specifically that she appeared in the form of an Indian woman, which makes (C) incorrect.

33. **(C)** "Juan Diego saw an apparition of the Mother of God" is the best answer to the question. In the first paragraph of the passage we are told: *Encima del cerro la Virgen María se le apareció y le habló en náhuatl.* (A) is not a good choice, because Juan picked the roses the third time he saw the Virgin, on December 12. Choice (B) is incorrect, since we are told that a sanctuary was built after December 12 when the Bishop saw the miraculous image on Juan's cloak. For the same reason (D) is not correct, since the Bishop saw the miraculous image of the Virgin on December 12, not the 9th.

34. **(B)** is correct. The details given in the first four paragraphs of the passage indicate that Juan Diego went to speak with the Bishop three times. This information makes all the other choices incorrect: (A) "seven times," (C) "twice," and (D) "four times."

35. **(D)** is the best answer, because the passage tells us "...*le comunicó el mensaje al Obispo, quien parecía no creer*" (...he communicated the message to the Bishop, who seemed not to believe). On Juan Diego's second visit, the Bishop also asked him to bring some kind of proof of the apparition. (A) is not the best answer, because the Bishop did, in fact, listen to Juan Diego's story. (B) is not correct; nothing in the information given

in the passage indicates that the Bishop "listened to him, but did not understand anything." (C) is not a good choice, given the Bishop's initial reaction ("he seemed not to believe"), and the fact that he later required Juan Diego to bring evidence to prove his account.

36. **(A)** "Roses blooming out of season" is the best answer to the question: "What did Juan Diego find on Tepeyac, that finally convinced the Bishop?" When Juan Diego told the Virgin that the Bishop wanted proof of the apparition, she told him to come back the next day, and she would give him evidence that would convince the Bishop. When Juan returned, "he saw that the barren hilltop was covered with Castilian roses, blooming out of season" (...*vio que la cima del cerro estéril estaba cubierta de rosas castellanas, florecidas fuera de temporada*). It is true that the image of the Virgin that miraculously appeared on Juan Diego's cloak also has a hand in convincing the Bishop, but Juan Diego did not actually "find" that on Tepeyac. (B) is not the best choice, since we are told that a basilica was eventually built there, not that Juan Diego found it "miraculously constructed" there. (C) is not a good choice; the passage indicates that Juan Diego's uncle was dying (*agónico*), but nothing is ever said about Juan Diego finding "a remedy that cured his uncle" on Tepeyac. (D) is incorrect. No information is given that would indicate that Juan found "a new clock made of an unknown cloth" on Tepeyac.

37. **(D)** is the best answer; the passage indicates that "the Bishop knelt down, amazed...the image of the Virgin, just as she had appeared on Tepeyac was engraved on his (Juan Diego's) cloak" (*El Obispo se arrodilló, maravillado,...la imagen de la Virgen, tal como la había visto en Tepeyac quedaba grabada en su capa*). (A) is not a good choice, since nothing in the passage supports the idea that the Bishop knelt before Juan Diego because "he wanted to show him the respect that he deserved." (B) is not the best choice; Juan Diego had only been to see the Bishop three times, so it is unlikely that the Bishop "was overwhelmed by Juan Diego's insistence." (C) is incorrect; the passage tells us that the Bishop fell to his knees because he was amazed at the proof that Juan Diego had brought: Castilian roses blooming out of season, and the miraculous image of the Virgin on Juan Diego's cloak. Nothing in the text indicates that he knelt down because "he wanted to get a closer look at the roses."

38. **(B)** is the correct answer. The passage indicates that after the Bishop saw the proof "a sanctuary was built immediately on Tepeyac" (*Un santuario fue construido de inmediato en Tepeyac*). (A) is not correct, since nothing is ever said about a mansion being built for Juan Diego. (C) is not

a good choice, because no information is given concerning "a country house for the Bishop." (D) is not the best choice; the text makes no reference to a store called La Morenita.

39. **(A)** is the best answer, since the Bishop required Juan Diego to bring proof that would back up his story of the apparition of the Virgin on Tepeyac. (B) is not correct, because no indication is given that the Bishop demanded that Juan Diego "go away and never come back." (C) is not a good choice, because we are told nothing about the Bishop requiring Juan Diego to give him a new cloak. (D) is incorrect; nothing in the passage suggests that the Bishop required Juan Diego "not to speak to him in náhuatl."

40. **(B)** is the correct answer. The story is told in the first person, and we do not know the narrator's name until his uncle addresses him in the fifth paragraph. (A) is not a good choice, since the passage indicates that Blas de Santillana is the narrator's father. (C) is not correct, because we are told that Gil Pérez is the narrator's uncle. (D) is incorrect; Dr. Godínez was Gil Blas's school teacher in Oviedo.

41. **(A)** is the best answer. The second paragraph of the passage tells us that Gil Blas's uncle, Gil Pérez, taught him how to read. (B) is not a good choice, since according to the text, Gil Blas already knew how to read when he went to Dr. Godínez's school. (C) is incorrect, because although the passage indicates that he is setting off for the University of Salamanca, it also tells us that his uncle taught him to read when he was very young. (D) is not the best choice; it was his uncle, not his parents, who taught him to read.

42. **(D)** is correct. According to the story, Gil Blas was leaving Oviedo to go to the University of Salamanca. (A) is not a good choice; Gil Blas could not leave Oviedo to go live with his uncle, because his uncle lived in Oviedo. (B) is incorrect, because Gil Blas was leaving Oviedo to go study at the University of Salamanca, not because he was planning to return to his hometown (Santillana). (C) is not correct, since Gil Blas was not leaving Oviedo because his parents threw him out of the house.

43. **(A)** is the best answer; it was his uncle, Gil Pérez, who told Gil Blas that he was sending him to the University of Salamanca, because he was intelligent, and could become an important man. (B) is not the best answer, because the passage says nothing of Dr. Godínez suggesting that Gil Blas go to the university. (C) is not a good choice, since the text indicates that it

was Gil Pérez's idea for his nephew to go to the university. (D) is not correct; we are told that Gil Blas liked the idea, but it originally came from his uncle, Gil Pérez.

44. **(B)** is the best answer; the narrator tells us that when he went to say goodbye to his parents, all they were able to give him were a hug and a lot of advice. (A) is not a good choice, since it was his uncle who gave him a mule and some money for the trip. (C) is not correct, since the passage never mentions anyone giving him "a black horse and a sword." (D) is incorrect, because nothing is ever said about "a new suit and several books."

45. **(C)** is the best answer. The narrator tells us that his uncle could not have proposed anything more to his liking, because he was anxious to see the world. (*Mi tío no podía proponerme cosa más de mi gusto, porque yo tenía ganas de ver el mundo.*) (A) The statement "he did not like it at all" is not a good choice, because the text indicates that Gil Blas liked the idea of going to the University of Salamanca. (B) "He got angry" does not correctly describe Gil Blas's reaction to the idea of going to Salamanca. (D) is not a good choice. Although Gil Blas "put on a sad face" when he was setting out on his trip, he did not "start to cry."

46. **(B)** is the correct answer. The narrative indicates that Lazarillo's father died in war. (A) is not a good choice, since, according to the passage, Tomé González was not poisoned by his wife. (C) is not the best choice, because, although we are told that Tomé González was put in jail, he did not die there. (D) is incorrect; the passage says nothing about Lazarillo's father drowning in the Tormes River.

47. **(A)** is the best choice, since the text states clearly that she "was earning so little that she decided to get married again" (...*ganaba tan poco que decidió casarse otra vez*). This makes all the other choices incorrect; (B) "because she was madly in love," (C) "because she was still very young and beautiful," and (D) "because Lazarillo was giving her a lot of problems."

48. **(C)** is the best response, because the passage indicates that after Lazarillo's father died, Antoña married Zaydé, which would make him Lazarillo's stepfather (*padrastro*). (A) is not the best choice; Lazarillo's father is identified as Tomé González, not Zaydé. (B) is not a good choice, because the name of the blind man who was passing through Salamanca is

not given in the story. (D) is not correct, since the text makes no reference to "Antoña's brother."

49. **(B)** is the best answer; the passage indicates that she consented to the blind man's request that Lazarillo go with him to be his guide. (A) is not correct; although Antoña was working at the inn (*mesón*), no indication is given that Lazarillo worked there also. (C) is not a good response, because there is no reference to Antoña enlisting Lazarillo in the army. (D) is not correct; no mention is made of Lazarillo's mother getting him a "job at the university."

50. **(B)** is the best answer. One of the things the narrator mentions in describing the state of the country at the time of Lazarillo's birth is that "Spain was the most powerful nation in the world" (...*España...era la nación más poderosa del mundo*). (A) is not a good choice; the passage tells us that Lazarillo was born "shortly after the discovery of America" (*El héroe de estas aventuras nació...un poco después del descubrimiento de América*), so the statement that when Lazarillo was born the New World had not been discovered yet is incorrect. (C) is not correct, since there is nothing in the story that would indicate that Lazarillo's parents "had a lot of money" when he was born. (D) is not the best choice; Lazarillo's father was killed in war, but since that happened when Lazarillo was very young, the statement that when Lazarillo was born his father had already died in war cannot be correct.

51. **(D)** is the best response. The passage tells us that Zaydé lost all of his money, abandoned his family, and never returned. (A) cannot be correct; according to the story, Tomé González (Lazarillo's father) was already dead when Antoña had to work as a maid, so it would be impossible for him to force her to do it. (B) is not a good choice, because we are told that Zaydé earned a lot of money. (C) is not correct, since there is nothing in the text that would indicate that "Lazarillo spent all the money."

52. **(B)** is the best answer. The description of him in the passage indicates that he is a "humble gardener." (A) is not correct, since there is nothing that would suggest that he is a "wealthy landowner from Querétaro"; on the contrary, he is described as "the authentic Mexican peasant" (*el auténtico campesino mexicano*). (C) is not a good choice; we are told that he sculpts trees and bushes into different shapes, but no mention is made of him taking pictures of them. (D) cannot be right, since the description of

Don José in the passage says that he is a man of few words (*de pocas palabras*).

53. **(D)** is the best answer. The passage indicates that Don José has never left his town in the state of Querétaro. This makes (A) and (B) incorrect, because he has neither (A) "travelled to many foreign countries," nor (B) "travelled only to large cities in Mexico." (C) is not a good choice; we are told that he is "not acquainted with the tendencies of modern art" (*no conoce las tendencias del arte moderno*), so it is not logical that he would be an expert (*perito*) in it.

54. **(A)** is the best answer. The article indicates that Don José has "one passion, nature" (*...tiene una pasión, la naturaleza...*). (B) is not a good choice, because we are told that Don José is "not acquainted with the tendencies of modern art" (*no conoce las tendencias del arte moderno*). (C) is incorrect, because the passage does not mention Don José in the context of taking care of the farm animals. (D) is not the best choice. We are told that "he is never in a hurry, since he doesn't live at the pace of the city" (*No tiene prisa nunca, pues no vive al ritmo de la ciudad*), which makes it unlikely that he would love "the hustle and bustle of urban life."

55. **(B)** is the best answer. What makes José Suárez's work unusual is that "he converts trees and bushes into works of art." (A) is not the best choice; he does not "only plant trees and bushes," but also takes care of the gardens on the hacienda. (C) is not a good choice; the passage tells us that "he is never in a hurry," (*No tiene prisa nunca*), so the statement that "he has to do his work at an accelerated pace" cannot be correct. (D) The passage reveals that Don José has understood that "one cannot make a distinction between art and daily life" (*no se puede hacer una distinción entre el arte y la vida de todos los días*), so the assertion that what makes his work unusual is that "he makes a clear distinction between art and daily life" cannot be correct.

56. **(D)** is the best of these choices. The passage tells us that "the hardest thing for him is finding the form that corresponds to the character and structure of each tree or bush" (*Lo más difícil para él es encontrar la forma que corresponde al carácter y estructura de cada árbol o arbusto.*). (A) is not correct, because the text makes no mention of it being difficult for Don José "to meditate on nature for many hours." (B) is not a good choice; the passage tells us that Don José is young for his almost 70 years, and it does not make reference to him having difficulty walking. (C) We are told that

Don José has never left his town in Querétaro, does not live at the rapid pace of the city, and is never in a hurry. In light of this, he would have no need "to get used to the feverish pace of the city."

57. **(D)** The correct answer is (D). Her nationality is mentioned in the first paragraph.

58. **(B)** Answer choice (B) is correct. In the second paragraph the author tells us that she races for the RLX Polo Sport team of the United States.

59. **(B)** The correct answer is (B). In paragraph two the author says that she earned a ranking of 32, when the minimum ranking in order to be invited to the Olympics was 30.

60. **(A)** The words in English in this passage most logically indicate that mountain biking was started in an English-speaking country. The correct answer is A.

61. **(C)** is the best answer. The other mountain bike races were mentioned in the third paragraph.

62. **(C)** The correct answer is (C). The author indicates that U.S. citizenship is highly sought after. The author gives no indication of choice (A), (B), or (D).

63. **(D)** Answer choice (D) is correct. The first paragraph explains that man had conquered immortality. The other items are mentioned, but are not the miraculous news itself.

64. **(B)** The correct answer is (B). In paragraph two, the author says he was happy. The other reactions were not those of the narrator.

65. **(A)** In paragraph five, it is stated that the injection will only take effect on those younger than 20 years old. Therefore (A) is the correct choice.

66. **(D)** is the correct answer. In paragraph six, the narrator compares the young immortals to the gods. The other choices are mentioned in relation to the older people only.

67. **(A)** The correct answer is (A). In paragraph eight, the narrator explains that the younger people thought of the older people as monsters.

Choices (B) and (D) are incorrect, because the young immortals did not see their parents with envy, nor as titans. Choice (C) seems plausible, but was not mentioned in the text.

68. **(C)**   The correct answer is (C). In the last paragraph the narrator explains that instead of feeling marginalized, he sympathized and understood the immortals' situation. Choices (A), (B) and (D) are incorrect because he was not afraid, angry, or disappointed in the end.

Section II

Part A

1. **(fastidiaba)**
    The verb "fastidiar" conjugates like the verb "gustar." It is in the imperfect here because of the ongoing nature of the feeling.

2. **(Los)**
    The noun "problemas" is masculine (like many nouns ending in -ma).

3. **(enormes)**
    The adjective agrees in number with the noun "problemas," not with the noun "apartamento."

4. **(primer)**
    The adjective "primero" shortens to "primer" before masculine singular nouns.

5. **(les)**
    The indirect object pronoun "les" is used because the agent showed them both the apartment.

6. **(dio)**
    The expression used here is "darse cuenta" (to realize). The verb "dar" is formed irregularly in the preterite.

7. **(los)**
    Instead of repeating the phrase "los padres," the definite article is used here.

8. **(los)**
    The direct object pronoun "los" refers to Antonio and Carmen.

9. **(la cual)**
    The relative pronoun here refers to Antonio's sister, and thus the feminine singular form is used.

10. **(necesitaban)**
    The imperfect is used here because of the ongoing nature of their need for money.

11. **(Los)**
   With days of the week, the definite article is needed. Because this sentence describes repetition, the plural form is needed.

12. **(sin/para)**
   The preposition used with "que" introduces the subjunctive form.

13. **(cuánto/cómo)**
   The interrogative here is used as an exclamation.

14. **(tienda)**
   The reference to merchandise refers to a store, and it agrees in number and gender with the noun and adjective used in the sentence.

15. **(pero)**
   The conjunction connects the two dependent clauses.

16. **(al)**
   Used with the infinitive, this contraction means "when."

17. **(para)**
   Used in this context, the word means "in order to."

18. **(lo/le)**
   Referring to the thief, the direct object pronoun in the used, though some speakers, when describing a singular masculine object, will use the indirect object pronoun.

19. **(se)**
   The reflexive pronoun agrees in number and subject with the verb used.

20. **(había)**
   The imperfect of "haber" is used to express the pluperfect, describing a past action.

SAMPLE INFORMAL WRITING SCORING HIGH

Querido Juan,

¡Acabo de ganar el premio del concurso estatal de ciencias! Mi equipo escolar fue al concurso ayer y ganó fácilmente contra los primeros dos equipos. Por fin nosotros ganamos contra el mejor equipo que ha ganado este torneo los últimos cinco años. Los miembros de mi equipo empataron al otro equipo cuando la pregunta final se hizo. Yo contesté la pregunta muy rápido y resultó que mi equipo ganó por unos dos puntos. ¡Qué alegre me sentí!

Espero que estés pasándolo bien este año.

Tu amigo,
Samuel

*With a good variety of vocabulary and verb tenses, this message clearly details the events leading up to the award. Very few errors (la **última** pregunta) are present to interfere.*

SAMPLE INFORMAL WRITING SCORING MID-RANGE

Querido Pepe,

Soy el ganador de un carro nuevo! Entré un concurso en una programa de televisión donde hacer cosas peligrosos como escalar montañas, comer insectos y nadar para largas distancias. Yo gané el concurso y recibé un carro para mí premio.

Ahora siento fabuloso y sé que tengo buena suerte. Mandame una carta cuando recibes éste. Te llevaré en mi carro algún día. ¡Adiós!

Bricio

*There is a good variety of vocabulary, but the gender agreement issues (**un** program, cosas **peligrosas**) and improper verb forms (donde **hacen**, y **recibí**) cause the letter to lose flow. It has some redeeming qualities (Te llevaré) but not enough to be considered in the higher category.*

SAMPLE INFORMAL WRITING SCORING LOW

Querida María,

¡Hola! ¿Que pasa? Esta fin de semana yo recibé un premio para montar los caballos. El premio es un medal brillante con caballo plato saltar. Después de gané el premio mi padres me tomaron a la cena elegante. Porque yo gané este premio, me siento como una persona especial. Todos mis amigos venieron a la ceremonia.

¿Cómo es su natación? Digame cuando te tienes una competición y yo lo asistiré. Yo te necisito más porque te echo de menos. Escribeme.

Yolanda

The majority of the verbs in this message are improperly formed (yo **recibí**, *Después de* **ganar**, *mis amigos* **vinieron**). *Several accents are missing (***Qué, Escríbeme***) and there are a few examples of the interference of English (un medal instead of* **una medalla**, *competición instead of* **competencia**, *tomaron instead of* **llevaron**, *Cómo es instead of Cómo* **está**). *The description of the medal is unclear and even confusing, making this message weak.*

SAMPLE FORMAL WRITING SCORING HIGH

El medio ambiente se considera una de los recursos más importantes de nuestras vidas, y por eso es loco que no hagamos nada cuando se contaminan los ríos, océanos y la terra de nuestro planeta. El medio ambiente, especialmente el agua, es algo en que necesitamos enfocarnos.

Cada día, según la Fuente 1, el medio ambiente se contamina con hidrocarburos, petróleo y aceites lubricantes. Dice que esto es un problema que no solo viene de accidentes pero es algo que podemos cambiar. También en la Fuente 3 hay algunas ideas que pueden ayudar a proteger el medio ambiente como no derrochar agua.

Lo que necesitamos entender es que si no protegemos el medio ambiente ahora, no habrá un medio ambiente limpio para la próxima generación. La Fuente 2 reconoce que cuesta mucho dinero mantener el medio ambiente y que sin la industria que aumenta la destrucción, muchos países no tendrían dinero. Pero también menciona que el medio ambiente nos da todo lo que necesitamos. Por eso, creo que no hay una mejor razón para protegerlo.

Lo difícil hacer es cambiar nuestra dependencia en la industria que crea contaminación del aire y del agua. Las fuentes dicen que esta vida que vivimos destruye el medio ambiente y nosotros y las compañías crean mucha de la contaminación del mundo. Será difícil cambiar, pero también será necesario. Según la Fuente 3, los ríos famosos como el Nilo y el Amazonas son contaminados. Si esto no despierta a la gente, no sé cómo.

El punto es que nosotros hemos creado la destrucción y ahora necesitamos repararla. Creo que es sumamente importante preservar el medio ambiente porque es tan frágil. Pero primero, antes de poder repararlo, nos toca hacer dos cosas. Necesitamos entender qué causa la contaminación para evitar eso. Segundo, necesitamos terminar nuestras costumbres destructivas. Si sólo hacemos esto, podemos comenzar de nuevo.

Content: This sample addresses the question well and supports the central theme with evidence from the three sources. There is a good introduction and conclusion with organized paragraphs.

Grammar: There are a few errors (**uno** de los recursos, no **sólo**, nosotros y las compañías **creamos**), but there is no pattern to them. The controlled use of various verb tenses shows advanced ability.

Vocabulary: This is a solid example of how to write with a wide variety of expressions (nos toca, de nuevo, lo difícil) and verbs without much repetition.

SAMPLE FORMAL WRITING SCORING MID-RANGE

Es muy importante proteger el medio ambiente en que nosotros vivimos porque todas las cosas que tenemos son de la naturaleza. Si no protegimos al medio ambiente, todas las cosas que usamos cada día morirá. Tres ejemplos de la contaminacion del mundo son el expansión del comercio de petróleo, la contaminacion de los ríos, y la infrastructura que destruye el mundo.

El expansión del comercio internacional de petróleo es muy importante para la economía de muchos de los países del mundo ahora. En los Estados Unidos, el petróleo es muy importante cada día par vivir, pero tambien es muy mal cuando los barcos contaminan los mares. La industria tiene cosas malas y cosas buenas. En la fuente uno, el autor describe que tal contaminación no sólo fue causada por accidentes de los busques pero son las operaciones de rutina que son peores. Es muy importante respetar nuestro medio ambiente porque es nuestra vida.

Más de la mitad de los rios grandes del mundo se contaminan. Ríos como el Nilo y el Congo en Africa se contaminan porque los seres humanos no protegen a su medio ambiente cada día. Estos rios son importantes porque los necesitamos para actividades normales como cepillando los dientes y para bebiendo. Es una necesidad para vida en el mundo y nosotros no la protegemos. En esta manera, es importante para cada persona que proteger el medio ambiente.

Hay varios otros ejemplos de la destruccion del medio ambiente en el mundo como la infrastructura que estamos construyendo en las ciudades. Toda la gente necesita realizar las malas cosas que destruyen al mundo cada día. Este es nuestro mundo y necesitamos protegerlo para vivir. Si no limpiamos los ríos, los mares, y protegemos a los especies, el mundo se morirá.

Content: In relatively well-organized paragraphs, the student addresses the question and works to support his ideas.

Grammar: Gender agreement is generally correct throughout this sample with only a few errors (**la** expansión, **las** especies). On occasion, accents are used correctly but not consistently (**destrucción**, **ríos**, **contaminación**). Subject/verb agreement is appropriate, but there are a few other verb errors (**protegemos,** para **beber**). There are a few errors (no sólo . . . **sino . . .**), but they are not serious.

Vocabulary: Some misspelled words (**buques, infraestructura**) and a false cognate (**darse cuenta**) are among the few mistakes here.

SAMPLE FORMAL WRITING SCORING LOW

El medio ambiente es una cosa lo que necisitamos proteger. Se incluye cosas como, los ríos, y simplemente es todo del mundo. Ahora, todo del mundo está contaminando al medio ambiente porque no piensan de los resultados de nuestros acciones. La necesidad en nuestras vidas especialmente con petróleo, es lo que resultan en la contaminación.

El petróleo es algo muy importante en la vida hoy. Lo necesitamos por coches y electricidad; y es importante pero es algo que causa muchas problemas con contaminación. Recibimos el petróleo en un barco, y de vez en cuando, puede ser un accidente, como dice Fuente 1. El petróleo en el agua se causa la contaminación con hidrocarburos. No solo es accidentes que se causan el contaminación, tambien son las cosas de toda el día. Los acietes lubricantes y la limpieza de los tanques de los busques que contienen el petróleo. Tambien el uso de aerosoles contamina no el agua pero el aire.

Hay dos grupos que contamina y los dos son diferentes. En los países ricos, personas destruye el medio ambiente porque quieren el coche mejor, la casa grande, y todas de las cosas materialistas; tambien no preservan a su agua. Ese destrucción no es necesario. En los países pobres, las personas destruyen al medio ambiente porque necesitan vivir. Ellos cortan arboles para crear leña para cocinar y mantener calor.

En conclusión, la contaminación y la destrucción del medio es una problema lo que necesitamos parar. Va a costar dinero para hacer y entonces mantener un medio ambiente limpio. Algunas personas hacen lo que necesitan hacer para vivir pero hay otros que pueden reducir su contaminación. Por fin, es bastante importante preservar el medio ambiente porque tenemos suerte para tener un mundo tan buena; y necesitamos preservar donde vivimos.

Content: This essay really does not address the question of why it is important to protect the environment. The student summarizes the causes of destruction without explaining what should be done to prevent such things.

Grammar: There is little and inconsistent accentuation of words, and the gender agreement fails repeatedly (**nuestras** acciones, **esa** destrucción). There is confusion between the use of "que" and "lo que" (una cosa **que** necesitamos proteger), and subject/verb agreement is often incorrect (se **incluyen** cosas, todo **el** mundo . . . no **piensa**). Many other grammatical errors make this essay weak.

Vocabulary: There is much repetition in this sample with the majority of the strong vocabulary coming straight from the sources.

Part B—Speaking

SAMPLE INFORMAL SPEAKING SCORING HIGH

—No, no lo he oído todavía. Estaba en mi casa y oía bien gritando en la calle pero yo no sabía quién era. ¿Tú sabes qué pasó ayer?

—Oh, fue Margarita. No sabía eso. Margarita es muy inteligente. ¿Qué será, qué era sus noticias? Tal vez consiguió algún premio . . . Yo no sé.

—Eso es una cosa muy buena para ella. Ella es muy inteligente y ella tiene que hacer eso aunque la universidad es muy lejos de aquí. Tiene que hacerlo, tiene que asistir allí.

—Sí, ella con una beca no tiene que pagar nada y no tenía mucho dinero y ahora puede asistir a la universidad de sus sueños que ella siempre ha querido ir.

—Tal vez, pero no creo que sí porque es una universidad muy buena y ella tiene que tomar esa oportunidad de ir de la casa y ellos pueden visitar el uno al otro en las vacaciones . . .

—Creo que voy a pasar por su casa a verla porque ésas son unas noticias muy grandes para ella y su familia. Le voy a decir que estoy muy entusiasmado con ella y darle buena suerte para su año próximo.

*While this is not free of errors (¿**Cuáles eran** sus noticias?, **está** muy lejos), it flows very naturally and shows great ease of expression The vocabulary and control of grammatical structures is excellent.*

SAMPLE INFORMAL SPEAKING SCORING MID-RANGE

—Sí, fue muy interesante. El presidente ganó la elección . . . y . . . el equipo de fútbol ha ganado también, ¿verdad?

—¿Qué? Ella es un poco loco porque vuelve a la casa de sus padres . . .

—¡Qué bueno! Pienso que ella va a . . . a hacer muy bien en la universidad esto otoño.

—Sí, es muy bueno que la universidad pagará por su educación y sus padres no deben ser preocupados por las finanzas.

—Sí, es un decisión muy complicada pero si la universidad va a pagar por su educación debe ir a esta universidad porque . . .

—Pienso que voy a pasar por su casa a verla porque no he ver ella por muchos meses y quiero ver ella.

*The vocabulary used here is rather standard. There are several grammatical errors of noun/adjective agreement (**loca, este** otoño, **una** decisión) as well as errors in pronoun use (**la** he **visto,** quiero ver**la**). There is a missed subjunctive formation (la universidad **pague**). The variety of verb tenses strengthens this sample, but the many other errors do not.*

SAMPLE INFORMAL SPEAKING SCORING LOW

—Sí, oigo las noticias de ayer y no estoy de acuerdo de . . .

—Sí eran las siete y pico cuando Margarita llegó a casa. Quiero ser gritando locamente a mi mamá y papá de esta manera.

—Um, . . . no me comprende una beca que pagará todos los gastos. Quiero comprender.

—Sí, creo . . . estoy de acuerdo con tú. Sus padres se han preocupados y quiero que no sean preocupado.

—Sí, será una decisión muy complicado. No quiero hacer una decisión como éste y es una decisión muy importante.

—Voy a paso por su casa a ver ella. No quiero llamar a Margarita ahora porque sus padres son muy preocupados y no quiero . . .

*A few of these prompts were not properly understood. This student seems to believe that the girl was yelling at her parents. There are frequent grammatical errors of all types (no **comprendo**, **contigo**, se han **preocupado**, **estén preocupados,** ver**la**) that make this difficult to follow. The vocabulary is repetitive and very simple as well.*

SAMPLE FORMAL ORAL PRESENTATION SCORING HIGH

Viajar a la Costa Norte es un viaje muy diferente que viajar a San Pedro en la Argentina. La Costa Norte es para el turista moderno pero ir a San Pedro es hacer un viaje con lo básico y natural.

San Pedro es reconocida por su abundancia natural y esfuerzo humano y tiene sus frutas tropicales que hace el orgullo de la gente sampedrina. En la tierra de San Pedro se cultiva la fruta y los cereales pero el mar también ofrece recursos naturales de comida. El río Paraná y la laguna hay lugares en que florecen y crecen otra fruta, la fruta del mar como los peces.

La Costa Norte es un lugar turístico y moderno con playas bellas y una extensa ribera. Hay pueblos y una exuberante flora y muchos sitios para visitar. La zona costera de Montecristi tiene playas escondidas y un parque nacional, tres importantes ríos y si buscas la naturaleza es el lugar para ti. También hay campos de golf y un centro comercial en Puerto Plata.

En mi opinión ir a la Costa Norte es mejor que . . . .

Content: There is a good introduction to this sample, and it appears that only the time limit interferes with the quantity. This description has many good ideas that are clearly expressed.

Grammar: Virtually free of errors (**florece y crece** otra fruta, **son** el orgullo), this is an excellent sample. The gender agreement is correctly used throughout.

Vocabulary: There are many advanced vocabulary items correctly used in the context.

SAMPLE FORMAL ORAL PRESENTATION SCORING MID-RANGE

Me gusta mucho más Montecristi que la Argentina y San Pedro porque Montecristi tiene muchos más aspectos turísticos como la playa que es virgen de descubrir y son escondidas y eso es importante porque no hay tantas personas y es mucho más fácil disfrutar en la playa cuando uno está solo.

En San Pedro, es más como un oasis para las personas que quieren comer porque no hay sólo pescados sino cosas como frutas también incluyendo duraznos, ciruelas, kiwis y otras comidas como la miel y hortalizas y el pescado es muy importante aquí como otros pescados.

Por eso después de surtarme en Montecristi cuando quiero comer, creo que en San Pedro voy a disfrutarme con mi familia y comer frutas increíbles y frescas y después podré ir a pescar con mi familia porque hay guías que pueden ayudarme a saber dónde hay los lugares mejores para pescar y eso es . . .

Content: There is a good amount of material with a considerable variety. Each location is described and evaluated clearly.

Grammar: The present tense is used well here, but there is only one other example of another verb tense (podré). The agreement of nouns and adjectives is correctly used.

Vocabulary: Several fruits are named, and there are a few good verbs used (disfrutar, pescar), but the vocabulary is not remarkable.

SAMPLE FORMAL ORAL PRESENTATION SCORING LOW

Los artículos en el subjeto del turismo la República Dominicana en específico la Costa Norte. Los artículos tiene información con frutales, actividades, la tierra, los ríos, y animales y otros cosas. Quiero visitar San Pedro y Costa Norte. Los dos ciudades tienen mucho para ofrecer a un visitante. Los ríos y todas las frutas en San Pedro van a ser muy divertidos ver y comer. Puedo nadar en los dos lugares y ir a la playa. Me parezco que la Costa Norte es más interesante para las personas activas que prefieres estar en el aire libre.

San Pedro es el nombre que el primero artículo y pesca frutales y los hombres naturales a la costa come mate y la economía de el es en turismo porque los hombres venden cosas a los turismo. En el artículo dos, exprese actividades si el campo de golf y la cultura y música que experiencia cuando estás allí.

Content: This very simple rewording of the information does not clearly synthesize the material.

Grammar: There are several errors throughout this sample of gender agreement (**otras** cosas), subject and verb agreement (artículos **tienen,** hombres . . . **tienen**), and use of prepositions (**en** la costa), as well as many others errors.

Vocabulary: There is interference from English (the word "subjeto" instead of "tema") and generally basic vocabulary. There are few vocabulary resources used to finish the description.

PRACTICE EXAM 3

AP Spanish Language

AP Spanish Language
Practice Exam 3

1. Ⓐ Ⓑ Ⓒ Ⓓ
2. Ⓐ Ⓑ Ⓒ Ⓓ
3. Ⓐ Ⓑ Ⓒ Ⓓ
4. Ⓐ Ⓑ Ⓒ Ⓓ
5. Ⓐ Ⓑ Ⓒ Ⓓ
6. Ⓐ Ⓑ Ⓒ Ⓓ
7. Ⓐ Ⓑ Ⓒ Ⓓ
8. Ⓐ Ⓑ Ⓒ Ⓓ
9. Ⓐ Ⓑ Ⓒ Ⓓ
10. Ⓐ Ⓑ Ⓒ Ⓓ
11. Ⓐ Ⓑ Ⓒ Ⓓ
12. Ⓐ Ⓑ Ⓒ Ⓓ
13. Ⓐ Ⓑ Ⓒ Ⓓ
14. Ⓐ Ⓑ Ⓒ Ⓓ
15. Ⓐ Ⓑ Ⓒ Ⓓ
16. Ⓐ Ⓑ Ⓒ Ⓓ
17. Ⓐ Ⓑ Ⓒ Ⓓ
18. Ⓐ Ⓑ Ⓒ Ⓓ
19. Ⓐ Ⓑ Ⓒ Ⓓ
20. Ⓐ Ⓑ Ⓒ Ⓓ
21. Ⓐ Ⓑ Ⓒ Ⓓ
22. Ⓐ Ⓑ Ⓒ Ⓓ
23. Ⓐ Ⓑ Ⓒ Ⓓ

24. Ⓐ Ⓑ Ⓒ Ⓓ
25. Ⓐ Ⓑ Ⓒ Ⓓ
26. Ⓐ Ⓑ Ⓒ Ⓓ
27. Ⓐ Ⓑ Ⓒ Ⓓ
28. Ⓐ Ⓑ Ⓒ Ⓓ
29. Ⓐ Ⓑ Ⓒ Ⓓ
30. Ⓐ Ⓑ Ⓒ Ⓓ
31. Ⓐ Ⓑ Ⓒ Ⓓ
32. Ⓐ Ⓑ Ⓒ Ⓓ
33. Ⓐ Ⓑ Ⓒ Ⓓ
34. Ⓐ Ⓑ Ⓒ Ⓓ
35. Ⓐ Ⓑ Ⓒ Ⓓ
36. Ⓐ Ⓑ Ⓒ Ⓓ
37. Ⓐ Ⓑ Ⓒ Ⓓ
38. Ⓐ Ⓑ Ⓒ Ⓓ
39. Ⓐ Ⓑ Ⓒ Ⓓ
40. Ⓐ Ⓑ Ⓒ Ⓓ
41. Ⓐ Ⓑ Ⓒ Ⓓ
42. Ⓐ Ⓑ Ⓒ Ⓓ
43. Ⓐ Ⓑ Ⓒ Ⓓ
44. Ⓐ Ⓑ Ⓒ Ⓓ
45. Ⓐ Ⓑ Ⓒ Ⓓ
46. Ⓐ Ⓑ Ⓒ Ⓓ

47. Ⓐ Ⓑ Ⓒ Ⓓ
48. Ⓐ Ⓑ Ⓒ Ⓓ
49. Ⓐ Ⓑ Ⓒ Ⓓ
50. Ⓐ Ⓑ Ⓒ Ⓓ
51. Ⓐ Ⓑ Ⓒ Ⓓ
52. Ⓐ Ⓑ Ⓒ Ⓓ
53. Ⓐ Ⓑ Ⓒ Ⓓ
54. Ⓐ Ⓑ Ⓒ Ⓓ
55. Ⓐ Ⓑ Ⓒ Ⓓ
56. Ⓐ Ⓑ Ⓒ Ⓓ
57. Ⓐ Ⓑ Ⓒ Ⓓ
58. Ⓐ Ⓑ Ⓒ Ⓓ
59. Ⓐ Ⓑ Ⓒ Ⓓ
60. Ⓐ Ⓑ Ⓒ Ⓓ
61. Ⓐ Ⓑ Ⓒ Ⓓ
62. Ⓐ Ⓑ Ⓒ Ⓓ
63. Ⓐ Ⓑ Ⓒ Ⓓ
64. Ⓐ Ⓑ Ⓒ Ⓓ
65. Ⓐ Ⓑ Ⓒ Ⓓ
66. Ⓐ Ⓑ Ⓒ Ⓓ
67. Ⓐ Ⓑ Ⓒ Ⓓ
68. Ⓐ Ⓑ Ⓒ Ⓓ

PRACTICE EXAM 3

AP Spanish Language

Total Test Time—2 hours and 50 minutes

SECTION I: Multiple Choice (Listening)

Time—1 hour and 30 minutes

Part A

(Approximate time—30 minutes)

(Listen to the audio recording on the accompanying CD—CD #2, Audio Track 4.)

<table>
<tr>
<td>

INSTRUCCIONES: Escucha los diálogos siguientes. Después, escucha las preguntas basadas en los diálogos que acabas de oír, y escoge la mejor respuesta de las que siguen. Llena el óvalo que corresponde en la hoja de respuestas.

</td>
<td>

DIRECTIONS: Listen to the following dialogues. Afterwards, listen to the questions based on the dialogues you have just heard, and choose the best answer from the choices that follow. Color in the corresponding oval on your answer sheet.

</td>
</tr>
</table>

Get ready for the first dialogue.

Dialogue Number 1

1. (A) En una cafetería

    (B) En un restaurante

    (C) En una cocina

    (D) En un bar

2. (A) El rustido de ternera con manzanas

    (B) La ensalada verde

    (C) Las costillas de cordero a la parrilla

    (D) El cochinillo asado

3. (A) Porque no puede comer cerdo

    (B) Porque siempre come ensaladas

    (C) Porque es vegetariano

    (D) Porque no le gusta la ternera

Dialogue Number 2

4. (A) Cambiarlos por otros

    (B) Devolverlos

    (C) Comprarlos

    (D) Regalarlos

5. (A) No son del agrado de la clienta

    (B) No son de la talla de la clienta

    (C) No son del color que la clienta quería

    (D) A la clienta no le gustan demasiado y además le quedan apretados

6. (A) Las etiquetas

    (B) El dinero para pagarlos

    (C) El comprobante de caja

    (D) La bolsa

7. (A) Se lo olvidó en casa

    (B) Se le perdió en el camino

    (C) No le dieron ninguno

    (D) Lo tiró con la bolsa

Dialogue Number 3

8. (A) Porque ha tenido examen

    (B) Porque el examen ha sido un desastre

    (C) Porque no se le da bien la política

    (D) Porque no le gustan las ciencias naturales

9. (A) Más de dos meses

    (B) Dos semanas

    (C) Dos meses

    (D) Dos días

10. (A) Las ciencias naturales

    (B) Por qué no sabía contestar las preguntas con todo lo que había estudiado

    (C) Las preguntas de política

    (D) El examen

11. (A) Entregar el examen en blanco

    (B) Las preguntas de ciencias naturales

    (C) Equivocarse de clase el día del examen

    (D) El examen de política

12. (A) Porque estaba nervioso

    (B) Porque es muy despistado

    (C) Porque es muy despiadado

    (D) Porque estaba preocupado

INSTRUCCIONES: Escucha los narrativos siguientes. Después, escucha las preguntas basadas en los que acabas de oír, y escoge la mejor respuesta de las que siguen. Llena el óvalo que corresponde en la hoja de respuestas.

DIRECTIONS: Listen to the following short narratives. Afterwards, listen to the questions based on the narratives you have just heard, and choose the best answer from the choices that follow. Color in the corresponding oval on your answer sheet.

Get ready for the first narrative.

Narrative Number 1

13. (A) El soccer

    (B) El béisbol

    (C) El fútbol americano

    (D) El baloncesto

14. (A) Una minoría

    (B) Ninguno

    (C) Una elite

    (D) Muchos

15. (A) Como un simple deporte

    (B) Como un espectáculo

    (C) Como el Día de Acción de Gracias

    (D) Como un gran negocio del espectáculo y una arraigada tradición

16. (A) Estar en la NFL

    (B) Jugar en las ligas universitarias

    (C) Participar en una Super Bowl

    (D) Participar en el gran circo

┌─────────────────────────┐
│ Narrative Number 2 │
└─────────────────────────┘

17. (A) Como un laragometraje

    (B) Como una película de ciencia ficción

    (C) Como una película de ciencia

    (D) Como un ejemplo de cine fantástico

18. (A) Cineasta

    (B) Escritor de best-sellers

    (C) Científico

    (D) Profesor

19. (A) Escribiendo novelas

    (B) Creando clónicamente especies extinguidas a partir del ADN

    (C) Rodando películas

    (D) Vendiendo los derechos cinematográficos de sus novelas

20. (A) Sobre dinosauarios

    (B) Sobre ciencia

    (C) Sobre los problemas de la ciencia

    (D) Sobre las películas

INSTRUCCIONES: Escucha las conferencias siguientes. Cada una durará aproximadamente cinco minutos. Es una buena idea tomar apuntes mientras escuchas las conferencias. En el examen habrá espacio para tus apuntes; usa tu propio papel para este examen de práctica. Al terminar cada conferencia, habrá pre-guntas basadas en la que acabas de oír. Escoge la mejor respuesta de las que siguen. Llena el óvalo que corresponde en la hoja de respuestas.

DIRECTIONS: Listen to the follow-ing lectures. Each will be approxi-mately five minutes in length. It would be a good idea to jot down some notes while you are listen-ing to the lectures. On the actual exam you will be provided a space for your notes; please use your own paper for this practice exam. At the end of each lecture, you will be presented with questions based on the lecture you have just heard. Choose the best answer from the choices that follow. Color in the corresponding oval on your answer sheet.

Lecture Number 1

21. ¿Cuál es el tema principal de esta conferencia?

   (A) La arquitectura de Barcelona

   (B) La polémica construcción de la Sagrada Familia

   (C) La arquitectura y la Naturaleza

   (D) Gaudí y su arquitectura

22. ¿Qué sirvió en mayor medida de fuente de inspiración a Gaudí?

   (A) La religión católica

   (B) La Naturaleza

   (C) El arte gótico

   (D) La arquitectura de la Grecia clásica

23. ¿Cuál es la principal característica de la obra de Gaudí?

   (A) La originalidad

   (B) La inspiración

   (C) Las imágenes religiosas

   (D) Las formas

24. ¿Qué edificio se considera la obra cumbre de Gaudí?

    (A) La Sagrada Familia

    (B) La iglesia de la colonia obrera Güell

    (C) La casa Milá

    (D) La Pedrera

25. ¿Cuál es el problema de la construcción de la Sagrada Familia?

    (A) No puede ser acabada.

    (B) Hay una polémica entre los que quieren acabarla y los que no.

    (C) Los bocetos originales se perdieron.

    (D) Hay que acabarla con las nuevas tecnologías.

> Lecture Number 2

26. Según el texto, se puede decir que...

    (A) todo el flamenco es gitano.

    (B) todo el flamenco proviene de la cultura gitana.

    (C) el flamenco tiene raíces de cuántos pueblos han pasado por el sur de España.

    (D) es una mezcla de las nuevas tendencias musicales.

27. ¿Cuál es la principal característica de la etapa del hermetismo?

    (A) El flamenco se mantiene encerrado en círculos familiares gitanos.

    (B) El flamenco se expande por toda Andalucía.

    (C) El flamenco se limita a los escenarios.

    (D) Sólo determinados estilos básicos se cultivan en esa época.

28. ¿Por qué los flamencólogos consideran negativa la "ópera flamenca"?

    (A) Porque se alejó de los cánones puristas

    (B) Por la aparición de figuras carismáticas

    (C) Porque irrumpía en los escenarios teatrales

    (D) Porque su cante estaba lleno de adornos

29. ¿Qué importante hecho tuvo lugar en Granada, en 1922?

    (A) Una reunión de intelectuales

    (B) El Concurso Nacional de Cante Jondo

    (C) Un festival para profesionales

    (D) El nacimiento de un mito del flamenco: Manolo Caracol

30. ¿Qué importancia tiene la guitarra dentro del flamenco?

    (A) Es un elemento imprescindible.

    (B) Es un elemento básico.

    (C) Es simplemente un elemento más.

    (D) Es de menor importancia que el cante y el baile.

STOP.
This is the end of Part A. You may check your answers to the
lecture questions, or you may go on to Part B.

Part B: Multiple Choice (Reading)
(Approximate time—60 minutes)

<table>
<tr>
<td>

INSTRUCCIONES: Lee con cuidado las lecturas siguientes. Después de cada una habrá varias oraciones o preguntas incompletas. Escoge la mejor respuesta basada en la lectura que acabas de leer. Llena el óvalo que corresponde en la hoja de respuestas.

</td>
<td>

DIRECTIONS: Carefully read the following passages for comprehension. After each passage there will be several incomplete statements or questions. Select the completion or answer that is the best, based on the passage you have just read. Color in the corresponding oval on your answer sheet.

</td>
</tr>
</table>

Passage Number 1

Miguel Hidalgo nació el 8 de mayo, 1753. Sus padres eran criollos, o sea, españoles nacidos en México. En 1810, a los 57 años de edad, era párroco en la pequeña población de Dolores, Guanajuato.

Linea
(5) El buen cura se había esmerado en ayudar a sus feligreses a mejorar su condición económica por medio de establecer industrias locales como la vinicultura, apicultura, curtiduría y la producción de seda. Al gobierno real, no le agradó esta iniciativa de parte de los aldeanos. El Virrey, Francisco Xavier de Venegas, mandó soldados para talar las moreras, cuyas hojas se usaban para alimentar los gusanos de seda, y para destruir los viñedos
(10) y las colmenas. Semejante injusticia de parte de los "gachupines," fue el colmo para el Padre Hidalgo. Durante 300 años los indígenas y mestizos habían sufrido bajo el yugo opresivo de los conquistadores primero y los colonizadores después.

Por la madrugada, el 16 de septiembre, 1810, un domingo, el cura
(15) sonó la campana de la iglesia en Dolores. Cuando los fieles acudieron, escucharon al Padre Hidalgo pronunciar el famoso "grito de Dolores," una llamada a la libertad. Incitó a los campesinos a que se rebelaran contra la tiranía de los "gachupines," y a que pusieran fin a su esclavitud.

El Padre se dirigió, con su ejército de campesinos armados con palos
(20) y machetes, a la Ciudad de México. Al principio, tuvieron éxito en sus batallas contra los soldados del Virrey. En Atontonilco Hidalgo se apoderó de una copia de la imagen de la Virgen de Guadalupe, para animar a sus seguidores a luchar por la libertad. Cuando llegó a la Capital, el ejército revolucionario había sufrido miles de bajas; muchos más o quedaban

(25) heridos, o desertaron. Por motivos desconocidos Hidalgo vaciló y no atacó la ciudad.

En la retirada las tropas realistas alcanzaron a las fuerzas de Hidalgo en el Puente de Calderón, cerca de Guadalajara, el 17 de enero, 1811, y los insurgentes sufrieron una derrota definitiva. Hidalgo, Allende y otros

(30) líderes de la rebelión huyeron al norte con la idea de pedirle ayuda al gobierno estadounidense.

Hidalgo, Allende, Aldama y Mariano Jiménez fueron traicionados y los realistas los capturaron cerca de Chihuahua el 21 de marzo, 1811. El tribunal militar los condenó a muerte, y a Hidalgo una corte eclesiástica lo

(35) despojó de su autoridad como cura. El 31 de julio, 1811, Hidalgo repartió dulces al pelotón de fusilamiento, y se le concedieron dos cortesías que a sus colegas no: lo fusilaron en el pecho en vez de la espalda, y le permitieron encararse con la muerte sin atarle las manos ni vendarle. Las cabezas fueron expuestas en las cuatro esquinas de la Alhóndiga de

(40) Granaditos en Guanajuato, cerca de donde apenas 10 meses antes Hidalgo había dado el "grito de Dolores."

31. ¿Por qué no atacó Hidalgo la Capital?

(A) Nadie sabía por qué.

(B) El ejército revolucionario tenía miedo y rehusó hacerlo.

(C) No había nadie con quien luchar en la Capital.

(D) Hidalgo sufrió una herida mortal.

32. ¿Qué importancia tenía para los revolucionarios la copia de la imagen de la Virgen?

(A) Servía para intensificar su fe en Dios.

(B) La Virgen representaba una llamada a la libertad.

(C) El ejército pensaba que con la copia de la imagen nadie moriría en la batalla.

(D) Ella misma había aparecido ante ellos exigiendo que atacaran a los "gachupines."

33. Miguel Hidalgo era

(A) un sacerdote católico.

(B) oficial en el ejército del Virrey.

(C) un campesino analfabeto.

(D) integrante del pelotón de fusilamiento.

34. ¿Qué hizo el Padre Hidalgo el 16 de septiembre, 1810?

(A) Traicionó a sus campatriotas en Chihuahua.

(B) Inició una rebelión en contra del gobierno colonial.

(C) Derrotó el ejército realista en el Puente de Calderón.

(D) Atacó el Palacio del Virrey en la Ciudad de México.

35. ¿Cómo murió Miguel Hidalgo?

(A) Sufrió un derrame cerebral.

(B) Contrajo una pulmonía mortal.

(C) Se suicidó en Chihuahua.

(D) Fue ejecutado.

36. ¿Por qué dio el Padre Hidalgo el "grito de Dolores"?

(A) Porque quería demostrar su apoyo al gobierno del Virrey

(B) Porque estaba enojado con sus feligreses

(C) Porque estaba harto de las injusticias del gobierno colonial

(D) Porque le pegaron un tiro al pecho

37. ¿A quiénes se refiere el término "gachupines"?

(A) A los campesinos que siguieron al Padre Hidalgo

(B) A los que estaban en control del gobierno en aquel entonces

(C) A todos los indígenas y mestizos

(D) A los rebeldes que se murieron en la lucha por la libertad.

38. En el Puente de Calderón

(A) los realistas derrotaron a los rebeldes.

(B) los rebeldes ganaron una victoria definitiva.

(C) el Padre Hidalgo fue asesinado.

(D) el ejército del Virrey fue derrotado.

39. ¿Qué hizo el Padre Hidalgo en Atontonilco?

(A) Repartió dulces al pelotón de fusilamiento.

(B) Prendió fuego a la iglesia.

(C) Renunció su autoridad como cura.

(D) Se apropió de un símbolo religioso.

Passage Number 2

Entre las tradiciones populares del continente americano, la riña de gallos se destaca por su popularidad. Fue importada de la "civilizada" Europa en la época de la conquista española. Es una fiesta popular, considerada por algunos como un deporte, por otros como una ceremonia o ritual, y por muchos como un espectáculo salvaje y sanguinario.

Casi todos los que asisten a estas luchas son hombres de un nivel económico y cultural pobre. Sin embargo, participan también mujeres y miembros de las clases privilegiadas. Tiene lugar en una "gallera," un espacio circular con un suelo blanco de arena fina, rodeado de graderías para los espectadores.

El espectáculo comienza cuando los entrenadores entran en el ruedo llevando sus respectivos animales cubiertos con capas de seda. Cada entrenador amarra el espolón en la pata derecha de su gallo. El espolón es el arma de ataque. Si es muy agudo, se reduce notablemente la duración de la lucha, pero si es menos agudo, se alarga el combate.

En el momento de que los entrenadores llevan sus animales al ruedo, teniéndoles por un cordel, el público puede apreciar de cerca su tamaño y su agresividad.

El juez levanta la campanilla y la mantiene en alto dos o tres minutos, mientras los espectadores hacen las apuestas. Pasado este tiempo se cortan los cordeles de los gallos y la verdadera lucha comienza. En las graderías hay un silencio absoluto cargado de expectación a la vez que los entrenadores estimulan a sus animales por medio de gritos.

Siguen los golpes, los saltos, los movimientos de ataque y defensa que fatigan a los luchadores. Finalmente uno se impone, y consigue herir a su enemigo con el espolón. Si la lucha es a muerte, viene el ataque final y uno de los animales queda sobre la arena manchada de sangre. El entrenador del vencedor se lanza al ruedo y abraza entusiasmado a su gallo, cubriéndolo con el manto de gala entre los aplausos, gritos y risas del público. El perdedor recoge tristemente su gallo muerto o herido, y

Linea / (5) / (10) / (15) / (20) / (25) / (30)

sale perdiéndose entre la confusión. El público abandona las graderías discutiendo animadamente. La trágica fiesta ha terminado; corren el vino y la cerveza, se comentan el espectáculo pasado y se prepara para el próximo.

[Adaptación de un artículo de *Siete Días Ilustrados* (Buenos Aires), by Peter Paz. Taken from *Sol y Sombra*, 3rd ed., Paul Pimsleur, Beverly Pimsleur, Frederick Suárez-Richard (New York: Harcourt Brace Jovanovich, Inc., 1983), pp. 136–138.]

40. En una lucha de gallos, el público es compuesto de

    (A) hombres pobres exclusivamente.

    (B) hombres y mujeres de todos los niveles sociales.

    (C) miembros de las clases privilegiadas solamente.

    (D) los entrenadores y el juez únicamente.

41. ¿De qué sirve el espolón amarrado a la pata derecha del gallo?

    (A) Es para atacar al adversario.

    (B) Es para defenderse de los entrenadores.

    (C) Es para agredir al público.

    (D) Es para complacer al juez.

42. ¿A qué se debe la presencia de la riña de gallos en las Américas?

    (A) Remonta a un rito precolombino de los indígenas americanos.

    (B) Vino de Europa durante la conquista española.

    (C) Originó en el continente africano.

    (D) Fue un invento de los conquistadores.

43. ¿Cuándo finaliza la lucha?

    (A) Cuando el juez se cansa de ver el espectáculo

    (B) Cuando el público guarda silencio

    (C) Cuando los entrenadores gritan animadamente

    (D) Cuando uno de los gallos no puede seguir luchando

44. ¿Qué efecto tiene un espolón poco agudo?

    (A) La pelea dura más tiempo.

    (B) El combate es más corto.

    (C) Los entrenadores gritan menos.

    (D) El público se disgusta.

45. ¿Qué es una gallera?

    (A) Asi un juez que se especializa en las luchas de gallos.

    (B) Asi se le llama al gallo que gana la lucha.

    (C) Es el lugar donde se realiza una lucha de gallos.

    (D) Es un criadero de gallos luchadores.

Passage Number 3

Pablo Benito Juárez figura entre los patriotas más venerados de México. Era zapoteco de pura raza, y luchó por salir de la pobreza en la tierra caliente de Oaxaca. Desempeñó cargos públicos desde Regidor del
Linea Ayuntamiento de Oaxaca hasta Presidente de la República.

(5)   Nació el 21 de marzo, 1806, en San Pablo Guelatao, en el estado de Oaxaca. Cuando tenía tres años fallecieron sus padres, y sus abuelos paternos se encargaron del bienestar de Benito y sus dos hermanas. Después de que se murieron sus abuelos, Benito fue a vivir con su tío, Bernardino Juárez.

(10)   Un día, cuando tenía doce años, cuidaba el rebaño de su tía. Le hicieron pláticas unos muleros que pasaban por allí, pero cuando se fueron, Benito se dio cuenta de que faltaba una de las ovejas. Otro muchacho se acercó y le contó que mientras que los muleros lo distraían, uno de sus compañeros le había robado el animal. En vez de enfrentarse a su tío, Benito huyó a la
(15) ciudad de Oaxaca.

    En Oaxaca trabajó para don Antonio Salanueva, un ecuadernador, quien lo cuidó bien y hasta se hizo su padrino. Allí aprendió muchas cosas, pero sobre todo don Antonio le inculcó la virtud de poner la honradez por encima de todo.

(20)   Benito era bajo, moreno, y muy fuerte físicamente. Era de temperamento reservado e imperturbable. Tuvo éxito en sus estudios y a los veinticinco años se hizo abogado.

(25) En 1843 se casó con Margarita Maza, y en 1844 fue nombrado Secretario de Estado por el Gobernador de Oaxaca. Dentro de pocos meses fue nombrado al Congreso Nacional donde sirvió durante tres años. En 1847 regresó a Oaxaca donde logró, con la ayuda de dos amigos, establecer un nuevo gobierno estatal. Se instaló como Gobernador y el año siguiente fue elegido a un mandato de cuatro años más.

(30) Las reformas sociales en beneficio de los zapotecos fueron el tema central de los cinco años que fue Gobernador de Oaxaca. Abrió cincuenta escuelas nuevas y abogó por la educación de las mujeres. Construyó caminos y abrió un puerto en la costa pacífica que había permanecido cerrado durante casi trescientos años. Logró pagar las deudas del estado y dejó la tesorería estatal en buenas condiciones cuando terminó su mandato.

(35) Jamás se aprovechó del cargo público para sacar beneficio propio.

46. Benito Juárez era hijo de

    (A) padres españoles.

    (B) criollos pobres.

    (C) padres indígenas.

    (D) mestizos adinerados.

47. ¿Qué le pasó a Benito en la infancia?

    (A) Quedó huérfano.

    (B) Se acostumbró a decir mentiras.

    (C) Tuvo que ir a vivir en la Ciudad de México.

    (D) Fue pisoteado por un mulo desbocado.

48. ¿Por qué huyó Benito a Oaxaca?

    (A) Quería de todo corazón conocer la ciudad.

    (B) Quería evitar un enfrentamiento con su tío.

    (C) Se había cansado de vivir en el campo.

    (D) Iba en busca de una oveja que se le perdió.

49. Durante su mandato como Gobernador de Oaxaca, Benito Juárez

    (A) hizo caso omiso de la pobreza de los zapotecos.

    (B) se aprovechó de su cargo público para enriquecerse.

    (C) efectuó muchas reformas sociales para ayudar a su gente.

    (D) aprendió a poner la honestidad por encima de todo.

50. ¿Cómo era Benito?

    (A) Alto, rubio y débil

    (B) Muy tonto, deshonesto y emotivo

    (C) Bastante guapo y poco inteligente

    (D) Bajo, moreno, fuerte y estoico

51. Benito Juárez se negó a

    (A) servir en el Congreso Nacional.

    (B) casarse con Margarita Maza.

    (C) abusar de cargo público para hacerse rico.

    (D) estudiar leyes.

Passage Number 4

Según Jorge Berrueta Vallín, ex director de Tequila Sauza, el segundo productor más grande del país, "El tequila constituye el licor nacional perfecto porque es mestizo, al igual que el pueblo mexicano: en parte indígena y en parte español." Como quiera que sea, el tequila se ha convertido en el símbolo líquido nacional del México actual.

La fama del tequila contradice sus orígenes humildes. Hace ya un milenio, los indígenas mexicanos aprendieron a extraer la savia dulce de las largas y carnosas hojas del agave, una planta espinosa del desierto, y a fermentarla luego para producir una bebida ligeramente alcohólica llamada pulque. Durante el gran imperio azteca, el pulque se usaba únicamente como bebida ritual de los sacerdotes, para mitigar el sufrimiento de los que iban a ser sacrificados a los dioses, como privilegio de los ancianos y como recompensa para los guerreros que habían demostrado su valentía.

Linea

(5)

(10)

(15) A diferencia de los indígenas, los invasores españoles eran grandes bebedores y ansiaban algo más fuerte que el pulque. Habían traído consigo el conocimiento del proceso de destilación que habían adquirido de los moros, y descubrieron que varias especies de la planta de agave producían un licor fuerte y transparente que llegó a conocerse con el nombre de mezcal.

(20) En 1893, un mezcal producido en un pueblo llamado Tequila, en Jalisco, ganó un premio en la Feria Mundial de Chicago con el nombre de "brandy de mezcal"; en 1910, una bebida similar, pero rebautizada como "vino tequila" mereció un trofeo en San Antonio, Texas, y el nombre de "tequila" se quedó.

[Excerpted from: "El tequila, regalo del sol," Selecciones Reader's Digest, February 1995, Vol. CIX, No. 651, pp. 54, 55.]

52. Durante el imperio azteca el pulque era

    (A) una bebida tomada libremente por toda la gente.

    (B) una bebida tomada solamente por ciertas personas.

    (C) más fuerte que el tequila.

    (D) completamente desconocido.

53. ¿Por qué el tequila es el "licor nacional perfecto" de México?

    (A) Porque fue importada de España por los conquistadores

    (B) Porque es mestizo, igual que el pueblo mexicano

    (C) Porque es una bebida muy fuerte

    (D) Porque solamente los mexicanos lo toman

54. ¿De qué se elabora el tequila?

    (A) De jugo de limón y sal

    (B) De jugo de frutas fermentado

    (C) De las flores del agave

    (D) De la savia fermentada del agave

55. Los invasores españoles

    (A) querían una bebida más fuerte que le pulque.

    (B) tomaban mucho menos licor que los aztecas.

    (C) no tomaban licor en absoluto.

    (D) trajeron el tequila de Europa.

56. El tequila y el pulque se diferencian en que

    (A) el pulque contiene mucho más alcohol.

    (B) el pulque carece de contenido alcohólico.

    (C) el tequila es destilado.

    (D) el tequila no es hecho de la planta agave.

Passage Number 5

El té asociado al placer, el té aliado a la salud, el té como tendencia fashion. Lo cierto es que esta infusión—que según la leyenda, nació en el año 2737 A.C—hoy está colonizando Buenos Aires. Catas, demostraciones de cómo se sirve en el Oriente, restaurantes de moda que piden sus propias mezclas a los especialistas y hasta seminarios para conocer sus íntimos secretos son algunas de las expresiones de este boom gourmet. Y como parte de esta movida tetera, también se presenta este mes, y hasta el 4 de agosto, la muestra del Museo Nacional de Arte Decorativo que expone antiguos cofres donde se guardaba el té bajo llave cuando éste era un producto más que de moda, de gran valor económico. Allí, se están dando charlas y ceremonias del té al estilo japonés, indio y marroquí. "Hay muchísimo interés de la gente que participa en las conferencias como, por ejemplo, la que dio Stephen Twining, décima generación de la famosa familia del té, que fue nuestro invitado especial", detalla Marina Christophersen, de la Asociación Amigos del Museo, entidad que organizó la exposición, luego de diez meses de trabajo, para recolectar fondos para mantener al museo en buenas condiciones.

Tomar el té en el hotel Alvear es un clásico del glamour de Buenos Aires desde los años 30 en adelante. Pero, a partir del año pasado, se perfiló una nueva tendencia: se amplió la concurrencia de gente joven. Hoy está de moda que mujeres de 30 y pico festejen sus cumpleaños en medio de la escenografía dorada de la Belle Epoque del hotel. "Es una forma

Linea

(5)

(10)

(15)

(20)

de mimarse: invitar a tus amigas a una salida bien distinta en un marco elegante y con un servicio de guantes blancos—describe Cecilia Nigro, (25) gerente de Relaciones Públicas del Alvear—. Pero no sólo están viniendo más mujeres jóvenes, también se ven a esa hora grupos de hombres, algunos hacen negocios mientras toman el té", dice.

Noemí Zlochisti, una de las dueñas de la tienda de té T & Co confirma que el consumo de té gourmet está de moda entre los jóvenes. "Se ve una corriente de interés por conocer y saber distinguir los distintos tipos. De (30) hecho, nosotros organizamos desde abril cursos intensivos de cata, que tienen mucho éxito."

Más allá de la tradición y de las modas que suelen ser efímeras, el té es, después del agua, la bebida más consumida del planeta. No es poca cosa.

[*Adapted from: Clarín, 27 julio de 2004, "La movida de té," por Dolores Vidal, Buenos Aires, Argentina.*]

57. ¿A quiénes se dirige este pasaje?

(A) A argentinos.

(B) A japoneses.

(C) A chinos.

(D) A indios.

58. Según el pasaje, ¿qué tiene que ver el té con el arte decorativo?

(A) Los antiguos recipientes del té tienen mucha decoración.

(B) La imagen del té aparece en mucha pintura contemporánea.

(C) Hay representaciones del té en las estatuas romanas.

(D) La gente de la clase alta quiere adornar sus casas con teteras.

59. En los años 30, ¿cuál era la tradición en el hotel Alvear?

(A) Organizaban exposiciones del té.

(B) Las mujeres invitaban a sus amigas a una fiesta elegante.

(C) Los hombres de negocio se reunían el tomar el té.

(D) La gente de la clase alta tomaba té.

60. En el contexto del pasaje, ¿a qué se refiere la palabra "cata"?

(A) El método de hacer el té.

(B) La ceremonia asociada con servir el té en el Oriente.

(C) Probar varios tipos del té.

(D) Las tiendas de té.

61. ¿Por qué se puede suponer que el té no va a desaparecer del mundo?

(A) Porque hoy el té es más popular que el agua.

(B) Porque el uso del té empezó hace 3300 años.

(C) Porque el té es la bebida más consumida en el mundo ahora, menos el agua.

(D) Porque hay muchas tiendas de té por todo el mundo.

62. ¿Qué sería el mejor título para este pasaje?

(A) El Museo Nacional de Arte Decorativo abre exposición.

(B) Inscríbanse al curso de té.

(C) Stephen Twining da conferencia del té.

(D) El té es la bebida de moda.

Passage Number 6

El Ballet Folclórico Nacional de México fue fundado en mayo de 1960 por una joven y talentosa bailarina, la maestra Silvia Lozano quien hasta la fecha ha sido su directora y la coreógrafa del mundialmente aclamado
Linea espectáculo.
(5)   A lo largo de sus primeros 44 años de existencia, el Ballet Folclórico Nacional de México ha contado con la colaboración de los más destacados investigadores y especialistas del folclor, la danza, la música y los trajes típicos de las diferentes regiones de la República Mexicana.

La idea de crear una base vino de la necesidad urgente de destinar
(10) los recursos técnicos y económicos para la conservación de este legado cultural mexicano en una cuestión étnica del baile mexicano. La Fundación del Ballet Folclórica Nacional de México para la conservación de la herencia cultural y nacional de los bailes mexicanos tiene como propósito

(15) primordial la investigación de los elementos auténticos de la cultura popular así como también las civilizaciones pre-hispánicas en las etapas diferentes del México Independiente.

En 1977 fue galardonado como la Compañía Oficial del Gobierno de México, representándolo a partir de entonces en su país así como en el extranjero. En su larga trayectoria se ha presentado en más de treinta (20) países de los cinco continentes, recibiendo innumerables premios y reconocimientos, identificándosele como uno de los principales Embajadores de la Cultura Mexicana.

Los bailes regionales de México desde los tiempos pre-hispánicos hasta nuestros días, son una herencia de valor incalculable que puede ser perdida (25) fácilmente por la nación mexicana.

Los métodos que se han seguido para mantener esta herencia cultural viva, se basan en las tradiciones orales que se han pasado desde los tiempos pre-hispánicos. Sin embargo, a causa de la naturaleza de este sistema, hay un riesgo que con el paso del tiempo, esta información y las tradiciones (30) pueden llegar a ser degradadas, modificadas y alteradas.

Las tradiciones que se recuperan, así como también los disfraces, la música y las coreografías que han sido desarrolladas por un grupo muy reducido de mexicanos, están en peligro de desaparecer a causa del proceso cultural, externo y natural que afecta a toda la población: los medios (35) masivos, así como también la globalización, las marcas de referencia a las que todos somos expuestos. Pero quizá el riesgo más grande está dentro de la desaparición física de bailarines, los coreógrafos, los maestros, los músicos y los taquígrafos y la herencia cultural que junto con ellos vive.

[Adapted from: *http://www.ballet-folc-nal.com.mx/espanol.htm*, Fundación Folclórica Nacional de México, 2004]

63. ¿Cuál es el propósito principal de este pasaje?

   (A) Dar la biografía de la bailarina Silvia Lozano.

   (B) Fomentar el interés en asistir a los conciertos del Ballet Folclórico Nacional de México.

   (C) Justificar la necesidad de recaudar fondos para el Ballet Folclórico de México.

   (D) Explicar la historia y la necesidad del Ballet Folclórico de México.

64. Según el pasaje, ¿cuál es el papel de Silvia Lozano con el Ballet Folclórico de México ahora?

    (A) Ella es la directora del Ballet.

    (B) Ella es la bailarina principal del Ballet.

    (C) Ella es la Embajadora de la Cultura Mexicana.

    (D) Ella se ha retirado de bailar.

65. ¿Cómo conserva el Ballet Folclórico de México los elementos auténticos de la cultura popular?

    (A) Encontrar los trajes típicos de varias regiones de México.

    (B) Colaborar con destacados investigadores.

    (C) Presenta el baile en cinco continentes del mundo.

    (D) Destinar recursos técnicos y económicos a la Fundación del Ballet Folclórica.

66. ¿El Ballet Folclórico de México presenta los bailes de que épocas de la historia del país?

    (A) Presenta los bailes del siglo pasado.

    (B) Presenta los bailes de la época después de la independencia de México.

    (C) Presenta los bailes de los tiempos pre-hispánicos hasta hoy.

    (D) Presenta los bailes de los tiempos pre-hispánicos.

67. ¿Por qué dice el autor que "con el paso del tiempo,…las tradiciones pueden llegar a ser degradadas, modificadas y alteradas"?

    (A) Porque tantos mexicanos llevan las tradiciones a países extranjeros.

    (B) Por el método de pasar las tradiciones oralmente.

    (C) Porque no hay suficiente recursos económicos para mantenerlas.

    (D) Porque el Gobierno de México no ha reconocido el Ballet Folclórico de México.

68. ¿Cuál es el proceso cultural que afecta a toda la población y sus bailes regionales?

   (A) La desaparición de los bailarines.

   (B) La falta de recursos técnicos.

   (C) El número reducido de mexicanos que se interesa por el baile.

   (D) Los medios masivos y la globalización.

STOP.
This is the end of Section 1. If you finish before the first hour and 30 minutes are up, you may check your work on this section only.

SECTION II

Total time—Approximately 1 hour and 40 minutes

Part A—Free Response (Writing)

Time—Approximately 80 minutes

INSTRUCCIONES: Hay varios espacios en blanco en el párrafo siguiente. A la derecha del párrafo, después de cada número hay un espacio en blanco y una palabra entre paréntesis. Primero lee el párrafo, entonces en la línea que sigue cada número, escribe la forma apropiada de la palabra entre paréntesis que complete la oración de una manera correcta y lógica. Para recibir todo el crédito posible, se debe deletrear todas las palabras correctamente y tener los acentos apropiados. Sólo se puede usar UNA palabra en cualquier espacio, y en unos casos, la palabra entre paréntesis NO cambiará de la forma original.

DIRECTIONS: There are several numbered blanks in the following passage. To the right of the passage, each number is followed by a blank and a word in parenthesis. Read the entire passage first, then on the line following each number, write the form that the word in parenthesis should take to make the sentence logical and grammatically correct. To receive full credit, all words must be spelled correctly and have the appropriate accents. Only ONE word may be inserted in any given spot, and in some cases, the word in parenthesis will not change from the suggested form.

(Approximate time—7 minutes)

Caminaba por la playa. Hacía __(1)__ calor opresivo y el sol brillaba intensamente. Pensaba en __(2)__ amigas, Sofia y Berta. Habían __(3)__ y yo estaba un poco preocupada de __(4)__. De pronto vi a Sofia __(5)__ en un banco. __(6)__ paré para hablar con ella. Hablamos por unos momentos de __(7)__ cosas. Cuando finalmente mencioné a Berta, Sofia me dijo que nunca __(8)__ verla otra vez. Comoquiera que __(9)__, no __(10)__ podía convencer que era buena idea reconciliarse.

1. _____ (uno)
2. _____ (mi)
3. _____ (discutir)
4. _____ (el)
5. _____ (sentado)
6. _____ (Se)
7. _____ (otro)
8. _____ (querer)
9. _____ (tratar)
10. _____ (lo)

INSTRUCCIONES: Hay varios espacios en blanco en los párrafos a continuación. A la derecha de estos párrafos, después de cada número hay un espacio en blanco. Lee primero cada pasaje luego completa las oraciones de una manera correcta y lógica, escribiendo una palabra lógica y correcta en cada espacio en blanco. Para recibir todo el crédito posible, se debe deletrear todas las palabras correctamente y tener los acentos apropiados. Sólo se puede usar UNA palabra en cualquier espacio.

DIRECTIONS: There are several blanks in the following paragraphs. To the right of the paragraphs, after each number there is a blank space. First read each passage then complete the sentences in a correct and logical way, writing the logical word in the blank. To receive all the possible credit, you should spell all the words correctly and have proper accents. You can only use ONE word in each space.

(Approximate time—10 minutes)

Desde joven, Marta siempre (11) sido una persona diligente y seria. No le interesa depender (12) nadie y sus compañeros de clase la consideran la persona (13) aplicada de la escuela. Sus familiares se preocupan (14) la tremenda cantidad de trabajo que tiene cada noche pero Marta nunca (15) queja. El año (16) espera matricularse en la universidad especializándose en la biología o la química. (17) desea hacerse doctora. Nadie duda del talento que tiene esa muchacha (18) padres también son médicos y muchos aún dicen que ella ya posee (19) madurez como la mayoría de adultos en su comunidad. Ojalá (20) mucho éxito en su futuro.

11. _____

12. _____

13. _____

14. _____

15. _____

16. _____

17. _____

18. _____

19. _____

20. _____

Informal Writing Task

—Escribe un mensaje en tu diario. Imagina que acabas de enterarte de que tu mejor amigo(a) va a mudarse a otro estado. Empieza el mensaje y

- describe qué noticias acabas de oír
- explica tu reacción a las noticias
- despídete.

Formal Writing Task

¿Qué impacto tiene la inmigración para la sociedad?

Fuente No. 1

FUENTE: Este artículo apareció en septiembre de 2006 en la página Web de la Organización de las Naciònes Unidas (la ONU) describiendo la inmigración.

Nuevas tecnologías podrían evitar fuga de cerebros de países en desarrollo, según CEPAL

Las nuevas tecnologías deberían servir para evitar la fuga de cerebros de los países en desarrollo hacia otros lugares, dijo hoy el asesor regional de la Comisión Económica para América Latina y el Caribe (CEPAL), Andrés Solimano.

El economista explicó que ésta es una de las conclusiones del proyecto de investigación "Movilidad Internacional del Talento" realizado por la CEPAL y la Universidad de las Naciones Unidas.

En una conferencia de prensa celebrada en la sede de la ONU antes de participar en un seminario sobre migración y desarrollo, Solimano resaltó que "la tendencia ha variado y ya no se produce un movimiento migratorio masivo de profesionales como ocurría hace 30 años".

"Ahora muchos migrantes son expertos en tecnologías de la información que no necesitan cambiar de residencia, ya que trabajan vía internet desde sus países de origen, aunque lo hagan para empresas extranjeras" apuntó.

El experto dijo que "no se quiere que los migrantes dejen todo en sus países de destino y regresen a los lugares donde nacieron, sino que se reconecten con sus países de origen realizando tareas para universidades u otros centros donde se formaron y de esta manera contribuir al desarrollo nacional de sus países".

En este sentido, pidió a los Estados menos desarrollados que revisen los sueldos de sus profesionales, eviten la politización de determinados cargos y que se esfuercen en "valorar las capacidades de su capital humano" para evitar que sus profesionales vayan a otros lugares en busca de mejores condiciones.

Con respecto a lo que pueden hacer los países de destino, Solimano citó el ejemplo del Reino Unido, que contribuye económicamente con universidades de los lugares de origen de muchos de los inmigrantes que trabajan en empresas británicas.

Esta compensación pretende fomentar la capacitación de potenciales expertos que podrían trabajar en el futuro en las empresas de países desarrollados.

Fuente No. 2

FUENTE: Este artículo apareció en el periódico El nuevo herald, publicado en Miami, en septiembre de 2006. Se titula "Inmigración afirma estar al día con las solicitudes."

Inmigración afirma estar al día con las solicitudes

KETTY RODRIGUEZ—El nuevo herald

La promesa de tramitar las solicitudes de inmigración en un plazo máximo de seis meses para el próximo octubre, será una meta cumplida según el propio Servicio de Inmigración y Ciudadanía (USCIS), que asegura haberse puesto al día en el retraso de millones de peticiones de ciudadanía, residencia permanente, asilo político y otros beneficios que por años se acumularon en la agencia.

De un retraso de 3.8 millones de solicitudes acumuladas en el 2004, el USCIS indicó que para julio del 2006 quedaban pendientes unas 140,000 de un total de 1.1 millones estancadas.

Inmigración considera que de estos 1.1 millones, muchos retrasos están relacionados con factores ajenos a la agencia como: el caso está esperando el resultado de la revisión de antecedentes criminales que hace el FBI, algunos candidatos deben tomar de nuevo el examen de naturalización, o la agencia está esperando evidencia adicional para completar el proceso de adjudicación.

Pese a que Inmigración celebra un triunfo, aún hay casos de personas que sufren la demora del procesamiento de sus solicitudes, a la vez que organizaciones estiman que con la rapidez con que la agencia está procesando las peticiones puede poner en riesgo la seguridad nacional, algo que la agencia rechazó rotundamente.

"Hemos eliminado el atraso sin comprometer la seguridad del país", aseguró Ana Santiago, una portavoz del USCIS en Miami.

La funcionaria explicó que Inmigración había recibido por primera vez del Congreso $500 millones en el 2001 para emplear a más personas y extender las horas de trabajo, con el fin de tramitar rápidamente las solicitudes.

"Miles de empleados del USCIS se han sacrificado y entrado a las 5 a.m. a sus oficinas para trabajar cada caso", agregó Santiago.

Sin embargo, organizaciones sin fines de lucro como NumbersUSA, que aboga por el control en la inmigración, criticó a la agencia federal por haberse comportando como "una factoría" a la hora de solicitudes, en lugar de garantizar la seguridad.

Según este grupo, Inmigración ha presionado a sus empleados y los ha empujado a trabajar con rapidez, prometiéndoles bonos de $500 a los que cumplan la meta.

La vocera del USCIS explicó que la compensación con bonos era una práctica común dentro del gobierno federal.

Por otro lado, hay alegaciones de retrasos y errores.

Wilmer, un nicaragüense de 35 años, está esperando desde diciembre del 2005 la cita para asistir a la ceremonia de juramentación que le dará la ciudadanía.

"Fui a la entrevista, aprobé el examen y hasta la fecha que no he recibido notificación de Inmigración... Ellos alegan que están esperando el resultado del FBI", declaró.

Para muchos activistas existe un problema de coordinación del USCIS con agencias de inteligencia que intervienen en la revisión de antecedentes criminales de los solicitantes.

Por otro lado, algunas fallas en la documentación afectan a los inmigrantes.

Marta puede perder su trabajo por un aparente error de Inmigración, que en lugar de enviar una citación para tomarse las huellas digitales a su nueva dirección, la envió a la anterior.

Por falta de huellas, la mujer no ha podido renovar el permiso de trabajo. "¿Quién se hace responsable si me despiden? No es mi culpa que hayan enviado la cita al lugar equivocado porque yo hice el cambio de dirección a tiempo", aseguró la señora, quien es madre soltera y el único sostén de su casa.

"Juegan con la estabilidad económica y emocional de las personas . . . Cada año me hacen sufrir con la renovación del permiso de trabajo", agregó Marta, quien está amparada por el TPS [Estatus de Protección Temporal].

Cada año debe disponer de $250 para renovar el permiso de trabajo que aún no llega.

También están otros ejemplos de inmigrantes que están esperando un ajuste de estatus y deben esperar años.

Al respecto, Santiago explicó que muchas veces Inmigración preparaba la documentación y procesaba un caso, pero la visa para el ajuste no estaba disponible.

"Las visas se agotan todos los años. El Congreso tiene un número limitado para cada categoría y, sencillamente, esas personas deben esperar no porque Inmigración no haga su trabajo, sino porque no hay una visa disponible", señaló la portavoz.

Esa es la situación de María, una venezolana que recibió su certificación laboral y está esperando la residencia desde hace dos años.

"Inmigración está procesando los casos de mayo del 2002, y para que llegue mi turno para una visa, debo esperar años . . . Yo pensaba que era una falla de Inmigración, pero no es así", afirmó la joven.

Fuente No. 3

(Listen to the audio recording on the accompanying CD—CD #2, Audio Track 5.)

FUENTE: Este informe, basado en un artículo de enero de 2004 de las Naciones Unidas, se titula "Annan pide a Unión Europea aumentar sus cuotas de inmigración legal."

PART B—Free Response (Speaking)

Informal Speaking

INSTRUCCIONES: Ahora tomarás parte en una conversación telefónica simulada. Primero, habrá 30 segundos para poder leer el esquema de la conversación. Próximo, oirás un mensaje y tendrás un minuto para leer de nuevo el esquema. Luego, comenzará la conversación telefónica siguiendo el esquema. En las partes indicadas, podrás hablar por 20 segundos; una señal indicará cuándo puedes empezar y dejar de hablar. Debes completar esta conversación de una manera lógica y detallada.

DIRECTIONS: You will now be asked to take part in a simulated phone conversation. First, there will be 30 seconds given for you to read the outline of the conversation. You will then hear a message and have one minute to read the outline again. Next, the phone conversation will start and follow the given outline. Where it is marked for you to speak, you will be given 20 seconds to respond; a tone signal will indicate when to start and stop speaking. You should complete the conversation as thoroughly as possible.

Read the following outline of the conversation.

A. (La conversación) [You will hear an answering machine message. Escucharás un mensaje en el contestador automático en la grabación.]

B. (La conversación) [The darkened lines represent what Fernando will say. Las líneas en gris representan lo que Fernando te dice.]

Te saluda y te hace una pregunta.

Tú — Salúdalo y contesta la pregunta detalladamente.

Continúa la conversación.

Tú — Descríbele los detalles.

Continúa la conversación.

Tú — Responde a la pregunta.

Continúa la conversación.

Tú — Responde a la pregunta y despídete.

(On the accompanying CD #2, play Audio Track 6. Record your answers on your recording device in the time allowed.)

Formal Oral Presentation

<table>
<tr>
<td>

INSTRUCCIONES: La siguiente pregunta se basa en el artículo impreso y una grabación. Primero, tendrás 5 minutos para leer el artículo impreso. Después escucharás una grabación; debes tomar apuntes mientras escuches. Entonces, tendrás 2 minutos para preparar tu respuesta y 2 minutos para grabar tu respuesta.

</td>
<td>

DIRECTIONS: The following question is based on the accompanying printed article and audio recording. First, you will have 5 minutes to read the printed article. Afterward, you will hear the audio recording; you should take notes while you listen. Then, you will have 2 minutes to plan your answer and 2 minutes to record your answer.

</td>
</tr>
</table>

Imagina que tienes que dar una presentación formal ante una clase de español sobre el siguiente tema:

El artículo que vas a leer es sobre la importancia de la educación física para el bien del estudiante; el informe que vas a oír tiene que ver con lo importante para el estudiante que desea tener éxito. En una presentación formal, describe lo que se requiere para tener éxito como estudiante.

Fuente No. 1

FUENTE: Este artículo apareció en *El nuevo herald* de Miami en septiembre de 2006. Se titula "La importancia de la educación física."

La importancia de la educación física

JAYNE GREENBERG

El programa de educación física juega un papel clave en la educación del estudiante. Estudios nacionales han demostrado que la actividad física es importante en el desarrollo de la mente y del cuerpo y contribuyen al desarrollo y competencia de la persona. También ayuda al estudiante a tomar decisiones acertadas y entender el valor de un estilo de vida activo.

Las Escuelas Públicas del Condado de Miami-Dade proporcionan a sus estudiantes la oportunidad de obtener un nivel óptimo de educación física, ofreciendo una gran variedad de actividades que estimulan el desarrollo del cuerpo humano. Estas actividades son esenciales y ayudan a desarrollar las destrezas físicas, mentales, emocionales y sociales de cada estudiante. Por medio de ellas, los estudiantes desarrollan intereses y habilidades que les animarán a mantener un sano estilo de vida.

De acuerdo a instituciones nacionales como la National Association for Sport and Physical Education (Asociación Nacional de Deportes y Educación Física) los beneficios de un buen programa de actividades físicas pueden afectar el rendimiento académico y el patrón de vida que el estudiante se traza personalmente. El estudiante saludable y activo físicamente es más propenso a estar mejor motivado académicamente, más alerta y exitoso en sus estudios.

Durante los años preescolares, la actividad física promueve las destrezas cognitivas. Cuando el estudiante entra en la adolescencia, esa misma actividad promueve su instinto a afrontar retos intelectuales, sociales y emocionales. En sus años escolares, la actividad física de calidad estimula al estudiante para competir, resolver problemas cooperando con otros y continuar con el ejercicio como una vía para conservar su buena salud y mantener hábitos saludables.

La educación física tiene un carácter único en los programas de enseñanza, ya que proporciona a los estudiantes la oportunidad de aprender a coordinar sus actividades físicas. El ejercicio previene enfermedades y lesiones, disminuye los índices de morbosidad y mortalidad prematuras, incrementa la salud mental, reduce la obesidad infantil e impide el desarrollo de enfermedades cardíacas, la diabetes tipo dos y otros graves problemas físicos. Existen muchas pruebas de que la conducta inactiva y sedentaria en los seres humanos puede empezar a una temprana edad. Al participar en el programa, los estudiantes aprenden actividades que los mantendrán saludables y se les enseña cómo incorporarlas a su vida cotidiana.

El distrito escolar tiene en vigor un programa de educación física que no solamente proporciona al estudiante un estilo de vida balanceado, sino que también le enseña los conocimientos necesarios para cumplir con los objetivos principales de nuestro programa de educación. El programa se ajusta a los requisitos del Competency-Based Curriculum en Educación Física y los Sunshine State Standards, the National Standards for Physical Education y el Informe SCANS, el cual prepara a los estudiantes que entran en la fuerza laboral.

El receso, aunque no está relacionado con la educación física, es esencial, sobre todo para los alumnos de la escuela primaria. El receso le ofrece al estudiante oportunidades de participar en actividades físicas que le ayudan a desarrollar un físico sano. También le enseña a resolver conflictos, a cooperar y respetar los reglamentos y a comunicar sus sentimientos en forma civilizada. Gracias al receso, los estudiantes también pueden concentrarse mejor en los estudios, lo que reduce su nivel de estrés y el desgaste mental. Como directora ejecutiva del Programa de Educación Física les insto a que motiven a sus hijos a participar de lleno en nuestro programa, para de esa forma graduar a estudiantes con un buen expediente académico y a la vez un físico saludable para los retos que les presentará la vida.

Fuente No. 2

(Listen to the audio recording on the accompanying CD—CD #2, Audio Track 7.)

FUENTE: El informe que vas a oír, basado en el artículo "Cómo ser el primero de la clase" del periódico *El nuevo herald* de Miami, apareció en septiembre de 2006.

PRACTICE EXAM 3

AP Spanish Language

Answer Key

Section I

Part A

1.	(B)	9.	(A)	17.	(C)	25.	(B)
2.	(D)	10.	(B)	18.	(B)	26.	(C)
3.	(C)	11.	(C)	19.	(D)	27.	(A)
4.	(B)	12.	(B)	20.	(A)	28.	(A)
5.	(D)	13.	(C)	21.	(D)	29.	(B)
6.	(C)	14.	(A)	22.	(B)	30.	(B)
7.	(D)	15.	(D)	23.	(A)		
8.	(B)	16.	(C)	24.	(A)		

Part B

31.	(A)	41.	(A)	51.	(C)	61.	(C)
32.	(A)	42.	(B)	52.	(B)	62.	(D)
33.	(A)	43.	(D)	53.	(B)	63.	(D)
34.	(B)	44.	(A)	54.	(D)	64.	(A)
35.	(D)	45.	(C)	55.	(A)	65.	(B)
36.	(C)	46.	(C)	56.	(C)	66.	(C)
37.	(B)	47.	(A)	57.	(A)	67.	(B)
38.	(A)	48.	(B)	58.	(A)	68.	(D)
39.	(D)	49.	(C)	59.	(D)		
40.	(B)	50.	(D)	60.	(C)		

Section II

Part A

1.	un	11.	ha
2.	mis	12.	de
3.	discutido	13.	más
4.	ellas	14.	por
5.	sentada	15.	se
6.	Me	16.	próximo/siguiente/entrante
7.	otras	17.	porque/pues
8.	quería	18.	cuyos
9.	tratara	19.	tanta
10.	la	20.	tenga

Note: Please see "Detailed Explanations of Answers"
for examples of responses to the essay and Part B.

PRACTICE EXAM 3

AP Spanish Language

Detailed Explanations of Answers

Section I

Part A

1.   **(B)**   The correct answer is (B) in a restaurant. (A) and (D) would not be appropriate. Even though in some bars and cafeterias meals are served, it is not usual that they would have such elaborate dishes as suggested by the waitress, or a house special. Neither would (C), in a kitchen, be adequate, since the presence of the waitress indicates that it is a place where there is service.

2.   **(D)**   The correct answer is (D)—*El cochinillo asado*. The waitress indicates that this is the house special. Choices (A), (B), and (C) are dishes that are served but are not the best on the menu, which is what the waitress recommended in the first place.

3.   **(C)**   The correct answer is (C) because he is a vegetarian. The other answers could be considered partially correct, but the dialogue does not establish them as completely correct. (A) could be correct, but all we know is that the man does not usually eat pork. (We do not know if he eats it from time to time, or if something prevents him from eating it.) Neither is (B) the most complete answer. We know that the man is going to eat salad that day, but not that it is the only thing he eats. Choice (D) is not correct because we don't know if he really doesn't eat it because he doesn't like it, or if he does like it but doesn't eat it because of a conviction. Choice (C) is the only answer that fully fits the dialogue.

4.   **(B)**   The correct answer is (B) return them. The saleswoman offered another possibility, (A) to change them, but the customer wanted to be refunded his money. Neither are the options (C) to buy them or (D) to give

them as a gift correct. The customer had already bought them, and it is never mentioned in the dialogue that the pants were a gift.

5. **(D)** The correct answer is (D) the customer did not like them, and besides, they were too tight for him. Choices (A) they were not to the customer's taste; (B) they were not the customer's size; and (C) they were not the color the customer wanted are only partially correct, since it is a combination of all three that the man expressed to the saleswoman.

6. **(C)** The correct answer is (C) the cash register receipt. Choice (D), the bag, is incorrect because the man explained that he threw it out. Choices (A), the tags, and (B), the money, are not appropriate because they are not mentioned in the dialogue.

7. **(D)** The correct answer is (D) he threw it out with the bag. Answers (A) he left it at home, (B) he lost it on the way, and (C) he wasn't given one are incorrect according to what the man explains to the saleswoman.

8. **(B)** The correct answer is (B) because the exam was a disaster. Answer (A) because he has had an exam would be only partially correct, while (C) because he doesn't like politics and (D) because he doesn't like natural sciences are false according to the content of the dialogue.

9. **(A)** The correct answer is (A) more than two months. Options (B), (C), and (D) are incorrect because they are less than the time the woman specified that Luis spent preparing for the exam.

10. **(B)** The correct answer is (B) because he could not answer the questions with all he had studied. Option (A) natural sciences would be incorrect because we do not know if Luis understood them or not. The only thing we know is that he did not know the answers to the questions. It would be possible to understand the questions without knowing how to answer them. For the same reason, choice (D) the exam is not correct. And (C) the questions on politics is incorrect, because the dialogue establishes that the questions were not on politics, but natural sciences.

11. **(C)** The disaster, according to Luis, was (C) missing class on the day of the exam. We cannot consider (D) the political exam correct, because Luis never got to take it; while (A) handing the exam in blank and (B) the natural sciences questions are only partially correct, since both are the consequences of the correct choice (C).

12. **(B)** The only correct choice is (B) because he's thrown off track. The other choices (A), (C), and (D) are false according to the dialogue.

13. **(C)** The correct response is (C) football. Choices (A), (B), and (D) are mentioned as sports which, although they are important, do not have as many fans as football.

14. **(A)** The most fitting answer is (A) a minority. Option (B) none is false, while (C) many is not suitable because it is too wide, and (D) an elite is not suitable since it is too restrictive, according to what the narrator explained.

15. **(D)** The correct answer is (D) as a spectacular and a revered tradition. Answer (A) simply as a sport is not correct because the passage makes it clear that it is more than a sport. Choices (B) as a show and (C) like Thanksgiving Day are only partially true, and are not as complete as (D).

16. **(C)** The correct answer is (C) to participate in the Superbowl. The other answers are not correct. (A) to be in the NFL is incorrect because a professional player already is. (B) to play in college leagues is not accurate because a professional player has already passed through them. (D) to participate in the "grand circus" if one considers the "grand circus" as a metaphor of the professional league would not be correct for the same reason as (A).

17. **(C)** The correct answer is (C) as a science movie. Choice (A) as a long footage (largometraje) is incorrect as it does not include any specification, and is not a valid classification. Neither (B) as a science fiction movie nor (D) as an example of a fantasy movie are correct, according to the explanation given in the narration.

18. **(B)** The correct answer is (B) writer of best-sellers. (A) Cineasta would not be correct because the text gives us to understand that he had been one in the past, but no longer was, by defining him as a former *cineasta*. (C) Scientist and (D) teacher are false.

19. **(D)** The correct answer is (D) selling the cinema rights of his novels. Choice (A) writing novels is only partially correct. Answers (B) and (C) are false.

20. **(A)**   The accurate answer is (A) on dinosaurs. (B) on science and (C) on the problems of science would be, according to the text, secondary themes in relation to the main theme of dinosaurs. They are therefore not complete answers like (A). Finally, choice (D) on movies is false.

21. **(D)**   The correct choice is (D), *Gaudí y su arquitectura.* Options (A), *La arquitectura de Barcelona*, (B), *La polémica construcción de la Sagrada Familia,* and (C), *La arquitectura y la Naturaleza*, are other topics that, at some point in the reading, are talked about, but none of them is the main subject.

22. **(B)**   The correct answer is (B), *La Naturaleza.* (A), *La religión católica*, is another source of inspiration, but it comes to him through his vision of Nature, so it would not be the most appropriate choice. (C), *El arte gótico,* and (D), *La arquitectura de la Grecia clásica*, are subjects that interested him, but was not the main source of inspiration for his work.

23. **(A)**   The main characteristic of Gaudí's works is (A), *La originalidad.* (B), *La inspiración*, is part of answer (A). (C), *Las imágenes religiosas*, cannot be considered as the main characteristic, from what the reading tells us. (D), *Las formas*, is too broad a concept to be a good choice to answer this question.

24. **(A)**   The correct answer is (A), *La Sagrada Familia.* Option (B), *La iglesia de la colonia obrera Güell*, is mentioned as one of the "rehearsals" for his main work, La Sagrada Familia. And (C), *La casa Milá*, and (D), *La Pedrera*, are the same building but, according to the lecture, it is not the most famous work of this architect.

25. **(B)**   The problem with the Sagrada Familia is (B), *Hay una polémica entre los que quieren acabarla y los que no.* (D), *Hay que acabarla con las nuevas tecnologías*, is part of the reason for the polemic, so it is not the most complete answer. Options (A) and (C) are false.

26. **(C)**   The correct answer is (C), *El flamenco tiene raíces de cuántos pueblos han pasado por el sur de España.* (A), *Todo el flamenco es gitano,* is not true, because this implies that all the performers are gypsies. (B), *Todo el flamenco proviene de la cultura gitana,* is false too. (D), *Es una mezcla de las nuevas tendencias musicales*, is not accurate either. The reading says that lately there is a fusion of flamenco with new tendencies, but not that flamenco, in general, comes from it.

27. **(A)** The correct answer is (A), *El flamenco se mantiene encerrado en círculos familiares gitanos.* Option (B) is not correct because flamenco is born and kept within family circles, so there is no further expansion at this time. According to the text, what is expanding is Andalusian folklore. (C) is not correct either because if used only for family parties and private celebrations, flamenco was not on the stages in this period. And (D) is not accurate because the reading doesn't establish which styles are cultivated at this time.

28. **(A)** The correct answer is (A) *Porque se alejó de los cánones puristas.* (B), *Por la aparición de figuras carismáticas,* (C), *Porque irrumpía en los escenarios teatrales,* and (D), *Porque su cante estaba lleno de adornos,* are other characteristics of this period, but they are not the reason for the negative opinion of flamenco scholars.

29. **(B)** The correct answer is (B), *El Concurso Nacional de Cante Jondo.* (A), *Una reunión de intelectuales,* is just the origin of this main event. (D), *El nacimiento de un mito del flamenco: Manolo Caracol,* didn't happen there. He became a myth with time. Finally, option (C), *Un festival para profesionales,* is false.

30. **(B)** The correct answer is (B), *Es un elemento básico.* (A), *Es un elemento imprescindible,* is not appropiate, because the text explains there are some ancient *cantes* without guitars. (C) and (D) are wrong choices too.

Part B

31. **(A)** "No one knew why" is the best choice. The text indicates that "por motivos desconodicos" (for unknown reasons) Hidalgo vacillated and did not attack the city. (B) is a poor choice since there was no mention of the army's being afraid, only that "many had been wounded or had deserted" prior to its arrival in the capital. (C) is not a logical choice given the fact that the army's purpose for going to the Capital was to attack the enemy there. (D) is incorrect since the reader learns later in the passage that on July 31, 1811 "lo fusilaron en el pecho" (they shot him in the chest) and "le permitieron encararse con la muerte sin atarle las manos ni vendarle" (they permitted him to face death without having his hands tied nor his eyes covered).

32. **(A)** "It served to intensify their faith in God" is the best choice. The text indicates that Hidalgo "se apoderó de ella...para animar a sus seguidores a luchar por la libertad" (Hidalgo took possession of it...to incite his followers to fight for liberty). (B) is not the best choice since it was Father Hidalgo's famous "grito de Dolores" that represented a call for liberty. (C) is a poor choice since no mention was made of the army's thoughts concerning this copy. According to the text, the revolutionary army "había sufrido miles de bajas" (had suffered thousands of losses) before its arrival at the Capital. (D) is incorrect since it was Father Hidalgo himself, and not the Virgin, who incited the troops to attack.

33. **(A)** (A) is the best answer. In the reading Miguel Hidalgo is referred to as *párroco* (parish priest), *cura,* (priest), and *Padre* (Father), all of which indicate that he was a Catholic priest. (B) cannot be correct, because Miguel Hidalgo was not an "officer in the Viceroy's army"; on the contrary, he was leading the rebellion against the Viceroy's forces. (C) is not a good choice; the fact that he was a priest precludes his being *analfabeto* (illiterate), and although he led the peasants (*campesinos*) in revolt, he was not one of them. He was a criollo, neither Indian nor mestizo. (D) is incorrect, because the text indicates that Hidalgo was executed by a firing squad (*pelotón de fusilamiento*), not that he was a member (*integrante*) of it.

34. **(B)** (B) is correct, because the passage tells us that on September 16, 1810, Father Hidalgo gave the "cry of Dolores," inciting the Indians and mestizos to rebel against the tyranny of the colonial government. (A) is not a good choice; we are told that Hidalgo and other leaders of the revolution were betrayed and captured near Chihuahua but there is no indication that Hildalgo "betrayed his fellow countrymen in Chihuahua." (C)

is not correct. The passage states exactly the opposite: the royalist troops defeated Hidalgo's army of peasants at the Bridge of Calderón (Puente de Calderón), January 17, 1811. (D) is not the best choice; we are told that Hidalgo led the rebels to Mexico City, but for unknown reasons he did not attack it.

35. **(D)** (D) is the correct answer. The passage indicates that he passed out candy to the firing squad, and was given the courtesy of being neither bound nor blindfolded; and shot in the chest instead of in the back. (A) is not right; Hidalgo did not die from a stroke (*derrame cerebral*). (B) is not a good choice, since the text says nothing about his "contracting a fatal (case of) pneumonia." (C) cannot be correct according to the information given in the passage. He was executed by a firing squad; he did not commit suicide.

36. **(C)** (C) is the best answer. The reading says that when the Viceroy sent soldiers to destroy the vineyards, mulberry trees, and beehives in Dolores, that was the last straw (*fue el colmo*) for Father Hidalgo. He was fed up with (*harto de*) such injustice on the part of the colonial government, and he gave the "cry of Dolores" to incite the peasants to revolt. (A) is not a good choice; Father Hidalgo did not want to "show his support for the Viceroy's government." (B) is not correct, because nothing is said in the passage to indicate that Father Hidalgo "was angry with his parishioners." (D) cannot be correct; Hidalgo gave the "cry of Dolores" because he wanted to stir up the Indians and mestizos to put an end to their slavery (*esclavitud*), not because "they shot him in the chest."

37. **(B)** (B) "Those who were in control of the government at that time" is the best answer to the question: "To whom does the term *gachupines* refer?" The word is used twice in the passage, one in the context of the Viceroy sending soldiers to destroy local industries: "*Semejante injusticia de parte de los 'gachupines,' fue el colmo para el Padre Hidalgo*," and again when Father Hidalgo instigated the revolt against the tyranny of the "*gachupines*" who had enslaved the peasants: "*Incitó a los campesinos a que se rebelaran contra la tiranía de los 'gachupines,' y a que pusieran fin a su esclavitud*." (A) is not a good choice; the text indicates that the crowd that followed Hidalgo was composed of *campesinos* (peasants), that is, Indians and mestizos who had been enslaved for 300 years: "*Durante 300 años los indígenas y mestizos habían sufrido bajo el yugo opresivo de los conquistadores primero y los colonizadores después*," In the same way (C) is also incorrect, since "gachupines" refers to the Spaniards who were in power, not the Indians and mestizos, who were slaves. (D) is not the best choice;

"the rebels who died in the fight for freedom" would be called *patriotas*, not *gachupines*.

38. **(A)** (A) is the correct answer. In the battle at the *Puente de Calderón* (Bridge of Calderón) "the royalists defeated the rebels." The passage tells us: "...*los insurgentes sufrieron una derrota definitiva.*" (...the rebels suffered a definitive defeat."). (B) is incorrect, since the rebels lost the battle; they did not "win a definitive victory." (C) is not a good choice; we are told that when his army was defeated at the *Puente de Calderón*, Hidalgo and other leaders of the revolution fled north, with the idea of asking the United States government for help. Hidalgo was not murdered (*asesinado*) in the battle at the Bridge of Calderón. (D) cannot be right according to the information given in the text. The Viceroy's army was not defeated at the Bridge of Calderón, but rather won a decisive victory over the rebel forces.

39. **(D)** (D) is correct, because the text specifically states: "*En Atontonilco Hidalgo se apoderó de una copia de la imagen de la Virgen de Guadalupe, para animar a sus seguidores a luchar por la libertad*" (In Atontonilco Hidalgo took possession of a copy of the image of the Virgin of Guadalupe, to encourage his followers to fight for freedom".) (A) is not a good choice; although we are told that Hidalgo did pass candy out to the firing squad, that was in Chihuahua, not Atontonilco. (B) is not correct, since nothing is said to indicate that he "set the church on fire." (C) is not correct, because Hidalgo never renounced his authority as a priest; he was divested of it by an ecclesiastical court, prior to his execution.

40. **(B)** (B) is the best answer, since the passage indicates that while the spectators are mostly men of the poorer economic and cultural classes, women and members of the privileged classes also attend: "*Casi todos los que asisten a estas luchas son hombres de un nivel económico y cultural pobre. Sin embargo, participan también mujeres y miembros de las clases privilegiadas.*" (A) is incorrect; the spectators are not "exclusively poor men." (C) is also incorrect, because the crowd is not composed of "only members of the privileged classes." (D) cannot be right; the crowd includes more people than just the trainers and the judge.

41. **(A)** (A) is the best answer. The spur that is tied onto the cock's right foot is used to attack his opponent: "*El espolón es el arma de ataque*" (The spur is the attack weapon). (B) is not a good choice, since the cock does not use the spur "to protect itself from the trainers." (C) is also incorrect, because the cock does not use the spur "to attack the crowd." (D) is a poor choice; the purpose of the spur is not "to please the judge."

42. **(B)**   (B) "It came from Europe during the Spanish conquest" best answers the question: "To what does cockfighting owe its presence in the Americas?" The passage informs us that it was imported to the Americas from "civilized" Europe during the period of the Spanish conquest: *"Fue importada de la 'civilizada' Europa en la época de la conquista española."* (A) is not a good choice, because "It goes back to a pre-Columbian ritual of the Native Americans" contradicts the statement in the text that says it was imported from Europe. (C) is incorrect; it did not "originate on the African continent." (D) is not the best choice, since nothing is said to indicate that cockfighting was an invention of the *conquistadores*. It already existed in Europe; they simply brought it to the New World.

43. **(D)**   (D) is the best answer. The fight is over "when one of the cocks cannot continue to fight." According to the information given in the passage, none of the other choices indicates a logical end to the fight. (A) is not correct, because nothing is said about the fight ending "when the judge gets tired of watching the show." (B) is not a good choice; we are told that after the fight begins the crowd becomes silent in anticipation of the outcome of the contest, so when the crowd gets quiet the fight is just beginning. (C) is not correct; the text says nothing about the fight ending "when the trainers shout in a lively way."

44. **(A)**   (A) "The fight lasts longer" is the best answer to the question: "What effect does a dull spur have?" The passage tells us that a sharp spur shortens the contest considerably, while a dull one makes it last longer: *"Si es muy agudo, se reduce notablemente la duración de la lucha, pero si es menos agudo, se alarga el combate."* (B) is not a good choice, because according to the text, if the spur is dull, the fight is longer, not shorter (*más corto*). (C) is not the best choice; "The trainers shout less" has no logical connection to a dull spur. (D) is not correct, because the effect of a dull spur is not that "the crowd gets upset," rather that the fight takes longer.

45. **(C)**   (C) is correct; a *gallera* is a cockfight arena, and is described in the passage as "a circular space with a floor of fine white sand surrounded by bleachers for the spectators" (*un espacio circular con un suelo blanco de arena fina, rodeado de graderías para los espectadores*). (A) is not a good choice, since the passage does not identify "a judge that specializes in cockfights" as a *gallera*. (B) is incorrect, because the text does not mention any special name for the cock that wins the match. (D) is not correct; a *gallera* is not a farm where fighting cocks are bred and raised (*criadero de gallos luchadores*).

46. **(C)** (C) is the correct answer. The passage indicates that he was full-blooded Zapotec (*Era zapoteco de pura raza*). This makes all of the other choices incorrect: (A) Spanish parents, (B) poor creoles, and (D) wealthy mestizos.

47. **(A)** (A) "He became an orphan" is the best answer, since the text tells us that at the age of three his parents died (*Cuando tenía tres años fallecieron sus padres...*). (B) is not a good choice; the passage says nothing of his "getting used to telling lies" but rather indicates that in don Antonio's house in Oaxaca he learned to put honesty above all else: *Allí aprendió muchas cosas, pero sobre todo don Antonio le inculcó la virtud de poner la honradez por encima de todo.* (C) is not the best choice, because while the text does mention that he served in the National Congress in 1844 (when he was 38 years old), which made it necessary for him to live in Mexico City, that does not fit into the time frame of the question: "*en la infancia*" (in his childhood). (D) is incorrect; the text mentions nothing of his being "trampled by a runaway mule."

48. **(B)** (B) "He wanted to avoid a confrontation with his uncle" is the best answer. Benito had lost one of his uncle's sheep, and instead of facing his uncle, he chose to run away to Oaxaca: *En vez de enfrentarse a su tío, Benito huyó a la ciudad de Oaxaca.* (A) is not the best answer, because, while it may have been true that "he wanted with all his heart to know the city," that was not his motive for running away. (C) is not a good answer, because Benito fled to Oaxaca to avoid facing his uncle, not because "he had gotten tired of living in the country." (D) is not correct; the passage tells us that he simply ran away, and nothing is mentioned of him "going in search of the sheep that he had lost."

49. **(C)** (C) is the best answer; the text says that "social reforms in benefit of the Zapotecs were the central theme of the five years that he served as governor of Oaxaca" (*Las reformas sociales en beneficio de los zapotecos fueron el tema central de los cinco años que sirvió como gobernador de Oaxaca*). (A) is not a good choice, since the last paragraph of the passage tells us that while he was the governor of Oaxaca he built 50 new schools and encouraged the education of women, which is a far cry from "ignoring the poverty of the Zapotecs." (B) is not correct, because the text indicates that he never took advantage of public office for personal gain (*Jamás se aprovechó del cargo público para sacar beneficio propio*). (D) is not right, because we are told that he learned the virtue of putting honesty above everything else when, at the age of 12, he began to work for don An-

tonio Salanueva in Oaxaca, not when he became the Governor of Oaxaca (He became Governor in 1847, when he was 41 years old).

50. **(D)** (D) is the best answer, since he is described in the passage as short, dark-skinned, and very strong physically, and as having a stolid and reserved temperament: *era bajo, moreno, y muy fuerte físicamente. Era de temperamento reservado e imperturbable.* (A) is incorrect; Benito was not "tall, blonde, and weak." (B) is not a good choice; he was not foolish (*tonto*), dishonest (*deshonesto*), or emotional (*emotivo*). The passage indicates that he was the opposite of all of these. (C) is not the best choice, since the text does not say if he was handsome or not, and it clearly indicates that he was very intelligent. He became a lawyer and a national political leader.

51. **(C)** (C) "abuse public office in order to get rich" is the best completion of the sentence: "Benito refused to…" The last sentence of the passage tells us that he never took advantage of public office for personal gain: *Jamás se aprovechó del cargo público para sacar beneficio propio.* All of the other choices are incorrect, because according to the information given in the text he did: (A) serve in the National Congress, (B) get married to Margarita Maza, and (D) study law.

52. **(B)** (B) is the best answer; the passage tells us that in the Aztec Empire pulque was drunk by the priest, sacrifice victims, old people, and warriors who had shown bravery in battle. (A) is not correct, since we are told that pulque was only drunk by certain people, and was not drunk freely by everyone. (C) is not the best choice; the passage clearly indicates that tequila is a stronger drink than pulque. (D) is not a good choice, because if the Aztecs drank it, then it could not be "completely unknown" to them.

53. **(B)** (B) is the best answer, because according to the first paragraph: "Tequila constitutes the perfect national liquor because it is mestizo, just like the Mexican people: part indigenous and part Spanish." (*"El tequila constituye el licor nacional perfecto porque es mestizo, al igual que el pueblo mexicano: en parte indígena y en parte español"*). (A) is not correct; the *conquistadores* did not import tequila from Spain, but rather invented it in the New World by distilling pulque. (C) is not a good choice; just because it is a "very strong drink" does not make it the perfect national liquor of Mexico. (D) is incorrect, because Mexicans are not the only ones who drink tequila; even if they were, that is not the reason that Jorge Berrueta gives for calling it the perfect national liquor.

54. **(D)**   (D) is the correct answer. Tequila is made from the fermented sap of the agave plant. (A) is not a good choice; although people may drink tequila with lime and salt, they are not mentioned in the passage, and tequila is not made from them. (B) is incorrect, because tequila is not made from fermented fruit juice. (C) is not the best choice, since tequila is made from the fermented sap of the agave, not its flower.

55. **(A)**   (A) is the correct answer; the passage states that "the Spanish invaders were great drinkers and longed for something stronger than pulque" (*…los invasores españoles eran grandes bebedores y ansiaban algo más fuerte que el pulque*). (B) is not a good choice, since the text indicates that one difference between the Aztecs and the Spaniards was that the Spaniards drank a lot (*A diferencia de los indígenas, los invasores españoles eran grandes bebedores…*). (C) The statement that the Spanish invaders "did not drink liquor at all" contradicts the information given in the passage, and so it cannot be correct. (D) is not the best choice, because the Spaniards did not bring tequila from Spain; they invented it in Mexico by distilling pulque to make a much stronger drink.

56. **(C)**   (C) "tequila is distilled" is the best completion for the sentence: "Tequila and pulque differ in that…" Tequila is made by distilling pulque, which is made by fermenting the sweet sap of the agave plant. (A) is incorrect, because in the passage it is clear that tequila contains much more alcohol than pulque. (B) is not the best choice; in the text pulque is described as being *"una bebida ligeramente alcohólica"* (a slightly alcoholic beverage), so the statement that "pulque lacks alcoholic content" is inaccurate. (D) is not a good choice because the passage tells us that both tequila and pulque are products of the agave plant.

57. **(A)**   The correct answer is (A). The passage mentions Buenos Aires, and so most logically is written for an Argentinean audience. The other nationalities are mentioned, but only with relation to the origins of tea.

58. **(A)**   The correct answer is (A). The first paragraph explains that the Decorative Art Museum has an exhibit of antique containers that held tea. There is no mention of the other three choices.

59. **(D)**   is the correct choice. Paragraph two states that drinking tea at the hotel was a pastime of the glamorous in the 1930's. The other choices were mentioned, but not in relation to the 1930's.

60. **(C)**   The correct answer is (C). In paragraph three the owner of the tea shop states that many people wish to try different types of teas, and therefore she organized a tea tasting. The other choices are mentioned, but are not logical meanings of the word "cata."

61. **(C)**   The correct answer is (C). The last paragraph states that tea is the most widely drunk beverage, after water. Choice (A) is false according to the passage. Choices (B) and (D) are mentioned in the article, but logically they do not provide evidence that tea will continue to be drunk around the world.

62. **(D)**   is the correct answer. The passage's principal idea is that tea is popular now. The other choices are details mentioned in the passage, but do not summarize it.

63. **(D)**   Choice (A) is incorrect because the biography of Silvia Lozano is not included in the passage. Choices (B) and (C) seem reasonable, but are not the principal purposes of the passage. The correct answer is (D).

64. **(A)**   The correct answer is (A). The first paragraph states that she is still the director of the ballet company today.

65. **(B)**   is the correct choice. In both the second and third paragraphs research and researchers are mentioned as the method of maintaining the authentic elements of folk dances.

66. **(C)**   The correct answer is (C). In both the third and fifth paragraphs, the Ballet Company is said to present dances from pre-hispanic cultures up through today.

67. **(B)**   In the sixth paragraph, it is explained that there is a risk of losing information through the oral tradition. Therefore, the correct answer is (B).

68. **(D)**   is the correct answer. In the seventh paragraph the author explains that the cultural process caused by mass media and globalization may cause the disappearance of the folk traditions of Mexico. The other choices are mentioned, but are not referred to as cultural processes that affect the entire population.

Section II

Part A—Writing

1. (un)

The definite article agrees with the masculine noun "calor." "Uno" shortens to "un" before all masculine singular nouns.

2. (mis)

The possessive adjective agrees in number with the noun it modifies, in this case "amigas."

3. (discutido)

The past participle is used in conjunction with the auxiliary "haber" to form the pluperfect.

4. (ellas)

The speaker is worried about her friends, both of whom are female; thus, feminine plural object of the preposition is used.

5. (sentada)

The past participle is used as an adjective here, and must agree in number and gender with the noun, Sofía.

6. (Me)

The pronoun forms part of the reflexive "pararse." The first person singular pronoun is used since the speaker is talking about herself.

7. (otras)

The adjective agrees in number and gender with the noun "cosas."

8. (quería)

The imperfect is used when reporting speech in the past.

9. (tratara)

The subjunctive is used after the indefinite "comoquiera." The imperfect subjunctive is appropriate because the imperfect "podía" is used in the other clause of the sentence.

10. **(la)**
The speaker could not convince Sofia, therefore, the feminine singular direct object pronoun is used.

11. **(ha)**
This completes the present perfect construction, agreeing in number with the stated subject.

12. **(de)**
This is part of the expression "to depend on", which in Spanish is "depender de."

13. **(más)**
This is part of the superlative expression "la más...de."

14. **(por)**
Meaning "about" this accompanies the expression "preocuparse" when expressing the reason.

15. **(se)**
This third-person singular pronoun is part of the reflexive verb "quejarse."

16. **(próximo/siguiente/entrante)**
This sentence describes her future plans, and the adjective "next" agrees in number and gender with the noun it modifies.

17. **(porque/pues)**
This is used to connect the two clauses presented in this sentence.

18. **(cuyos)**
The relative pronoun "whose" agrees in number and gender with the noun it modifies.

19. **(tanta)**
The comparative "as much" agrees in number and gender with the noun it modifies.

20. **(tenga)**
The present subjunctive is used after "Ojalá" to complete the idiomatic expression "tener éxito" to agree with the subject indicated.

SAMPLE INFORMAL WRITING SCORING HIGH

Querido diario,

Acabo de entender que Ricardo va a mudarse a California. Es posible que yo no lo veré nunca. Recibí estas noticias cuando estaba desayunando esta mañana. Mamá me dijo que es posible que Ricardo vaya a mudarse. Primero, no la creí pero hoy Ricardo me dijo que es verdad, y su padre tiene un trabajo nuevo.

Estoy muy triste porque Ricardo ha sido mi mejor amigo por cinco años.

Yo no sé cómo voy a estar sin Ricardo. Estoy un poco enfadado porque no he tenido suficiente tiempo para despedirse a Ricardo. Pienso ir a su casa ahora para comer con él su última cena en esta ciudad. Espero que esté alegre en California.

*The variety of verb tenses used here makes this seem very natural. There are a few errors (no lo **vea, despedirme de** Ricardo) but it thoroughly explains how the student heard and reacted to the news.*

SAMPLE INFORMAL WRITING SCORING MID-RANGE

Querido diario,

No paso un buen día hoy. Acabo de oír que mi mejor amiga Elizabeth va a mudarse con su familia al fin de este mes. Se muda a Nueva York porque su padre recibe un trabajo a la universidad que es mejor de su trabajo ahora a Virginia. Yo estoy muy triste y no sé que voy a ser sin ella. Ella vivía en mi calle para diez años y se vemos todos los días.

No estoy contenta con estas noticias pero yo pienso que ella va a gustar la ciudad de Nueva York. ¡Yo puedo visitarle! Debemos tener un buen tiempo antes del fin de mes. Tengo que hacer mi tarea ahora. ¡Adiós!

*There are a few verb tense problems (paso instead of **pasé,** recibe instead of **recibió**, vivía instead of **vivió**) in this message. The incorrect structures with "gustar" (ella va a gustar instead of **le** va a gustar) and divertirse (tener un buen tiempo) as well as preposition errors (**en** la universidad, **por** diez años) cause interference, but the sentences are relatively detailed and more descriptive.*

SAMPLE INFORMAL WRITING SCORING LOW

Hoy es Martes, y no es una buena día. Primero tenía escuela y fue muy difícil entonces vengo a casa y recibe malas noticias. Madre me dice que mi mejor amigo, Juan, va a mudarse desde Virginia a California; su padre recibe una oportunidad para ganar más dinero en una trabaja nueva. Me alegro de que su padre tiene un trabajo mejor pero estoy triste que mi mejor amigo va a salir. Ojalá que Juan puede visitar algun tiempo. Pues ahora tengo despedirse a Juan; no puede escribir nada más.

*There are numerous errors in this short message. The improper capitalization (**martes**), incorrect gender (**un buen** día, **un trabajo nuevo**), subject/ verb agreement (tengo **que despedirme**, no **puedo** escribir) and wrong verb tense (**tuve, vine**) make it difficult to read. This message has great potential for the present subjunctive, but each opportunity is missed (su padre **tenga**, que Juan **pueda**). Not one of these sentences is solid.*

SAMPLE FORMAL WRITING SCORING HIGH

La inmigración ha afectado cada parte del mundo. Cada pais, cada lugar, cada persona tiene una opinion del tema, y entonces hay muchos opiniones. Para mí, como en las fuentes aquí, hay dos puntos de vista. Los dos tienen valor y es posible que los dos sean correctos.

El primer punto de vista muestra y describe muchas cosas que ocurren con la inmigración. Por ejemplo, es muy común encontrar a personas que no tienen ni trabajo ni dinero porque las personas de otros paises han tomado las posiciones. En los Estados Unidos los extranjeros de México, por ejemplo, son buenos trabajadores con mucho deseo de ayudar a sus familias. Ellos trabajan por mucho menos dinero que los americanos y entonces los jefes creen que pueden gastar menos dinero pagando menos a sus empleados.

El otro punto de vista es que la inmigración puede y debe ayudar a los paises. Kofi Annan ha dicho que sin la ayuda de la inmigración, la población de Europa va a disminuir a 400 millones en el año 2010. La economía de Europa ya depende del trabajo de los extranjeros.

Finalmente, hay algunas personas que creen que es posible aprovecharse de los dos mundos sin causar problemas. Los expertos saben que las personas de otros paises tienen mucho talento tecnologico. Creen que los extranjeros pueden ayudar a empresas trabajando de sus propios paises y entonces no tienen que dominar la población.

Yo creo que la inmigración tiene mas ventajas que desventajas porque los extranjeros pueden traer otros puntos de vista a la sociedad, y pueden enseñar como dos civilizaciones pueden sobrevivir juntos, ayudando el uno al otro.

Content: Several points are made here with supporting details. There is excellent organization of paragraphs between the clear introduction and conclusion.

Grammar: Though many accents are not present (**país, tecnológico, cómo**), the verb conjugations are accurate throughout. The gender and number agreement is also accurate.

Vocabulary: There is great variety of vocabulary used here with little repetition. The various verbs included reflect an extensive vocabulary base.

SAMPLE FORMAL WRITING SCORING MID-RANGE

Como el artículo de las Naciones Unidas indica, los migrantes necesitan a otra nación y otra nación necesita a los migrantes. La inmigración tiene un tremendo impacto en todo el mundo. La nación que recibe a los migrantes recibe unas ventajas y desventajas como la nación que deja salir a los migrantes. Ultimatamente, la inmigración es una parte más importante para todos.

Las naciones que los migrantes vienen de tienen unas cosas buenas y unas malas de la inmigración. Lo bueno es que los migrantes ganan el dinero para sus servicios. Las familias de estas personas entonces reciben el dinero. Estas personas pueden comprar comida, ropa y otras cosas necesarias para la vida. Este trabajo lleva el dinero a la nación y es bastante necesario. Lo malo, como notó el primero artículo, es que el desarollo de la nación original no avanza. Porque los migrantes están fuera de su país, no están allí para ayudar.

Los países adónde van los migrantes se mejoran por los migrantes. Hay mejor economía y el trabajo es terminado. Los migrantes anade a la cultura de su nueva nación y los del lugar aprenden mucho de otra cultura. Una gran variedad emergen de ropa, de lengua, y de comida. Como el artículo del *Nuevo herald* escribe, la securidad de la nación se pregunta. La discuón sobre quién debe ser permitido está hablando mucho. Usualmente cuando la inmigración está llevando la conversación, los derechos están discutido. La inmigración lleva todos los tipos de preguntas, algunas morales.

Bueno o malo, la inmigración es una parte esencial a la economía de las naciones, las de los migrantes y las del trabajo. Es también una parte esencial a la cultura de un lugar. Sin la inmigración el mundo sería muy diferente. Esperamente, la inmigración será una parte de la vida por un tiempo largo.

Content: With generally clear presentation, the paragraphs are well organized. There is an introduction and conclusion.

Grammar: There are some awkward structures that reflect interference from English (Las naciones **de donde vienen** los migrantes tienen . . .). The passive voice is not properly used ("es terminado" instead of "se completa" or "se hace" and "está hablando" instead of "se presenta").

Vocabulary: There is confusion with some verbs ("emergen" instead of "resulta" and "se pregunta" intead of "se pone en riesgo"). A few words are misspelled (**seguridad, Últimamente**), but overall there is a relatively good mix of expressions used.

SAMPLE FORMAL WRITING SCORING LOW

Muchas personas tienen aspectos diferentes en inmigración. Un parte de la sociedad cree que esta es una cosa buena pero el otro parte cree que es una cosa mal. Hay muchas explanaciones sobre la inmigración y los impactos la tiene para la sociedad.

Un problema que la inmigración tiene para la sociedad es sobre dinero. El Congreso había recibido $500 millones para "emplear a más personas y extender las horas de trabajo" para los inmigrantes. A veces hay inmigración illegal y la organización se llama NumbersUSA trabaja con el control de la inmigración legal y illegal. Pero en los Estados Unidos es necesario tener la inmigración porque necesitamos personas trabajan en cosas como construciona y otras formas difíciles del trabajo. Pero hay problemas como los inmigrantes no pueden vivir una vida éxito pero es mejor como la vida de su país original.

En Europa, el población dice que la "inmigración será una solución inevitable." Ellos necesitan los inmigrantes en Europa para trabajar y dan las personas de Europa una economía "más justa, más rica, más fuerte, y más joven." Ellos tienen una economía pobre y vieja" pero con los migrantes ellos pueden tener una economía rica.

La inmigración tiene impactos que puede ayudar la economía y sociedad de los países pero esta puede afecta las abilidades de tener los trabajos y otras cosas. Pero como Kofi Annan dijo, "Los migrantes necesitan a Europa, pero Europa también necesita a los migrantes."

Content: There are organized paragraphs but not many supporting ideas.

Grammar: The connecting word "que" is left out of a few structures (la organización **que** se llama, los impactos **que** tiene). There are some misspelled words (**illegal**). There is a misused comparative form (es mejor **que**) and several other grammatical mistakes (**esto** puede **afectar**).

Vocabulary: Some words are confused ("tienen aspectos diferentes" instead of "tienen **perspectives/opiniones** diferentes" and "explanaciones" instead of "explicaciones") or misspelled (**construcción**). There seem to be few vocabulary resources to develop this essay better.

Part B—Speaking

SAMPLE INFORMAL SPEAKING SCORING HIGH

—Bueno, vamos a Colombia, Venezuela y la Argentina y vamos a pasar dos semanas en cada país, seis semanas en total. Va a ser divertido y tengo ganas de ir pronto.

—Bueno, vamos a hacer una viaje a Latinoamérica y va a ser muy interesante porque estudiaremos la flora y fauna silvestre de estos países. Va a ser muy divertido y quiero ir muy pronto.

—Necesitas tener más de 15 años y necesitas el permiso de tus padres y también tienes que haber estudiado mucho español.

—Claro que sí, eso está bien conmigo. Si quieres hablar mañana, está bien. Tengo que ir a la escuela mañana pero podemos hablar después de las cinco. Bueno, adiós.

*This is an excellent sample because of its natural flow and nearly flawless grammar (**un** viaje). Each question is answered thoroughly and clearly.*

SAMPLE INFORMAL SPEAKING SCORING MID-RANGE

—Vamos a Puerto Rico y vamos a pasar tres semanas allí y vamos a estudiar mucho de las culturas de este lugar.

—Este viaje es muy interesante. Vamos a ir a Puerto Rico y estudiamos… vamos a ver a muchos monumentos y vamos a ir a…

—Tienes que estar en la clase de español de AP y tienes que pagar $2.000 para ir, para pagar el vuelo y la escuela y todo entonces no necesitamos un hotel.

—Sí, mañana es bien. Podemos encontrar a la una en mi cuarto y puedes preguntarme . . .

*This sample shows good grammar in general (**está** bien, encontrar**nos**) with some variety of verb tenses (**estudiaremos**). The answers are fine, but they do not have rich vocabulary or many details. Some answers are unfinished.*

SAMPLE INFORMAL SPEAKING SCORING LOW

—Uds. van a Costa Rica y a . . . esperamos piensan pasar dos o tres semanas posible más pero no sé.

—Este viaje es más importante por el Club de español a Latinoamérica. Vamos a Costa Rica para desarrollar una escuela en la ciudad y en el pueblo . . .

—Necesitas tener 15 años o más. Necesitas participar en el club en la escuela. Necesitas tiene un boleto de equipo y tarjetas . . .

—Uh, mañana es posible pero no sé porque necesito una niñera por mi bebé. Mi bebé está muy enfermo y si puedo habla contigo . . . no . . .

*There are several errors with verb forms (esperamos **poder** pasar, Necesitas **tener**, puedo **hablar**), as well as when answering the question with "ustedes" that should have been answered with the "nosotros" form. There are errors with por/para (**para** el Club, **para** mi bebé). Several other errors in these simple sentences add to the weak overall feel of this sample.*

SAMPLE FORMAL ORAL PRESENTATION SCORING HIGH

Apoyar es lo que se debe hacer para asegurar el éxito de un estudiante. Lograr, tener éxito, es un término general que puede significar lo que se quiere. La definición estudiantil es sacar las mejores notas porque es una manera de determinar su propio nivel de esfuerza e inteligencia. Para tener éxito, un estudiante necesita los recursos, el apoyo y un modelo de lo que uno debe hacer para lograr.

Aunque muchos estudiantes como nosotros tenemos muchos recursos, hay demasiado jóvenes que vienen de situaciones con menos oportunidades. Hay jóvenes con la capacidad de ser listos que forman parte de la delincuencia juvenil o que viven en lugares peligrosos donde lograr en la escuela no se considera una opción. Ellos también merecen las mismas oportunidades y los especialistas deben implementar programas para ayudar a la seguridad de todos los alumnos.

Tener el apoyo de su propia familia es la mejor manera de motivar un estudiante a aprender. Además de la escuela, muchos estudiantes participan en deportes o tocan la música pero esto aumenta el nivel de estrés. Es mejor si ellos dan su apoyo al éxito escolar como primer enfoque.

Muchos jóvenes no tienen buenos ejemplos que seguir en sus vidas. No es bastante decirles lo que deben hacer entonces necesitan un buen ambiente para estudiar y modelos del éxito que imitar.

Tener éxito puede ser fácil si los estudiantes tienen los recursos y el apoyo de sus padres y e. . . .

Content: This well-organized and well-supported description provides several good ideas. The presentation is clear and thorough.

Vocabulary: There are many advanced verbs and a variety of adjectives, all used properly with one exception (**esfuerzo**).

Grammar: The use of a verb as a subject adds to the sophistication of this sample. The subject and verb agreement is correctly used throughout this sample. The agreement of number and gender is correct with one error (**demasiados** jóvenes).

SAMPLE FORMAL ORAL PRESENTATION SCORING MID-RANGE

Éxito es una cosa determinada por los códigos sociales de ahora. Es natural pensar que éxito viene de dinero o felicidad pero éxito significa diferentes cosas para cada persona, especialmente en el aula. Hay unas cosas comunes que cada persona necesita hacer para tener algún nivel de éxito en la escuela.

Primero, hay que negar la presión y el estrés. Esas dos cosas resultan muchas veces en trabajo malo. Necesitas controlarlo en casa. Muchos padres quieren que sus hijos hacen todo perfectamente y son mejores en la escuela. Eso no ayuda al estudiante. Al contrario, su trabajo sufre.

Segundo, hay que dar responsibilidades a los estudiantes. Cuando tienen responsabilidad, pueden desarrollar sus proficiones en la clase sin mucha ayuda. Es un ventaje enseñarse cosas que pueden ayudarse sin otros.

La tercera parte tiene que ver con la casa. Fuente número dos organiza una lista de diez cosas importantes. Número seis menciona la organización. Estudiantes que tienen horarios pueden tener éxito porque saben qué hacer. Tienen las mismas cosas que hacer cada día entonces es habitual y no es difícil hacer qué es necesario.

Todo esto está conectado. Los padres dan responsabilidad a los estudiantes. Los estudiantes pueden controlar su ambiente con estructura y un horario. Finalmente, hay tiempo. . . .

Content: Though the time runs out before a full conclusion is explained, there is a good introduction and good supporting ideas before the conclusion. The ideas are well-organized.

Vocabulary: There are a few mispronounced words (**una ventaja, responsabilidad**), but the majority of the words are used correctly.

Grammar: The definite article is mistakenly left out when speaking in general terms (**El** éxito, **La** responsabilidad, **Los** estudiantes), but the overall gender agreement is correct. The subjunctive is missed (padres quieren que sus hijos **hagan ...** y **sean),** but most of the grammar is correctly used.

SAMPLE FORMAL ORAL PRESENTATION SCORING LOW

Hoy en día hay mucho estrés tener éxito en la escuela y hacer que necesitan para ser la persona perfecta. Por eso, muchos niños se converten depresados y no creen que pueda sobresalir el presión. Algunos doblan a drogas o otras formas de lastimarse y otros, cuyos padres no les orgullan, reciben acciones violentes en las casas cuando vuelvan desde escuela. Aunque a muchas organizaciones que tratan disminuir este estrés y las otras problemas, como NOVA y TRUST, los estudiantes también tener que trabajar a tener éxito.

Primero, un estudiante que sabe que quiere tener éxito necesita que ser bien organizado. Como el profesor del fuente 2 dice, "organiza el horario de estudio y sé disciplinado con él." Pero también es importante su tarea y apuntes. Puede preguntar al profesor a explanar una idea o una problema que no es claro. Si se tiene organización, también se disminuye el estrés.

Otro modo de tener éxito es participar en otras actividades afuera de la escuela. Como el fuente uno dice "actividades extraescolares ... les llevan de un otro lado." Un estudiante que tiene más que sólo el estrés escolar estará mejor listo para hacer las cosas de la escuela.

En conclusión, los estudiantes sí deben trabajar y hacer sus tarea y deben ser bien organizado para mejorar las posibilidades de tener éxito.

Content: There are good ideas presented here in a clear and logical order.

Vocabulary: There is a lot of interference from English ("depresados" instead of "deprimidos," "doblan" instead of "resultan tomar," "orgullan" instead of "apoyan," and "explanar" instead of "explicar").

Grammar: The agreement of number and gender is sporadically correct, but there are errors throughout (**la** presión, acciones **violentas, los otros** problemas, **su** tarea). Many other errors of varying types cause this to be weak.

TRANSCRIPTS

AP Spanish Language Appendix

EXAM 1 TRANSCRIPT

AP Spanish Language

SECTION I

Part A

Get ready for the listening part of the Advanced Placement practice examination in Spanish.

DIRECTIONS: Listen to the following dialogues. Afterwards, listen to the questions based on the dialogues you have just heard and choose the best answer from the choices that follow. Color in the corresponding oval on your answer sheet.

Get ready for the first dialogue.

Dialogue Number 1

Vendedora:	Buenos días, señor. ¿En qué puedo servirle?
Cliente:	Buenos días. Quisiera ver esa camisa colorada que está en el escaparate.
Vendedora:	Por supuesto. En seguida se la traigo. (pausa breve) Aquí la tiene.
Cliente:	Ah, sí, me gusta mucho. ¿La tiene en talla 30?
Vendedora:	¡Cómo no!, pero me parece que le va a quedar chica.
Cliente:	No es para mí. Es para mi hermano. Mañana será su cumpleaños. ¿Cuánto cuesta?
Vendedora:	Se la puedo dejar por 100 nuevos pesos.
Cliente:	¡100 pesos! ¿Por qué tan cara?
Vendedora:	Pues como ve, se trata de la última moda importada de París. Seguro que a su hermano le va a encantar.

Cliente:	A lo mejor tiene razón, pero no puede valer más de 70 pesos.
Vendedora:	Bueno, señor, para Ud. se la dejo por 80, pero no se lo vaya a decir a todo el mundo.
Cliente:	¡De acuerdo! Aquí tiene los 80 pesos.
Vendedora:	Muchas gracias, señor. Le aseguro que no se va a arrepentir. ¿Quiere que se la envuelvo como regalo?
Cliente:	Sí, por favor.

1. ¿Dónde está el señor?

2. ¿Quién va a cumplir años mañana?

3. ¿Por qué es tan cara la camisa?

Dialogue Number 2

Rosa:	Ay, Chepe, de veras debiera haber hablado con mi mamá antes de hacer este viaje tan precipitado. No quiero que se preocupe por mi cuenta.
Chepe:	Dale, Rosa, no tengas cuidado. ¿No dejaste un recado con Paula?
Rosa:	Pues, sí, pero no sé si hice bien. Tú sabes cómo es mi hermana. Es muy irresponsable, y además es capaz de no darle el recado a mi mamá por puro despecho.
Chepe:	Eso sí, Paula tiene fama de ser rencorosa. Pues, ni modo. Por el momento, sólo podemos esperar que cumpla.
Rosa:	¿Y si no? ¿Qué hago? Mi mamá no va a saber por qué tardo ni dónde estoy, y se va a afligir mucho.
Chepe:	Puede ser, pero tú ya eres grande, y tu mamá sabe que eres muy responsable, y que puedes cuidarte a ti misma. ¿No crees?
Rosa:	Por supuesto, pero siempre le aviso si voy a tardar en llegar a casa.
Chepe:	Tranquilízate, mi vida. Cuando lleguemos a la casa de tu tía puedes llamarla por teléfono para explicarle todo y decirle que estás bien. Así te vas de la duda de si Paula le comunicó el mensaje que le encargaste. ¿Qué te parece?

Rosa: Pues, sí, mi amor, tienes toda la razón. Eso es lo que voy a hacer.

4.   ¿Quién es Paula?

5.   ¿Por qué está preocupada Rosa?

6.   ¿Qué le sugiere Chepe a Rosa?

7.   Según Chepe, ¿Cómo es Paula?

Dialogue Number 3

Carlos: Apúrate, Juan, ya sale el tren. Si perdemos éste, no vamos a llegar a tiempo para la boda de mi prima.

Juan: No te preocupes, Carlos. Tu tío nos dijo que si tomaramos el rápido de las tres, llegaríamos a Morón con tiempo de sobra.

Carlos: Espero que así sea, pues no quiero llegar tarde. (A otro pasajero): Oiga, señorita, ¿me puede decir más o menos cuánto tarda este tren en llegar a Morón?

Señorita: Pues, éste no va a Morón. Va a Florencio Varela, y no para hasta llegar. El tren para Morón sale de Once. Éste acaba de salir de Constitución.

Juan: ¡Ay, no puede ser! Nos equivocamos de tren otra vez. Esto es lo que me toca por confiar en ti, Carlos.

8.   ¿Adónde quieren ir Juan y Carlos?

9.   ¿Por qué Carlos quiere que Juan se apure?

10. ¿Qué tren deberían tomar para llegar a tiempo?

11. ¿De dónde sale el rápido para Morón?

12. ¿Cómo se equivocaron de tren?

DIRECTIONS: Listen to the following short narratives. Afterwards, listen to the questions based on the narratives you have just heard and choose the best answer from the choices that follow. Color in the corresponding oval on your answer sheet.

Get ready for the first narrative.

Narrative Number 1

Juan Carlos iba medio dormido, parado e inmóvil. El viaje era un rito que repetía todos los días, ida y vuelta, menos los domingos y ferias nacionales. Mañana sería Navidad y esperaba con toda su alma que el boleto de lotería que acababa de comprar fuera el que ganara el premio gordo este año. Para él la lotería no era un vicio, sino más bien una diversión obligatoria. Compraba un número sólo una vez al año, en el gran sorteo de Navidad, y eso desde hacía veinte años.

Hasta entonces siempre había comprado el número 16, la edad que tenía cuando conoció a su esposa, Carmela, y para él eso fue el suceso más oportuno de su vida. A pesar de su perseverancia, la mala suerte le había seguido implacablemente. Pues hoy ni siquiera le tocó la buena suerte de encontrar un asiento desocupado en el tren, y tuvo que hacer todo el viaje a casa de pie. Sin embargo, tenía un presagio de que su vida iba a cambiar.

En cada parada subía más gente, y tanto el calor humano como el mal olor que lo acompañaba se volvían insoportables. Juan pensaba en cómo le iba a regañar su esposa por haber derrochado más dinero en ese juego del infierno, y se le ocurrió que si hubiera lotería en el infierno, y si tuviera la mala suerte de ir a parar allí (como se lo aseguraba Carmela), ¿cuál sería el premio si le tocara el boleto ganador?

13. ¿Por qué estaba Juan Carlos en el tren?

14. ¿Qué esperaba Juan Carlos con toda su alma?

15. ¿Por qué siempre compraba el boleto número 16?

16. ¿Qué opinaba Carmela con respecto a la costumbre de su marido de jugar a la lotería en Navidad?

Narrative Number 2

Ayer por la tarde en el Paraninfo ha sido premiado el novelista Javier Requetemacho por su obra más reciente, *Alba de la mujer*. Según el acta del jurado del concurso, se le reconoce la elevada calidad literaria de su novela y su comprensión nada despreciable del papel de la mujer en la sociedad actual.

Requetemacho, catedrático que ejerce su tarea educativa en la Facultad de Filosofía y Letras, en su discurso de respuesta, ha acentuado la rapidez con la que ha ido la mujer ocupando los sitios que antes sólo estaban reservados para el varón y ha apuntado que esto ha sido piedra de escándalo en no pocos hogares, incluso el suyo. Ha elogiado el escritor la valentía con la cual se ha hecho valer la hembra a pesar de los muchos obstáculos con los que se ha encontrado sobre la marcha de la realización de su ser.

En una conferencia de prensa posterior al acto solemne, ha manifestado el premiado, con cierta emotividad, que, a pesar de sus convicciones, le choca mucho que hoy en día la mujer salga sola a la calle y que lleve pantalones. En casa suya, según él, sólo los lleva él. A esto añadió el distinguido hombre de letras que la semana pasada se le huyó de casa la mujer.

17. ¿Con quién ha hablado el novelista?

18. ¿Qué piensan los jueces de Requetemacho?

19. ¿Cuál de las fraces es la más exacta?

20. ¿De qué es el discurso de Requetemacho?

DIRECTIONS: Listen to the following lectures. Each will be approximately five minutes in length. It would be a good idea to jot down some notes while you are listening to the lectures. At the end of each lecture, you will be presented with questions based on the lecture you just heard. Choose the best answer from the choices that follow. Color in the corresponding oval on your answer sheet.

Get ready for the first lecture.

Lecture 1

Un fenómeno bastante común en la América Latina, como lo es en varias otras partes del mundo, es la creación de santos populares, o sea personas reales o ficticias que han llegado a ser percibidas en la imaginación colectiva de la gente como verdaderos santos, y poseedores de poderes milagrosos.

Los santos populares no cuentan con la aprobación de la Iglesia Católica, pues no han pasado por el proceso de beatificación dictado por ella. Aunque el culto a los santos populares está proscrito según el dogma oficial, una inmensa cantidad de creyentes católicos reverencia las imágenes de estos santos, acude a capillas y santuarios construidos en su honor, les lleva ofrendas y les hace súplicas.

En algunos casos el santo es el producto de un sincretismo sutil que durante el transcurso de siglos ha entretejido dioses paganos y leyendas precolombinas con personajes y ritos cristianos. Un ejemplo de esto es el famoso "Maximón" de Guatemala que ha llegado a ser venerado, tanto entre la población indígena como entre los ladinos.

Otras veces el origen del santo remonta a una persona que por algún acontecimiento en su vida amerita, en los ojos de sus compatriotas, el derecho de ser llamada santa. Así sucedió con una jovencita argentina, Deolinda Correa, que vivía en la Provincia de San Juan, a mediados del siglo diecinueve. Resultó que su padre y su esposo se fueron a La Rioja para unirse a las fuerzas de Facundo Quiroga, dejándola sola con su hijito recién nacido. Además de la tremenda tristeza y soledad que sentía, algunos hombres del lugar querían enamorarla y lo hostigaban constantemente. Prefiriendo arriesgarse la vida en vez de serle infiel a su marido, huyó de su pueblo con su hijito en brazos, y emprendió a pie el arduo viaje a La Rioja para encontrar a sus hombres. Como no conocía el camino, se perdió, y cuando ya no pudo seguir, cayó y se murió de sed. Unos arrieros hallaron su cadáver, junto con su hijito, que pudo sobrevivir por haber amamentado de su madre muerta.

Mucha gente consideró este hecho como milagroso y fue erigido una capilla en el mismo sitio donde fueron encontrados. Llegó a ser conocida como la Difunta Correa, y cada año miles de peregrinos llegan a su capilla, a pesar de que el Obispado Argentino haya amonestado a todos los fieles católicos que debieran abstenerse de ese culto profano.

Inclusive, se encuentran esparcidos por todos los caminos de la República santuarios construidos en honor de ella. Muchas veces si una persona piensa hacer un viaje, llena una botella con agua y la deposita en uno de los santuarios, pidiéndole a la Difunta Correa que la proteja por el camino. Asimismo, si un viajero se salva de un accidente grave por el camino, lleva el volante u otra pieza del vehículo en que viajaba a un santuario como ofrenda para agradecerle a la Difunta Correa haberle salvado la vida.

Nunca faltan quienes se aprovechan de la fe de los devotos para sacarles dinero, y existe un enorme negocio en torno de la Difunta Correa que incluye de todo desde hoteles y compañías de transporte hasta la comercialización de infinidad de artículos vinculados con el culto, incluso piedras y paquetes de tierra del lugar.

This is the end of Lecture 1. Please respond to the corresponding questions in your book.

Lecture 2

En México, el Día de los Muertos, llamado también el Día de los Difuntos, se celebra el 2 de noviembre, de acuerdo con el calendario católico. Los ritos que se llevan a cabo esa fecha no son netamente cristianos, más bien representan una maraña de creencias y tradiciones de las culturas de los indígenas precolombinos y las de los Conquistadores.

Cuando los españoles llegaron a México los habitantes indígenas ya realizaban fiestas en honor de los difuntos en el día que en su calendario correspondía al 2 de noviembre. En su afán por convertir a los aztecas paganos al cristianismo, los padres católicos se esforzaron por destrozar los ídolos y la mayor parte de sus escrituras sagradas, y se esmeraron en reemplazar las fiestas paganas con ritos de índole cristiano. Cuando los misioneros impusieron el catolicismo a los aztecas, y otros grupos indígenas, éstos no tuvieron más remedio que someterse a la religión de sus conquistadores. Los padres creían que habían logrado erradicar las prácticas paganas entre sus feligreses, pero no fue así. Las mismas creencias y tradiciones que existían por tantos siglos antes de la llegada de los europeos, se dan expresión en la forma de celebrar el Día de los Muertos en la actualidad. Algunas de las prácticas siguen iguales que hace siglos, y en otros casos, permanece la antigua creencia pagana, sólo que se expresa de una forma que se asemeja más a ritos cristianos.

La Iglesia Católica no se opone a que sus fieles construyan altares caseros, enciendan velas, y recen a la Virgen, rogándole que vele por sus seres queridos que ya murieron. Los aztecas cumplían ritos semejantes en una celebración en honor de la diosa de la tierra y de la muerte, Cuatlicue, a fin de complacer a la diosa y agradar a los miembros fallecidos de su clan. Los aztecas ofrecían a los difuntos comidas que a ellos les gustaban mientras vivían, una costumbre que persiste en la celebración actual del 2 de noviembre. Los familiares preparan la comida y la bebida favorita del muerto, y las colocan en una ofrenda junta con atole, cigarros, café, tortillas y posesiones personales del difunto.

La costumbre de dar regalos unos a otros durante las fiestas en honor de los difuntos remonta a los tiempos precolombinos, y ha desembocado en la práctica actual de obsequiar calaveras de dulce. La ofrenda del hogar se adorna con roscas y pan de muerto (pan dulce con anís) que representan las almas de los fallecidos. Casi siempre colocan una foto del ser querido en el altar, junto con imágenes de la Virgen y otros santos, y las flores amarillas del cempazúchil. En la antigüedad los aztecas también usaban esta flor en su culto de la muerte, y quemaban incienso de copal, una costumbre vinculada con esta celebración que sobrevive hasta el día de hoy.

Todo esto se hace a fin de agradar a las almas, pues se cree que disfrutan de la esencia de las comidas que se les ofrece. Por el mismo motivo los familiares suelen limpiar y adornar las tumbas de sus seres queridos, y a veces la familia pasa toda la noche en el cementerio para acompañarle al difunto. Las velas encendidas en el altar y en el cementerio sirven para alumbrarle el camino al alma que regresa a su casa.

Así como los aztecas de antaño creían que al fallecer un familiar se convertía en un miembro invisible del clan, también creen muchos mexicanos de hoy que sus seres queridos muertos sólo han pasado a otra fase de vida, y que por lo menos una vez al año vuelven de ultratumba para gozar de las atenciones de su familia.

Hoy día en México, muchas personas ya no celebran el Día de los Muertos como antes. A medida que cada vez más gente abandona las zonas rurales y se traslada a los grandes centros urbanos, especialmente a la capital, en busca de trabajo y una vida mejor, muchas de las fiestas tradicionales celebradas todos los años en el campo, como el Día de los Muertos, están cayendo en desuso.

This is the end of Lecture 2. Please respond to the corresponding questions in your book.

SECTION II

Part A — Writing

Formal Writing Task

> **DIRECTIONS:** Listen to the following recording and then write your essay in your test booklet.

Fuente No. 3

El ser humano, aunque nos parezca extraño, ha nacido para desplazarse de forma bípeda, es decir sobre sus dos poderosas extremidades inferiores, las más fuertes de su físico y, por lo tanto . . . para correr.

Si nos preocupa la mejora de nuestro estado físico, es recomendable realizar ejercicios aeróbicos, y el correr es el mejor sistema para conseguirlo, ¿quieres saber por qué?

El trabajo aeróbico produce una mejor circulación sanguínea a la vez que una mejor oxigenación de la sangre, una mayor capacidad para quemar grasas acumuladas y, acompañado de sesiones de estiramientos, también una mayor movilidad articular y mejora del tono muscular. Los efectos positivos de este deporte se manifiestan en el aparato esquelético, muscular, respiratorio, circulatorio y a nivel emocional.

Cuando nos movemos vigorosamente de una forma regular por 20 minutos o más, el corazón se vuelve más fuerte y más eficiente, bombeando más sangre con menos latidos. Con el tiempo, esta clase de ejercicio aeróbico que nos mantiene respirando fuerte mientras nuestra sangre circula rápidamente aumenta el número y tamaño de nuestros vasos sanguíneos en los tejidos y esto incrementa el suministro de sangre. Cuando hacemos ejercicios fuertes, la sangre circula más rápido a través de estos vasos expandidos, proporcionando oxígeno y nutrientes a todo nuestro cuerpo y eliminando más rápidamente los desperdicios. En una primera fase, cuando aún no estamos entrenados, las únicas sensaciones que podremos advertir al esforzarnos serán las del pulso cardíaco acelerado y la respiración más rápida y afanosa. Sólo a base de entrenamiento empieza el corazón a bombear más sangre en cada contracción para ahorrar energía y responder de manera más adecuada a las solicitudes de esfuerzo.

Hemos ya mencionado en otras ediciones que el ejercicio funge también como un tratamiento alternativo y adecuado para la depresión. Se ha observado que el ejercicio vigoroso aumenta los niveles de una hormona que se encuentra en la sangre y que actúa como tranquilizante y analgésico natural para combatir el dolor y cambios de ánimo.

Por otro lado el descubrimiento de las endorfinas, en relación al ejercicio y su función en el organismo, se ha hecho muy popular en corto tiempo ya que se produce una sensación de complacencia y satisfacción cuando las personas se ejercitan por largas e intensas sesiones, lo cual ayuda a mejorar la parte emocional y ayuda a un bienestar general.

(You now have 5 minutes to plan your essay and
40 minutes to write your essay in your test booklet.
Stop the audio CD and write your essay.)

Part B — Speaking

Simulated Conversation

(NARRADOR/A)   Ahora tienes treinta segundos para leer el siguiente esquema de la conversación.

(30 seconds)

(NARR.)   Imagina que oyes un anuncio en tu colegio invitando a los estudiantes a participar en un espectáculo de talento. Después de oírlo discute con tu mejor amiga Gloria la posibilidad de participar en él.

(M)   Oye amigo, ¿te dicen tus colegas que cantas como un ángel? Cuando bailas, ¿para la gente a admirar tu gracia? Si posees cierta presencia en el escenario te invitamos a participar en el espectáculo "Todo el talento nuestro". Queremos poetas, cantantes, bailadores, cómicos y más. Todos están invitados a mostrar lo suyo. Vamos a organizar un programa que nadie olvidará. Todos los aspirantes deben venir el lunes, veinte de octubre al teatro escolar a las cuatro de la tarde. ¡Anímate! ¡No te lo pierdas!

(NARR.)   Ahora usa el próximo minuto para leer otra vez el esquema de la conversación.

(1 minute)

Ahora comenzará el anuncio.

(30 seconds)

Ahora comenzarás la conversación con tu amiga Gloria.

(F)   ¿Aquí en nuestra escuela van a hacer tal espectáculo? ¡Increíble!

           TONE (20 seconds) TONE

(F)   Sí, sí, ya lo creo. Y tú que has pasado años cantando con gusto, pues ¿por qué no piensas en esta oportunidad?

           TONE (20 seconds) TONE

(F)   Mira, además de cantar, bailas divinamente. No debes tener miedo en absoluto, ¿verdad?

           TONE (20 seconds) TONE

(F)   Sabes que te apoyo totalmente y si quieres te puedo acompañar al teatro ese día. Sería muy divertido, ¿no crees?

           TONE (20 seconds) TONE

(F)   Entonces prepárate bien antes del lunes. Oye, me tengo que ir. Te veo por la mañana, ¿no?

           TONE (20 seconds) TONE

(Stop the audio CD and resume the test in the book.)

Formal Oral Presentation

Fuente No. 2

Juliet García, primera hispana directora de una universidad en EEUU

La doctora Juliet Villareal García, quien recibió en el Kennedy Center de Washington el Premio Hispanic Heritage, es la primera latina que llegó a dirigir una universidad en Estados Unidos. Villareal García, nació en 1949 en Brownsville (Texas). Se convirtió en 1992 en presidenta de la Universidad de Texas en Brownsville (UTB), luego de ser durante seis años presidenta del Texas Southmost College (TSC). Durante su presidencia de UTB-TSC, instituciones que comparten un campus común, el alumnado conjunto creció de 7.358 a más de 12.000, un aumento de un 56%. La educadora fue elevada en el otoño de 2000 al Salón de la Fama de las Mujeres de Texas por sus logros de toda una vida en la Educación.

Además, en 1993 la revista Hispanic Business la consideró por primera vez uno de los 100 Hispanos Más Influyentes en Estados Unidos, distinción que la publicación ha repetido en varias ocasiones.

Al terminar en 1994 el régimen del "apartheid" en Sudáfrica, el Consejo Estadounidense de Educación y la Agencia de Estados Unidos para el Desarrollo Internacional (USAID) seleccionaron a un grupo de educadores, que incluyó a García, para ayudar a las universidades en ese país.

En 1995, la revista Texas Hispanic la reconoció como una de las mujeres latinas más influyentes en el estado. Desde ese mismo año, la educadora es invitada anualmente a hablar en el programa de la Universidad de Harvard para líderes de Educación Superior.

Ha sido también presidenta del Consejo Estadounidense de Educación, la organización más importante del país en el ramo, al representar a unas 1.800 universidades.

García está graduada de Comunicaciones y Lingüística en la Universidad de Texas en Austin, y tiene estudios de posgrado en Lenguaje e Inglés en la Universidad de Houston.

También tiene estudios pos-doctorales en el Instituto de Administración Educacional de la Escuela de Gobierno JFK en Harvard, en el Instituto de Tecnología de Massachusetts y en la Escuela de Negocios de Londres. García está casada con Oscar E. García, y juntos tienen dos hijos mayores y cuatro nietos.

(You now have two minutes to plan your answer and two
minutes to record your answer on your recording
device. Stop the audio CD.)

This is the end of Practice Exam 1.

EXAM 2 TRANSCRIPT

AP Spanish Language

SECTION I

Part A

Get ready for the listening part of the Advanced Placement practice examination in Spanish.

> **DIRECTIONS**: Listen to the following dialogues. Afterwards, listen to the questions based on the dialogues you have just heard and choose the best answer from the choices that follow. Color in the corresponding oval on your answer sheet.

Get ready for the first dialogue.

Dialogue Number 1

Olga:	Dígame.
Luis:	Olga, soy Luis.
Olga:	¡Qué alegría! ¡Cuánto tiempo sin saber nada de ti! ¿Cómo estás? Hace tiempo que quiero llamarte, pero parece que has cambiado de teléfono...
Luis:	De teléfono, de casa, de ciudad y...de vida. ¡Me he casado!
Olga:	¿Cómo? Pero, ¿pero cuándo ha sido eso? ¿Quién es la afortunada esposa?
Luis:	Fue todo muy de prisa. ¿Recuerdas que iba a hacer un crucero por el mar Báltico, en Semana Santa?
Olga:	Sí, me lo comentaste la última vez que nos vimos, en marzo, creo.

Luis: Fue un viaje maravilloso, en el que conocí a Rebeca, mi esposa. Fue muy romántico. Amor a primera vista. Al cabo de una semana, le propuse matrimonio y ella aceptó. Nos casamos hace diez días. Y ahora estoy en Wellington.

Olga: ¿En el hotel Wellington?

Luis: ¡No! En Wellington, Nueva Zelandia. Rebeca es de aquí y dirige la empresa de su familia.

Olga: ¡Cuántos cambios! Pero al menos, ya tengo adonde ir a pasar las vacaciones...

1.   ¿Por qué no había podido la mujer hablar con su amigo?

2.   ¿Cuál es la gran noticia que comenta el hombre?

3.   ¿Qué insinúa la mujer sobre sus futuras vacaciones?

Dialogue Number 2

Mujer: No sé qué hacer. Creo que hay un ratón en mi apartamento.

Hombre: Tendrías que comprar esas trampas de alambre y colocar un trocito de queso, para atraparlo.

Mujer: Uy, no sé. No creo que fuera capaz de usarla. Seguro que al cabo de unos días te encuentras al pobre bicho estrangulado.

Hombre: Bueno, entonces deberías tratar de cazarlo con esos papeles encolados que se colocan en las esquinas.

Mujer: ¿Y luego qué? ¿Tengo que matarlo con una escoba?

Hombre: Supongo que algo así...

Mujer: No, no me convence mucho la idea. ¿Qué otras opciones me quedan?

Hombre: Me parece que, o compras veneno y lo esparces por el suelo, o llamas a un exterminador para que acabe con él.

Mujer: ¡Claro! ¿Cómo no se me había ocurrido antes? En estos casos, siempre es mejor recurrir a un profesional.

4. ¿Cuál es el problema de la mujer?

5. ¿Por qué no quiere la mujer comprar una trampa de alambre?

6. ¿Cuál es el inconveniente del papel encolado, según la mujer?

7. ¿Quién matará al ratón, finalmente?

Dialogue Number 3

Hombre: Hola. ¿Había llamado usted para un arreglo en la cocina?

Mujer: Sí. Hace tiempo me dijeron que vendrían a arreglar el horno, pero nadie vino. Ahora tampoco funcionan los pilotos de los fogones.

Hombre: Nadie me había notificado que hubiera averías en este piso antes de esta mañana. Pero no se preocupe, ahora miraré qué es lo que pasa.

Mujer: ¿Cree que podrá arreglarla?

Hombre: No lo sé. De momento veo que los pilotos de los fogones están oxidados. Y el horno tiene un olor muy extraño. ¿Lo ha limpiado últimamente?

Mujer: Sí. Y el conducto del gas parece ser muy viejo.

Hombre: No sólo es muy viejo, sino que tiene un pequeño agujero. Eso provoca un escape del gas y, para prevenir accidentes, los pilotos se bloquean y no funcionan. Me temo que va a tener que cambiar de cocina.

8. ¿Qué avería notifica la señora?

9. ¿Cuándo le notificaron al técnico la avería en el piso de la señora?

10. ¿Cómo está el conducto del gas?

11. ¿Por qué se bloquean los pilotos?

12. ¿Cuál es la solución final que da el técnico a la señora?

DIRECTIONS: Listen to the following short narratives. Afterwards, listen to the questions based on the narratives you have just heard and choose the best answer from the choices that follow. Color in the corresponding oval on your answer sheet.

Get ready for the first narrative.

Narrative Number 1

Junto a las costas africanas, cerca del desierto del Sáhara, se hallan las Islas Canarias, un archipiélago que, pese a los kilómetros que lo separan de la Península Ibérica, forma parte de España. Los antiguos pobladores canarios, llamados guanches, rompían la imagen prototipo que el mundo tiene de los españoles, bajitos, de pelo moreno y ojos oscuros. Los guanches eran altos, con la piel bronceada por el sol, rubios y de ojos azules o verdes. Estas características físicas, tan distintas a las de cualquier otro pueblo cercano, son de difícil explicación, pero algunos estudiosos del tema afirman que eso se debe a que los guanches son descendientes de los habitantes de la legendaria Atlántida, un continente del que se dice que, hace muchos años, se hundió para siempre bajo el mar. Los que apoyan esta teoría afirman que las Islas Canarias son los picos de la Atlántida que el agua nunca llegó a cubrir.

13. ¿Dónde están las Islas Canarias?

14. ¿Cómo eran los guanches, físicamente?

15. ¿Cuál es la explicación de este físico particular que dan algunos estudiosos?

16. ¿Qué afirman sobre las Islas Canarias los que apoyan esta teoría?

Narrative Number 2

España es un país de la Comunidad Europea que, a pesar de no ser demasiado grande (tiene un territorio aproximadamente del tamaño del estado de Tejas), posee en su interior una gran diversidad de culturas. Esta riqueza cultural es debida, especialmente, al diferente desarrollo histórico de sus distintas regiones. Todo ello ha dado lugar a que haya cuatro idiomas distintos en el país. Uno, que se habla en toda España, es el castellano, al que se conoce internacionalmente como español, y que es la misma lengua que se habla en Latinoamérica. Sin embargo, esta denominación tan genérica, aunque está muy extendida, no sería apropiada, porque los otros tres idiomas que se hablan en España también son "españoles." En Galicia, situada al noroeste de la Península Ibérica, se habla también gallego. En la zona de Cataluña, se habla, además del castellano, catalán. Finalmente, en el País Vasco, en el noreste de España, se habla vasco (que ellos llaman "euskera"). Castellano, catalán, vasco y gallego son idiomas oficiales en el estado español. Pero a quien quiera visitar el país, le bastará con hablar castellano para entenderse con la gente de cualquier región.

17. ¿De qué tamaño es España?

18. ¿Por qué no es apropiada la denominación de "español" para definir el castellano, según el narrador?

19. ¿Qué idioma tiene que hablar un visitante para entenderse con la gente de cualquier región?

20. ¿Cuál es el tema principal de esta narración?

Lecture 1

Seguramente, si se hiciera una encuesta preguntando a la gente cuál ha sido el mayor genio de la literatura en el mundo entero, la respuesta más popular sería William Shakespeare. Pero también es muy probable que el segundo nombre más votado fuera el de Miguel de Cervantes.

El literato español, prácticamente contemporáneo de Shakespeare, se ganó la fama de su nombre con una extensa obra que ha sido traducida a decenas de idiomas: El ingenioso hildalgo Don Quijote de la Mancha, llamada popularmente "El Quijote" o "Don Quijote." Pocas personas que no hayan estudiado, al menos superficialmente, un poco de la historia de la literatura española, sabrían nombrar cualquier otra obra de Cervantes. La fama de "El Quijote" dejó prácticamente a la sombra el resto de sus creaciones literarias para un lector corriente. Sin embargo, la variedad y extensión de sus escritos es muy amplia y merece la pena ser estudiada.

Pero como le sucede a cualquier escritor, las peripecias de la vida de Miguel de Cervantes tienen una gran relevancia en las obras que escribió. A diferencia de Shakespeare, Cervantes inició su carrera literaria a los 38 años, una edad bastante avanzada, especialmente teniendo en cuenta que la expectativa de vida en aquella época era muy inferior a la actual. Comenzar a escribir en plena madurez le dio, sin embargo, la posibilidad de tratar sobre cualquier tema desde un punto de vista bien arraigado, con un enfoque adulto y sensato. Además, su atribulada existencia le brindó la oportunidad de haber pasado por todo tipo de experiencias, muchas de las cuales quedarían reflejadas en su obra.

Miguel de Cervantes Saavedra nació en Alcalá de Henares, una localidad cercana a la actual capital de España, en 1547. Llevado por la pasión de la juventud, cuando contaba con 22 años embarcó hacia Italia para unirse a las fuerzas del ejército español.

El joven Cervantes, siendo ya soldado, participó heroicamente en la histórica batalla de Lepanto, en la que resultó herido en el brazo, un hecho del que el autor se enorgullecería durante el resto de su vida. Con el paso del tiempo, el pueblo llano, tan dado a las exageraciones, acabaría llamando al literato con el sobrenombre de "el manco de Lepanto," aunque en realidad la herida del brazo no llegó a dejarlo manco.

Miguel de Cervantes Saavedra murió en Madrid, donde residió en los últimos años de su vida, el 23 de abril de 1616.

Como ya hemos comentado antes, Cervantes comenzó a escribir en su edad madura. Su primera obra la escribe en 1585 con La Galatea, una novela pastoril. Los críticos la consideran una obra mediocre, por su lánguido relato y la poca calidad de los versos que se intercalan en él. Sin embargo en ella queda patente la sólida formación literaria del autor, que concocía a fondo las doctrinas renacentistas de origen clásico gracias a profundas lecturas de las obras de Aristóteles y Platón, entre otros, a los que alude a menudo en sus escritos. También es bien sabido que el escritor había leído a los autores italianos y españoles más relevantes de su período y que conocía las ideas esenciales de la filosofía humanística. Así pues, la importancia de La Galatea es, precisamente, la de ser la primera obra del literato.

Su tardía entrada en la literatura no le permitió una obra especialmente prolífica, pero eso no fue obstáculo para que dejara escritos en todos los géneros literarios. En poesía, el autor de Alcalá de Henares no destacó especialmente. Él mismo era consciente de sus limitaciones en el género. Pero el escritor compensaba la falta de musicalidad de sus poemas con inteligentes resagos irónicos, emotivos y autobiográficos. Sus más destacados poemas son "Al túmulo de Felipe I" y "Viaje al Parnaso." Este último es un comentario detallado en el que Cervantes repasa a los más famosos escritores de la época, entre los cuales se cita a él mismo, no sin cierta tristeza.

El teatro de Miguel de Cervantes es mucho más conocido que su obra poética. Sus primeras obras, de estilo humanista de inspiración clásica, se representaron con gran éxito. A esta etapa pertenece El cerco de Numancia, cuyos personajes son alegóricos (como la Guerra, la Fama,…) con la intención de exaltar el espíritu heroico español.

Cuando Lope de Vega escribió las nuevas reglas teatrales, Cervantes, viendo la gran acogida que tenían las obras de este nuevo autor, aceptó su reforma. De todos modos, sus obras conservarían un tono personal a la hora de definir a sus personajes, firma típica de la literatura cervantina. De este período destacan dos comedias: una romántica, desarrollada en el típico ambiente de pícaros y gitanos, Pedro de Urdemalas, y otra de carácter autobiográfico, Los baños de Argel.

Pero sin duda alguna, sus obras teatrales más celebradas fueron los Entremeses, de gran vivacidad y colorido en sus personajes. El más conocido de los ocho que escribió es El retablo de las maravillas.

Por último, El ingenioso hidalgo Don Quijote de la Mancha, es la obra cumbre en la carrera de Cervantes y, seguramente, la más importante en la historia de la literatura española. Gracias a ella, se puede decir que Miguel de Cervantes fue el primer novelista moderno. La extensa obra se publicó en dos partes, escritas con varios años de diferencia. Las desventuras del hidalgo manchego que, trastornado por la lectura de los libros de caballerías, se convierte en caballero andante y recorre los caminos, en compañiá de un escudero, para ayudar a los débiles, darán la vuelta al mundo.

This is the end of Lecture 1. Please respond to the corresponding questions in your book.

Lecture 2

Durante la Edad Media, los pueblos musulmanes comenzaron a extenderse rápidamente por el mundo romanizado. Su influencia sobre los países a los que fueron llegando se notó en la economía, en la política y, muy especialmente, en la cultura. Esta influencia fue muy importante en los territorios que hoy constituyen España.

El islam hispánico tuvo una historia de siete siglos y dejaría una huella trascendental para la cultura española. Los primeros ejércitos musulmanes comenzaron a asentarse en la Península Ibérica en el siglo VIII después de Cristo. Hasta entonces, los pueblos musulmanes eran básicamente agrarios y su economía se basaba en la ganadería y la agricultura. Pero cuando no pudieron practicar estas actividades de una manera estable, se convirtieron en pueblos guerreros y conquistadores. Como principal justificación a esta necesidad de conquistar otros territorios se refugiaron en una religión aglutinante, el islamismo. En la base de esta religión está la lucha para someter a los pueblos "infieles," es decir, a todos aquellos que no compartieran sus creencias religiosas.

Los musulmanes fueron entrando en la Península Ibérica y conquistando tierras sin encontrar demasiada resistencia en el estado visigodo, muy debilitado por la falta de cohesión y las intrigas personales. Treinta años les fueron suficientes para dominar casi toda la Península (con excepción de dos pequeñas zonas en el Norte, las que hoy conforman Asturias y el País Vasco, aproximadamente). El islam hispánico se convierte entonces en un emirato dependiente, o sea, una provincia dependiente del califa de Damasco y las tierras conquistadas pasan a llamarse Al-Andalus. Este nombre evolucionará hasta nuestros días para denominar a la región sur de la España actual, Andalucia.

Posteriormente, Abderramán I toma el poder en Córdoba e instaura el Emirato independiente, que se extenderá desde 756 hasta 912, cuando la economía, mucho más fortalecida y una clase política firmemente asentada propician que Abderramán III instaure el Califato Independiente. Córdoba se convierte entonces en la capital. Es la época de mayor esplendor, tanto política, económica como urbanísticamente, del mundo musulmán hispano.

Pero setecientos años dejaron muchas marcas bien arraigadas en el pueblo español. Para empezar, la influencia islámica ha dejado como herencia un montón de palabras adaptadas del árabe. Todos los vocablos del español que comienzan por "al" proceden del musulmán, como por ejemplo, almohada, alcantarilla, aljibe,...También en muchos nombres geográficos hay una raíz islámica. Especialmente en el sur de España, hay muchas poblaciones que comienzan por "guadal." Ésa era la palabra que los musulmanes utilizaban para referirse al río. Y ciudades, pueblos y ríos han heredado esa raíz: Guadalajara, Guadalquivir, Guadalete, etcétera.

La agricultura, una de las actividades principales de los territorios visigodos, se renovó inmensamente con la llegada de los musulmanes. Los hispanomusulmanes perfeccionaron los sistemas de regadío con norias, acequias y canales. Además de innovarse en las técnicas agrícolas, se extiende el cultivo del olivo y se intensifican los frutales, como el limonero, el naranjo y la vid.

El mundo hispano musulmán comienza a desarrollarse en la industria y el comercio. La industria minera fue la de más importancia, especialmente en oro, plata, plomo y mercurio. También la industria artesanal se expande enormemente, especialmente en la fabricación textil, con el algodón, la lana y la seda. Además, Toledo se convierte en un esencial foco de la fabricación de armas. Otras industrias artesanales son la de cerámicas y azulejos, la orfebrería y los cueros.

No hay que olvidar tampoco que fueron los musulmanes quienes introdujeron la técnica oriental de la fabricación de pasta de papel, que con el paso de los años se difundiría por el resto de la Europa cristiana.

Pero para sacar provecho de todo este poder de la industria artesanal era necesario establecer unas redes comerciales adecuadas. El comercio interior tenía lugar entre las distintas poblaciones del Al-Andalus y su centro era el mercado, llamado "zoco." Alrededor de éste se iban agrupando los artesanos. Las comunidades judías, que contaban con la aprobación y el respeto de los dirigentes musulmanes, fueron una parte importante de este esplendor comercial. Para trasladarse de un pueblo a otro en el comercio, por mar se empleaba la navegación de cabotaje y por tierra se hacía a través de las calzadas romanas.

Y como objeto de canje en el comercio, los musulmanes utilizaban dos tipos de monedas: el dinar (de oro, procedente de las minas de Sudán y del comercio con Oriente) y el dirhem (de plata). En la Alta Edad Media los reinos cristianos no poseían metales preciosos y es por ello que las monedas musulmanas eran muy buscadas y atesoradas. Incluso llegaron a utilizarse para ser reacuñadas y convertidas en moneda cristiana.

This is the end of Lecture 2. Please respond to the corresponding questions in your book.

SECTION II

Part A — Writing

Formal Writing Task

> **DIRECTIONS:** Listen to the following recording and then write your essay in your test booklet.

Fuente No. 3

"El problema del agua"

En el mes de noviembre de 1999, el Consejo Mundial del Agua hizo públicos los resultados de unos estudios que indicaban que más de la mitad de los ríos del mundo están contaminados o secos, por lo que sus aguas no pueden o no deberían emplearse para consumo humano o riego. En esos ríos se incluyen no sólo ríos europeos, sino también grandes ríos asiáticos como el río Amarillo en China o africanos como el Nilo en África. El estudio indicaba que de los grandes ríos sólo se salvan de la contaminación el río Amazonas y el río Congo. En el mismo estudio se concluía que los daños al medio ambiente (incluyendo la carencia de agua potable), han provocado en este siglo más desplazados que las guerras.

En España, por ejemplo, la mayoría de sus ríos están contaminados y llenos de basuras y, a pesar de ser el país europeo con mayores problemas de agua, es de los que más se consume (o derrocha) y de los que está más barata. Es importante saber que el agua es un bien escaso y necesaria y hay que cuidarla al máximo para no derrochar.

Pequeñas acciones diarias nos pueden ahorrar mucha agua: cerrar bien los grifos (los goteos consumen mucho), utilizar bocas en grifos y duchas de las que ahorran agua (de venta en cualquier ferretería), cerrar el grifo al cepillarte los dientes, afeitarte, enjabonarte en la ducha o enjabonar los platos, no tirar de la cadena innecesariamente y meter en las cisternas una o dos botellas llenas (así se ahorra mucho y no se pierde eficacia), cerrar ligeramente la llave de paso del agua de tu casa bajará la presión y ahorrará más de lo que parece, no usar lavavajillas o lavadora, a menos que estén llenos ...

Muchas veces se piensa que la solución está en construir embalses, aunque éstos inunden zonas de gran valor ecológico. Sin embargo, la auténtica solución pasa por no derrochar agua, no contaminar la que tenemos y evitar el calentamiento global del planeta. Claro, que a veces, pagar la multa por contaminar es más barato que dejar de contaminar. Ya lo decía Quevedo (1580-1645), "poderoso caballero es don dinero".

(You now have 5 minutes to plan your essay and
40 minutes to write your essay in your test booklet.
Stop the audio CD and write your essay.)

Part B — Speaking

Simulated Conversation

(NARRADOR/A)   Ahora tienes treinta segundos para leer el esquema de la conversación.

(30 seconds)

(NARR.)   Imagina que te encuentras en la calle con tu vecino Fernando. Escucha lo que te cuenta.

Usa el próximo minuto para leer otra vez el esquema de la conversación.

(1 minute)

Ahora comenzará la conversación.

(M)   Oye, ¿oíste las noticias de ayer?

TONE (20 seconds) TONE

(M)   Mira, eran las siete y pico de la tarde cuando Margarita, la hija de los Ramírez, llegó a casa y bajó de su coche saltando y gritando locamente "¡Mamá, papá!"

TONE (20 seconds) TONE

(M)   Pues, parece que después de numerosas entrevistas y tal la joven ha ganado una beca que le pagará todos los gastos para poder asistir a la universidad en el otoño.

TONE (20 seconds) TONE

(M)   Estoy de acuerdo. Sus padres se han preocupado un montón por las finanzas pero ahora se sentirán muy aliviados, ¿no crees?

TONE (20 seconds) TONE

(M)   Claro, claro. Lo que les inquieta a los Ramírez es el hecho de que esa universidad queda tan lejos de aquí. Será una decisión muy complicada, ¿no?

TONE (20 seconds) TONE

(M)   Tienes toda la razón. Bueno, sé que ustedes son buenos amigos y quería compartir esas noticias contigo. ¿Piensas llamar a Margarita ahora o vas a pasar por su casa a verla?

TONE (20 seconds) TONE

(Stop the audio CD and resume the test in the book.)

Formal Oral Presentation

Fuente No. 2

Costa Norte, el interminable paraíso dominicano

Playas hay muchas, tantas como destinos turísticos en el Caribe, pero muy pocas cuentan con tantos atractivos naturales como las que conforman la costa norte de República Dominicana. Una extensa ribera que supera los 600 kilómetros de clara agua de mar y donde abundan amplios e intrincados balnearios rodeados de pueblos y exuberante flora que rememora los tiempos aún vírgenes del Descubrimiento.

Comenzando por la zona cercana a Montecristi, donde se perfila una de las regiones naturales más protegidas en el país y continuando por Puerto Plata, situada entre una esbelta cordillera y el amplio océano Atlántico, hasta llegar a Samaná donde perdura la imagen del paraíso tropical.

Con sobrecogedoras costas abruptas, arrecifes de barrera, playas casi escondidas y amplias zonas verdes que conforman un parque nacional, Montecristi cuenta con el panorama único dado por cayos, manglares, lagunas costeras, bahía y la desembocadura de tres importantes ríos. Un escenario cuán perfecto para dar rienda suelta al viajero que busca la naturaleza. Destacándose precisamente el paisaje, que además de contar con una vegetación endémica es morada de una valiosa fauna compuesta por diversas aves tropicales, manatíes y las impasibles tortugas verdes.

De hecho, la zona costera de Montecristi está ubicada casi bajo el nivel del mar, lo que permite la entrada del agua de la mar en algunos lugares y su asiento en las terrazas construidas para atrapar la sal del líquido evaporado, convirtiendo la comarca en una importante productora de sal.

El núcleo urbano cuenta con historia y personajes de coraje y valentía. Allí se encuentra el Museo Máximo Gómez, lugar donde el militar dominicano tuvo el célebre encuentro con el apóstol de la independencia cubana José Martí.

Sobre un lado del pueblo se destaca El Morro, que no es una edificación colonial, sino una protuberancia de tierra en forma de camello echado y rodeada de una singular playa con arena áspera y rojiza, donde el fuerte oleaje golpea el acantilado. Un esbelto montículo que parece anunciar el arribo al lugar deseado y que por largos años sirvió como faro imaginario a los marinos.

Muchas son las atracciones turísticas que conforman este enclave costeño, destacándose los más de treinta balnearios que acicalan su costa y donde se distinguen Sosua, Cabarete y Playa Dorada, ésta última en una muy bien delimitada demarcación que ofrece más de quince recintos hoteleros de cuatro y cinco estrellas, campo de golf, restaurantes y centro comercial, siendo su esmerado servicio de "todo incluido", incluyendo hospedaje, comidas y bebidas por un precio determinado, su mejor oferta.

Sin embargo, a esta oferta debemos agregar un importante paisaje natural que incluye extensas zonas rurales de interés turístico y ecológico con importantes elevaciones y un caudaloso río. Además, el visitante tiene la oportunidad de visitar el pintoresco pueblo, su plaza principal con algunas reminiscencias de arquitectura victoriana, estilo precisamente importado por inmigrantes, la vieja fortaleza española San Felipe, un parque nacional con interesante jardín botánico y una enorme estatua de Cristo, versión más pequeña de su igual en Río de Janeiro, que corona la loma Isabel de Torres y a donde se llega por medio de un teleférico.

Además de Playa Dorada, Puerto Plata cuenta con la recién remozada Long Beach o Playa del Pueblo, como muchos le llaman, delineada por un malecón a donde acuden los lugareños a disfrutar de la mar, el sol, la buena cocina dominicana y su rica música popular.

(You now have two minutes to plan your answer and two minutes to record your answer on your recording device. Stop the audio CD.)

This is the end of Practice Exam 2.

EXAM 3 TRANSCRIPT

AP Spanish Language

SECTION I

Part A

Get ready for the listening part of the Advanced Placement practice examination in Spanish.

DIRECTIONS: Listen to the following dialogues. Afterwards, listen to the questions based on the dialogues you have just heard and choose the best answer from the choices that follow. Color in the corresponding oval on your answer sheet.

Get ready for the first dialogue.

Dialogue Number 1

Camarera:	¿Saben ya los señores qué van a pedir?
Hombre:	Bueno,... Mis compañeros de trabajo me han dicho que todo aquí está muy bueno pero, ¿cuál es la especialidad de la casa?
Camarera:	El cochinillo asado. Nuestro cocinero lo prepara de una manera especial, durante varios días, para que quede muy tierno. Pruébelo, es realmente delicioso.
Hombre:	No, la verdad es que yo no suelo comer mucho cerdo. ¿Qué más nos recomienda?
Camarera:	También tenemos unas excelentes costillas de cordero a la parrilla, o si lo prefiere, rustido de ternera con manzanas...
Hombre:	No, no me convence demasiado. ¿No tienen nada más?

Camarera: ¿Al señor no le gustan mis sugerencias?

Mujer: Es que mi marido es vegetariano.

Camarera: En ese caso, ¿qué le parece una ensalada verde?

Hombre: Veo que es lo único que podremos comer.

Camarera: Así, ¿ensalada para dos?

Mujer: No, por favor. Yo sí comeré ese delicioso cochinillo...

1.   ¿Dondé se desarrolla la escena?

2.   ¿Cuál es el mejor plato de la casa?

3.   ¿Por qué no le gustan al cliente las sugerencias de la camarera?

Dialogue Number 2

Mujer: Buenos días. ¿En qué puedo servirle? ¿Quiere ver algo concreto o prefiere mirar por su cuenta?

Hombre: No, yo venía porque quería devolver estos pantalones que compré el otro día en este mismo departamento.

Mujer: A ver, déjeme ver de qué modelo se trata. ¿Cuál es el problema? ¿Tienen algún defecto?

Hombre: No, es que no me acaba de convencer el color y, además me vienen un poco ajustados.

Mujer: Bueno. No hay problema. Sólo tiene que darme el recibo de compra y le abonaré las 5.000 pesetas que pagó por ellos. O si quiere, puede canjearlos por otra prenda.

Hombre: No, quiero el dinero pero...La verdad es que no tengo el recibo. Debí haberlo tirado a la basura con la bolsa, sin darme cuenta.

Mujer: En ese caso, me temo que no voy a poder devolverle su dinero. El cartel dice bien claro que para cualquier cambio o devolución es necesario presentar el recibo de caja.

4.   ¿Qué es lo que quiere hacer el hombre con los pantalones?

5. ¿Cuál es el problema de los pantalones?

6. ¿Qué es lo que ha perdido el cliente?

7. ¿Qué le pasó al recibo de compra?

Dialogue Number 3

Mujer: Luis,¡vaya cara que traes! ¿Qué te pasa, hombre?

Hombre: Es que hoy he tenido examen de política y...ha sido un desastre.

Mujer: Pero si llevabas más de dos meses preparándote para esta prueba. ¿Cómo te ha ido tan mal?

Hombre: Yo al principio tampoco lo entendía. Cuando miré la hoja con las preguntas, no sabía contestar ninguna.

Mujer: Es extraño. A ti siempre te ha ido muy bien en política.

Hombre: Y me sigue yendo bien. Lo que pasó es que, cuando entregué el examen en blanco, me di cuenta de que... ¡estaba en la clase de ciencias naturales!

Mujer: ¡Eres un auténtico despistado!

8. ¿Por qué trae mala cara Luis?

9. ¿Cuánto tiempo llevaba Luis preparando para el examen?

10. ¿Qué es lo que Luis no entendía?

11. ¿Cuál fue el desastre, según Luis?

12. ¿Por qué se equivocó de clase Luis, según la mujer?

DIRECTIONS: Listen to the following short narratives. Afterwards, listen to the questions based on the narratives you have just heard and choose the best answer from the choices that follow. Color in the corresponding oval on your answer sheet.

Get ready for the first narrative.

Narrative Number 1

Dicen que es el deporte que más dinero mueve en Estados Unidos y el que cuenta con más aficionados, por encima del béisbol y del baloncesto de la NBA. El fútbol americano (como lo llamamos los españoles para diferenciarlo del europeo, al que ellos denominan "soccer") hace tiempo que dejó de ser un simple deporte para convertirse en un gran negocio del espactáculo y en una tradición tan arraigada a la cultura americana como el pavo asado del día de Acción de Gracias. Los niños estadounidenses sueñan con llegar a ser un día estrellas del fútbol americano, pero son una minoría los que llegan a formar parte de las ligas universitarias, y sólo una exclusiva elite de ellos tiene acceso a ese gran circo de juego y dinero que es la NFL. Una vez alcanzada la liga profesional, el gran hito para un jugador es llegar a participar en una Super Bowl.

13. ¿Cuál es el deporte más popular en Estados Unidos?

14. ¿Cuántos niños estadounidenses llegan a formar parte de las ligas universitarias?

15. ¿Cómo considera el fútbol americano la narradora?

16. ¿Cuál es el hito de un jugador profesional?

Narrative Number 2

Steven Spielberg asegura que "Parque Jurásico" no es ni un film de ciencia ficción ni un ejemplo de cine fantástico, sino una película de ciencia, a secas, porque lo que en ella se narra muy bien pudiera suceder hoy en día. También afirma que se han necesitado 65 millones de años para realizar el famoso largometraje, porque ése ha sido el tiempo que ha pasado desde que los gigantescos dinosaurios poblaron la Tierra hasta que los avances científicos han permitido especular con la creación clónica de especies extinguidas a partir del ADN. Michael Crichton, el autor de la novela en la que se basa el film, se ha convertido en uno de los más famosos escritores de "best sellers" de los útimos años en Estados Unidos. Antiguo cineasta, el novelista ha conseguido suculentos beneficios vendiendo los derechos cinematográficos de sus obras a las grandes productoras de Hollywood. Crichton, a quien siempre le ha apasionado el tema de los dinosaurios, dijo que desde hace mucho tiempo tenía ganas de escribir algo sobre ellos, muy ligado con la ciencia y los problemas que ésta puede llegar a causar.

17. ¿Cómo clasifica Spielberg "Parque Jurásico"?

18. ¿Cuál es la profesión de Michael Crichton, según el texto?

19. ¿Cómo ha conseguido Crichton grandes beneficios?

20. ¿Sobre qué tema quería escribir Crichton desde hace mucho tiempo?

Lecture 1

A cualquiera que haya visitado Barcelona seguramente le habrá impresionado ver las altas torres de la Sagrada Familia, los curvados bancos de mosaico del Parque Güell o las fantasmagóricas formas de La Pedrera. Estos edificios y muchos más de características muy diversas forman parte inseparable del paisaje arquitectónico de la capital catalana y llaman la atención por su originalidad. Todos ellos llevan una misma firma: la del famoso arquitecto catalán Antoni Gaudí.

Gaudí nació en 1852 y desde muy joven se dedicó en cuerpo y alma al estudio y la creación arquitectónica. El que llegara a ser un arquitecto fuera de lo normal no significa que fuera autodidacta. Antoni Gaudí fue a la escuela de los Escolapios, tomó clases en el taller de Eudald Puntí y acudió, durante ocho años, a la Escuela de Arquitectura, a la vez que trabajaba como delineante para algunos de sus profesores.

Pero además de estos estudios más dirigidos hacia la arquitectura, Gaudí también asistió a los cursos de Filosofia y Estética de la Universidad Literaria. Todos estos conocimientos y experiencias se fueron entremezclando en su mente y se concentraron en un único esfuerzo: la creación arquitectónica. Al contrario que otros colegas suyos, el arquitecto catalán nunca dio clases ni conferencias, ni se sintió atraído por la erudición, los negocios o la política. Tampoco se casó nunca. Todo en su vida era por y para la arquitectura, para la creación de sus obras o para ayudar a salvar edificios en precario estado de conservación, como hizo con la Catedral de Ciudad de Mallorca, entre otros.

Este interés monotemático ha dado lugar a todo tipo de especulaciones sobre su vida privada y su personalidad, pero lo que realmente interesa saber de Antoni Gaudí queda claramente reflejado en sus creaciones.

Para Gaudí la arquitectura era algo más que el arte de proyectar casas y edificios. La concebía como la creación de la unidad a través de la diversidad: como de distintos elementos, básicos u ornamentales, y a través de diferentes talleres de artesanía (de cerámica, de hierro forjado, etc.) podía crearse un todo.

La originalidad de su obra no la consiguió por la invención de materiales nuevos, o el uso de estructuras que rompían los moldes de la época. Siempre utilizó para crear sus edificios los medios más comunes de su tiempo: piedras, ladrillos, muros y hierro. Su originalidad estaba en la forma y el colorido que tomaban sus obras a medida que se iban levantando del suelo.

A menudo solía comentar el arquitecto que la originalidad consistía en volver a los orígenes, y para él, el origen de todo está en la Naturaleza. Gaudí aprendió directamente de la Naturaleza, gracias a su innato espíritu de observación. Meticulosamente estudiaba el cielo, la tierra, los hombres y las formas de las plantas, etcétera. Analizaba los fenómenos de la naturaleza para sintetizarlos en su obra. Todo lo natural se convirtió en el mejor modelo para sus creaciones: acantilados, flores, animales, árboles,...

Otra fuente de inspiración de la que bebió el renombrado arquitecto fue la religión católica, de la que era un devoto y fiel seguidor. Historias del Apocalipsis o de los Testamentos le proporcionaron imágenes simbólicas que aparecen en algunas de sus creaciones.

Uno de los factores que más repercutió en la extensa obra de Antoni Gaudí fue la labor de mecenazgo que sobre él tuvieron Eusebi Güell y la familia del marqués de Comillas. La protección artística que éstos le brindaron permitió que el genial arquitecto pudiera dedicarse plenamente a su labor creadora, con total libertad y gran abundancia de medios. Esto fue providencial para Gaudí, cuyos complicados esquemas mentales tardaban largo tiempo en materializarse en obras completas.

Su carácter perfeccionista hizo que Gaudí no diera por concluidas muchas de sus obras. Siempre encontraba algo que mejorar, algo que retocar, algún aspecto que transformar. Cuando le llegó la muerte, tras ser atropellado por un tranvía a los 74 años de edad, en 1926, aún le quedaba mucho trabajo por terminar en varios de sus edificios, pero especialmente en el que era más importante para él: la Sagrada Familia.

No obstante, hay una trilogía de obras de Gaudí que constituyen el nudo de su estilo: las Misiones de África, en Tánger (un proyecto que nunca llevó a cabo), la iglesia de la colonia obrera Güell, en Santa Coloma de Cervelló y el templo de la Sagrada Familia, en Barcelona. Desgraciadamente, la destrucción del archivo Gaudí sólo nos ha dejado del proyecto de las Misiones dos fotografías. De la iglesia de la colonia obrera sólo está acabada la cripta. Pero estos dos ensayos son el antecedente de la obra caudal del maestro, la Sagrada Familia.

Como ya se ha comentado anteriormente, la muerte del gran arquitecto, en 1926, dejó el templo inacabado, aunque se conservaban todos los bocetos y proyectos que Gaudí tenía en su estudio. Sólo había concluido la cripta, el ábside y la fachada del Nacimiento, con grandes esculturas naturalistas, y uno de los nueve campanarios. Al poco tiempo se concluyeron otros tres.

Hoy en día, continúa la labor de construcción del gran templo, no sin cierta polémica, porque los arquitectos más puristas consideran que no se debería terminar con toda la tecnología moderna, como se está haciendo, mientras que otros opinan que, como sucedía en las grandes catedrales de la antigüedad, el tiempo iba superponiendo estilos y técnicas. El visitante podrá ver el gran contraste entre la zona levantada en la época gaudiniana y la más moderna (con cuatro campanarios más). Mientras prosigue la polémica, prosiguen también las obras en la Sagrada Familia.

This is the end of Lecture 1. Please respond to the corresponding questions in your book.

Lecture 2

El mundo entero tiene la noción de que el flamenco es el baile típico y característico de la cultura española. Se piensa que en cualquier región de España que se visite, todos los habitantes sabrán bailar, cantar y tocar flamenco. Pero no hay nada más lejano a la realidad.

El flamenco nació en Andalucía. En todos los rincones del arte flamenco se pueden encontrar raíces de la larga lista de pueblos que, en un momento u otro de la historia, han pasado por el sur de la Península Ibérica. Así pues, hay reminiscencias judías, musulmanas, gitanas,… Una mezcla de culturas que fueron dejando su huella en la gente del sur de España ayudó a configurar lo que, con el paso del tiempo, se convertiría en el flamenco.

A partir del siglo pasado, la historia más documentada del flamenco se estructura en cuatro grandes etapas claramente definidas.

La primera de ellas se desarrolla desde 1800 hasta 1860 y los estudiosos del flamenco han acordado llamarla la época del "hermetismo." Durante estos años, el cante estuvo encerrado en círculos familiares gitanos, donde era cultivado por los miembros de la familia para celebrar todo tipo de acontecimientos, como bautizos, bodas o cualquier otra festividad. Pero este hermetismo con el que los flamencólogos han querido denominar esta incipiente etapa del arte flamenco fue relativo, porque se limitó al cante flamenco puro o gitano. Paralelamente, se expandía un folklore andaluz mucho más extrovertido. El flamenco se debe en gran parte a la cultura gitana, pero sólo en determinados estilos básicos, no en su totalidad.

La segunda etapa cubre los años que separan 1860 de 1910, y se la ha llamado la época de los "cafés cantantes." En los Cafés Cantantes el flamenco encontró un espacio escénico, un escenario más definido, que sería el precursor de los "tablaos" del siglo XX. Los primeros Cafés Cantantes hacen su aparición hacia 1842, pero su influencia en la historia del arte flamenco no fue de demasiada relevancia hasta los años sesenta del siglo XIX.

La tercera etapa de la historia del flamenco se extiende desde 1910 hasta 1936 y su principal característica es que el flamenco irrumpe en los escenarios teatrales. Un público amplio acudía a los teatros a presenciar cantes cargados de adornos, que se alejaban de las formas más puras. Esta época es conocida por el nombre de "'Opera flamenca." Muchos flamencólogos consideran que ésta fue la peor época para el flamenco y también la más negativa. De todos modos, también hay que entender que la fase de la ópera flamenca tuvo algunos aspectos positivos, como por ejemplo la expansión del flamenco a otros ámbitos, la aparición entre los artistas de figuras emblemáticas y carismáticas, la inclusión en el flamenco de influencias de estilos de origen americano,—más livianos pero que no por ello han de ser despreciados—, etc.

Por último, la cuarta etapa agrupa los años que se extienden desde 1940 hasta nuestros días. Esta etapa se distingue principalmente por una continua evolución del flamenco, el auge de festivales y concursos, el reconocimiento internacional del flamenco como arte universal y una vuelta a los cánones más puristas, sin dejar de lado las nuevas tendencias y las fusiones con otros estilos musicales, como el jazz o el rock, entre otros muchos.

Pero a la hora de recordar la historia del flamenco, no se puede dejar de mencionar la gran importancia que tuvo el Concurso Nacional de Cante Jondo que se celebró en Granada en 1922. El Concurso fue promovido por un grupo de intelectuales de la época, entre los que se encontraban nombres tan relevantes como el de los compositores Manuel de Falla y Turina, o los escritores Federico García Lorca y Juan Ramón Jiménez. La razón principal de que se organizaran este histórico evento era su temor a que el flamenco pudiera desaparecer. El Concurso tuvo un éxito fuera de lo común. Los organizadores, en su intento de preservar lo más puro del arte flamenco, prohibieron la participación a los artistas profesionales, limitando la opción a concurso a todos aquellos que no cobraran por ello, con lo cual el nivel de participación se mermó bastante. Finalmente, el vencedor fue un niño de 12 años que estaba llamado a convertirse en una de las figuras más míticas del flamenco: Manolo Caracol. El Concurso Nacional de Cante Jondo tuvo tanta trascendencia que el flamenco se abrió a una elite intelectual que antes lo desconocía prácticamente por completo.

Por otra parte, la guitarra flamenca es el verdadero puntal y cimiento del flamenco. Sólo en casos esporádicos, como en el caso de cantes muy antiguos, se podía llegar a prescindir de la guitarra. En todos los demás, la guitarra es un elemento indispensable cuando se habla de flamenco.

En los últimos tiempos, especialmente en la segunda mitad de este siglo, la guitarra flamenca ha sido uno de los elementos que más ha evolucionado. Unos cambios tan amplios raramente se deben a una sola persona, pero en este caso, gran parte de esta evolución se debe a Paco de Lucía. Su extraordinaria calidad como guitarrista ha logrado poner en el primer término del flamenco a la guitarra. La admiración y el respeto que han despertado su arte ha hecho que un sinfín de jóvenes guitarristas trataran de seguir sus pasos, cosa que está haciendo que la nueva cosecha artística tenga un nivel muy alto.

Otros famosos guitarristas de todos los tiempos han sido Sabicas, El Niño Ricardo, Montoya, Melchor de Marchena,... y de la generación que encabeza Paco de Lucía hay que destacar a Manolo Sanlúcar, Enrique de Melchor, Paco Cepero, Gerardo Núñez o El Niño de Pura, entre otros.

This is the end of Lecture 2. Please respond to the corresponding questions in your book.

SECTION II

Part A — Writing

Formal Writing Task

> **DIRECTIONS:** Listen to the following recording and then write your essay in your test booklet.

Fuente No. 3

Annan pide a Unión Europea aumentar sus cuotas de inmigración legal

"Los migrantes necesitan a Europa, pero Europa también necesita a los migrantes", dijo hoy Kofi Annan, Secretario General de la ONU en el Parlamento Europeo, donde urgió a la Unión Europea aumentar sus cuotas de inmigración legal.

Al recibir el premio 2004 Andrei Sakharov para la Libertad de Pensamiento, Annan subrayó que una Europa cerrada a la inmigración sería "más pobre, más débil y más vieja", mientras que si abriera sus políticas migratorias, se convertiría en una región "más justa, más rica, más fuerte y más joven".

Sin inmigración, agregó, la población de la Unión Europea disminuiría a menos de 400 millones para el año 2050 y, si esto ocurriera, "sus economías se contraerían y sus sociedades se estancarían", advirtió.

En su discurso, el titular de la ONU recordó que este panorama no es privativo de Europa, sino que también se presenta en la Federación de Rusia, en Japón y en otros países asiáticos, para los que la inmigración será una solución inevitable.

Frente a estas perspectivas, alentó a los Estados europeos a abrir sus políticas de inmigración legal permanente y temporal para trabajadores calificados y no calificados.

Asimismo, les pidió considerar objetivos como la unificación familiar y la mejora económica de las personas que migran.

El Secretario General reconoció las dificultades que supone el fenómeno migratorio, pero recordó que, por otra parte, los inmigrantes hacen contribuciones enormes en el campo de la ciencia, la academia, los deportes, las artes y los gobiernos.

Durante su participación también se refirió a los refugiados, para quienes pidió protección adecuada.

Destacó que siete de cada diez refugiados huyen a países en desarrollo donde los recursos y los derechos humanos son menos sólidos que en Europa. En este sentido, Annan llamó a la Unión Europea a ayudar a los países pobres a fortalecer su capacidad para proteger y albergar a los refugiados.

(You now have 5 minutes to plan your essay and
40 minutes to write your essay in your test booklet.
Stop the audio CD and write your essay.)

Part B — Speaking

Simulated Conversation

(NARRADOR/A)   Ahora tienes treinta segundos para leer el siguiente esquema de la conversación.

(30 seconds)

(NARR.)   Imagina que recibes un mensaje telefónico del editor del periódico escolar que quiere entrevistarte para la próxima edición. Después de oírlo, vuelve a llamarlo para hablar de la entrevista.

(M)   Buenas tardes. He entendido que vas a hacer un viaje con el Club de español a Latinoamérica. Quisiera entrevistarte para poder escribir un artículo describiendo el viaje en nuestro próximo periódico. Llámame cuando puedas, por favor.

(NARR.)   Ahora usa el próximo minuto para leer otra vez el esquema de la conversación.

(1 minute)

Ahora comenzará la llamada.

(M)   ¿Qué tal? Para comenzar, para este viaje ¿adónde van ustedes y cuánto tiempo piensan pasar allí?

TONE (20 seconds) TONE

(M)   Qué interesante Me gustaría saber más de este viaje que Uds. van a hacer.

TONE (20 seconds) TONE

(M)   Parece fenomenal. ¿Qué requisitos hay para poder participar?

TONE (20 seconds) TONE

(M)   Bueno, gracias por tu tiempo y si se me ocurre alguna pregunta, ¿podemos continuar esta conversación mañana?

TONE (20 seconds) TONE

(Stop the audio CD and resume the test in the book.)

Formal Oral Presentation

Fuente No. 2

Cómo ser el primero de la clase

Sacar las mejores notas es el objetivo de todos los estudiantes y los padres deben ayudar contribuyendo a crear un ambiente familiar que facilite el estudio sin añadir presión, especialmente a los más pequeños.

"La concentración es el principal problema durante la educación infantil, sobre todo cuando los niños van el primer año al colegio. Los niños se ven incapaces de prestar atención de manera constante por eso es fundamental que controlen sus distracciones en el aula y los padres deben contribuir a enseñarles en casa cómo conseguirlo", afirma Adolfo Torrecilla, profesor de Literatura y muy vinculado a temas y desarrollo de la educación.

Cuando las familias no son numerosas concentran todas sus energías en lograr una educación variada para sus hijos y sin darse cuenta les cargan de actividades extraescolares que les llevan de un lado a otro: de clases de música, a la práctica de la natación, el tenis o el fútbol, además de cursos de idiomas.

El profesor Torrecilla afirma que es fundamental que el alumno tenga afán de superación para conseguir que sus notas sean las primeras de la clase. "Los padres tienen una labor importante para conseguir que su hijo se ilusione con aprender cada día más. Un alumno curioso y con ganas de aprender tiene un porcentaje más alto de lograr el éxito en los estudios".

Lograr un buen ambiente de estudio es primordial para tener buenas notas. "Recomiendo que no se estudie ni con la radio ni con la televisión puesta. Tampoco es aconsejable estudiar escuchando música. Internet sólo debe utilizarse para momentos puntuales de consulta durante el estudio, sino se corre el peligro de utilizar otros instrumentos que dispersan la concentración", comenta Torrecilla.

El profesor apunta algunas claves que no deben perderse de vista durante el transcurso del curso escolar.

1. Tomar nota de las indicaciones del profesor favorece la atención en la clase durante sus explicaciones, y también ayudará más tarde a recordar en casa la exposición.

2. Llevar al día los deberes ayudará a plantear cualquier duda que surja al día siguiente en el aula.

3. Pregunta todas las dudas en clase, no salgas sin tener claro cualquiera de las cosas, incluso aquellas que puedas considerar nimias.

4. Estudiar el último día antes del examen no es nada productivo. Huye de los atracones de última hora.

5. Estudia primero lo que más te cueste; será más fácil, cuando el cansancio haga mella, enfrentarse a lo que más te gusta.

6. Organiza el horario de estudio y sé disciplinado con él.

7. Mejora tu atención en el aula. Evita bromas a destiempo que distraigan tu atención.

8. Cuida cómo merece todo el material escolar. Resulta desolador estudiar sobre libros desvencijados que atraen poco a la lectura o que la dispersan con dibujos en los márgenes.

9. Atender a las necesidades de un compañero además de reforzar los lazos entre alumnos, ayuda a comprobar que también puedes aprender de tus compañeros.

10. Sé constante en el aprendizaje y escucha con atención.

(You now have two minutes to plan your answer and two
minutes to record your answer on your recording
device. Stop the audio CD.)

This is the end of Practice Exam 3.

GLOSSARY

AP Spanish Language

ENGLISH-TO-SPANISH
& SPANISH-TO-ENGLISH

ENGLISH-TO-SPANISH GLOSSARY

AP Spanish Language

Use the English-to-Spanish glossary that appears on the following pages to prepare your answers for the essay and spoken portions of the exam. You can look up words in English that you feel would enhance your answers and learn their Spanish equivalent.

After the English-to-Spanish glossary is a Spanish-to-English version. Use this one to learn the meanings of Spanish words that you were unfamiliar with from the questions or passages.

action – *n.* – *la acción*

actor – *n.* – *el actor*

actress – *n.* – *la actriz*

after – *prep.* – *después de*

airline – *n.* – *la aerolinea*

airplane – *n.* – *el avión*

alley – *n.* – *el callejón*

almost – *adv.* – *casi*

always – *adv.* – *siempre*

ancient – *adj.* – *antiguo*

angry (to get) – *v.* – *enfadarse (enojarse, molestarse)*

ankle – *n.* – *el tobillo*

announcer – *n.* – *el (la) locutor (a)*

apple – *n.* – *la manzana*

arm – *n.* – *el brazo*

aroma – *n.* – *el aroma*

arrive – *v.* – *llegar*

artist – *n.* – *el artista*

athletic – *adj.* – *atlético*

attempt – *v.* – *intentar*

attend – *v.* – *asistir a*

audience – *n.* – *el público*

aunt – *n.* – *la tía*

autumn – *n.* – *el otoño*

avenue – *n.* – *la avenida*

back – n. – la espalda

bacon – n. – el tocino

bad – adj. – malo, mal

banana, plantain – n. – el plátano (la banana)

bathroom – n. – el baño

bathtub – n. – la tina

beach – n. – la playa

beard – n. – la barba

beautiful – adj. – bello

bed – n. – la cama

bedroom – n. – el dormitorio (alcoba)

beer – n. – la cerveza

before – prep. – antes de

begin – v. – empezar

believe – v. – creer

better – adj. – mejor

big – adj. – grande

bird – n. – el pájaro

birth – n. – el nacimiento

birthday – n. – el cumpleaños

black – adj. – negro

blind – adj. – ciego

blue – adj. – azul

boar – n. – el jabalí

boat – n. – el bote, la barca, el barco

book – n. – el libro

bookstore – n. – la librería

boring – adj. – aburrido

born (to be) – v. – nacer

boss – n. – el jefe

bother – v. – molestar

box – n. – la caja

boy – n. – el niño

bread – n. – el pan

bring – v. – traer

bronchitis – n. – la bronquitis

brother – n. – el hermano

brown – adj. – marrón, pardo

brush – v. – cepillarse

building – n. – el edificio

bull – n. – el toro

bus – n. – el ómnibus (autobús; microbús; la guagua)

business – n. – el negocio

businessman – n. – el hombre de negocios

butter – n. – la mantequilla

buy – v. – comprar

cake – n. – la torta

car – n. – el auto, automóvil, coche, carro

carry – v. – llevar

cat – n. – el gato

cathedral – n. – la catedral

chair – n. – la silla

change – v. – cambiar

cheese – *n.* – *el queso*

chemist – *n.* – *el químico*

chemistry – *n.* – *la química*

chest – *n.* – *el pecho*

chicken – *n.* – *el pollo*

Christmas – *n.* – *la(s) Navidad(es)*

city – *n.* – *la ciudad*

clean – *adj.* – *limpio*

climate – *n.* – *el clima*

clothing – *n.* – *la ropa*

coat – *n.* – *la chaqueta, el saco, el abrigo*

coffee – *n.* – *el café*

coffin – *n.* – *el ataúd*

cold – *adj.* – *frío*

colleague – *n.* – *el colega*

comb – *n.* – *la peinilla*

comb (one's hair) – *v.* – *peinarse*

comet – *n.* – *el cometa*

computer – *n.* – *el ordenador*

conference – *n.* – *la consulta*

corn – *n.* – *el choclo (maíz)*

couch – *n.* – *el sillón*

courageous – *adj.* – *valiente*

course – *n.* – *el curso*

courteous – *adj.* – *cortés*

cow – *n.* – *la vaca*

crime – *n.* – *el delito, el crimen*

crisis – *n.* – *la crisis*

crowd – *n.* – *la muchedumbre*

cup – *n.* – *la taza*

cure – *n.* – *la cura*

daughter – *n.* – *la hija*

daughter-in-law – *n.* – *la nuera*

day – *n.* – *el día*

death – *n.* – *la muerte*

deer – *n.* – *el ciervo (venado)*

departure – *n.* – *la salida*

desk – *n.* – *el escritorio*

dessert – *n.* – *el postre*

die – *v.* – *morir*

difficult – *adj.* – *difícil*

dining room – *n.* – *el comedor*

diploma – *n.* – *el diploma*

dirty – *adj.* – *sucio*

disappointment – *n.* – *la decepción*

doctor – *n.* – *el (la) doctor (a)*, (*el médico*)

dog – *n.* – *el perro*

door – *n.* – *la puerta*

down (to go) – *v.* – *bajar*

downtown – *n.* – *el centro*

drama – *n.* – *el drama*

drawing – *n.* – *el dibujo*

dream – *n.* – *el sueño*

dream – *v.* – *soñar*

dress (oneself) – v. – *vestirse*

dresser – n. – *la cómoda (el toca-dor)*

drink – v. – *beber (tomar)*

drive – v. – *manejar (conducir, guiar)*

drunk (to get) – v. – *emborracharse*

eagle – n. – *el águila*

ear – n. – *la oreja*

early – adv. – *temprano*

easy – adj. – *fácil*

eat – v. – *comer*

elbow – n. – *el codo*

elevator – n. – *el ascensor*

engineer – n. – *el ingeniero*

enough – adv. – *bastante*

enter – v. – *entrar*

entrance, lobby – n. – *la entrada*

envelope – n. – *el sobre*

eulogy – n. – *el elogio*

event – n. – *el suceso*

expensive – adj. – *caro*

eyeglasses – n. – *los anteojos, las gafas, los espejuelos, los lentes*

eyelashes – n. – *las pestañas*

eyelids – n. – *los párpados*

eye – n. – *el ojo*

face – n. – *la cara*

factory – n. – *la fábrica*

fainting – n. – *el desmayo*

fall (down) – v. – *caer (se)*

family – n. – *la familia*

fantastic – adj. – *fantástico*

far – adv. – *lejos*

farm – n. – *la granja*

farmer – n. – *el agricultor*

fat – adj. – *gordo*

father – n. – *el padre*

fear – n. – *el miedo*

female – n. – *la hembra*

field – n. – *el campo*

film – n. – *la película*

film director ("auteur") or producer – n. – *el cineasta*

fingernails – n. – *las uñas*

fingers – n. – *los dedos*

fire – n. – *el fuego*

fireplace; chimney – n. – *la chime-nea (el hogar)*

fish – n. – *el pescado, pez*

fishing – v. – *pescar*

flight – n. – *el vuelo*

floppy disk – n. – *el disco flexible*

fly – v. – *volar*

forehead – n. – *la frente*

forget – v. – *olvidar*

fragile – adj. – *frágil*

funny – adj. – *divertido*

game – *n.* – *el juego*

garden – *n.* – *el jardín*

glass – *n.* – *el vaso*

goat – *n.* – *la cabra*

God – *n.* – *Dios*

gold – *n.* – *el oro*

good – *adj.* – *bueno*

goodbye – *adiós, hasta luego*

granddaughter – *n.* – *la nieta*

grandfather – *n.* – *el abuelo*

grandmother – *n.* – *la abuela*

grandson – *n.* – *el nieto*

grapes – *n.* – *las uvas*

grass (tended, not wild) – *n.* – *la hierba*

great-grandfather – *n.* – *el bisabuelo*

great-grandmother – *n.* – *la bis-abuela*

green – *adj.* – *verde*

greet – *v.* – *saludar*

grow (get) tired – *v.* – *cansarse*

grow – *v.* – *crecer, cultivar*

guide (book) – *n.* – *la guía*

guide (person) – *n.* – *el guía*

hair – *n.* – *el cabello (pelo)*

ham – *n.* – *el jamón*

hand – *n.* – *la mano*

handsome – *adj.* – *guapo*

happy – *adj.* – *feliz, contento*

hard – *adj.* – *duro, difícil*

hard disk – *n.* – *el disco duro*

hatchet – *n.* – *un hacha*

hate – *v.* – *odiar*

head – *n.* – *la cabeza*

health – *n.* – *la salud*

healthy – *adj.* – *sano (a)*

hear – *v.* – *oír, escuchar*

heel – *n.* – *el talón*

hen – *n.* – *la gallina*

hips – *n.* – *las caderas*

hope – *n.* – *la esperanza*

horse – *n.* – *el caballo*

house (big) – *n.* – *la casona*

house – *n.* – *la casa*

hunger – *n.* – *hambre (f.)*

husband – *n.* – *el marido, esposo*

image – *n.* – *la imagen*

intelligent – *adj.* – *inteligente*

interesting – *adj.* – *interesante*

internal – *adj.* – *interior*

intersection – *n.* – *la bocacalle*

iron – *n.* – *el hierro*

joke – *n.* – *la chanza, el chiste, la broma*

journalist – *n.* – *el periodista*

joy – *n.* – *la alegría*

judge – *n.* – *el juez*

keep – *v.* – *mantener*

keyboard – *n.* – *el teclado*

king – *n.* – *el rey*

kitchen – *n.* – *la cocina*

kite – *n.* – *la cometa*

knee – *n.* – *la rodilla*

know – *v.* – *saber (conocer)*

lamp – *n.* – *la lámpara*

language – *n.* – *el idioma*

last night – *adv.* – *anoche*

late – *adv.* – *tarde*

later – *adv.* – *luego (después)*

lawyer – *n.* – *el abogado*

learn – *v.* – *aprender*

leave – *v.* – *irse (partir, salir)*

lecture – *n.* – *la conferencia*

less – *adv.* – *menos*

letter – *n.* – *la carta*

lettuce – *n.* – *la lechuga*

light – *n.* – *la luz*

like – *v.* – *gustar*

lip – *n.* – *el labio*

listen to – *v.* – *escuchar*

living room – *n.* – *la sala*

long – *adj.* – *largo*

look at – *v.* – *mirar*

lose – *v.* – *perder(ie)*

love – *n.* – *el amor*

luck – *n.* – *la suerte*

luggage – *n.* – *el equipaje*

lunch – *n.* – *el almuerzo*

machine – *n.* – *la máquina*

magazine – *n.* – *la revista*

mail – *n.* – *el correo*

mailman – *n.* – *el cartero*

make (do) – *v.* – *hacer*

male – *n.* – *el varón*

man (big) – *n.* – *el hombrón*

map – *n.* – *el mapa*

market – *n.* – *el mercado*

marvelous – *adj.* – *maravilloso*

mean – *adj.* – *mezquino*

meat – *n.* – *la carne*

mechanic – *n.* – *el mecánico*

microwave oven – *n.* – *el microon-das*

milk – *n.* – *la leche*

mirror – *n.* – *el espejo*

misfortune – *n.* – *la desgracia*

money – *n.* – *el dinero*

moon – *n.* – *la luna*

more – *adv.* – *más*

morning – *n.* – *la mañana*

mother – *n.* – *la madre*

motorcycle – *n.* – *la moto*

mountain – *n.* – *la montaña*

mountain climbing – *n.* – *el alpinismo*

mouse – *n.* – *el ratón*

mouth – *n.* – *la boca*

move – *v.* – *mover(se) (mudarse)*

moviehouse – *n.* – *el cine*

muscles – *n.* – *los músculos*

nail – *n.* – *el clavo*

name – *n.* – *el nombre*

near – *adv.* – *cerca*

neck – *n.* – *el cuello*

necklace – *n.* – *el collar*

need – *v.* – *necesitar*

neighbor – *n.* – *el vecino (el prójimo)*

neighborhood – *n.* – *el vecindario*

nephew – *n.* – *el sobrino*

never – *adv.* – *nunca*

newspaper – *n.* – *el periódico, diario*

niece – *n.* – *la sobrina*

night – *n.* – *la noche*

night table – *n.* – *el velador*

nightmare – *n.* – *la pesadilla*

noise – *n.* – *el ruido*

nose – *n.* – *la nariz*

notes – *n.* – *los apuntes*

nothing – *pro./adv.* – *nada*

nurse – *n.* – *la enfermera*

occupation – *n.* – *el oficio*

old – *adj.* – *viejo (antiguo)*

older – *adj.* – *mayor*

olive – *n.* – *la aceituna*

order (as in public order) – *n.* – *el orden*

order (to do something) – *n.* – *la orden*

order, ask – *v.* – *pedir(i, i)*

out (to go) – *v.* – *salir*

outer – *adj.* – *exterior*

oven; furnace – *n.* – *el horno*

owe – *v.* – *deber*

painting – *n.* – *el cuadro*

pants – *n.* – *los pantalones*

paper – *n.* – *el papel*

parachuting – *n.* – *el paracaidismo*

park – *v.* – *estacionarse*

parking lot – *n.* – *la plaza de estacionamiento*

passenger – *n.* – *el (la) pasajero (a)*

passport – *n.* – *el pasaporte*

pay – *v.* – *pagar*

peach – *n.* – *el durazno*

pear – *n.* – *la pera*

pencil – *n.* – *el lápiz*

people – *n.* – *la gente*

photo – *n.* – *la foto*

physician – *n.* – *el médico (el doctor)*

physicist – *n.* – *el físico*

pig – *n.* – *el cerdo (el chancho, el puerco, el marrano)*

pink – *adj.* – *rosa (rosado)*

play – *v.* – *jugar*

player – *n.* – *el (la) jugador (a)*

poem – *n.* – *el poema*

poet – *n.* – *el poeta*

poison (to) – *v.* – *intoxicar, envenenar*

police – *n.* – *la policía*

politician – *n.* – *el político*

Pope – *n.* – *el papa*

potato – *n.* – *la papa (patatas)*

prefer – *v.* – *preferir*

pregnant – *adj.* – *embarazada*

prepare – *v.* – *preparar*

presence – *n.* – *la presencia*

pretty – *adj.* – *bonito*

price – *n.* – *el precio*

prick, wound – *v.* – *pinchar*

priest – *n.* – *el cura*

printer – *n.* – *la impresora*

problem – *n.* – *el problema*

prophet – *n.* – *el profeta*

purple – *adj.* – *morado (violeta)*

pyramid – *n.* – *la pirámide*

queen – *n.* – *la reina*

quiet – *adj.* – *callado*

rabbit – *n.* – *el conejo*

radio – *n.* – *el radio*

read – *v.* – *leer*

reading – *n.* – *la lectura*

reason – *n.* – *la razón*

record player – *n.* – *el tocadiscos*

red – *adj.* – *rojo, colorado*

referee – *n.* – *el árbitro*

refrigerator – *n.* – *el refrigerador, la heladera (nevera)*

remember – *v.* – *recordar*

rent – *v.* – *alquilar*

responsibility – *n.* – *la responsabilidad*

rest – *v.* – *descansar*

return – *v.* – *regresar (volver)*

rice – *n.* – *el arroz*

rich – *adj.* – *rico*

ring – *n.* – *el anillo*

river – *n.* – *el río*

roof; ceiling – *n.* – *el techo*

rooster – *n.* – *el gallo*

run – *v.* – *correr*

sad – *adj.* – *triste*

salad – *n.* – *la ensalada*

salesman – *n.* – *el vendedor*

sand – *n.* – *la arena*

say (tell) – *v.* – *decir*

school (high) – *n.* – *el colegio*

school – *n.* – *la escuela*

sea – *n.* – *el mar*

secret – *n.* – *la confidencia*

see – *v.* – *ver*

sell – *v.* – *vender*

send – *v.* – *enviar, mandar*

sensitive – *adj.* – *sensible*

sentence – *n.* – *la frase*

series – *n.* – *la serie*

shark – *n.* – *el tiburón*

shave – *v.* – *afeitar(se)*

sheep – *n.* – *la oveja*

sheets – *n.* – *las sábanas*

shirt – *n.* – *la camisa*

shoe – *n.* – *el zapato*

shopping – *v.* – *ir de compras*

short – *adj.* – *corto, bajo*

shoulders – *n.* – *los hombros*

shovel – *n.* – *la pala*

shower – *n.* – *la ducha*

sick (person) – *n.* – *el (la) enfermo(a)*

sidewalk – *n.* – *la acera (vereda)*

signature – *n.* – *la firma*

silent (to be) – *v.* – *callar*

silver – *n.* – *la plata*

singer – *n.* – *el cantante*

sink – *n.* – *el lavamanos*

sister – *n.* – *la hermana*

sit down – *v.* – *sentarse*

sleep – *v.* – *dormir*

small – *adj.* – *chico, pequeño*

smile – *n.* – *la sonrisa*

smoke – *n.* – *el humo*

smoke – *v.* – *fumar*

snack – *n.* – *la merienda*

snorkel – *v.* – *bucear*

soccer – *n.* – *el fútbol*

society – *n.* – *la sociedad*

sock – *n.* – *el calcetín, la media*

sofa – *n.* – *el sofá*

soldier – *n.* – *el soldado*

some – *adj.* – *poco*

someone – *n.* – *alguien*

something – *n.* – *algo*

sometimes – *adv.* – *a veces*

son – *n.* – *el hijo*

son-in-law – *n.* – *el yerno*

spinach – *n.* – *la espinaca*

sport – *n.* – *el deporte*

square – *n.* – *la plaza*

squirrel – *n.* – *la ardilla*

stairs – *n.* – *las escaleras*

stand – *v.* – *pararse, ponerse de pie, levantarse*

star – *n.* – *la estrella*

still – *adv.* – *todavía*

stop – *v.* – *detenerse (pararse)*

store – *n.* – *la tienda*

store clerk – *n.* – *el (la) dependiente*

strawberry – *n.* – *la fresa*

street – *n.* – *la calle*

strong – *adj.* – *fuerte*

student – *n.* – *el (la) estudiante*

subway – *n.* – *el subterráneo (metro)*

success – *n.* – *el éxito*

sugar – *n.* – *el azúcar*

suitcase – *n.* – *la maleta*

sun – *n.* – *el sol*

superior – *adj.* – *superior*

surgeon – *n.* – *el cirujano*

sweetheart – *n.* – *el amorcito*

swim – *v.* – *nadar*

switch (light) – *n.* – *el conmutador*

system – *n.* – *el sistema*

table – *n.* – *la mesa*

tablecloth – *n.* – *el mantel*

tailor – *n.* – *el sastre*

talk – *v.* – *hablar (conversar)*

tap – *n.* – *el grifo (la llave)*

tape recorder – *n.* – *la grabadora*

teacher – *n.* – *el (la) profesor (a)*

team – *n.* – *el equipo*

technician – *n.* – *el técnico*

television – *n.* – *la televisión*

temperament – *n.* – *el temperamento*

Thanksgiving – *n.* – *el Día de Acción de Gracias*

theme – *n.* – *el tema*

then – *adv.* – *entonces*

thighs – *n.* – *los múslos*

thin – *adj.* – *flaco*

think – *v.* – *pensar*

thirst – *n.* – *la sed*

thus – *adv.* – *así*

time – *n.* – *la vez*

tip – *n.* – *la propina*

tired – *adj.* – *cansado*

tolerate – *v.* – *soportar*

tongue – *n.* – *la lengua*

too much – *adv.* – *demasiado*

tooth – *n.* – *los dientes*

towel – *n.* – *la toalla*

tower – *n.* – *la torre*

train – *n.* – *el tren*

travel – *v.* – *viajar*

trolley – *n.* – *el tranvía*

turf – *n.* – *el césped*

turkey – *n.* – *el pavo*

turtle – *n.* – *la tortuga*

typist – *n.* – *el mecanógrafo*

unaware (to be) – *v.* – *ignorar*

uncle – *n.* – *el tío*

up (to get) – *v.* – *levantarse (pararse)*

up (to go) – *v.* – *subir*

vacation – *n.* – *las vacaciones*

vase – *n.* – *el florero, el jarrón*

vegetables – *n.* – *las verduras (las legumbres)*

vulgar – *adj.* – *vulgar*

waist – *n.* – *la cintura*

wait – *v.* – *esperar, aguardar*

walk – *v.* – *caminar (andar)*

want – *v.* – *querer*

watch – *n.* – *el reloj*

watch – *v.* – *observar, vigilar*

water – *n.* – *el agua*

watermelon – *n.* – *la sandía*

waves – *n.* – *las olas*

weak – *adj.* – *débil*

wedding – *n.* – *las bodas, el casamiento*

well – *adj.* – *bien*

whale – *n.* – *la ballena*

white – *adj.* – *blanco*

wife – *n.* – *la esposa, la señora, la mujer*

win – *v.* – *ganar*

wind – *n.* – *el viento*

window – *n.* – *la ventana*

wine – *n.* – *el vino*

wood – *n.* – *la madera*

work – *v.* – *trabajar*

worse – *adj.* – *peor*

wrist – *n.* – *la muñeca*

write – *v.* – *escribir*

writer – *n.* – *el (la) escritor (a)*

yard – *n.* – *el patio*

yellow – *adj.* – *amarillo*

yesterday – *adv.* – *ayer*

young man – *n.* – *el muchacho, el joven*

young woman – *n.* – *la muchacha, la joven*

SPANISH-TO-ENGLISH GLOSSARY

AP Spanish Language

a veces – *adv.* – sometimes

abogado – *n.* – (m.) lawyer

abrigo – *n.* – (m.) coat

abuela – *n.* – (f.) grandmother

abuelo – *n.* – (m.) grandfather

aburrido – *adj.* – boring

acción – *n.* – (f.) action

aceituna – *n.* – (f.) olive

acera (vereda) – *n.* – (f.) sidewalk

actor – *n.* – (m.) actor

actriz – *n.* – (f.) actress

adiós, hasta luego – goodbye

aerolinea – *n.* – (f.) airline

afeitar(se) – *v.* – shave

agricultor – *n.* – (m.) farmer

agua – *n.* – (f.) water

aguardar – *v.* – wait

águila – *n.* – (m.) eagle

alegría – *n.* – (f.) joy

algo – *n.* – something

alguien – *n.* – someone

almuerzo – *n.* – (m.) lunch

alpinismo – *n.* – (m.) mountain climbing

alquilar – *v.* – rent

amarillo – *adj.* – yellow

amor – *n.* – (m.) love

amorcito – *n.* – (m.) sweetheart

anillo – *n.* – (m.) ring

anoche – *adv.* – last night

anteojos – *n.* – (m.) eyeglasses

antes de – *prep.* – before

antiguo – *adj.* – ancient, old

aprender – *v.* – learn

apuntes – *n.* – (m.) notes, as those you take in class

árbitro – *n.* – (m.) referee

ardilla – *n.* – (f.) squirrel

arena – n. – (f.) sand

aroma – n. – (m.) aroma

arroz – n. – (m.) rice

artista – n. – (m.) artist

ascensor – n. – (m.) elevator

así – adv. – thus

asistir a – v. – attend

ataúd – n. – (m.) coffin

atlético – adj. – athletic

auditorio – n. – (m.) audience

auto – n. – (m.) car

autobús – n. – (m.) bus

automóvil – n. – (m.) car

avenida – n. – (f.) avenue

avión – n. – (m.) airplane

ayer – adv. – yesterday

azúcar – n. – (m.) sugar

azul – adj. – blue

bajar – v. – down (to go)

bajo – adj. – short

ballena – n. – (f.) whale

baño – n. – (m.) bathroom

barba – n. – (f.) beard

barca – n. – (f.) boat

barco – n. – (m.) boat

bastante – adv. – enough

beber (tomar) – v. – drink

bello – adj. – beautiful

bien – adj. – well

bisabuela – n. – (f.) great-grand-mother

bisabuelo – n. – (m.) great-grand-father

blanco – adj. – white

boca – n. – (f.) mouth

bocacalle – n. – (f.) intersection

boda – n. – (f.) wedding

bonito – adj. – pretty

bote – n. – (m.) boat

brazo – n. – (m.) arm

bronquitis – n. – (f.) bronchitis

bucear – v. – snorkel

bueno – adj. – good

caballo – n. – (m.) horse

cabello (pelo) – n. – (m.) hair

cabeza – n. – (f.) head

cabra – n. – (f.) goat

cadera – n. – (f.) hip

caer(se) – v. – fall

café – n. – (m.) coffee

caja – n. – (f.) box

calcetín – n. – (f.) sock

callado – adj. – quiet

callar – v. – silent (to be)

calle – n. – (f.) street

callejón – n. – (m.) alley

cama – n. – (f.) bed

cambiar – *v.* – change

caminar (andar) – *v.* – walk

camisa – *n.* – (f.) shirt

campo – *n.* – (m.) field

cansado – *adj.* – tired

cansarse – *v.* – grow (get) tired

cantante – *n.* – (m.) singer

cara – *n.* – (f.) face

cargo – *n.* – (m.) responsibility

carne – *n.* – (f.) meat

caro – *adj.* – expensive

carro – *n.* – (m.) car

carta – *n.* – (f.) letter

cartero – *n.* – (m.) mailman

casa – *n.* – (f.) house

casamiento – *n.* – (m.) wedding

casi – *adv.* – almost

casona – *n.* – (f.) house (big)

catedral – *n.* – (f.) cathedral

centro – *n.* – (m.) downtown

cepillarse – *v.* – brush

cerca – *adj.* – near

cerdo – *n.* – (m.) pig

cerveza – *n.* – (f.) beer

césped – *n.* – (m.) turf

chancho – *n.* – (m.) pig

chanza, chiste – *n.* – (f.) joke

chaqueta – *n.* – (f.) coat

chico – *adj.* – small

chimenea (hogar) – *n.* – (f.) fire-place; chimney

choclo – *n.* – (m.) corn

ciego – *n.* – (m.) blind person

ciego – *adj.* – blind

ciervo (venado) – *n.* – (m.) deer

cine – *n.* – (m.) moviehouse

cineasta – *n.* – (m.) film director

cintura – *n.* – (f.) waist

cirujano – *n.* – (m.) surgeon

ciudad – *n.* – (f.) city

clavo – *n.* – (m.) nail

clima – *n.* – (m.) climate

coche – *n.* – (m.) car

cocina – *n.* – (f.) kitchen

codo – *n.* – (m.) elbow

colega – *n.* – (m.) colleague

colegio – *n.* – (m.) school (high)

collar – *n.* – (m.) necklace

colorado – *adj.* – red

comedor – *n.* – (m.) dining room

comer – *v.* – eat

cometa – *n.* – (m.) comet

cometa – *n.* – (f.) kite

cómoda (el tocador) – *n.* – (f.) dresser

comprar – *v.* – buy

conejo – *n.* – (m.) rabbit

conferencia – n. – (f.) lecture

confidencia – n. – (f.) secret

conmutador – n. – (m.) switch (light)

conocer – v. – know

consulta – n. – (f.) conference

contento – adj. – happy

correo – n. – (m.) mail

correr – v. – run

cortés – adj. – courteous

corto – adj. – short

crecer – v. – grow

creer – v. – believe

crisis – n. – (f.) crisis

cuadro – n. – (m.) painting

cuello – n. – (m.) neck

cultivar – v. – grow

cumpleaños – n. – (m.) birthday

cura – n. – (f.) cure

cura – n. – (m.) priest

curso – n. – (m.) course

deber – v. – owe

débil – adj. – weak

decepción – n. – (f.) disappointment

decir – v. – say (tell)

dedo – n. – (m.) finger

delito – n. – (m.) crime

demasiado – adv. – too much; adj. – too many

dependiente – n. – (m.) store clerk

deporte – n. – (m.) sport

descansar – v. – rest

desgracia – n. – (f.) misfortune

desmayo – n. – (m.) fainting

después de – prep. – after

detenerse (pararse) – v. – stop

día – n. – (m.) day

Día de Acción de Gracias – n. – (m.) Thanksgiving

diario – n. – (m.) newspaper

dibujo – n. – (m.) drawing

diente – n. – (m.) tooth

difícil – adj. – difficult

dinero – n. – (m.) money

Dios – n. – God

diploma – n. – (m.) diploma

disco duro – n. – (m.) hard disk

disco flexible – n. – (m.) floppy disk

divertido – adj. – funny

doctor (a) – n. – (m.) doctor (physician)

dormir – v. – sleep

dormitorio (la alcoba) – n. – (m.) bedroom

drama – n. – (m.) drama

ducha – n. – (f.) shower

durazno – n. – (m.) peach

duro, difícil – adj. – hard

edificio – n. – (m.) building

elogio – n. – (f.) eulogy

embarazada – adj. – pregnant

emborracharse – v. – drunk (to get)

empezar – v. – begin

enfadarse (molestarse) – v. – angry (to get)

enfermera – n. – (f.) nurse

enfermo(a) – n. – (m.) sick person

ensalada – n. – (f.) salad

entonces – adv. – then

entrada – n. – (f.) entrance, lobby

entrar – v. – enter

enviar – v. – send

equipaje – n. – (m.) luggage

equipo – n. – (m.) team

escalera – n. – (f.) stair

escribir – v. – write

escritor (a) – n. – (m.) writer

escritorio – n. – (m.) desk

escuchar – v. – hear

escuela – n. – (f.) school

espalda – n. – (f.) back

espejo – n. – (m.) mirror

espejuelos – n. – (m.) eyeglasses

esperanza – n. – (f.) hope

esperar – v. – wait

espinaca – n. – (f.) spinach

esposa – n. – (f.) wife

esposo – n. – (m.) husband

estacionarse – v. – park

estrella – n. – (f.) star

estudiante – n. – (m.) student

éxito – n. – (m.) success

exterior – adj. – outer

fábrica – n. – (f.) factory

fácil – adj. – easy

familia – n. – (f.) family

fantástico – adj. – fantastic

feliz – adj. – happy

firma – n. – (f.) signature

físico – n. – (m.) physicist

flaco – adj. – thin

florero – n. – (m.) vase

foto – n. – (f.) photo

frágil – adj. – fragile

frase – n. – (f.) sentence

frente – n. – (f.) forehead

fresa – n. – (f.) strawberry

frío – adj. – cold

fuego – n. – (m.) fire

fuerte – adj. – strong

fumar – v. – smoke

fútbol – n. – (m.) soccer

gafas – n. – (f.) eyeglasses

gallina – n. – (f.) hen

gallo – n. – (m.) rooster

ganar – v. – win

gato – n. – (m.) cat

gente – n. – (f.) people

gordo – adj. – fat

grabadora – n. – (f.) tape recorder

grande – adj. – big

granja – n. – (f.) farm

grifo (la llave) – n. – (m.) tap

guagua – n. – (f.) bus

guapo – adj. – handsome

guía – n. – (f.) guide (book)

guía – n. – (m.) guide (person)

gustar – v. – like

hablar (conversar) – v. – talk

hacer – v. – make (do)

hacha – n. – (f.) hatchet

hambre – n. – (f.) hunger

heladera – n. – (f.) refrigerator

hembra – n. – (f.) female

hermana – n. – (f.) sister

hermano – n. – (m.) brother

hierba – n. – (f.) grass (tended, not wild)

hierro – n. – (m.) iron

hija – n. – (f.) daughter

hijo – n. – (m.) son

hombre de negocios – n. – (m.) businessman

hombro – n. – (m.) shoulder

hombrón – n. – (m.) man (big)

horno – n. – (m.) oven; furnace

humo – n. – (m.) smoke

idioma – n. – (m.) language

ignorar – v. – unaware (to be)

imagen – n. – (f.) image

impresora – n. – (f.) printer

ingeniero – n. – (m.) engineer

inteligente – adj. – intelligent

interesante – adj. – interesting

interior – adj. – internal

intoxicar – v. – poison

ir de compras – v. – shopping (to go)

irse – v. – leave

jabalí – n. – (m.) boar

jamón – n. – (m.) ham

jardín – n. – (m.) garden

jarrón – n. – (m.) vase

jefe – n. – (m.) boss

juez – n. – (m.) judge

jugador (a) – n. – (m.) player

jugar – v. – play

labio – n. – (m.) lip

lámpara – n. – (f.) lamp

lápiz – n. – (m.) pencil

largo – *adj.* – long

lavatorio – *n.* – (m.) sink

leche – *n.* – (f.) milk

lechuga – *n.* – (f.) lettuce

lectura – *n.* – (f.) reading

leer – *v.* – read

legumbre – *n.* – (f.) vegetable

lejos – *adj.* – far

lengua – *n.* – (f.) tongue

levantar – *v.* – raise, lift

levantarse (*pararse*) – *v.* – up (to get)

librería – *n.* – (f.) book store

libro – *n.* – (m.) book

limpio – *adj.* – clean

llegar – *v.* – arrive

llevar – *v.* – carry

locutor – *n.* – (m.) announcer

luego – *adv.* – later

luna – *n.* – (f.) moon

luz – *n.* – (f.) light

macho – *n.* – (m.) male

madera – *n.* – (f.) wood

madre – *n.* – (f.) mother

maíz – *n.* – (m.) corn

maleta – *n.* – (f.) suitcase

malo, mal – *adj.* – bad

mañana – *n.* – (f.) morning

mandar – *v.* – send

manejar (*conducir, guiar*) – *v.* – drive

mano – *n.* – (f.) hand

mantel – *n.* – (m.) tablecloth

mantener – *v.* – keep

mantequilla – *n.* – (f.) butter

manzana – *n.* – (f.) apple

mapa – *n.* – (m.) map

máquina – *n.* – (f.) machine

mar – *n.* – (m.) sea

maravilloso – *adj.* – marvelous

marido – *n.* – (m.) husband

marrano – *n.* – (m.) pig, hog

marrón (*pardo*) – *adj.* – brown

más – *adv.* – more

mayor – *adj.* – older

mecánico – *n.* – (m.) mechanic

mecanógrafa – *n.* – (m.) typist

media – *n.* – (f.) sock

médico – *n.* – (m.) physician

mejor – *adj.* – better

menos – *adv.* – less

mercado – *n.* – (m.) market

merienda – *n.* – (f.) snack

mesa – *n.* – (f.) table

microondas – *n.* – (m.) microwave oven

miedo – *n.* – (m.) fear

mirar – *v.* – look at

molestar – *v.* – bother

montaña – *n.* – (f.) mountain

morado (violeta) – *adj.* – purple

morir – *v.* – die

moto – *n.* – (f.) motorcycle

mover(se), mudarse – *v.* – move

muchacha, la joven – *n.* – (f.) young woman

muchacho, el joven – *n.* – (m.) young man

muchedumbre – *n.* – (f.) crowd

muerte – *n.* – (f.) death

mujer – *n.* – (f.) wife, woman

muñeca – *n.* – (f.) wrist

músculo – *n.* – (m.) muscle

múslo – *n.* – (m.) thigh

nacer – *v.* – born (to be)

nacimiento – *n.* – (m.) birth

nada – nothing

nadar – *v.* – swim

nariz – *n.* – (f.) nose

Navidad(es) – *n.* – (f.) Christmas

necesitar – *v.* – need

negocio – *n.* – (m.) business

negro – *adj.* – black

nieta – *n.* – (f.) granddaughter

nieto – *n.* – (m.) grandson

niño – *n.* – (m.) boy

noche – *n.* – (f.) night

nombre – *n.* – (m.) name

nuera – *n.* – (f.) daughter-in-law

nunca – *adv.* – never

observar – *v.* – watch

odiar – *v.* – hate

oficio – *n.* – (m.) occupation

oír – *v.* – hear

ojo – *n.* – (m.) eye

ola – *n.* – (f.) wave

olvidar – *v.* – forget

ómnibus – *n.* – (m.) bus

orden – *n.* – (f.) order (do something)

orden – *n.* – (m.) order (public order)

ordenador – *n.* – (m.) computer

oreja – *n.* – (f.) ear

oro – *n.* – (m.) gold

otoño – *n.* – (m.) autumn

oveja – *n.* – (f.) sheep

padre – *n.* – (m.) father

pagar – *v.* – pay

pájaro – *n.* – (m.) bird

pala – *n.* – (f.) shovel

pan – *n.* – (m.) bread

pantalones – *n.* – (m.) pants

papa (patatas) – *n.* – (f.) potato

papa – *n.* – (m.) Pope

papel – *n.* – (m.) paper

paracaidismo – *n.* – (m.) parachuting

pararse – *v.* – stand

párpados – *n.* – (m.) eyelids

partido – *n.* – (m.) game (party)

partir – *v.* – leave

pasajero (a) – *n.* – (m.) passenger

pasaporte – *n.* – (m.) passport

patio – *n.* – (m.) yard

pavo – *n.* – (m.) turkey

pecho – *n.* – (m.) chest

pedir – *v.* – order, ask

peinarse – *v.* – comb (one's hair)

peinilla – *n.* – (f.) comb

película – *n.* – (f.) film

pensar – *v.* – think

peor – *adj.* – worse

pequeño – *adj.* – small

pera – *n.* – (f.) pear

perder – *v.* – lose

periódico – *n.* – (m.) newspaper

periodista – *n.* – (m.) journalist

perro – *n.* – (m.) dog

pesadilla – *n.* – (f.) nightmare

pescado – *n.* – (m.) fish

pescar – *v.* – fish

pestañas – *n.* – (f.) eyelashes

pez – *n.* – (m.) fish

pinchar – *v.* – to prick, wound

pirámide – *n.* – (f.) pyramid

plata – *n.* – (f.) silver

plátano – *n.* – (m.) banana, plantain

playa – *n.* – (f.) beach

plaza de estacionamiento – *n.* – (f.) parking lot

plaza – *n.* – (f.) square

poco – *adj.* – some

poema – *n.* – (m.) poem

poeta – *n.* – (m.) poet

policía – *n.* – (f.) police

político – *n.* – (m.) politician

pollo – *n.* – (m.) chicken

ponerse de pie – *v.* – stand

postre – *n.* – (m.) dessert

precio – *n.* – (m.) price

preferir – *v.* – prefer

preparar – *v.* – prepare

presencia – *n.* – (f.) presence

pretender – *v.* – aspire to

problema – *n.* – (m.) problem

profesor (a) – *n.* – (m.) teacher

profeta – *n.* – (m.) prophet

prójimo – *n.* – (m.) neighbor

propina – *n.* – (f.) tip

puerco – *n.* – (m.) pig

puerta – *n.* – (f.) door

querer – v. – want

queso – n. – (m.) cheese

química – n. – (f.) chemistry

químico – n. – (m.) chemist

radio – n. – (m.) radio

ratón – n. – (m.) mouse

razón – n. – (f.) reason

recordar – v. – remember

refrigerador – n. – (f.) refrigerator

regresar – v. – return

reina – n. – (f.) queen

reloj – n. – (m.) watch

revista – n. – (f.) magazine

rey – n. – (m.) king

rico – adj. – rich

río – n. – (m.) river

rodilla – n. – (f.) knee

rojo – adj. – red

ropa – n. – (f.) clothing

rosa (rosado) – adj. – pink

ruido – n. – (m.) noise

sábana – n. – (f.) sheet

saber – v. – know

saco – n. – (m.) coat

sala – n. – (f.) living room

salida – n. – (f.) departure

salir – v. – out (to go)

salud – n. – (f.) health

saludar – v. – greet

sandía – n. – (f.) watermelon

sano – adj. – healthy

sastre – n. – (m.) tailor

sed – n. – (f.) thirst

señora – n. – (f.) wife, Mrs.

sensible – adj. – sensitive

sentarse – v. – sit down

serie – n. – (f.) series

siempre – adv. – always

silla – n. – (f.) chair

sillón – n. – (m.) couch

sistema – n. – (m.) system

sobre – n. – (m.) envelope

sobrina – n. – (f.) niece

sobrino – n. – (m.) nephew

sociedad – n. – (f.) society

soez – adj. – mean, vile

sofá – n. – (m.) sofa

sol – n. – (m.) sun

soldado – n. – (m.) soldier

soñar – v. – dream

sonrisa – n. – (f.) smile

soportar – v. – tolerate

subir – v. – up (to go)

subterráneo (metro) – n. – (m.) subway

suceso – n. – (m.) event

sucio – adj. – dirty

sueño – n. – (m.) dream

suerte – n. – (f.) luck

superior – adj. – superior

talón – n. – (m.) heel

tarde – adv. – late; *n. –* (f.) afternoon

taza – n. – (f.) cup

techo – n. – (m.) roof; ceiling

teclado – n. – (m.) keyboard

técnico – n. – (m.) technician

televisión – n. – (f.) television

tema – n. – (m.) theme

temperamento – n. – (m.) temperament

temprano – adv. – early

tía – n. – (f.) aunt

tiburón – n. – (m.) shark

tienda – n. – (f.) store

tina – n. – (f.) bathtub

tío – n. – (m.) uncle

toalla – n. – (f.) towel

tobillo – n. – (m.) ankle

tocadiscos – n. – (m.) record player

tocino – n. – (m.) bacon

todavía – adv. – still

toro – n. – (m.) bull

torre – n. – (f.) tower

torta – n. – (f.) cake

tortuga – n. – (f.) turtle

trabajar – v. – work

traer – v. – bring

tranvía – n. – (m.) trolley

tren – n. – (m.) train

triste – adj. – sad

uña – n. – (f.) fingernail

uva – n. – (f.) grape

vacaciones – n. – (f.) vacation

vaca – n. – (f.) cow

valiente – adj. – courageous

vaso – n. – (m.) glass

vecindario – n. – (m.) neighborhood

vecino – n. – (m.) neighbor

velador – n. – (m.) night table

vendedor – n. – (m.) salesman

vender – v. – sell

ventana – n. – (f.) window

ver – v. – see

verde – adj. – green

verdura – n. – (f.) vegetable

vestirse – v. – dress (oneself)

vez – n. – (f.) time

viajar – v. – travel

viejo – adj. – old

viento – n. – (m.) wind

vigilar – v. – watch

vino – n. – (m.) wine

volar – *v.* – fly

volver – *v.* – return

vuelo – *n.* – (m.) flight

vulgar – *adj.* – vulgar

yerno – *n.* – (m.) son-in-law

zapato – *n.* – (m.) shoe

NOTES

AP Spanish Language

NOTES

AP Spanish Language

NOTES

AP Spanish Language

NOTES

AP Spanish Language

NOTES

AP Spanish Language

NOTES

AP Spanish Language

The ESSENTIALS®
of LANGUAGE

Each book in the **LANGUAGE ESSENTIALS** series offers all the essential information of the grammar and vocabulary of the language it covers. They include conjugations, irregular verb forms, and sentence structure, and are designed to help students in preparing for exams and doing homework. The **LANGUAGE ESSENTIALS** are excellent supplements to any class text or course of study.

The **LANGUAGE ESSENTIALS** are complete and concise, with quick access to needed information. They also provide a handy reference source at all times. The **LANGUAGE ESSENTIALS** are prepared with REA's customary concern for high professional quality and student needs.

Available Titles Include:

French   *Italian*

German   *Spanish*

REA'S
PROBLEM SOLVERS

PROBLEM SOLVERS
Physics

The Perfect Resource for:
• any class
• any exam
• any problem

A Reference for Life

The PROBLEM SOLVERS® are comprehensive supplemental textbooks designed to save time in finding solutions to problems. Each PROBLEM SOLVER® is the first of its kind ever produced in its field. It is the product of a massive effort to illustrate almost any imaginable problem in exceptional depth, detail, and clarity. Each problem is worked out in detail with a step-by-step solution, and the problems are arranged in order of complexity from elementary to advanced. Each book is fully indexed for locating problems rapidly.

Accounting	Genetics
Advanced Calculus	Geometry
Algebra & Trigonometry	Linear Algebra
Automatic Control Systems/Robotics	Mechanics
Biology	Numerical Analysis
Business, Accounting & Finance	Operations Research
Calculus	Organic Chemistry
Chemistry	Physics
Differential Equations	Pre-Calculus
Economics	Probability
Electrical Machines	Psychology
Electric Circuits	Statistics
Electromagnetics	Technical Design Graphics
Electronics	Thermodynamics
Finite & Discrete Math	Topology
Fluid Mechanics/Dynamics	Transport Phenomena

If you would like more information about any of these books,
complete the coupon below and return it to us or visit your local bookstore.

Research & Education Association
61 Ethel Road W., Piscataway, NJ 08854
Phone: (732) 819-8880   **website: www.rea.com**

Please send me more information about your Problem Solver® books.

Name _____

Address _____

City _____ State _____ Zip _____

REA's Test Preps
The Best in Test Preparation

- REA "Test Preps" are **far more** comprehensive than any other test preparation series
- Each book contains up to **eight** full-length practice tests based on the most recent exams
- **Every** type of question likely to be given on the exams is included
- Answers are accompanied by **full** and **detailed** explanations

REA publishes over 70 Test Preparation volumes in several series. They include:

Advanced Placement Exams (APs)
Art History
Biology
Calculus AB & BC
Chemistry
Economics
English Language & Composition
English Literature & Composition
European History
French Language
Government & Politics
Latin
Physics B & C
Psychology
Spanish Language
Statistics
United States History
World History

College-Level Examination Program (CLEP)
Analyzing and Interpreting Literature
College Algebra
Freshman College Composition
General Examinations
General Examinations Review
History of the United States I
History of the United States II
Introduction to Educational Psychology
Human Growth and Development
Introductory Psychology
Introductory Sociology
Principles of Management
Principles of Marketing
Spanish
Western Civilization I
Western Civilization II

SAT Subject Tests
Biology E/M
Chemistry
French
German
Literature
Mathematics Level 1, 2
Physics
Spanish
United States History

Graduate Record Exams (GREs)
Biology
Chemistry
Computer Science
General
Literature in English
Mathematics
Physics
Psychology

ACT - ACT Assessment
ASVAB - Armed Services Vocational Aptitude Battery
CBEST - California Basic Educational Skills Test
CDL - Commercial Driver License Exam
CLAST - College Level Academic Skills Test
COOP & HSPT - Catholic High School Admission Tests
ELM - California State University Entry Level Mathematics Exam
FE (EIT) - Fundamentals of Engineering Exams - For Both AM & PM Exams

FTCE - Florida Teacher Certification Examinations
GED - (U.S. Edition)
GMAT - Graduate Management Admission Test
LSAT - Law School Admission Test
MAT - Miller Analogies Test
MCAT - Medical College Admission Test
MTEL - Massachusetts Tests for Educator Licensure
NJ HSPA - New Jersey High School Proficiency Assessment
NYSTCE - New York State Teacher Certification Examinations
PRAXIS PLT - Principles of Learning & Teaching Tests
PRAXIS PPST - Pre-Professional Skills Tests
PSAT/NMSQT
SAT
TExES - Texas Examinations of Educator Standards
THEA - Texas Higher Education Assessment
TOEFL - Test of English as a Foreign Language
TOEIC - Test of English for International Communication
USMLE Steps 1,2,3 - U.S. Medical Licensing Exams

Research & Education Association
61 Ethel Road W., Piscataway, NJ 08854
Phone: (732) 819-8880   **website: www.rea.com**

Please send me more information about your Test Prep books.

Name _____

Address _____

City _____ State _____ Zip _____

REA's Test Prep Books Are The Best!
(a sample of the <u>hundreds of letters</u> REA receives each year)

" I am writing to congratulate you on preparing an exceptional study guide. In five years of teaching this course I have never encountered a more thorough, comprehensive, concise and realistic preparation for this examination. "
Teacher, Davie, FL

" I have found your publications, *The Best Test Preparation...*, to be exactly that. "
Teacher, Aptos, CA

" I used yo[...] % — thank you! "

" Y[...] nk you. "

" I rece[...] I congratulate

" Your A[...] t impressive. "

[...] r! "